CONSPIRACY INVESTIGATIONS

Criminal Investigation Series

Michael Flax

Copyright © 2005 Michael Flax

LawTech Custom Publishing Co., Inc.

(949)498-4815   Fax: (949)498-4858

E-mail: info@LawTechCustomPublishing.com

www.LawTechCustomPublishing.com

Comments and suggestions are welcome.

v.06.24.05

pp. 421

ISBN: 1-889315-45-1

Michael Flax retired January 2005, as assistant special agent in charge, Department of Homeland Security, Immigration and Customs Enforcement, San Diego, California. He has also served as a special agent with the Internal Revenue Service, Criminal Investigative Division, Bureau of Alcohol, Tobacco and Firearms, and the United States Customs Service, Office of Investigation.

Michael has directed investigations involving violations of federal laws including drugs, money laundering, arms and strategic technology investigations, computer crimes, customs fraud and intellectual property rights violations, and asset forfeiture. He has directed several highly successful international covert operations involving drugs and arms and strategic technology investigations.

Michael has spoken at national meetings and conventions as a subject matter expert and he has received a number of commendations and awards, including the Commissioner's Trade Enforcement Strategy Award and nominated Special Agent of the Year.

Contents at a Glance

Contents

Table of Articles and Figures

Chapter 8

Chapter 9

Chapter 10

Chapter 1

Introduction To Conspiracy

OVERVIEW

Conspiracy laws are some valuable tools for law enforcement agencies to disrupt and dismantle major criminal organizations. In this Chapter you will learn the definition of conspiracy, the different types of conspiracies, the history of the conspiracy law, the motivations for groups to engage in conspiracies and commit the substantive acts to accomplish the crime and why law enforcement finds conspiracy a valuable tool.

CHAPTER OBJECTIVES

1. Understand and recognize the various types of conspiracies such as, historical, ongoing, chain, wheel, and combination.
2. Know the history of the conspiracy law.
3. Learn the motivations of criminal organizations to engage in offenses to commit financial crimes, crimes against persons, drug violations and terrorism.
4. Learn why criminal organizations engage in conspiracies to commit financial crimes, crimes against persons, drug violations and terrorism.
5. Learn why law enforcement chooses to use the conspiracy law to disrupt and dismantle criminal organizations.

DEFINITION OF CONSPIRACY

Conspiracy is two or more persons who agree to commit an unlawful act in furtherance of the object of the conspiracy. Conspiracy is a separate crime from the crime that was the unlawful act that was in furtherance of the object of the conspiracy.

TYPES OF CONSPIRACIES

Historical

Many conspiracy cases are made by criminal investigators who gather evidence to link together individual legal and illegal acts used in a broad scheme to accomplish the object of the conspiracy. These cases are different from the more proactive investigations that use undercover agents, informants or wiretaps to prove their cases. For example, special agents regularly analyze drug seizures at the Mexican border for common links, such as registered owners of the vehicles used for the smuggling. Together with the information gained from the cooperation of the load drivers and other investigative techniques that will be discussed later, they are on their way to initiating a criminal conspiracy case.

Ongoing

Conspiracies can have a continuous objective. An organization that engages in the illegal smuggling of cocaine into the United States has as the object of the conspiracy a crime that does not end with the smuggling of just one load of cocaine. The objective of the conspiracy, the illegal importation of cocaine into the United States does not end until the organization is dismantled or the final overt act, unlike an agreement between two people to rob a particular bank.

Chain Conspiracy

A chain conspiracy is used to describe a conspiracy where the members are linked by a common purpose to achieve a single objective and their roles and activities are further linked by the acts taken over time to achieve their common objective.

Figure 1.1 Marijuana Smuggling Chain

CHAIN

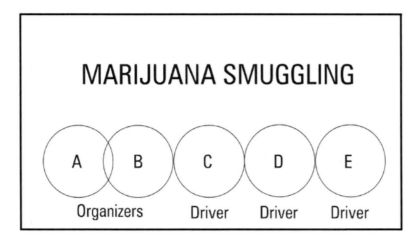

In above example, A and B agree to smuggle marijuana into the United States from Mexico, C joins the conspiracy by agreeing to drive the loads of marijuana from the interior of Mexico to a storage facility just south of the Mexican/United States border. D agrees to smuggle the marijuana from the storage facility to a load house in the United States. E agrees to drive the marijuana from the load house to the buyers of the marijuana in Los Angeles.

Wheel Conspiracy

In a wheel conspiracy there is a hub of organizers that enter into an agreement to achieve multiple objectives. Each of the objectives is a spoke of the wheel. Inside the hub are those organizers who have full knowledge of the existence of the other spokes. Those outside of the hub only have knowledge of the objective of their spoke.

WHEEL

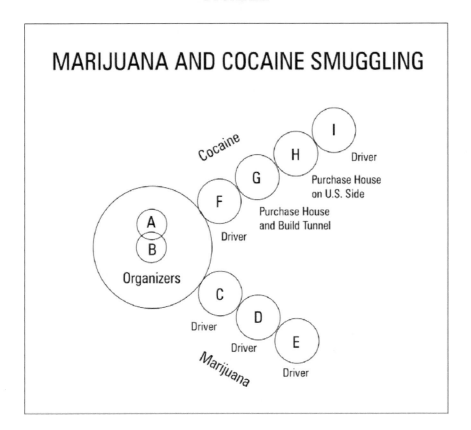

MARIJUANA AND COCAINE SMUGGLING

In the example above, A and B agree to smuggle cocaine and marijuana into the United States from Mexico. They decide to protect the organizations by settings up two separate organizations, one to smuggle the marijuana and the other to smuggle the cocaine. The marijuana organization, the first spoke of the hub, is set up the same as in the chain conspiracy. A and B agree to smuggle marijuana into the United States from Mexico. C joins the conspiracy by agreeing to drive the loads of marijuana from the interior of Mexico to a storage facility just south of the Mexican/United States border. D agrees to smuggle the marijuana from the storage facility to a load house in the United States. E agrees to drive the marijuana from the load house to the buyers of the marijuana in Los Angeles.

The second spoke of the hub, is more complex due to the value of the cocaine in comparison to the marijuana. A and B are still the organizers of the organization. F agrees to drive the cocaine from the interior of

Mexico to a safe house near the Mexican/United States border. G purchased a house on the border of Mexico and the United States. G then built a tunnel that connected to a sewer drain that went into the United States. H purchased a residence on the United States side next to an exit of the sewer system. H would receive the cocaine that was smuggled through the sewer into the United States. I joined the conspiracy to drive the cocaine from the United States border to Los Angeles to the buyers.

In this example, A and B would be liable for all the crimes committed by both the marijuana and cocaine smuggling organizations, they are the hub of the wheel conspiracy. While C, D and E would be responsible only for the marijuana conspiracy and F, G, H and I would only be responsible for the cocaine conspiracy. As you will learn later, it is the agreement and intent that play a major role in liability for the crimes committed in furtherance of objective of the conspiracy.

Combination Conspiracy

There are times when neither a wheel conspiracy nor a chain conspiracy accurately defines the organization. This normally occurs when the hub has very few organizers with multiple objectives and the chains vary substantially in length. With spokes that represent from two to numerous people one could hardly draw a wheel at all.

HISTORY OF THE CONSPIRACY LAW

Conspiracy, Title 18, USC, Section 371 first appeared as Section 30 of "An act to amend, existing laws, relating to Internal Revenue, and for other purposes" enacted on March 2, 1867. That act, except for an omitted not relevant provision, is almost precisely in its present form. It was carried into the revision of the United States Statutes of 1873-4 in the Crimes against the Operations of the Government section. On January 1, 1910, it was carried into the Criminal Code where it now appears.

MOTIVATIONS TO ENGAGE IN CONSPIRACY OFFENSES

Financial Crimes

Greed for money is the primary motivator for financial crimes as well as many other crimes. Money laundering is a financial crime that takes the proceeds from unlawful activities and makes that money appear to be legitimate so it may be used by the organizations for a lavish living style or to make legitimate investments to further hide their illegal source of funds.

Other examples of financial crimes include insurance fraud, high yield investment schemes, bank fraud and embezzlement. Insurance fraud could include arson to defraud the insurance company for the value of the property or an inventory that didn't exist. High Yield investment schemes defraud people and companies out of millions of dollars each year. These schemes include purchasing stocks or certificates at a substantial discount to their face value, but in reality they are worthless. You would be surprised by how many people are cheated out of their money each year in schemes were people believe they are buying valuable property at a substantial discount. One of the schemes active for the last few years is a Canadian lottery scheme. It preys on the elderly, who are contacted by phone by individuals identifying themselves as a Customs official. They are told they won a lottery in Canada and only need to pay the duties on the money prior to the money being sent into the United States. Banks are cheated out money by a variety of schemes. Recently, a group of real estate buyers and an appraiser conspired to defraud banks buying mortgages by buying properties and selling them to each other for artificially inflated prices with the assistance of a certified appraiser who falsify the appraisals. After the property was flipped several times they paid a person to sign a contract to purchase the home. The buyer was able to obtain a mortgage from the bank because they appeared to be putting down a large down payment. The conspirators were taking advantage of liberalized loan documentation requirements for buyers who put down a large down payments that results in high loan to value ratios. The co-conspirators then split the profit. After a couple of months the property was in default and repossessed by the bank and only then the banks realize the property value was over inflated.

Embezzlement is converting money or assest from an individual or company for personal use. In complex embezzlement schemes it may require the complicity of several well-placed people.

Examples Of Financial Crimes

Figure 1.3 Press Release United States Attorney's Office

Corey Kemp   Glenn K. Holck   Stephen M. Umbrell

RELEASE (202) 514-6XXX TDD (202) 514-1XXX

June 29 2004

WHITE, KEMP, AND 10 OTHERS CHARGED IN PHILADEPHIA CORRUPTION CASE

PHILADELPHIA

United States Attorney Patrick L. Meehan, F.B.I. Special Agent-in-Charge Jeffrey Lampinski, and I.R.S. Special Agent-in-Charge Jerome Lisuzzo announced the indictment of 12 defendants, including attorney Ronald A. White, former Philadelphia City Treasurer Corey Kemp, and the president and regional vice-president of Commerce Bank/Pennsylvania, N.A., in a case alleging corruption in connection with financial transactions of the City of Philadelphia and other deals involving Kemp.

The indictment alleges that White corrupted City Treasurer Kemp, from January 2002 through October 16, 2003, by making payments and giving other benefits to Kemp. In exchange, Kemp followed White's direction regarding the decisions Kemp was required to make regarding the employment of financial service companies to carry out bond transactions, and other matters. Kemp's decisions created large financial gains for White and those White favored.

"The nameplate on the desk of the City Treasurer may have read Corey Kemp but Ron White was calling the shots," said Meehan. "This is an indictment not only of the defendants but of a pay to play culture that can only breed corruption."

Figure 1.3 Press Release United States Attorney's Office (cont.)

The indictment states that, throughout 2002 and 2003, White showered Kemp with payments and other gratuities, with the intent to influence Kemp in his official actions. These gifts included at least $10,000 paid in 2002, a $10,350 deck for Kemp's house in 2003, a trip to the Super Bowl in San Diego in January 2003 (including transportation by private jet and limousine, and a ticket to the game), tickets and limousine rides to all three days of the NBA All-Star events in Philadelphia in February 2002, and numerous other meals, parties, and choice tickets to sports and entertainment events. The indictment asserts that White also held out the promise of vast future riches, assuring Kemp secret participation in what White represented would be lucrative financial opportunities in the development of the Philadelphia International Airport and a racetrack/casino proposed at the Philadelphia Naval Yard.

"There was a seemingly endless stream of benefits in exchange for control that Kemp was more than willing to surrender," said Meehan. "In effect, the public trust was being bought and sold." The indictment states that in exchange for these benefits, Kemp permitted White to direct Kemp's decision-making as Treasurer of the City. On a daily basis, White instructed Kemp regarding which providers to select for participation in City transactions, and which to exclude, and Kemp followed those instructions. Kemp successfully recommended that White himself be hired as counsel in City bond deals, more frequently than any other attorney, earning White $633,594 in fees during Kemp's tenure. Kemp also repeatedly recommended the selection of a printing company nominally controlled by White's paramour, defendant Janice Renee Knight, which earned $308,632 in City bond deals during the same period. On one occasion, according to the indictment, Kemp told a financial advisor to the City that White would be paid $35,000 on a deal just for the hell of it, even though White didn't really do anything. Kemp then informed White of the same thing, saying, "you got your boy sitting in, in the Treasurer's seat, man that's what we do, man, take care of each other."

White also profited by directing Kemp to award City business to firms favored by White, which in turn, to obtain White's access and influence, paid White legal fees and retainers, gave additional business to Knight's printing company, and made contributions to politicians, charities, and other causes White favored. One of the firms that benefited from White and Kemp's corrupt scheme was Commerce Bank. The indictment charges that Commerce Bank/Pennsylvania president Glenn K. Holck and regional vice-president Stephen M. Umbrell themselves made favorable and

Figure 1.3 Press Release United States Attorney's Office (cont.)

otherwise unavailable loans to Kemp, such as for 100% financing on his house at a time that Kemp had extremely poor credit, and paid benefits to White knowing that White exerted influence over Kemp. As a result, Kemp favored Commerce Bank in the award of a $30 million line of credit and other transactions. With respect to the line of credit, after Commerce submitted its bid to the City in a closed bidding process with other banks, Kemp told White on May 28, 2003, "just some advice in the future, cause they submitted their proposal first, right? Tell them don't submit it first, because I can tell you what came in, and then you can tell them how to beat the s——." White so advised Holck and Umbrell. Kemp then informed Holck and Umbrell what offer would win the deal.

The indictment rests in part on conversations monitored by the government pursuant to judicial authorization for approximately nine months during 2003. During that time, according to the indictment, White and Kemp openly discussed their criminal scheme, in which Kemp permitted White to take over Kemp's official decision-making in exchange for benefits from White and others. For example, on February 12, 2003, while discussing the selection of financial services firms favored by White, White stated: "well, we moving s——, ain't we Corey? ...there ain't nobody in it but me and you now." Kemp replied, "That's it, everybody else out the picture, huh?"

During 2003, White occasionally promised Kemp that, if Philadelphia Mayor John F. Street, whom White supported and who employed Kemp, were reelected in November 2003, White would continue to benefit Kemp and Kemp would become financially set. For example, on August 25, 2003, White stated to Kemp, "the key for us right now, man, is to concentrate on getting John elected, so it gives us four more years to do our thing. If we get four more years, Corey, we should be able to set up, you know, I mean and for you we maybe only talking about only two, you know what I mean?" Kemp said, "That's good, that's good, that's cool."

The indictment states further that in permitting White to direct his official actions, Kemp knew his actions not only benefited White and White's interests but also the political candidates White supported, including the Mayor. White and Kemp agreed that when White demanded political contributions from financial services firms to the Mayor's campaign, the firms had to make them or face the loss of the ability to obtain City business. On August 26, 2003, discussing that matter, White said to Kemp, "either you down or you ain't with it."

Figure 1.3 Press Release United States Attorney's Office (cont.)

Kemp replied, "right, cause if they don't, if they ain't with us they ain't gonna get nothing." White said, "that's right." Kemp said, "you know, you just hate to say it but that's the way it is, man, I mean, this is election time, this is time to either get down or lay down, man, I mean, come on, to me, personally it's not even a hard decision."

The indictment states that in furthering his political agenda White was motivated by financial gain rather than political conviction. It recounts a conversation he had on September 24, 2003, when he stated to a fellow fundraiser, (the whole thing, man, you know I don(t care about none of this s—-, man, none of this politics s—- means nothing to me. What we want to do is, we business people, we want to protect our f—-ing investment, and we need to talk about how we gonna do that if John loses."

The indictment further alleges that:

During the spring and summer of 2003, Kemp and White engaged in an effort to extort an investment broker at Legg Mason, Inc. in Baltimore, Maryland. When White and Kemp learned that the broker was interested in obtaining City of Philadelphia business, they acted to try to extract from the broker his assistance in getting work in Baltimore for White and for Knight's printing company, and later demanded a $5,000 campaign contribution to the Mayor of Philadelphia. When the broker did not deliver, his request for business was summarily denied.

In August 2003, White, with Kemp's assistance, demanded a $25,000 campaign contribution for Mayor Street's campaign from a Philadelphia financial advisory firm, in exchange for a ticket to the Mayor's box at the Philadelphia Eagles season opener and the opportunity to obtain City business from Kemp.

White, at the behest of defendants Charles LeCroy and Anthony C. Snell, who were executives of J.P. Morgan, submitted a false invoice to J.P. Morgan seeking the payment of $50,000 for legal work which White did not actually perform on a Mobile, Alabama bond transaction. LeCroy and Snell arranged this payment, which was made on May 30, 2003, against the intent of their employer, in order to secure White's assistance in obtaining business for J.P. Morgan in Philadelphia, which could result in personal benefit for LeCroy and Snell.

In May 2003, Kemp traveled to New York City to play a fictitious role at a business meeting conducted by White and defendant La-Van Hawkins. The purpose was to deceive a person with whom Hawkins

Figure 1.3 Press Release United States Attorney's Office (cont.)

wished to do business into believing that Hawkins had available funds, from the Philadelphia pension fund, to engage in the transaction.

Kemp engaged in other fraudulent schemes.

First, Kemp and defendant Francis D. McCracken, the pastor of St. James Chapel Church, Church of God in Christ, in Reading, submitted false statements to Commerce Bank in order to obtain an advance of $115,898.37 on a loan made by Commerce to the Church. By falsely representing that work had been done to refurbish the Church, Kemp and McCracken were able to obtain over $50,000, which they diverted for their personal benefit, concealing their fraud by laundering proceeds through a series of bank accounts they controlled. They also discussed a plan to use an additional $50,000 of the funds loaned to the Church to make an investment on their personal behalf in a private investment opportunity being offered by Ronald White regarding development of a racetrack/casino at the Philadelphia Naval Yard. This plan did not come to fruition, however, by the time the defendant's criminal conduct came to light.

Second, Kemp and McCracken perpetrated a fraud on a state-funded welfare-to-work program. Third, Kemp and an attorney, Rhonda M. Anderson, established a business to assist individuals in making claims against unclaimed funds held by the City or having payments made for lost or misplaced bonds issued by the City. Kemp received cash for his participation in this business even though, as he explained to Anderson, he was the City official charged with making such payments and was not permitted to receive cash payments in connection with the performance of his duties.

The defendants in this case are:

1. Ronald A. White, 54, an attorney, of Sedgwick Street in Philadelphia. White is charged with conspiracy to commit honest services fraud, 22 counts of wire fraud, four counts of mail fraud, two counts of extortion, and five counts of making false statements to the FBI. If convicted on all counts, he faces a maximum sentence of 555 years imprisonment and an $8.25 million fine.

2. Corey Kemp, 34, the former City Treasurer, of King Fisher Drive in Birdsboro, Pennsylvania. Kemp is charged with conspiracy to commit honest services fraud, 20 counts of wire fraud, 15 counts of mail fraud, two counts of extortion, three counts of making false statements to a bank, four counts of money laundering, and one count

Figure 1.3 Press Release United States Attorney's Office (cont.)

of filing a false tax return. If convicted on all counts, he faces a maximum sentence of 798 years imprisonment and a $10.75 million fine.

3. Glenn K. Holck, 44, the president of Commerce Bank/Pennsylvania, who resides on Greenbriar Lane in Newtown, Pennsylvania. Holck is charged with conspiracy to commit honest services fraud, eight counts of wire fraud, and one count of mail fraud. If convicted on all counts, he faces a maximum sentence of 185 years imprisonment and a $2.5 million fine.

4. Stephen M. Umbrell, 44, the regional vice-president of Commerce Bank/Pennsylvania, who resides on Cornell Drive in Delran, New Jersey. Umbrell is charged with conspiracy to commit honest services fraud, eight counts of wire fraud, and one count of mail fraud. If convicted on all counts, he faces a maximum sentence of 185 years imprisonment and a $2.5 million fine.

5. La-Van Hawkins, 46, a Detroit businessman. Hawkins is charged with conspiracy to commit honest services fraud, four counts of wire fraud, and four counts of committing perjury before the federal grand jury, which investigated this case. If convicted on all counts, he faces a maximum sentence of 125 years imprisonment and a $2.5 million fine.

6. Janice R. Knight, 40, a businesswoman, of Wade Drive in Cherry Hill, New Jersey. Knight is charged with conspiracy to commit honest services fraud, three counts of wire fraud, and three counts of making false statements to the FBI. If convicted on all counts, she faces a maximum sentence of 80 years imprisonment and a $1.75 million fine.

7. Charles LeCroy, 49, a former managing director of the southeast regional office of J.P. Morgan, who resides in Winter Park, Florida. LeCroy is charged with two counts of wire fraud. If convicted on both counts, he faces a maximum sentence of 40 years imprisonment and a $500,000 fine.

8. Anthony C. Snell, 44, a former vice-president of J.P. Morgan, who resides in Smyrna, Georgia. Snell is charged with two counts of wire fraud. If convicted on both counts, he faces a maximum sentence of 40 years imprisonment and a $500,000 fine.

9. Denis Carlson, 49, a senior vice-president of Janney Montgomery Scott, who resides on Mermaid Lane in Philadelphia. Carlson is charged with two counts of making false statements to the FBI agents investigating this case; it is alleged that Carlson

Figure 1.3 Press Release United States Attorney's Office (cont.)

misrepresented his relationship with White and his purpose in giving Corey Kemp the free use of a vacation condominium Carlson owned. If convicted on both counts, he faces a maximum sentence of 10 years imprisonment and a $500,000 fine.

10. Francis D. McCracken, 54, the pastor of the St. James Chapel Church, Church of God in Christ, who resides on North 3rd Street in Reading, Pennsylvania. McCracken is charged with three counts of making false statements to a bank, four counts of money laundering, and six counts of mail fraud. If convicted on all counts, he faces a maximum sentence of 290 years imprisonment and a $3.25 million fine.

11. Jose Mendoza, 44, of Elm Street in Reading, Pennsylvania. Mendoza was a worker employed by McCracken, and allegedly assisted in the preparation of a false statement submitted to Commerce Bank. He is charged with one count of making a false statement to a bank, and if convicted, faces a maximum sentence of 30 years imprisonment and a $1 million fine.

12. Rhonda M. Anderson, 30, of Walnut Park Drive in Philadelphia. Anderson is an attorney who allegedly participated in a fraudulent scheme with Kemp. She is charged with one count of mail fraud, and if convicted, faces a maximum sentence of 20 years imprisonment and a $250,000 fine.

This case was investigated by the Federal Bureau of Investigation, with the assistance of the Internal Revenue Service, the Philadelphia District Office of the Securities and Exchange Commission, the Office of the Comptroller of the Currency, and the Pennsylvania Attorney General's Office, Medicaid Fraud Control Section.

UNITED STATES ATTORNEY'S OFFICE Contact: RICH MANIERI EASTERN DISTRICT, PENNSYLVANIA Public Affairs Suite XXX, XXX Chestnut Street 215-861-8XXX Philadelphia, PA 19106

Note: On May 9, 2005 defendants Corey Kemp, Glenn Holck and Stephen Umbrell were convicted by a jury in Philadelphia of participating in a corruption scheme.

Figure 1.4 United States Department of Justice Press Release

FOR IMMEDIATE RELEASE THURSDAY, SEPTEMBER 28, 2000 (202) 514-2XXX WWW.USDOJ.GOV TDD (202) 514-1XXX

KOCH INDUSTRIES INDICTED FOR ENVIRONMENTAL CRIMES AT REFINERY

WASHINGTON, D.C. - A federal grand jury in Corpus Christi, Tex., today returned a 97-count indictment against Koch Industries Inc., Koch Petroleum Group, L.P., and four corporate employees charging them with environmental crimes at a Texas oil refinery.

The defendants are charged with violating federal air and hazardous waste laws at Koch Petroleum Group's West Plant refinery near Corpus Christi. The indictment also charges the defendants with conspiracy and making false statements to Texas environmental officials.

The West Plant is subject to Clean Air Act standards that limit emissions of benzene. In 1977, the EPA added benzene to the list of hazardous air pollutants based on scientific reports strongly suggesting an increased incidence of leukemia in humans exposed to benzene. The Clean Air Act also requires owners and operators of oil refineries like the West Plant to submit an annual report to federal and state regulators certifying that their refineries comply with benzene regulations.

Under the Act, the West Plant was required to comply with the federal benzene standards by April, 1993, but Koch Petroleum Group applied for and received a compliance waiver until January, 1995. The indictment alleges that in 1995, Koch Industries and Koch Petroleum Group were informed by an employee that the West Plant had at least 91 metric tons of uncontrolled benzene in its liquid waste streams, some 15 times greater than the 6 metric ton limit that applied to the refinery.

"Companies that produce dangerous pollutants simply cannot focus on profit and efficiency at the expense of a community's health," said Lois Schiffer, Assistant Attorney General in charge of the environment at the Justice Department. "We will continue to find and prosecute those who would flout our environmental laws."

The indictment charges Koch Industries and Koch Petroleum Group with violating the Clean Air Act by, among other things, failing to install required emission control devices in 1995 on certain waste management units, such as its oil-water separators, wastewater sewers, and oil and wastewater tanks.

Figure 1.4 United States Department of Justice Press Release (cont.)

In addition, the indictment alleges that a device that Koch Petroleum Group installed in January 1995 to destroy benzene fumes from two oil-water separators, the Thermatrix Thermal Oxidizer, could not handle the high levels of benzene routed to it, and it would often shut down for extended periods of time.

According to the indictment, when the Thermatrix shut down, the West Plant continued to operate and Koch Industries and Koch Petroleum Group intentionally vented large amounts of untreated benzene fumes directly to the atmosphere through a bypass stack. The benzene released through the bypass stack exceeded 10 pounds per 24-hour period on several occasions, and Koch Industries and Koch Petroleum Group did not report these releases to the National Response Center. As a result, Koch Industries and Koch Petroleum Group and have been charged with violating the Comprehensive Environmental Response, Compensation and Liability Act for failing to immediately report to the National Response Center the discharges of a hazardous substance, namely benzene, from its West Plant.

The defendants then made false and misleading statements to the Texas Natural Resource Conservation Commission to conceal the extent of the refinery's noncompliance with the Clean Air Act, according to the indictment, and falsely certified in a report filed in 1996 that the refinery complied with the benzene regulations.

"The Texas Natural Resource Conservation Commission takes very seriously its responsibility to enforce all environmental laws to protect public health and the environment," said TNRCC Executive Director Jeff Saitas. "We continue to work closely with state and federal task force members on this and other environmental criminal matters."

David L. Lamp of Woodlands, Texas, was plant manager of the West Plant from November 1991 until June 1994, when he was promoted to Vice President for Marketing of the Koch Refining and Chemical Group. In May 1996, Lamp became vice president of Texas operations for Koch Refinery Company, which later became Koch Petroleum Group. Lamp is charged with conspiracy to violate the Clean Air Act and conspiracy to make false statements to Texas environmental officials; with operating the West Plant in violation of the Clean Air Act; and with making false statements to Texas environmental officials. If convicted, Lamp faces a maximum penalty of 25 years imprisonment and $1.25 million in fines.

Vincent A. Mietlicki of Andover, Kan., was an attorney in the legal department of Koch Industries, Inc. and subsequently the

Figure 1.4 United States Department of Justice Press Release (cont.)

environmental manager of the West Plant. Mietlicki is charged with conspiracy to violate the Clean Air Act and conspiracy to make false statements to Texas environmental officials; with operating the West Plant in violation of the Clean Air Act; and with two counts of making false statements to Texas environmental officials. If convicted, Mietlicki faces maximum penalties of 35 years imprisonment and $1.75 million in fines.

John C. Wadsworth of Wichita, Kan., was vice president and plant manager of the West Plant from 1994 until 1996. Wadsworth is charged with conspiracy to violate the Clean Air Act and conspiracy to make false statements to Texas environmental officials. Wadsworth is also charged with operating the West Plant in violation of the Clean Air Act. If convicted, Wadsworth faces maximum penalties of 20 years imprisonment and $1 million in fines.

James W. Weathers, Jr. of Andover, Kan., was environmental engineer from 1992 until 1996, when he became manager of the environmental department at the West Plant. Weathers is charged with conspiracy to violate the Clean Air Act and conspiracy to make false statement to Texas environmental officials. Weathers is also charged in the indictment with two counts of making false statements to Texas environmental officials. Weathers faces maximum penalties of 20 years imprisonment and $1 million in fines if convicted.

Koch Industries and its subsidiary Koch Petroleum Group face a maximum statutory penalty of $48.5 million. Alternatively, under federal law, the companies may be subject to fines of twice the pecuniary gain realized from the criminal offenses, in lieu of the maximum penalty under the applicable statutes. According to the indictment, Koch Industries and Koch Petroleum Group earned profits of more than $176 million in 1995, while operating the refinery in violation of the Clean Air Act. One goal of the alleged conspiracy was to maximize profits and avoid shutting down the refinery, which did not meet environmental standards.

The case was investigated by the Texas Environmental Enforcement Task Force, comprised of federal and state agencies, including the FBI, the EPA's Criminal Investigation Division, and the Texas Natural Resource Conservation Commission's Special Investigations Unit. The case is being prosecuted by the Department of Justice Environmental Crimes Section.

"Today's indictments demonstrate the importance of close cooperation with our state and federal task force partners," said Steve Herman, EPA's Assistant Administrator for Enforcement and

Figure 1.4 United States Department of Justice Press Release (cont.)
Compliance Assurance. "We will continue to work vigorously with other enforcement agencies to ensure that the public is protected from chemical pollution in the air." An indictment is a formal charge that a defendant has committed a criminal violation of federal law. Every defendant is presumed innocent unless and until proven guilty.

CRIMES AGAINST PERSONS

Crimes against persons include hate crimes, organized crime and emotional crimes such as murder or assault. Organizations like the Ku Klux Klan bring together individuals with a common hatred for the purpose of committing unlawful activities to further their beliefs. Organized crime commits crimes against persons to control their competition from infringing upon their territory or to persuade their victims to cooperate with them. The scale of these organizations can vary widely. Street gangs that engage in extortion, murder, robbery and other crimes in their neighborhood sometimes attempt to expand their influence to other neighborhoods. When this happens, the gangs use violence to achieve their goals or to protect their territory. Other organizations such as Jamaican gangs or Asian gangs operate in a larger geographical area that requires more people. They still have the same motivations and use the same tools of crimes against persons to achieve their objectives. There also can be cooperation between the gangs as in a supplier and buyer relationship.

People are motivated to kill their spouse out of emotional response from disputes or to get out of the marriage. They then may engage in a conspiracy with another person to murder their spouse. This can be a strictly professional fee for service arrangement as in a hired killer or a person motivated by the love of the victim's spouse.

Figure 1.5 Example of a Crime Against Persons

FOR IMMEDIATE RELEASE CONTACT: U.S. ATTORNEY'S OFFICE

JANUARY 23, 2004

MARVIN SMILON, HERBERT HADAD, MICHAEL KULSTAD

FBI PUBLIC INFORMATION OFFICE

JOSEPH A. VALIQUETTE (212) 637-2XXX, JAMES M. MARGOLIN (212) 384-2XXX, 2XXX, NYPD PAUL BROWNE (646) 610-6XXX

LUCHESE ACTING BOSS CONVICTED OF RACKETEERING AND MURDER

DAVID N. KELLEY, the United States Attorney for the Southern District of New York, PASQUALE D(AMURO, the Assistant Director in Charge of the New York Office of the FBI, and RAYMOND W. KELLY, the New York City Police Commissioner, announced today that LOUIS DAIDONE, 56, the Acting Boss of the Luchese Organized Crime Family of La Cosa Nostra, was convicted in Manhattan federal court on racketeering and loan sharking charges that included two homicides.

According to the evidence introduced at trial, DAIDONE participated in the criminal activities of the Luchese Crime Family from the early 1980(s up to at least January 2000. DAIDONE began as a Soldier, then rose to Acting Capo, Consigliere, and, most recently, Acting Boss of the Family.

DAIDONE was convicted of two racketeering (or (RICO() counts, which each included charges that DAIDONE participated in two homicides, the February 1989 murder of Thomas Gilmore and the August 1990 murder of Bruno Facciolo. The third racketeering act charged DAIDONE with participating in a long-term, wide-ranging loan sharking conspiracy that involved the making of extortionate loans, the financing of those loans, and the collection of those loans by extortionate means. DAIDONE was found guilty of all three racketeering acts in both of the racketeering counts.

With respect to the Gilmore homicide, according to the evidence introduced at trial, DAIDONE and two Luchese associates stalked Gilmore until they found him alone outside his home in Queens, then ran up behind him and shot him in the head and neck.

Regarding Facciolo, DAIDONE lured Facciolo to an ambush, where DAIDONE and two other members of the Luchese Crime

> ## Figure 1.5 Example of a Crime Against Persons (cont.)
>
> Family stabbed and shot Facciolo to death. Then DAIDONE and the others placed a canary in Facciolo(s mouth as a symbol to deter others who might cooperate with the authorities, and left Facciolo(s body in the trunk of his car, parked on a Brooklyn street where it was discovered several days later.
>
> Count Three charged DAIDONE with committing witness tampering by murdering Bruno Facciolo because Facciolo was suspected of cooperating with the authorities. The evidence at trial showed that the Luchese Family(s suspicions about Facciolo were unfounded.Counts Four and Five charged DAIDONE with being part of conspiracies to make (extortionate extensions of credit,(and to collect such extensions of credit, otherwise known as (loansharking.(
>
> DAIDONE was convicted on all counts, and faces a mandatory minimum sentence of life in prison without the possibility of parole. DAIDONE is scheduled to be sentenced before United States District Judge RICHARD M. BERMAN on April 28, 2004, at 2:30 p.m.
>
> Mr. KELLEY praised the efforts of the Federal Bureau of Investigation and the New York Police Department in conducting the investigation.
>
> Assistant United States Attorneys KARL METZNER and DIANE GUJARATI are in charge of the prosecution.

DRUGS

Drugs are smuggled into the United States and sold because of the huge profits they provide. The profits are so huge that organizations can afford to buy protection to move their drugs through countries by buying off political, law enforcement and military officials who guarantee safe passage. These organizations require a lot of people to grow, cultivate, package, ship, smuggle and distribute their drugs and then smuggle the proceeds back to the organizers. Conspiracy is the necessary method to accomplish their objectives because of the complexities of the crime. It also offers the organization an opportunity to make the most money from its venture. In each step of the smuggling process the value of the drugs increases because of the inherent risk of moving the drugs from a controlled environment through the border and to the streets of the United States, where many law enforcement agencies are engaged in enforcing the narcotic laws.

Examples Of Drug Cases

Figure 1.6 U.S. Department of Justice Press Release

FOR IMMEDIATE RELEASE May 20, 2003
For more information contact: Mary H. Vaira, DEA PIO (215) 861-3XXX

May 20—Today, as a result of a two-year investigation, a major heroin organization that operated from the source of supply in Colombia to New York/Newark and to the streets of Philadelphia, was dismantled. This Colombian-Dominican trafficking organization was totally exposed from the retail street level managers, couriers, and wholesalers to the source of supply in Medellin, Colombia. Twenty-one arrest warrants and seven search warrants were issued in Philadelphia, along with arrest and search warrants in New York, Newark and Colombia resulting in 30 arrests which took place early this morning in the four locations mentioned above. This operation in all the locations mentioned above has arrested 45 defendants, and seized approximately 14 kilograms of heroin and $320,000 to date.

James M. Kasson, Special Agent in Charge of the Drug Enforcement Administration, Philadelphia Division, stated that this investigation, which covers heroin trafficking from the "farm to the arm" is very significant due to the extremely high purity level of heroin in the City of Philadelphia. "Philadelphia has had the highest heroin purity in the country for a number of years. When I arrived here I started a 'Heroin Initiative' to focus on the extreme heroin problem in Philadelphia and in the surrounding areas. This investigation targets the heroin problem in Philadelphia. This investigation also tells me that this city is no longer just a user city, but it is now a major Gateway city for heroin."

The arrest warrants and search warrants in Philadelphia were authorized by Federal Magistrate Judge Melinson on Friday, May 16, 2003. Sixteen members of the Franklin Santos Drug Trafficking Organization were arrested by DEA agents and Philadelphia Police Department Task Force Officers early this morning, four guns and gram quantites of crack and heroin were seized along with $3,400 USC. Four persons were arrested in Newark along with $37,000 and four vehicles, five persons were arrested in New York along with four and a half kilograms of heroin and $125,000. Four individuals were arrested in Colombia this morning. At the same time DEA agents, and police officers executed search warrants at seven locations in Philadelphia, one was a storefront and six were private residences.

Figure 1.6 U.S. Department of Justice Press Release (cont.)

Kasson, United States Attorney Patrick Meehan, and Philadelphia Police Commissioner Sylvester Johnson, announced these arrests this afternoon at a joint press conference. Mr. Meehan stated that, "This was a dangerous organization whose tentacles reached well beyond the borders of the Delaware Valley. This case demonstrates the value of teamwork among federal and state law enforcement officials, as well as the critical role of cooperation among US Attorney and DEA offices from across the country. In particular, I thank Commissioner Sylvester Johnson and the men and women of the Philadelphia Police Department for their support and efforts in this case."

The target of the investigation was the Franklin Santos Heroin Organization. According to affidavits filed in support of the arrests and search warrants, Santos, a Dominican national, 34 years of age, living at 7400 Roosevelt Blvd, in Philadelphia was supplied by a heroin organization based in Colombia. Santos headed the Philadelphia organization along with Carlos Tapia, who previously lived in Philadelphia but moved to New York due to pressure from law enforcement. They imported heroin from Colombian sources of supply in kilogram quantities. The heroin was brought to the northeast and then was transported to Philadelphia to be sold by Dominican traffickers. The Santos Organization is responsible for distributing kilogram quantities of heroin throughout Philadelphia. Three street level distribution locations have been identified.

Investigative leads identified members of the organization in New York, Newark and Medellin, Colombia. DEA offices along with the Colombian National Police then conducted their own investigations.

During the investigation, DEA agents seized approximately thee and one half kilograms of heroin in Philadelphia in February 2003. This heroin seizure occurred when the organization had attempted to deliver a heroin shipment into Philadelphia from New York. In April 2003, approximately four kilograms of heroin were seized from members of the organization in New York as couriers were riding on a bus destined for Philadelphia. Later in the month, two kilograms of heroin were seized from a courier in Colombia as the heroin was being prepared to be sent to the US.

The defendants in this investigation are charged with conspiracy to possess with intent to distribute, in excess of one kilogram of heroin and also with possessing with intent to distribute heroin.

Figure 1.6 U.S. Department of Justice Press Release (cont.)

This case will be prosecuted by the Eastern District of Pennsylvania. If convicted the defendants could receive sentences of up to life in prison.

DEA would also like to thank the US Customs Service, Immigration and Naturalization Service, US Marshal's Service and the Pennsylvania State Police Canine Unit for their assistance in this investigation.

Figure 1.7 U.S. Department of Justice Press Release

News Release FOR IMMEDIATE RELEASE January 12, 2004

Cash Smuggling Case at O'Hare Airport *Ex-Royal Jordanian Airlines Mgr. Sentenced*

JAN 12 - CHICAGO, IL - Another chapter was closed late last week in an illicit cash smuggling scheme as a former assistant station manager for Royal Jordanian Airlines at O'Hare International Airport was sentenced to 41 months prison on currency charges. Adnan Aldarawsheh, of Willow Springs, Illinois, a naturalized citizen from Jordan, was sentenced for being part of an illegal drug ring and using his position with the airline to help smuggle United States currency abroad. The over 1.5 million dollars seized in the case consisted of profits for transporting and supplying the drug pseudoephedrine into the United States as a precursor in the manufacturing of the illegal drug methamphetamine, commonly known as "crystal meth" or "crank."

Aldarawsheh and his co-conspirator, Mazen Abdallah, also a naturalized citizen from Jordan, were charged in Federal court with violating U.S. currency laws as Customs Inspectors at O'Hare Airport seized $651,817 in undeclared cash from Abdallah in January 2002. Abdallah attempted to leave the U.S. on an international flight with the seized cash but failed to declare it to border inspectors. Federal law requires that anyone traveling into or out of the United States with more that $10,000 in currency or monetary instruments

Figure 1.7 U.S. Department of Justice Press Release (cont.)

must declare such funds to border inspectors through a declaration known as a Currency and Monetary Instruments Report. Abdallah is scheduled for sentencing within the next few months.

An investigation of Abdallah led agents of the U.S. Immigration and Customs Enforcement (ICE), the FBI and the DEA to a larger case revealed the source of the currency as Jubran Dighlawi. Dighlawi, a resident of California, was operating a large-scale pseudoephedrine-trafficking operation. The pseudoephedrine was smuggled into the United States from Canada, stored in Detroit and Chicago, and later transported to the West Coast. Dighlawi and others then sold the pseudoephedrine to Mexican drug traffickers for use in manufacturing the illegal drug methamphetamine. Proceeds from the sale of the pseudoephedrine were then returned to Chicago area operatives, where Aldarawsheh, using his position as an airline employee, helped smuggle the cash outside of the United States. One method used to smuggle the cash was to stuff it in empty cereal boxes that were packed in Abadallah's suitcase.

"This investigation showed exemplary coordination between the U.S. Immigration and Customs Enforcement, the FBI and the Drug Enforcement Administration," said DEA's Associate Special Agent in Charge William J. Segarra. "The money seized by ICE at O'Hare Airport assisted the overall investigation into methamphetamine traffickers operating in California Superlabs."

Aldarawsheh and Abdallah both pleaded guilty in October to one count each of violating Title 18 United States Code, Section 371 (Conspiracy), Title 31 United States Code, Section 5316 (Currency and Monetary Instrument Reporting Requirements), and Title 31 United States Code, Section 5332 (Bulk Currency Smuggling). United States Attorney Patrick Fitzgerald of the Northern District of Illinois prosecuted the case.

TERRORISM

Terrorists are motivated to commit crimes to accomplish their political and religious goals. It is a form of a hate crime, but its tentacles extend to financial crimes, fear crimes, intellectual property right crimes and drugs. These crimes are committed to finance terrorist activities or to create fear in the targets of their objectives. The objective of the conspiracy that lead to the events of September 11th were motivated by the political and religious beliefs of Al Qaeda and its hatred of the United States. The acts were intended to create fear in the people of the United States. It took a large number of determined people all around the world to commit the crimes of September 11th. The conspiracy includes the organizers, the financiers, the people who trained the hijackers at the camps of Al Qaeda, the people who knowingly housed the hijackers, and many others. The crime could not have been committed without forming a conspiracy.

WHY CONSPIRACIES ARE FORMED TO COMMIT CRIMES

Some crimes necessitate large numbers of people to commit. To manufacture, smuggle and distribute large quantities of drugs it takes a lot of people. Other times, conspiracies provide isolation from the crime to avoid detection and/or prosecution. If the organizers can control the organization from a country with a corrupt government that would provide them protection they can enjoy the fruits of their crimes without the risk of going to jail. Conspiracies can be used to compartmentalize the various units so that detection by law enforcement of one unit does not put the entire organization in jeopardy. Profits can be maximized by vertically integrating the operations. Drug organizations can make the most profits by producing the drugs and selling them at the wholesale or retail level. However, this increase in profits comes with higher risks from law enforcement.

Why Conspiracy Laws Are Used By Law Enforcement To Dismantle Criminal Organizations

Conspiracy laws allow law enforcement agencies to dismantle an entire organization because of their ability to charge all members of the conspiracy for the acts of each other. Even those members of the conspiracy who provide lawful services in furtherance of the unlawful object of the conspiracy can be charged. Conspiracy laws are tools to go after the organizers and management of the conspiracy who are isolated from the individual unlawful acts. Persons who cannot be convicted of aiding and abetting or as an accessory because a crime was never consummated, may still be punished for the conspiracy. Law enforcement can use the conspiracy laws in a proactive manner using investigative techniques such as wiretaps, or undercover operatives or building historical cases with evidence and witnesses. When large organizations are taken down there is huge media attention with favorable press coverage that gives the public a positive image of law enforcement. The dismantling of criminal organizations allows law enforcement to seize the proceeds, assets and property used to facilitate the crime. Removing the financial gains for the crime is a major blow to the organizations. The Federal asset forfeiture laws allow the forfeited assets to be used by the law enforcement agencies to fight crime.

SUMMARY

Conspiracy laws are a valuable tool for law enforcement to disrupt and dismantle major criminal organizations. Conspiracy is defined as at least two people who agree to commit an unlawful act in furtherance of the object of the conspiracy. The object of the conspiracy can be lawful.

DISCUSSION QUESTIONS

1. How can conspiracy laws be used to disrupt and dismantle major criminal organizations?
2. Why do criminals form conspiracies?
3. Describe a wheel conspiracy, a chain conspiracy and a combination conspiracy.

ADDITIONAL READINGS

Department of Justice, United States Attorney's Manual, http://www.usdoj.gov/usao/eousa/foia_reading_room, Title, Section 9.27, Principals of federal prosecution

Legal Issues

OVERVIEW

While conspiracy laws are valuable tools for law enforcement, they present the investigator with many challenges. How do you prove the existence of an agreement among the participants, you are not going to find a written agreement. In this chapter we will explore the elements of the crime, how participants enter and leave a conspiracy, venue, the exception to the hearsay rule and special relationship in a conspiracy such as husband and wife or undercover agents and another person.

CHAPTER OBJECTIVES

1. Know the elements of the conspiracy statute, 18, USC, Section 371.
2. Understand the requirements needed to meet each of the elements of the conspiracy statute.
3. Know Wharton's rule and how it applies to the conspiracy statute.
4. Know how special relationship such as husband and wife are affected by the conspiracy statutes.
5. Understand why some conspiracy laws require an overt act while others don't.
6. Know the liability that accrues to a co-conspirator for the acts of others in a conspiracy.
7. Be able to determine the venue for a conspiracy charge.
8. Know why determining the duration of a conspiracy is important.
9. Understand the importance of the hearsay exception.

ELEMENTS OF CONSPIRACY

The elements of conspiracy, Title 18, USC, Section 371 are:
- Two or more persons
- Agreement to commit offenses against the United States or
- Agreement to defraud the United States and
- An overt act in furtherance thereof

Once all of the above elements are present, the offense of conspiracy in complete and chargeable. As a practical matter, even though the crime is complete not all crimes are prosecuted. The prosecutor will consider whether the case has jury appeal, if the object of the conspiracy is likely to offend the jury and the strength of the evidence. The United States Attorney does not want to lose a case, it is the responsibility of the criminal investigator to present a provable case. At the federal level, each United States Attorney sets priorities for the types of cases they will prosecute. The volume of cases presented for prosecutions in relation to the number of assistant united states attorneys available to handle those case will have a signification impact on how many and which cases are chosen for prosecution. Some cases that are a violation of both state and federal statutes will be given to the state to prosecute. Other cases may be given back to an agency for administrative remedy, like a violation of the Internal Revenue laws.

The Agreement

The agreement is the essential essence of the crime of conspiracy and it is a separate crime from the unlawful act that is in furtherance of the object of the conspiracy. It is the agreement that distinguishes conspiracy from aiding and abetting. While you do not have to prove actual words or a written agreement, you must show a meeting of the minds to deliberately commit an unlawful act. You must show intent to further, promote and cooperate to commit the unlawful acts in furtherance of the object of the conspiracy. Evidence must be developed to show that the conspirators acted together with a common understanding of their objective and intent. Some of the techniques used to develop this evidence will be discussed in the chapter on Investigative Techniques.

Two Or More Persons

While this element seems self-explanatory there are special relationships that require examination and an exception to the rule.

Wharton's Rule

Wharton's rule is a concept that if two people are required for the completion of an unlawful act, then they cannot be charged with conspiracy. For example, for adultery two people are necessary for the crime, therefore while the two might be charged for the crime of adultery they could not also be charged with conspiracy. In a drug distribution case it is necessary to sell or transfer the drugs to a buyer, therefore they could not be charged with conspiracy to distribute.

Special Relationships

Corporations

Corporations are legal separate entities and can be charged as a co-conspirator. A corporation can conspire with its officers and employees. However, one corporate officer acting along without consulting with other persons could not be charged with conspiracy. It is also possible to charge one person with conspiracy when the identities of the other co-conspirators are unknown.

Partners

A partnership is not a separate legal entity and cannot be charged with conspiracy.

Attorney and Clients   IMPORTANT

If an attorney advises conspirators before or during the commission of the conspiracy, with knowledge of the conspiracy and for the purpose of furthering the object of the conspiracy, he can be charged as a co-conspirator.

Employer and Employee

If an employee knows of the unlawful nature of the transactions being carried on and they continue to work to accomplish the unlawful ends they can be charged with conspiracy. This is true even if the employee received nothing more than his legal wages.

Landlord and Tenant

Even if a landlord knows of an illegal activity being conducted on his leased premises and does nothing to stop it he cannot be charged with conspiracy. This is true because he is not part of the agreement, however, he may be guilty of aiding and abetting.

Husband and Wife

The conspirators may be husband and wife.

Government Undercover Agent and Another Person

An undercover agent or confidential informant has no intent to achieve a criminal purpose. Therefore, he cannot be one of the two persons required for a conspiracy.

Object Of The Conspiracy

The agreement is between two or more persons to commit an unlawful act in furtherance of the objective of the conspiracy. The object of the conspiracy may be unlawful in itself, or the means to be employed for its accomplishments are unlawful or a lawful act that is corrupt, dishonest or fraudulent, but not a crime. The objective of the conspiracy may be impossible to accomplish.

Overt Acts

As previously stated in the Elements of the Crime section of this chapter, an overt act is not required for all conspiracy charges. Common law is derived from historical court cases and for crimes that were known to be bad such as murder or robbery. This is still true for many widely used federal conspiracy statues including conspiracy to violate federal drug laws, conspiracy to violate the Money Laundering Control Act, conspiracy to violate the RICO Act and conspiracy to violate the Export Administration Act. In theory, these conspiracies are so dangerous to society that the agreement itself is enough to complete the crime.

Some statutes require an overt act in furtherance of the crime to show intent. In these statutes after there is an agreement it is the overt act that marks the point where the crime of conspiracy is complete. Once that point is reached all of those who agreed to the conspiracy become liable for the crime of conspiracy. The intent is the key element of completion of the crime. There must be intent to be part of the agreement and intent to achieve the objective. Each conspirator must know that there is a plan and the overall purpose of the plan. They do not have to know all the details, the identity of other conspirators or what each person contributes to the plan. Just knowing that a conspiracy exists without participation does not make a person a party to the conspiracy.

It is important to prove the extent of the knowledge of each participant since conspiracies can have multiple objectives. A party to a conspiracy is responsible for any substantive offense committed by him or any other co-conspirator in furtherance of the conspiracy. If a participant knows about and agrees to participate in a conspiracy to import marijuana and the organizers also import cocaine and they have not agreed to the cocaine conspiracy they cannot be charged with the conspiracy to import cocaine or the crimes committed in furtherance of that objective. However, if crimes are committed that were not specifically agreed to, but could have been reasonably foreseen as a consequence of accomplishing the original objective, then all the conspirators would be liable for those substantive crimes. In our example of a person who agreed to participate in a conspiracy to import marijuana, if he knew that armed escorts would protect the loads while crossing the United States border and a federal agent was shot by those escorts, he would be liable for that murder. He should have been able to reasonably foresee that a shooting might occur at the border.

Late Joiners To A Conspiracy

A late joiner is not liable for criminal acts of co-conspirators committed prior to his joining the conspiracy, but those acts are admissible against him for the purpose of proving the conspiracy. A late joiner to a conspiracy does not create a new conspiracy.

Venue

The venue for the conspiracy is any district where:

1. The agreement was formed
2. Any overt act was committed by any of the co-conspirators

If the offenses began or were committed upon the high seas, or elsewhere out of the jurisdiction of any particular State or district, the venue lies in the district in which any one of two or more of the offenders are arrested or first brought. If the offenders are not arrested or brought into any district, an indictment may be filed in the district of the last known residence of any one of two or more joint offenders, or if there is no such residence known the indictment may be filed in the District of Columbia.

Duration Of The Conspiracy

The conspiracy ends if the objective of the conspiracy has been met, if the co-conspirators agree to terminate the conspiracy, or with the commission of the last overt act if the objective of the conspiracy is never achieved. These same conditions begin to run the statute of limitations. Determining the duration of the conspiracy and when it ends is important because only statements made during the course of the conspiracy are admissible under the rule concerning declarations by co-conspirators, co-conspirators can be held criminally responsible for acts committed by co-conspirators prior to the termination of the conspiracy and termination is critical for the statue of limitations purposes.

The Hearsay Exception

The Federal Rules of Evidence allow out-of-court statements made during the course of and in furtherance of the conspiracy by a member of a conspiracy to be admissible against other members of the conspiracy. The government must prove that a conspiracy existed, the defendant and the declarant were both members of the conspiracy at the time the statement was made and the statement was made both during the course of and in furtherance of the conspiracy.

FEDERAL CONSPIRACY LAWS

The general conspiracy statute is Title 18, USC, Section 371, however many more federal statues have conspiracy charges. The following are the federal conspiracy statutes:

1. 8 U.S.C. § 1252 - Apprehension and Deportation of Aliens
2. 8 U.S.C. § 1327 - Aiding or Assisting Certain Aliens to Enter
3. 10 U.S.C. § 881 - Article 81 Conspiracy
4. 15 U.S.C. § 1 - Trusts etc., in Restraint of Trade Illegal; penalty
5. 15 U.S.C. § 2 - Monopolizing Trade a Felony; penalty
6. 15 U.S.C. § 3 - Trusts in Territories or District of Columbia Illegal; combination a felony
7. 15 U.S.C. § 8 - Trusts in Restraint of Import Trade Illegal; penalty

8. 15 U.S.C. § 714m - Crimes and Offenses

9. 16 U.S.C. § 831t - Offenses; fines and punishment

10. 18 U.S.C. § 224 - Bribery in Sporting Contests

11. 18 U.S.C. § 241 - Conspiracy Against Rights

12. 18 U.S.C. § 286 - Conspiracy to Defraud the Government with Respect to Claims

13. 18 U.S.C. § 351 - Congressional, Cabinet, and Supreme Court Assassination, Kidnapping, and Assault; penalties

14. 18 U.S.C. § 371 - Conspiracy to Commit Offense or to Defraud United States

15. 18 U.S.C. § 372 - Conspiracy to Impede or Injure Officer

16. 18 U.S.C. § 757 - Prisoners of War or Enemy Aliens

17. 18 U.S.C. § 793 - Gathering, Transmitting, or Losing Defense Information

18. 18 U.S.C. § 794 - Gathering or Delivering Defense Information to Aid Foreign Government

19. 18 U.S.C. § 894 - Collection of Extensions of Credit by Extortionate Means

20. 18 U.S.C. § 956 - Conspiracy to Injure Property of Foreign Government

21. 18 U.S.C. § 1117 - Conspiracy to Murder

22. 18 U.S.C. § 1201 - Kidnapping

23. 18 U.S.C. § 1511 - Obstruction of State or Local Law Enforcement

24. 18 U.S.C. § 1751 - Presidential and Presidential Staff Assassination, Kidnapping, and Assault; penalties

25. 18 U.S.C. § 1752 - Temporary Residences and Offices of the President and Others

26. 18 U.S.C. § 1792 - Mutiny and Riot Prohibited

27. 18 U.S.C. § 1831 - Economic Espionage

28. 18 U.S.C. § 1832 (Theft of Trade Secrets

29. 18 U.S.C. § 1962(d) - RICO

30. 18 U.S.C. § 2153 - Destruction of War Material, War Premises, or War Utilities

31. 18 U.S.C. § 2154 - Production of Defective War Material, War Premises, or War Utilities

32. 18 U.S.C. § 2155 - Destruction of National-Defense Materials, National-Defense Premises or National-Defense Utilities

33. 18 U.S.C. § 2156 - Production of National-Defense Materials, National-Defense Premises or National-Defense Utilities

34. 18 U.S.C. § 2192 - Incitation of Seamen to Revolt or Mutiny

35. 18 U.S.C. § 2252 (Certain Activities Relating to the Sexual Exploitation of Minors

36. 18 U.S.C. § 2252A (Certain Activities Relating to Material Constituting or Containing Child Pornography

37. 18 U.S.C. § 2271 - Conspiracy to Destroy Vessels

38. 18 U.S.C. § 2384 - Seditious Conspiracy

39. 18 U.S.C. § 2385 - Advocating Overthrow of Government

40. 21 U.S.C. § 846 - Attempt and Conspiracy

41. 26 U.S.C. § 7214 - Offenses by Officers and Employees of the United States

42. 31 U.S.C. § 3729 - False Claims

43. 40 U.S.C. § 193h - Prosecution and Punishment of Offenses; procedure

44. 42 U.S.C. § 1973j - Same; Civil and Criminal Sanctions Depriving or Attempting to Deprive Persons of Secured Rights

45. 42 U.S.C. § 2272 - Violation of Specific Rights

46. 42 U.S.C. § 2273 - Violation of Sections

47. 42 U.S.C. § 2274 - Communication of Restricted Data

48. 42 U.S.C. § 2277 - Disclosure of Restricted Data

49. 47 U.S.C. § 509 - Prohibited Practices in Contests of Knowledge, Skill, or Chance Influencing, Prearranging, or Predetermining Outcome

50. 50 U.S.C. § 783 - Conspiracy to Establish Totalitarian Dictatorship

51. 50 U.S.C. App. § 462 - Selective Service Act Racketeer Influenced and Corrupt Organizations Act (RICO)

On October 15, 1970, the Organized Crime Control Act of 1970 became law; Title IX of the Act is the Racketeer Influenced and Corrupt Organizations Statute, 18, USC, Sections 1961 - 1968. The purpose of the RICO statute is the elimination of the infiltration of organized crime and racketeering into legitimate organizations operating in interstate commerce. There are nine state and thirty-five federal offenses specifically listed as racketeering activity. The nine state offenses are murder, kidnapping, gambling, robbery, arson, and bribery, dealing in obscene materials and dealing in narcotics or other dangerous drugs. In addition to its criminal provisions, RICO gives private parties and the federal government civil causes of action against violators. Attempts and conspiracies to commit the listed crimes are covered by RICO.

Figure 2.1 U.S. Department of Justice Press Release

NEWS RELEASE

FOR IMMEDIATE RELEASE DECEMBER 11 2003

CONTACT: MELODIE RYDALCH (801) 325-3XXX

GRAND JURY RETURNS INDICTMENT CHARGING MEMBERS, ASSOCIATES OF SOLDIERS OF THE ARYAN CULTURE WITH VIOLATIONS OF RICO, VIOLENT CRIME IN AID OF RACKETEERING ACTIVITY

SALT LAKE CITY — Members of a criminal organization, which law enforcement officers and prosecutors believe use violent criminal conduct and promotion of white supremacist ideology inside and outside of Utah correctional institutions to gain and maintain power, face a federal indictment today charging them with 13 violations of the Racketeer Influenced and Corrupt Organizations (RICO) Conspiracy and Violent Crime in Aid of Racketeering Activity (VICAR).

The indictment follows an investigation lead by the FBI and member agencies of its Joint Terrorism Task Force; the Salt Lake Area Metro Gang Unit and its participating agencies; the Utah Department of Corrections; and other local, state, and federal law enforcement agencies.

Agencies involved in the JTTF include the FBI, the IRS, the Salt Lake City Police Department, the U.S. Secret Service, the Weber County Sheriff's Office, ATF, U.S. Department of Homeland Security Bureau of Immigration and Customs Enforcement, U.S. Treasury Department Office of Inspector General for Tax Administration, the Ogden Police Department, the Utah Department of Public Safety, Federal Air Marshals, the Salt Lake County Sheriff's Office, and the Utah Department of Corrections.The Salt Lake Area Gang Unit includes the FBI, ATF, U.S. Marshals, the U.S. Attorney's Office, Utah DPS, Utah Department of Corrections, the Utah Division of Youth Corrections, Salt Lake County Sheriff's Office, the Granite School District, and city police departments from Salt Lake City, West Valley City, South Salt Lake City, South Jordan, West Jordan, Midvale, Murray, and Sandy.

The case is being prosecuted by four Assistant U.S. Attorneys, Leshia M. Lee-Dixon, David J. Schwendiman, Richard McKelvie, and Robert A. Lund, and Salt Lake Assistant District Attorney Vince Meister. Twelve members of the Soldiers of the Aryan Culture (SAC) are named in the indictment which was returned December 4, 2003, and unsealed in federal court Wednesday afternoon.

Figure 2.1 U.S. Department of Justice Press Release (cont.)

Defendants charged in indictments are presumed innocent unless or until proven guilty in court.

Charged in the indictment are Tracy David Swena, aka TinMan; John Arthur McGee, aka Cajun; Steve Mark Swena, aka Taz; David Fink, aka Castle; Mike Main, aka M & M; Mark Isaac Snarr, aka Snuff; Lee Ervin Heyen, aka Dallas; Lance Vanderstappen, aka Lil Lance, Cub; Jason Bates, aka Kid; Andrew Beck, aka Nutz, Bandit; Dennis Judd; and Jeff Schirado, aka Sherwood.

Main, Snarr and Judd were arrested by the FBI Wednesday morning. Schirado, Steve Mark Swena, Heyen, Fink, Vanderstappen, McGee, Beck and Bates are incarcerated at the Utah State Prison. Tracy David Swena is in a federal prison. Initial appearances were Wednesday afternoon for the three arrested this week. Initial appearances for other defendants are scheduled this week before U.S. Magistrate Judge Samuel Alba. Tracy David Swena will have an initial appearance scheduled in January.

The indictment alleges that the defendants were members and associates of SAC, a criminal organization whose members engaged in acts of violence, including conspiracy to commit murder, attempted murder, extortion, and conspiracy to distribute narcotics, operating principally in the state of Utah and within Utah correctional institutions. The indictment alleges SAC is an enterprise with members working together for a common purpose in achieving the objectives of the enterprise.

The hierarchy of SAC, according to the indictment, includes "generals," "lieutenants," "sergeants," and "soldiers." Under the direction of generals and lieutenants of the enterprise, the defendants participated in unlawful and other activities in furtherance of the conduct of the enterprise's affairs, the indictment charges.

According to the indictment, SAC accepts members by invitation only. New members must be sponsored by lieutenants and sergeants. The indictment outlines the process new members must follow to become a member of SAC.

According to the indictment, SAC requires its members to read specific types of white supremacy literature to learn more about the movement. In addition, SAC has a "manual" or code of conduct which outlines the rules and guidelines members must follow. It also outlines enforcement policies and what action will be taken to maintain discipline and punish those who violate the rules.

> ### Figure 2.1 U.S. Department of Justice Press Release (cont.)
>
> The indictment charges three defendants, Tracy David Swena, Steve Mark Swena, and Mark Isaac Snarr, with a violation of the federal RICO statute. The indictment details nine predicate offenses prosecutors are relying on to establish a pattern of racketeering activity. Federal law outlines what kinds of crimes or categories of crimes can serve as predicates to make up a pattern of racketeering activity. These are generally serious kinds of crime commonly associated with organized criminal activity — for example, murder, extortion, debt collection, drug dealing, or kidnapping. They do not have to be federal crimes. In the SAC indictment, eight of the nine predicate offenses are violations of state criminal laws.
>
> The three charged in the RICO conspiracy count and the other nine defendants in the also are charged with various violations of the VICAR statute. The VICAR counts in the indictment draw on the same racketeering activities and acts outlined in the RICO count.

THE USA PATRIOT ACT

On October 26, 2001, The Uniting and Strengthening America by Providing Appropriate Tools Required to Intercept and Obstruct Terrorism Act of 2001, known as the USA Patriot Act, was signed into law. A week after the September 11th attack the Bush Administration introduced the bill. The Act was a compromise version of the Anti-Terrorism Act of 2001 that was intended to strengthen the nations' defense against terrorism. The Act made major changes to laws including Wiretap Statute, Electronic Communications Privacy Act, Computer Fraud and Abuse Act, Foreign Intelligence Surveillance Act, Pen Register and Trap and Trace Statutes and the Bank Secrecy Act.

The Act expanded law enforcement's authority to use trap and trace and pen register devises. Prior law was written to apply to the telephone industry to collect numbers dialed on a telephone line and the originating number. The Act redefined pen register as a "device or process which records or decodes dialing, routing, addressing, or signaling information transmitted by an instrument or facility from which a wire or electronic communication is transmitted." The change in definition allowed law enforcement to capture Internet information, covering electronic mail, Web surfing, and all other forms of electronic communications.

IMPORTANT

A change to the wiretap law added crimes of terrorism or production/dissemination of chemical weapons as predicate offenses as a crime for which an application for a wiretap can be made. It also added offenses relating to the intentional, unauthorized access to a protected government computer to obtain and communicate classified information for a clandestine foreign source that could be used to injure the United States or a foreign nation as felonies and a predicate offense for a wiretap.

The Act changed rule 6(e)(3)(c) of the Federal Rules of Criminal Procedures to allow grand jury material involving foreign intelligence or counterintelligence to be shared with any Federal law enforcement, intelligence, protective, immigration, national defense, or national security official in order to assist the official receiving the information in the performance of their official duties.

Prior to the enactment of the Patriot Act, a court order for a wiretap or pen register was only good for the judicial district of the issuing court. The Act allowed the courts to issue orders for the installation of a surveillance device anywhere in the United States. This is an important tool for law enforcement with the mobility of today's criminals. The Act also adds a crime to Title 31 for bulk currency smuggling.

The complaint below was the first time that section was used for prosecution.

Figure 2.2 Sample Complaint

1	
2	**UNITED STATES DISTRICT COURT**
3	**SOUTHERN DISTRICT OF CALIFORNIA**
4	

UNITED STATES DISTRICT COURT

SOUTHERN DISTRICT OF CALIFORNIA

FILED

'03 JUL -2 AM 11:42

CLERK, U.S. DISTRICT COURT
SOUTHERN DISTRICT OF CALIFORNIA

BY: _____ DEPUTY

)
) Magistrate's Case No.
)
UNITED STATES OF AMERICA)
)
VS.) **COMPLAINT**
)
) 31 USC SS. 5332
)
Alvaro OBESO-Valenzuela) Bulk Cash Smuggling Out of the United States
)
) '03 mg15674

The undersigned complainant being duly sworn states:

COUNT ONE

That on or about July 1, 2003, within the Southern District of California, **Alvaro OBESO-Valenzuela**, did knowingly and intentionally conceal in his vehicle more than $10,000.00 in US currency and attempt to transfer such currency from a place within the United States, to a place outside the United States, with the intent to evade a currency reporting requirement; in violation of Title 31, United States Code, Section 5332

And the complainant states that this complaint is based on the attached statement of facts, which is incorporated herein by reference.

_____
Richard D. Krahn
Senior Special Agent, U.S. Customs Service

Sworn to before me and subscribed in my presence, this _____ day of _____, 2003.

_____
United States Magistrate/Judge

Page 1

Figure 2.2 Sample Complaint (cont.)

<u>PROBABLE CAUSE STATEMENT</u>

I, Senior Special Agent Richard Krahn, declare under penalty of perjury, that the following is true and correct:

On July 1, 2003, Agents of the San Diego Financial Task Force were conducting vehicle southbound operations at the San Ysidro, California, Port of Entry.

On July 1, 2003, at approximately 1010 hours, Agent Krahn encountered a 1997 Ford Thunderbird, silver in color and bearing California license 3XLH030 attempt to depart the United States. The 1997 Ford was driven by a sole occupant later identified as Alvaro OBESO-Valenzuela. At this time, the vehicle traffic at the border entrance into Mexico was stopped and sporadically moving when Agent Krahn noticed OBESO attempt to change lanes and go around other stopped vehicles.

Agent Krahn approached OBESO and requested that he turn off the engine to the vehicle. Initially, Agent Krahn spoke to OBESO in the English language, when OBESO informed the agent in the Spanish language that he did not understand. Agent Krahn continued in the Spanish language and asked OBESO if he had anything to declare, where he was going, what he was bringing into Mexico, if he had more than $10,000.00 in currency, who owned the vehicle, what was the purpose of the trip, where was he coming from and if he had any firearms. OBESO replied that he did not have anything to declare and that he was not bringing anything into Mexico, that he owned the car, that he had driven from Los Angeles and was going to Tijuana to see a family member. Agent Krahn again asked OBESO if had more than $10,000.00 in currency or anything else to declare, to which he replied "nada." Agent Krahn requested the keys to the trunk of the vehicle and observed a 24 pack of Sprite. Agent Krahn observed and noted that OBESO appeared to be evasive giving one-word answers to the questions and avoiding eye contact. Additionally, Agent Krahn made note and observed there to be two keys on the key chain, the trunk appeared to be unusually clean and empty and the interior of the vehicle also to be unusually clean and to have little or no personal possessions except for several items that appeared to be strategically placed. Agent Krahn escorted OBESO to the Secondary Inspection area for more intensive search purposes.

OBESO was escorted to the Security Office where a pat-down search of OBESO was conducted for the purposes of officer safety and contraband detection yielding negative results. During the search of OBESO, the inspectors asked OBESO 3 times, if OBESO had more than $10,000.00 in currency on his person or in the vehicle. OBESO looked downward and said "no." Additionally, OBESO made two more negative declarations for currency to the inspectors.

In the Secondary area, Agent Krahn requested a Canine Enforcement Officer, to utilize his assigned canine to screen the 1997 Ford for narcotics and contraband.

Figure 2.2 Sample Complaint (cont.)

The officer observed the canine to exhibit a "positive" alert sourced to the driver's side rear quarter panel interior. Agent Krahn then requested an x-ray of the vehicle with the Mobil Truck X-ray. The x-ray of the vehicle revealed what appeared to be a number of packages concealed in the driver's side rear quarter panel.

Agent Krahn conducted an intensive search of the 1997 Ford and discovered 7 blocks of US currency concealed in the driver's side interior quarter panel located behind the rear speaker. Agent Krahn noted that each package was fastened with rubber bands and tightly wrapped in clear plastic. Various denominations of bills were noted to be contained in each package. The 7 packages totaled approximately $156,980.00 in US currency.

On July 1, 2003, at approximately 1405 hours, Agent Krahn advised Alvaro OBESO-Valenzuela that he was under arrest for attempting to smuggle US currency out of the United States. A San Diego Police Department detective advised OBESO of his Constitutional Rights (Miranda), in the Spanish language. OBESO said that he understood his rights and agreed to make statements to the investigating agents. OBESO also waived notification to the Mexican Consulate.

In summary, Alvaro OBESO-Valenzuela stated that he owned the vehicle (1997 Ford) for approximately 2 months, that he was instructed to loan the car to an unknown person and that he was instructed to drive to Tijuana, Mexico, where he was to meet and give the car to a female. OBESO admitted that this was his second trip to Mexico, to deliver the car to the female.

OBESO explained that he did not know there was US currency in the vehicle and that he did not put the money in the car. OBESO stated that "CHENO LNU" (Last Name Unknown) had purchased the 1997 Ford for OBESO because OBESO had a California driver's license. OBESO was to have the car to use except when "LILLY LNU" needed the car in Mexico. Then OBESO was supposed to deliver the vehicle to Mexico. OBESO stated that yesterday, CHENO instructed OBESO to meet an unknown person in Los Angeles and for OBESO to let the person borrow the car for awhile. CHENO then instructed OBESO to drive the car to Tijuana today and meet LILLY. OBESO admitted that he knows that CHENO and others are involved in narcotics trafficking.

OBESO told the investigating officers that he knows the currency reporting requirements, as OBESO has crossed the border many times and has read the signs posted about reporting $10,000.00 or more in US currency.

In his possession at the time of arrest, OBESO had several documents including deposit slips showing cash deposits into the Mexican bank account of the wife of OBESO, Blanca Hilda OBESO-Soberanes. ($9,234.06 on May 28, 2003 and $8,000.00 on June 16, 2003.)

Individual State Statutes

Most states contain anti-conspiracy laws modeled after the federal statutes and a growing number of white-collar criminal prosecutions have included allegations of conspiracy.

Canadian Law

Canada has a number of conspiracy statutes. Under their laws relating to terrorism they have ten separate statutes that have conspiracy violations. Their treason statute has a provision for conspiracy. Other laws that have conspiracy statutes including gambling, drugs, sabotage, forgery, weapons trafficking, bribery, fraud on government, municipal corruption, perjury, obstructing justice, prison breach, obscene materials, child pornography, murder, assault with a weapon, sexual assault, kidnapping, abduction, theft, unauthorized use of a computer, robbery, extortion, breaking and entering and arson.

International Criminal Court

The International Criminal Court was established by the Rome Statute of the International Criminal Court on July 17, 1998, when 120 States participating in the "United Nations Diplomatic Conference of Plenipotentiaries on the Establishment of an International Criminal Court" adopted the Statute. This was the first ever permanent, treaty based, international criminal court established to promote the rule of law and ensure that the gravest international crimes do not go unpunished.

The Statute sets out the Court's jurisdiction, structure and functions and it provides for its establishment sixty days after sixty States have ratified or acceded to it, which happen on April 11, 2002. Anyone who commits any of the crimes under the Statute after this date will be liable for prosecution by the Court. The seat of the Court is The Hague in the Netherlands.

Member States, as well as the United Nation Security Council can refer situations to the Office of the Prosecutor for investigations. The Prosecutor also has the power to initiate investigations if it is determined that there is a reasonable basis to proceed with an investigation. The Pre-Trial Chamber can issue a warrant for arrest if the Prosecutor satisfies the Chamber that there are reasonable grounds to believe that the person has committed one of the crimes under the Statute. The arrested person will appear before a competent judicial authority to determine the lawfulness of their arrest and apply for bail. The accused is entitled to appear before the Trial Chamber within a reasonable time for confirmation of the charges. The Trial Chamber will ensure that trials are fair and expeditious. The maximum sentence that can be imposed by the Court is thirty years. Oversight management of the Court is provided by the Assembly of States Parties, a body composed of all parties to the Statute.

Figure 2.3 Case Study: Multicore, LTD.

Multicore was a front company for the Iranian government headquartered in London, England. The company was established to acquired aircraft, missile and other parts needed by the Iranian government for its weapons programs. The sale of these parts to a company outside the United States without a proper license is unlawful. Multicore LTD. established a branch office in Bakersfield, California to acquire the parts then ship them to a sister company in Singapore to be transshipped to Iran. On December 7, 2001, special agents from the U.S. Customs Service and the Defense Criminal Investigative Service executed a search warrant on the residence of Saeed Homayouni and a warehouse in Bakersfield, California. The agents seized a total 16 pallet and one crate of military aircraft and other spare parts valued at over $1.5 million.

Sample Indictment

As you read the indictment which starts on the next page, notice how skillfully Assistant United States Attorney George Hardy laid out the violations, objectives and overt acts.

Figure 2.4 Sample Indictment

FILED

00 DEC 19 PM 3:59

CLERK, U.S. DISTRICT COURT
SOUTHERN DISTRICT OF CALIFORNIA

BY: _____ DEPUTY

UNITED STATES DISTRICT COURT

SOUTHERN DISTRICT OF CALIFORNIA

February 2000 Grand Jury

00 CR 3843 J

UNITED STATES OF AMERICA,
 	
          Plaintiff,
 	
          v.
 	
MULTICORE LTD. (1),
SOROOSH HOMAYOUNI (2),
     aka "Peter Harris",
SAEED HOMAYOUNI (3),
     aka "Joe Barry",
     aka "Sid Hamilton",
YEW LENG FUNG (4),
     aka "Pamela Fung",
 	
          Defendants.
	Criminal Case No._____
	
	I N D I C T M E N T
	
	Title 18, U.S.C., Sec. 371 -
	Conspiracy to Defraud the United
	States, and to Commit Offenses
	Against the United States; to
	wit, Title 22, U.S.C.,
	Sec. 2778 - Arms Export Control
	Act; Title 50, U.S.C., App.,
	Sec. 2401 et seq. - Export
	Administration Act; Title 50,
	U.S.C., Sec. 1701 et seq. -
	International Emergency
	Economic Powers Act;
	Title 18, U.S.C., Sec. 1956 -
	Money Laundering

     The Grand Jury charges:

A.   Introductory Allegations:

     · At all times material to this Indictment:

     <u>Persons and Entities</u>

     1.   MULTICORE LTD. was a business entity headquartered at 1a

Dorset Street W1H 3FD, London, England, with a branch office located

at 800 New Stine Road, Suite 6, Bakersfield, California, in

//

GDH:nlv(xxx):San Diego
12/19/00

9

Figure 2.4 Sample Indictment (cont.)

1   the business of purchasing and exporting United States military

2   aircraft and missile parts, without registering or obtaining

3   appropriate licenses from the United States government.

4   2.   SOROOSH HOMAYOUNI, aka "Peter Harris", was a shareholder of

5   MULTICORE LTD., and resided in London, England.

6   3.   SAEED HOMAYOUNI, aka "Joe Barry" and "Sid Hamilton", was an

7   agent of MULTICORE LTD. who resided and worked out of the branch

8   office at 800 New Stine Road, Suite 6, Bakersfield, California.

9   4.   YEW LENG FUNG, aka "Pamela Fung", was an agent of MULTICORE

10 LTD. who worked out of the London headquarters office, and

11 periodically visited and worked out of the branch office at 800 New

12 Stine Road, Suite 6, Bakersfield, California.

13   5.   Rowland Diesel Parts was a fictitious business entity in

14 Vista, California, identified by SAEED HOMAYOUNI, aka "Joe Barry", as

15 the shipper of military aircraft and missile parts to Singapore.

16   The Statutes and Regulations

17   6.   The Arms Export Control Act (22 U.S.C. § 2778) authorizes

18 the President of the United States to control the export of "defense

19 articles" by including items, particularly military aircraft and

20 missile parts, on the United States Munitions List. Persons or

21 entities desiring to export from the United States an item on the

22 United States Munitions List must first register with, and then obtain

23 a license from, the United States Department of State, Office of

24 Defense Trade Controls.

25   7.   It is a felony to wilfully violate the requirements of the

26 Arms Export Control Act, including the requirement that those in the

27 business of exporting articles, or in the business of brokering

28 activities with respect to exporting defense articles, must register

2

Figure 2.4 Sample Indictment (cont.)

1 and obtain a license from the Office of Defense Trade Controls, before

2 exporting defense articles.

3   8.   The Export Administration Act (50 U.S.C. App. § 2401 et

4 seq.) authorizes the United States Department of Commerce, Office of

5 Export Enforcement, to control the export of "goods and technology"

6 by including items on the Control List, maintained by the Secretary

7 of Commerce.

8   9.   It is a felony to wilfully violate, or conspire, or attempt

9 to violate any provision of the Export Administration Act. The Act

10 requires those who wish to export items on the Control List, and those

11 who possess items on the Control List, with intent to export the goods

12 or technology in violation of export controls, or having reason to

13 believe the goods or technology would be so exported, to obtain a

14 license from the Department of Commerce.

15   10.   The International Emergency Economic Powers Act (50 U.S.C.

16 § 1701, et seq.), among other things, authorizes the President of the

17 United States to impose trade sanctions on a country, in response to

18 the unusual and extraordinary threat to the national security, foreign

19 policy, and economy of the United States presented by that country.

20 By Executive Orders, the President of the United States imposed such

21 sanctions on Iran and the Government of Iran.

22   11.   It is a felony to wilfully violate or attempt to violate any

23 order or regulation issued under the authority of the International

24 Emergency Economic Powers Act.

25   12.   The Money Laundering statute (18 U.S.C. § 1956) prohibits,

26 among other things, the transfer of monetary instruments or funds to

27 a place in the United States from or through a place outside the

28 United States with the intent to promote the carrying on of specified

3

Figure 2.4 Sample Indictment (cont.)

1 unlawful activity. Specified unlawful activity includes violations
2 of the Arms Export Control Act, the Export Administration Act, and the
3 International Emergency Economic Powers Act.
4   The Iranian Military
5   13. Prior to 1979, during the reign of the most recent Shah of
6 Iran, the United States sold numerous weapons systems to Iran,
7 including the F-14 Tomcat fighter aircraft, the F-4 Phantom fighter
8 aircraft, the F-5 Tiger fighter aircraft, and the Hawk Missile System.
9   14. Following the overthrow of the Shah, and the resulting trade
10 embargo with Iran, the Government of Iran has been unable to legally
11 obtain from the United States spare parts and components for these
12 weapons systems.
13 B.   The Conspiracy
14   15. Beginning at a date unknown, and continuing to on or about
15 December 7, 2000, within the Southern District of California, and
16 elsewhere, defendants MULTICORE LTD., SOROOSH HOMAYOUNI, SAEED
17 HOMAYOUNI, and YEW LENG FUNG did knowingly and intentionally combine,
18 conspire, confederate and agree together, and with others unknown, to
19 defraud the United States, and to commit offenses against the United
20 States; to wit, to violate provisions of 22 U.S.C. § 2778 (Arms Export
21 Control Act), 50 U.S.C. App. § 2401, et seq. (Export Administration
22 Act), 50 U.S.C. § 1701, et seq. (International Emergency Economic
23 Powers Act), and 18 U.S.C. § 1956(a)(2) (Money Laundering).
24 C.   Objects of the Conspiracy
25   16. It was part of the conspiracy that defendants MULTICORE
26 LTD., SOROOSH HOMAYOUNI, SAEED HOMAYOUNI, and YEW LENG FUNG would and
27 did defraud the United States by circumventing, defeating, and
28 frustrating statutes, regulations, and executive orders, passed,

4

Figure 2.4 Sample Indictment (cont.)

1 promulgated, and issued for the purpose of controlling the exportation

2 of military aircraft and missile parts.

3   17. It was a further part of the conspiracy that defendants

4 MULTICORE LTD., SOROOSH HOMAYOUNI, SAEED HOMAYOUNI, and YEW LENG FUNG

5 would and did violate provisions of the Arms Export Control Act (22

6 U.S.C. § 2778), by wilfully failing to register with the Department

7 of State, Office of Defense Controls, while engaged in the business

8 of exporting defense articles, and the business of brokering

9 activities with respect to exporting defense articles, and by wilfully

10 exporting defense articles without first obtaining a license from the

11 Department of State, Office of Defense Trade Controls.

12   18. It was a further part of the conspiracy that defendants

13 MULTICORE LTD., SOROOSH HOMAYOUNI, SAEED HOMAYOUNI, and YEW LENG FUNG

14 would and did violate provisions of the Export Administration Act (50

15 U.S.C. App. § 2401, et seq.), by possessing goods and technology with

16 intent to export said goods and technology in violation of export

17 controls, and knowing, and having reason to believe said goods and

18 technology would be so exported.

19   19. It was a further part of the conspiracy that defendants

20 MULTICORE LTD., SOROOSH HOMAYOUNI, SAEED HOMAYOUNI, and YEW LENG FUNG

21 would and did violate provisions of the International Emergency

22 Economic Powers Act (50 U.S.C. § 1701, et seq.), by wilfully violating

23 and attempting to violate Executive Orders prohibiting trade with Iran

24 and the Government of Iran.

25   20. It was a further part of the conspiracy that defendants

26 MULTICORE LTD., SOROOSH HOMAYOUNI, SAEED HOMAYOUNI, and YEW LENG FUNG

27 would and did violate the Money Laundering Statute (18 U.S.C. § 1956),

28 by transporting, transmitting, and transferring, and attempting to

5

Figure 2.4 Sample Indictment (cont.)

1   transport, transmit, and transfer monetary instruments and funds to

2   California, from London, England, with the intent to promote the

3   carrying on of specified unlawful activity; that is, violations of the

4   Arms Export Control Act, the Export Administration Act, and the

5   International Emergency Economic Powers Act.

6   D.   Methods and Means of the Conspiracy

7   21.   In furtherance of the conspiracy and to effect the objects

8   of the conspiracy, the following methods and means, among others, were

9   used:

10   a.   MULTICORE LTD., SOROOSH HOMAYOUNI, and YEW LENG

11   FUNG would and did solicit requests for

12   quotations from vendors of military aircraft and

13   missile parts throughout the United States.

14   b.   MULTICORE LTD., SOROOSH HOMAYOUNI, SAEED

15   HOMAYOUNI, and YEW LENG FUNG would and did

16   negotiate final purchase prices for the parts and

17   either accept delivery of the parts in

18   Bakersfield, California, or direct the vendor to

19   ship the parts directly to a transshipper in

20   Singapore.

21   c.   MULTICORE LTD., SOROOSH HOMAYOUNI, SAEED

22   HOMAYOUNI, and YEW LENG FUNG would and did pay

23   for the parts using checks drawn on a Bank of

24   America account in San Francisco, California;

25   which account had been funded by transfers of

26   funds from Barclays Bank, London, England.

27   d.   MULTICORE LTD., SAEED HOMAYOUNI and YEW LENG FUNG

28   would and did store parts that had been shipped

Figure 2.4 Sample Indictment (cont.)

1   to Bakersfield, California, in private storage

2   facilities, pending exportation.

3   e.   MULTICORE LTD., and SAEED HOMAYOUNI, would and

4   did establish a fictitious business entity,

5   called "Rowland Diesel Parts", in Vista,

6   California, and identify this entity as the

7   "shipper" on packages of military aircraft and

8   missile parts being exported to a transshipper in

9   Singapore.

10   f.   MULTICORE LTD. would and did control and monitor

11   all transactions from its headquarters in London,

12   England.

13   g.   MULTICORE   LTD.,   SOROOSH   HOMAYOUNI,   SAEED

14   HOMAYOUNI, and YEW LENG FUNG undertook the

15   aforementioned activities without first obtaining

16   licenses from the United States Department of

17   Commerce, or the Department of State.

18   E.   Overt Acts

19   22. In furtherance of the conspiracy and to effect the objects

20   of the conspiracy, the following overt acts, among others, were

21   committed in the Southern District of California:

22   a.   On or about October 28, 1996, MULTICORE LTD., and

23   SOROOSH   HOMAYOUNI,   aka   "Peter   Harris",

24   telephonically contacted Vernitron Corporation,

25   San Diego, California, to discuss the purchase of

26   a "synchro" (part #TX23-4G3), a part subject to

27   export controls.

28   //

7

Figure 2.4 Sample Indictment (cont.)

1   b.   On or about February 11, 1997, MULTICORE LTD.,

2   and SOROOSH HOMAYOUNI, aka "Peter Harris", faxed

3   a purchase order to Vernitron Corporation, San

4   Diego, California, purchasing 30 "synchros" (part

5   #TX23-4G3).

6   c.   On or about March 29, 1997, MULTICORE LTD.,

7   caused Vernitron Corporation to ship 10

8   "synchros" (part #TX23-4G3) from San Diego,

9   California, to Singapore.

10   d.   On or about April 25, 1997, MULTICORE LTD.,

11   caused Vernitron Corporation to ship 20

12   "synchros" (part #TX23-4G3) from San Diego,

13   California, to Singapore.

14   e.   On or about June 7, 1997, SAEED HOMAYOUNI, aka

15   "Joe Barry", faxed a Service Agreement

16   Application to Precise Communications, 1330 E.

17   Vista Way, Vista, California, seeking to

18   establish answering service for "Rowland Diesel

19   Parts", a fictitious business entity.

20   f.   On or about September 10, 1997, MULTICORE LTD.,

21   and SOROOSH HOMAYOUNI, aka "Peter Harris", faxed

22   to Vernitron Corporation, San Diego, California,

23   a request for quote for a "synchro control" (part

24   #CT23-4G), a part subject to export controls.

25 //

26 //

27 //

28 //

8

Figure 2.4 Sample Indictment (cont.)

g.   On or about September 23, 1997, MULTICORE, LTD., and SOROOSH HOMAYOUNI, aka "Peter Harris", caused Vernitron Corporation, San Diego, California, to fax a price quote and delivery schedule for a "synchro control" (part #CT23-4G).

h.   On or about December 22, 1997, MULTICORE LTD., and SOROOSH HOMAYOUNI, aka "Peter Harris", faxed a purchase order to Vernitron Corporation, San Diego, California, purchasing 10 "synchro controls" (part #CT23-4G).

i.   On or about February 2, 1998, MULTICORE LTD., and SOROOSH HOMAYOUNI, aka "Peter Harris", faxed a letter to Vernitron Corporation, San Diego, California, identifying a shipping account number to be used to ship the "synchro controls" (part #CT23-4G).

j.   On or about February 7, 1998, MULTICORE LTD., caused Vernitron Corporation, San Diego, California, to ship 10 "synchro controls" (part #CT23-4G) to Singapore.

k.   On or about February 8, 1999, MULTICORE LTD., and SOROOSH HOMAYOUNI, aka "Peter Harris", faxed a request to Eclipse Aeronautical, Oceanside, California, for pricing information for a "half quick coupling" (part #A51H9182-1), a part unique to the F-14 Tomcat fighter aircraft, and a "connector" (part #MS27484T8B44-S).

//

9

Figure 2.4 Sample Indictment (cont.)

1.　On or about February 9, 1999, MULTICORE LTD., and YEW LENG FUNG, aka "Pamela Fung", faxed a request to Eclipse Aeronautical, Oceanside, California, for pricing information for a "seal assembly" (part #A51B90919-13), a part unique to the F-14 Tomcat fighter aircraft.

m.　On or about June 2, 2000, MULTICORE LTD., and SOROOSH HOMAYOUNI, aka "Peter Harris", faxed an invoice to Eclipse Aeronautical, Oceanside, California, purchasing 10 "half quick couplings" (part #A51H9182-1).

n.　On or about June 9, 2000, SOROOSH HOMAYOUNI, aka "Peter Harris", telephonically spoke with a representative of Eclipse Aeronautical in Oceanside, California, regarding the price of the "half quick couplings" (part #A51H9182-1).

o.　On or about June 9, 2000, MULTICORE LTD. caused Eclipse Aeronautical, Oceanside, California, to ship 10 "half quick couplings" (part #A51H9182-1) to Bakersfield, California, where it was picked up and paid for by SAEED HOMAYOUNI, aka "Sid Hamilton".

p.　On or about May 28, 1999, MULTICORE LTD., and SOROOSH HOMAYOUNI, aka "Peter Harris", faxed an invoice to Mackenzie Aircraft Company, Carlsbad, California, purchasing a "cable assembly" (part #080-021-001), a part unique to the F-14 Tomcat fighter aircraft.

10

Figure 2.4 Sample Indictment (cont.)

q. On or about June 1, 1999, MULTICORE LTD. caused Mackenzie Aircraft Company, Carlsbad, California, to ship 1 "cable assembly" (part #080-021-001) to Bakersfield, California, where it was picked up and paid for by SAEED HOMAYOUNI, aka "Sid Hamilton".

r. On or about October 2, 2000, MULTICORE LTD., and SOROOSH HOMAYOUNI, aka "Peter Harris", caused Mackenzie Aircraft Company, Carlsbad, California, to fax a quotation for a "motor" (part #3602-4) to MULTICORE LTD.

s. On or about October 19, 2000, MULTICORE LTD. and YEW LENG FUNG, aka "Pamela Fung", faxed a request to Mackenzie Aircraft Company, Carlsbad, California, for pricing information for an "adaptor techtronic" (part #103-0028-00).

t. On or about October 20, 2000, MULTICORE LTD. and YEW LENG FUNG, aka "Pamela Fung", caused Mackenzie Aircraft Company, Carlsbad, California, to fax a quotation for an "adaptor techtronic" (part #103-0028-00).

u. On or about November 27, 2000, MULTICORE LTD. and YEW LENG FUNG, aka "Pamela Fung", faxed a request to Mackenzie Aircraft Company, Carlsbad, California, for pricing information for a "seal" (part #2183975).

v. On or about November 28, 2000, MULTICORE LTD. and YEW LENG FUNG, aka "Pamela Fung", caused

11

Figure 2.4 Sample Indictment (cont.)

1   Mackenzie Aircraft Company, Carlsbad, California,

2   to fax a quotation for a "seal" (part #2183975).

3   w.   On or about November 30, 2000, MULTICORE LTD. and

4   YEW LENG FUNG, aka "Pamela Fung", faxed a request

5   to   Mackenzie   Aircraft   Company,   Carlsbad,

6   California, for pricing information for a "dummy

7   load", part "#L205-1222".

8   x.   On or about December 1, 2000, MULTICORE LTD. and

9   YEW   LENG   FUNG,   aka   "Pamela   Fung",   caused

10   Mackenzie Aircraft Company, Carlsbad, California,

11   to fax a quotation for a "dummy load", part

12   "#L202S-1222".

13   23.   In furtherance of the conspiracy and to effect the objects

14   of the conspiracy, the following overt acts, among others, were

15   committed outside the Southern District of California:

16   a.   On or about April 25, 2000, MULTICORE LTD. and

17   SOROOSH HOMAYOUNI, aka "Peter Harris, purchased

18   a "correlation cursor", a part unique to the Hawk

19   Missile System, from Bright Lights USA, Inc.,

20   Barrington, New Jersey.

21   b.   On or about October 10, 2000, MULTICORE LTD., and

22   SAEED HOMAYOUNI, aka "Sid Hamilton" received

23   delivery   of   a   "correlation   cursor"   in

24   Bakersfield, California, from Bright Lights USA,

25   Inc., Barrington, New Jersey.

26   c.   On or about July 2, 1999, MULTICORE LTD., and

27   SOROOSH HOMAYOUNI, aka "Peter Harris", purchased

28   20 "electron tubes", parts unique to the F-4

12

Figure 2.4 Sample Indictment (cont.)

1		Phantom fighter aircraft, from Imaging and
2		Sensing Technology, Horseheads, New York.
3	d.	On or about September 8, 1999, SAEED HOMAYOUNI,
4		aka "Sid Hamilton", received delivery of 7
5		"electron tubes" in Bakersfield, California,
6		from Imaging and Sensing Technology, Horseheads,
7		New York.
8	e.	On or about October 5, 1999, SAEED HOMAYOUNI
9		wrote a check to cash in the amount of $4454.55,
10		for the purchase of a cashiers check payable to
11		Imaging and Sensing Technology.
12	f.	On or about November 30, 2000, MULTICORE LTD.,
13		and YEW LENG FUNG, aka "Pamela Fung", requested
14		pricing information from Intertrade Aviation
15		Corp, Huntington Beach, California, for a
16		"leading edge, aircraft" for the F-5 Tiger
17		fighter aircraft.
18	g.	On or about July 31, 2000, MULTICORE LTD.
19		purchased 40 "impeller wheels", parts unique to
20		the F-14 Tomcat fighter aircraft, from Lee Air
21		Company, Sun Valley, California.
22	h.	On or about August 4, 2000, SAEED HOMAYOUNI, aka
23		"Sid Hamilton" received delivery of, and paid
24		for, the 40 "impeller wheels" purchased from Lee
25		Air Company, Sun Valley, California.
26	i.	On or about December 17, 1999, SOROOSH HOMAYOUNI
27		signed an application for a letter of credit,
28		guaranteeing payment in the amount of

13

Figure 2.4 Sample Indictment (cont.)

approximately $327,000, to Derco Aerospace, Inc., Milwaukee, Wisconsin, for the manufacture and delivery of 5 "generators", parts unique to the F-5 Tiger fighter aircraft.

j.   On or about October 14, 1999, MULTICORE LTD., and SOROOSH HOMAYOUNI wire transferred $60,000 from Barclays Bank, London, England, to Bank of America, San Francisco, California.

k.   On or about November 19, 1999, MULTICORE LTD. wire transferred $160,000 from Barclays Bank, London, England, to Bank of America, San Francisco, California.

l.   On or about December 20, 1999, MULTICORE LTD. wire transferred $327,990 from Barclays Bank, London, England, to Bank of America, San Francisco, California.

m.   On or about May 23, 2000, MULTICORE LTD. wire transferred $122,000 from Barclays Bank, London, England, to Bank of America, San Francisco, California.

n.   On or about July 25, 2000, MULTICORE LTD. wire transferred $100,000 from Barclays Bank, London, England, to Bank of America, San Francisco, California.

//
//
//
//

14

Figure 2.4 Sample Indictment (cont.)

```
 1            o.     On or about August 2, 2000, MULTICORE LTD. wire
 2                   transferred $200,000 from Barclays Bank, London,
 3                   England, to Bank of America, San Francisco,
 4                   California.
 5   All in violation of Title 18, United States Code, Section 371.
 6       DATE:  December 19, 2000.
 7                                          A TRUE BILL:
 8
 9                                          Foreperson
10
   GREGORY A. VEGA
11   United States Attorney
12
13   By:
       GEORGE D. HARDY
14     Assistant U.S. Attorney
15
16
17
18
19
20
21
22
23
24
25
26
27
28

                                15
```

SUMMARY

A co-conspirator can withdraw from a conspiracy, but they are responsible for all the crimes committed to the point of their withdrawal, in addition to the charge of conspiracy. A person can join a conspiracy after it has been formed and they are responsible for all the crimes committed after their joining in addition to the charge of conspiracy. Conspiracy is a separate chargeable crime. The agreement is the essential essence of the crime of conspiracy. It is the agreement that distinguishes conspiracy from aiding and abetting. While you do not have to prove actual words or written agreement, you must show a meeting of the minds to deliberately commit an unlawful act.

DISCUSSION QUESTIONS

1. How can you prove the existence of an agreement to commit an unlawful act?
2. Explain Wharton's rule.
3. Give examples of lawful and unlawful overt acts.
4. What is the venue for a charge of conspiracy?

ADDITIONAL READING

Department of Justice, United States Attorney's Manual, Criminal Resource Manuel http://www.usdoj.gov/usao/eousa/foia_reading_room Title 9, Chapter 14

BIBLIOGRAPHY

U.S. Customs, law course for Customs officers

U.S. Code Annotated, Title 18

Electronic Privacy Information Center, www.epic.org

International Criminal Court, www.ici-cpi.int

Department of Justice, United States Attorney's Manuel, www.usdoj.gov

Department of Justice Canada, Canadian Justice System, Chapter 46, www.canada.justice.gc.ca

Press Release - U.S. Department of Justice, Grand Jury returns indictment charging members, associates of soldiers of the Aryan culture with violations of RICO, violent crime in aid of racketeering activity dated December 11, 2003, www.usdoj.gov/.

www.findlaw.com/case code

www.usdoj.gov

www.dea.gov

Chapter 3

Financial Crimes

OVERVIEW

In this chapter you learned about different types of financial crimes. You will study materials that will examine in detail some of the different types of schemes being used to commit financial crimes. You will also read an actual indictment for bankruptcy fraud.

CHAPTER OBJECTIVES

1. Understand the motives to commit financial crimes.
2. Be able to identify the different types of financial crimes.
3. Know some of the elements of the financial crimes.
4. Know the effects of financial crimes on the economy.
5. Understand why the conspiracy statutes are used to prosecute violators of financial crimes.

DEFINITION OF FINANCIAL CRIMES

Financial crimes encompass a wide variety of crimes that are motivated by the greed for money. These crimes include illegal procurement and contract fraud, anti-trust violations, health care fraud, environmental crimes, financial institution fraud, intellectual property crimes, telemarketing fraud, securities/commodities fraud, insurance fraud, bankruptcy fraud and money laundering.

HEALTH CARE FRAUD

Health care fraud involves the over charging for goods and services. Sometimes the good are never delivered or not needed. Other times people are given medical procedures or medicines that are not needed. Doctors, pharmacists, nurses, physical therapists or equipment suppliers commit these crimes. It is estimated that the cost of health care fraud to government and private insurers exceeds 95 billion dollars a year with the government programs like Medicaid and Medicare picking up about 44 percent of that lost.

According to the FBI, people who file phony auto insurance claims and stage car accidents defraud the insurance companies out of nearly 20 billion dollars a year. That translates into about $200 a year more for your car insurance.

United States Code, Title 18 § 347 Health Care Fraud

Whoever knowingly and willfully executes, or attempts to execute, a scheme or artifice

(1) To defraud any health care benefit program; or

(2) To obtain, by means of false or fraudulent pretenses, representations, or promises, any of the money or property owned by, or under the custody or control of, any health care benefit program, in connection with the delivery of or payment for health care benefits, items, or services, shall be fined under this title or imprisoned not more than 10 years, or both. If the violation results in serious bodily injury (as defined in section 1365 of this title), such person shall be fined under this title or imprisoned not more than 20 years, or both; and if the violation results in death, such person shall be fined under this title, or imprisoned for any term of years or for life, or both.

Figure 3.1 Government Administrative Office Summary of Report on Health Care Fraud May 1996

Health Care Fraud: Information Sharing Proposals to Improve Enforcement Efforts

GAO Report to the Banking Minority Member, Subcommittee on National Security, International Affairs and Criminal Justice, House Committee on Government Reform and Oversight

EXECUTIVE SUMMARY

Purpose

Health care fraud burdens the nation with enormous financial costs, while threatening the quality of health care. Estimates of annual losses due to health care fraud range from 3 to 10 percent of all health care expenditures—between $30 billion and $100 billion based on estimated 1995 expenditures of over $1 trillion. In late 1993, the Attorney General designated health care fraud as the Department of Justice's number two enforcement priority, second only to violent crime initiatives.

In response to a request from the former Chairman and subsequent agreements with the current Ranking Minority Member, House Subcommittee on National Security, International Affairs and Criminal Justice, Committee on Government Reform and Oversight, GAO's report focuses on information-sharing issues that may affect health care anti-fraud enforcement efforts. Specifically, this report discusses (1) the extent of federal and state immunity laws protecting persons who report health care fraud-related information and (2) the advantages and disadvantages of establishing a centralized health care fraud database to enhance information sharing and support enforcement efforts.

Background

The size and complexity of the health care industry present considerable challenges for government and industry fraud investigators. Federal enforcement agencies responsible for investigating health care fraud include the Federal Bureau of Investigation (FBI); the U.S. Postal Inspection Service; and various Offices of Inspector General, such as that within the Department of Health and Human Services (HHS). Moreover, most states have established insurance fraud bureaus or units that investigate health care fraud. Also, many private insurance carriers have established special units to investigate fraud within their health plans. In addition, a group of private sector health insurers and public sector enforcement agencies has established the National Health Care

Figure 3.1 Government Administrative Office Summary of Report on Health Care Fraud May 1996 (cont.)

Anti-Fraud Association (NHCAA), which represents a cooperative effort to address health care fraud.

Over the years, the administration and Congress have considered proposals to enhance information sharing among the federal, state, and private entities involved in health care anti-fraud enforcement. In considering such proposals, decision makers have been confronted with the inherent conflicts between the dual public policy goals of (l) supporting the role of private entities in the investigation and prosecution of fraud and (2) protecting innocent people and organizations against unsubstantiated allegations made in bad faith or with malice. On the one hand, some proposals have called for federal immunity legislation to provide protection—from defamation of character and other civil lawsuits—for persons (including private insurance company employees) who report suspected fraud. The purpose of such immunity law would be to encourage the reporting of suspected fraud to law enforcement agencies.

On the other hand, concerns have been raised about the need to incorporate safeguards to provide individuals with protection against bad faith allegations. Safeguards that have been considered include requirements governing the specificity and credibility of reported information and provisions giving individuals legal recourse against bad faith allegations that could seriously damage an individual's life and livelihood if publicly disclosed.

Other proposals have called for establishment of a national, centralized database of health care fraud-related information. The purpose of such a database would be to coordinate federal, state, and local anti-fraud enforcement efforts by providing a national data collection program for information about persons or entities involved in health care fraud.

To obtain perspectives on these issues, GAO contacted key government and private organizations. GAO also surveyed all 50 state insurance commissioners.

Results in Brief

GAO identified no immunity provision on the federal level designed to protect persons who report suspected health care fraud to law enforcement agencies. One existing federal immunity provision would protect persons reporting health care fraud-related information, but it applies only to persons who report information about the Medicare and Medicaid programs to peer review contractors operating under those programs. Private insurers and other health care claims processors are provided no federal immunity protection for reporting health care fraud-related information concerning other public or private health plans. While most states have enacted immunity laws protecting insurers, these laws vary in terms of the protection provided. Legislation (S. 1088, 104th Cong.) awaiting congressional consideration at the time of GAO's review would expand existing federal immunity law to protect persons providing information about fraud in any health plan (public or private) to either HHS or Justice.

Almost all of the federal and state officials as well as representatives of insurance companies and health care providers interviewed by GAO supported the concept of an expanded federal immunity law, including appropriate safeguards to protect against unsubstantiated allegations made in bad faith. The responses to GAO' survey of state insurance commissioners indicated broad support for both state and federal immunity laws. Many of the field officials GAO interviewed said that a federal immunity law, to be most useful, should be broader than the provisions included in S. 1088 by providing immunity protection to (1) persons sharing fraud-related information with any applicable federal or state enforcement entity and (2) insurers sharing such information with other insurers. Some of these officials noted that the latter approach involves greater risks because of the possibility that insurers could use the information inappropriately to discriminate against health care providers.

There is no centralized national database to track criminal activity in the health care system that would assist federal, state, and industry anti-fraud enforcement efforts. Recent congressional and administration proposals would have established health care fraud databases containing information about health care system participants (such as license revocations and criminal convictions) and ongoing health care fraud investigations, but none of these were implemented. Ss 1088 proposes to establish a centralized health care fraud database of final adverse actions including criminal convictions civil judgments, and negative licensing or certification actions accessible by federal and state government agencies and health insurers.

Most of the law enforcement and industry officials GAO interviewed saw benefits in and supported the establishment of a database of final adverse actions; however, many of the others did not

> **Figure 3.1 Government Administrative Office Summary of Report on Health Care Fraud May 1996 (cont.)**
>
> consider the potential benefits essential to enforcement efforts. Many of the officials also suggested that enforcement benefits probably would accrue from centralized databases that contain information about (1) ongoing health care fraud investigations and/or (2) suspected fraud reported by persons to enforcement or regulatory agencies. However, officials were concerned that such databases pose risks in terms of unauthorized disclosure and use of the information. In addition to these issues, there are also uncertainties about the cost of developing and operating a centralized database.

ENVIRONMENTAL CRIMES

Environmental crimes involve the poisonous polluting and the disposal of industrial chemicals like asbestos, Freon, medical waste and thousands of industrial chemicals. The more hazardous the material the more it cost to properly handle, store, and dispose of it legally.

Chlorofluorocarbons (CFCs) is known by its brand name, "Freon." In 1987, an international agreement was signed by more than 160 countries to completely phase out CFC production by the year 2000 because of its ozone-depleting characteristic. Diminishing supply and continuing demand has created a huge black market. The product is still being produced in Mexico and some smugglers make more money smuggling Freon than marijuana.

An off chute of the environmental fraud is lab fraud involving fraudulent testing/analysis designed to show compliance and serve as the basis for false statements to regulatory government agencies. Another form of lab fraud is fraudulent lab results to induce companies or individuals to contract for unnecessary environmental services.

FRAUD AGAINST THE GOVERNMENT

The United States Government is one of the largest purchasers of goods and services in the world. Kickbacks, false claims and fraudulently inflated contracts are typical of the violations that occur.

ANTITRUST

The primary federal antitrust law is the Sherman Antitrust Act. The Act makes it a violation for making contracts that unreasonably restrain trade, and attempting to form and maintain a monopoly in an industry.

FINANCIAL INSTITUTION FRAUD

Financial institution fraud includes bank failures, check fraud, counterfeit negotiable instruments, check kiting and loan fraud. Due to the regulatory agencies involved in policing the banks, we have not seen as many bank failures due to criminal activity since the peak of the saving and loan crisis in 1992. During the late 1980s and early 1990s, a majority of the fraud reported by financial institutions related to bank insider abuse. Since that time, the availability of personal information through information networks has made external fraud relating to check fraud and counterfeit negotiable instruments schemes one of the primary violations.

Criminal activity for loan fraud has continued to increase and become more complex. They include multi-transactional frauds involving groups of people from top management to industry professionals who assist in the loan application process. These professionals include real estate attorneys, loan brokers, appraisers and accountants.

United States Code, Title 18

§ 1001 Statements or entries generally

(a) Except as otherwise provided in this section, whoever, in any matter within the jurisdiction of the executive, legislative, or judicial branch of the Government of the United States, knowingly and willfully:

(1) Falsifies, conceals, or covers up by any trick, scheme, or device a material fact;

(2) Makes any materially false, fictitious, or fraudulent statement or representation; or

(3) Makes or uses any false writing or document knowing the same to contain any materially false, fictitious, or fraudulent statement or entry; shall be fined under this title or imprisoned not more than 5 years, or both.

You will see this statute noted on most government documents you sign or documents that have some connection to the government such as mortgage applications that are funded or insured by the government.

§1005. Bank entries, reports and transactions

Whoever, being an officer, director, agent or employee of any Federal Reserve bank, member bank, depository institution holding company, national bank, insured bank, branch or agency of a foreign bank, or organization operating under section 25 or section 25(a) of the Federal Reserve Act [12 USCU 601 et seq., 611 et seq.], without authority from the directors of such bank or company, branch, agency, or organization, issues or puts in circulation any notes of such bank or company, branch, agency, or organization; or

Whoever, without such authority, makes, draws, issues, puts forth, or assigns any certificate of deposit, draft, order, bill of exchange, acceptance, note, debenture, bond, or other obligation, or mortgage, judgment or decree; or Whoever makes any false entry in any book, report, or statement of such bank, company, branch, agency, or organization with intent to injure or defraud such bank, company, branch, agency, or organization, or any other company, body politic or corporate, or any individual person, or to deceive any officer of such bank, company, branch, agency, or organization, or the Comptroller of the Currency, or the Federal Deposit Insurance Corporation, or any agent or examiner appointed to examine the affairs of such bank, company, branch, agency, or organization, or the Board of Governors of the Federal Reserve System; or

Whoever with intent to defraud the United States or any agency thereof, or any financial institution referred to in this section, participates or shares in or receives (directly or indirectly) any money, profit, property, or benefits through any transaction, loan, commission, contract, or any other act of any such financial institution shall be fined not more than $1,000,000 or imprisoned not more than 30 years, or both.

§1031. Major fraud against the United States

(a) Whoever knowingly executes, or attempts to execute, any scheme or artifice with the intent

(1) To defraud the United States; or

(2) To obtain money or property by means of false or fraudulent pretenses, representations, or promises, in any procurement of property or services as a prime contractor with the United States or as a subcontractor or supplier on a contract in which there is a prime contract with the United States, if the value of the contract, subcontract, or any constituent part thereof, for such property or services is $1,000,000 or more shall, subject to the applicability of subsection 3) of this section, be fined not more than $1,000,000, or imprisoned not more than 10 years, or both.

(b) The fine imposed for an offense under this section may exceed the maximum otherwise provided by law, if such fine does not exceed $5,000,000 and

(1) The gross loss to the Government or the gross gain to a defendant is $500,000 or greater; or

(2) The offense involves a conscious or reckless risk of serious personal injury.

(3) The maximum fine imposed upon a defendant for a prosecution including a prosecution with multiple counts under this section shall not exceed $10,000,000.

§1344. Bank fraud

Whoever knowingly executes, or attempts to execute, a scheme or artifice

(1) To defraud a financial institution; or

(2) To obtain any of the moneys, funds, credits, assets, securities, or other property owned by, or under the custody or control of, a financial institution, by means of false or fraudulent pretenses, representations, or promises; shall be fined not more than $1,000,000 or imprisoned not more than 30 years, or both.

INTELLECTUAL PROPERTY CRIMES

Enforcement of intellectual property crimes protects American jobs. Intellectual property crimes pose a significant threat to the health and viability of the United States economy. The International Anti-Counterfeiting Coalition estimated that U.S. companies lost $200 billion in 1997 due to worldwide copyright, trademark and trade secret infringement. The Business Software Alliance estimates that 25% of all business software programs used by U.S. companies is pirated, in some countries that figure soars to 99%. The Motion Picture Export Association of America claims that counterfeit videotapes cost their industry approximately $750 million a year, while the International Federation for the Phonographic Industry estimates that piracy of compact discs costs their industry hundreds of millions of dollars a year. The American Society of Industrial Security has estimated the losses attributable to the theft of trade secrets to be at least $2 billion a month.

Intellectual property crimes cheats the U.S. of tax revenues, adds to the national trade deficit, subjects consumers to health and safety risks and leaves consumers without any legal recourse when they are financially or physically injured by counterfeit products. Counterfeit products such as airplane parts, pharmaceuticals, baby formulas and children's toy, often are manufactured using inferior materials and rarely undergo any type of quality control.

Many counterfeiters hail from foreign countries, such as South Korea, Vietnam, or Russia. They are frequently organized in a loosely knit network of importers and distributors who use connections in China, southeast Asia or Latin America to have their counterfeit and imitating products made inexpensively by grossly underpaid laborers, including child labor. There is strong evidence that organized criminal groups have moved into intellectual crime and that they are using the profits generated from these crimes to facilitate other illegal activities.

United States Code, Title 18

§2320. Trafficking in counterfeit goods or services

(a) Whoever intentionally traffics or attempts to traffic in goods or services and knowingly uses a counterfeit mark on or in connection with such goods or services shall, if an individual, be fined $2,000,000 or imprisoned not more than 10 years, or both, and, if a person other than an individual, be fined not more than $5,000,000. In the case of an offense by a person under this section that occurs after that person is convicted of another offense under this section, the person convicted, if an individual, shall be fined not more than $5,000,000 or imprisoned not more than 20 years, or both, and if other than an individual, shall be fined not more than $15,000,000.

§2319. Criminal infringement of a copyright

(a) Whoever violates section 506(a) (relating to criminal offenses) of title 17 shall be punished as provided in subsections (b) and (c) of this section and such penalties shall be in addition to any other provisions of title 17 or any other law.

(b) Any person who commits an offense under section 506(a)(1) of title 17

(1) Shall be imprisoned not more than 5 years, or fined in the amount set forth in this title, or both, if the offense consists of the reproduction or distribution, including by electronic means, during any 180day period, of at least 10 copies or phonorecords, of 1 or more copyrighted works, which have a total retail value of more than $2,500;

(2) Shall be imprisoned not more than 10 years, or fined in the amount set forth in this title, or both, if the offense is a second or subsequent offense under paragraph (1); and

(3) Shall be imprisoned not more than 1 year, or fined in the amount set forth in this title, or both, in any other case.

(c) Any person who commits an offense under section 506(a)(2) of title 17, United States Code

(1) shall be imprisoned not more than 3 years, or fined in the amount set forth in this title, or both, if the offense consists of the reproduction or distribution of 10 or more copies or phonorecords of 1 or more copyrighted works, which have a total retail value of $2,500 or more;

(2) shall be imprisoned not more than 6 years, or fined in the amount set forth in this title, or both, if the offense is a second or subsequent offense under paragraph (1); and

(3) Shall be imprisoned not more than 1 year, or fined in the amount set forth in this title, or both, if the offense consists of the reproduction or distribution of 1 or more copies or phonorecords of 1 or more copyrighted works, which have a total retail value of more than $1,000.

§2318. Trafficking in counterfeit labels for phonorecords, etc.

Trafficking in counterfeit labels for phonorecords, copies of computer programs or computer program documentation or packaging, and copies of motion pictures or other audio visual works, and trafficking in counterfeit computer program documentation or packaging

(a) Whoever, in any of the circumstances described in subsection () of this section, knowingly traffics in a counterfeit label affixed or designed to be affixed to a phonorecord, or a copy of a computer program or documentation or packaging for a computer program, or a copy of a motion picture or other audiovisual work, and whoever, in any of the circumstances described in subsection () of this section, knowingly traffics in counterfeit documentation or packaging for a computer program, shall be fined under this title or imprisoned for not more than five years, or both.

The International Anti-Counterfeiting Coalition is an industry organization dedicated to protecting their member's industry, American jobs and the public against counterfeit products. They produce a comprehensive report that is a valuable learning tool on why counterfeit products hurt the American public. (For additional information, see Additional Readings at the end of this chapter.)

Figure 3.2 Former FBI Chief's Comments on Counterfeiting

Introduction

Mr. James Moody, former chief of the Federal Bureau of Investigation's Organized Crime/Drug Operations Division declared that counterfeiting would become "the crime of the 21st century."

— *George W. Abbott, Jr. and Lee S. Sporn, Trademark Counterfeiting § 1.01 (2001).*

The DOJ's own prosecution guidelines for intellectual property offenses contain the following pertinent passage:

The importance of intellectual property to the national economy, and the scale of intellectual property theft, led the Department of Justice to designate intellectual property crime as a "priority" for federal law enforcement. As the U.S. Attorneys' Manual recognizes, "from time to time the Department establishes national investigative and prosecutorial priorities. These priorities are designed to focus Federal law enforcement efforts on those matters within the Federal jurisdiction that are most deserving of Federal attention and are most likely to be handled effectively at the Federal level." U.S. Attorneys' Manual 9-27.230(B)(1) (comment).

Intellectual property crimes were formally designated a "priority" by Deputy Attorney General Eric Holder on July 23, 1999. Deputy Attorney General Eric Holder, Remarks at Press Conference Announcing the Intellectual Property Rights Initiative (Jul. 23, 1999) (http://www.cybercrime.gov/dagipini.html). In announcing the Intellectual Property Rights Initiative, Deputy Attorney General

Figure 3.2 Former FBI Chief's Comments on Counterfeiting (cont.)

Holder stated that the Department of Justice, the Federal Bureau of Investigation and the United States Customs Service had concluded that they must make investigating and prosecuting intellectual property crime "a major law enforcement priority." In making the announcement, he noted that as the world moves from the Industrial Age to the Information Age, the United States' economy is increasingly dependent on the production and distribution of intellectual property. Currently, the U.S. leads the world in the creation and export of intellectual property and related products.

Deputy Attorney General Holder also observed, "At the same time that our information economy is soaring, so is intellectual property theft." Since intellectual property theft undermines the federally established copyright and trademark systems, it is especially appropriate that investigation and prosecution of these crimes be a federal law enforcement priority. United States Department of Justice Prosecuting Intellectual Property Crimes Manual   http://www.usdoj.gov/criminal/cybercrime/ipmanual/06ipma.htm#VI.A.1.a. (Section six of this manual is entitled: Charging and Other Strategy Considerations for Infringement Cases). The manual was drafted by the Computer Crime and Intellectual Property Section (CCIPS) of the Department of Justice and the entire manual can be accessed at http://www.usdoj.gov/criminal/cybercrime/ipmanual. htm.

Economic Impact of Counterfeiting

The size and scope of product counterfeiting has skyrocketed in recent years. The United States economy is losing millions of dollars in tax revenue and tens of thousands of jobs because of the manufacture, distribution and sale of counterfeit goods. This decrease in revenue results in fewer schools, hospitals, police, roads, etc. The actions of counterfeiters also make it harder for legitimate retailers to compete in the marketplace.

Counterfeiting results in decreased retail sales and lost jobs as honest intellectual property owners are forced to cut back work forces because of decreased sales.

Counterfeiters are not innocent little con artists or isolated street peddlers simply trying to make a few extra dollars. The truth is they steal from the corporations, steal from the community, steal from the consumers they deceive and are only concerned with lining their own pockets.

Figure 3.2 Former FBI Chief's Comments on Counterfeiting (cont.)

(1) The Business Software Alliance estimates the cost of software piracy alone to be about $12 billion a year.

(2) The International Chamber of Commerce estimates that seven percent of the world trade is in counterfeit goods and that the counterfeit market is worth $ 350 billion. George W. Abbott, Jr. and Lee S. Sporn, *Trademark Counterfeiting* § 1.03[A][2] (2001).

(3) In 1982 the International Trade Commission estimated counterfeiting and piracy losses at 5.5 billion. In 1996, that number stood at $200 billion. (Bank robberies, by contrast, involve less than $50 million per year, but seem to garner more public attention and more law enforcement resources). *S. Rep. No. 104-177, 104th Cong., 1st Sess. 1-2 (1995);* George W. Abbott, Jr. and Lee S. Sporn, *Trademark Counterfeiting* § 1.03[A][2] (2001).

(4) Counterfeit automobile parts, like brake pads, cost the auto industry alone over $12 billion dollars in lost sales. If these losses were eliminated the auto industry could hire 200,000 additional workers. George W. Abbott, Jr. and Lee S. Sporn, *Trademark Counterfeiting* § 1.03[A][2] (2001); Richard C. Noble, *From Brakes to Plugs to Engines, Counterfeiters Produce, Push Parts,* Flint J., September 3, 1995; H.R. Rep. No. 104-556 (1996), *reprinted in* 1996 U.S.C.C.A.N. 1074, 1075.

(5) Lost tax revenue costs New York City alone approximately $350 million a year in lost revenue- *Joseph Scott, He Is the Fashion Police, New York, March 6, 1995, at 38.*

According to a 1993 Business Wire release, product counterfeiting is believed to cost www.iacc.org California $7.5 billion a year and 25, 000 jobs. In Michigan, a piracy rate of 14.7% translates into $64.7 million in retail losses and $34.9 million in lost tax revenue. *BSA Seeks to Sink Software Pirates,* Grand Rapids Business Journal, vol. 20, No. 18, pg. 3 (May 6, 2002).

Organized Crime/Terrorism & Counterfeiting

Examples

Low risk of prosecution and enormous profit potential have made criminal counterfeiting an attractive enterprise for organized crime groups. Congress recognized organize crime's increasing role in the theft of intellectual property when it made trademark counterfeiting and copyright piracy predicate acts under the federal RICO statute (see 18 U.S.C. § 1961). Recently, ties have been established between counterfeiting and terrorist organizations who use the sale of fake

Figure 3.2 Former FBI Chief's Comments on Counterfeiting (cont.)

goods to raise and launder money. Consider these facts about the presence of organized criminal and terrorist groups in the underground counterfeiting and piracy markets:

(1) Operation Green Quest — a multi-agency task force established by the Treasury Department and aimed at identifying, disrupting and dismantling the terrorist financial infrastructure and sources of funding — has specifically recognized counterfeit merchandise schemes as a source of terrorist funding. *Green Quest, Finding the Missing Piece of the Terrorist Puzzle,* available at http://www.customs.ustreas.gov/xp/cgov/enforcement/investigative _priorities/greenquest.xml.

(2) In February 2003, federal prosecutors in Brooklyn, NY charged six men with importing up to 35 million counterfeit cigarettes from China into the United States. The men were accused of importing the fake cigarettes, then selling them through a tax free business located at an upstate New York Indian reservation and also through the website http://www.smokecheap.com. The cigarettes were allegedly imported into the United States in 5 separate shipments through New Jersey ports over a two-tear period. The charging documents stated that the counterfeiters hid the cigarettes in shipping containers behind kitchen pots. According to the prosecutors, the men were under investigation in Europe for cigarette smuggling. Two of the defendants were also charged with importing counterfeit batteries from China via Lithuania. William Glaberson, *6 Are Charged With Selling Millions of Counterfeit Marlboros,* The New York Times, February 21, 2003, at sec. B, pg. 3; John Marzulli, *Fake Marlboro Men Busted in Smuggling Ring,* Daily News (New York), February 21, 2003

(3) On February 28, 2003, Mohamad Hammoud was sentenced to 155 years in prison for helping to lead a cigarette smuggling operation that sent money to Hezbollah. *Ringleader Gets Maximum Sentence in Scheme to Help Hezbollah,* available at http://www.foxnews.com/story/0,2933,79909,00.html

(4) In the Philippines, underground CD production lines are often heavily secured sites equipped with hidden cameras for early detection and surveillance purposes. Syndicates move the equipment in piece by piece to avoid detection. Dave L. Llorito, *Loose Rules Make CD Pirates Feel at Home Here,* The Manila Times (January 2, 2003)(a three part article); *Lax Rules Give CD Pirates a New Home in the Philippines,* The Straits Times (January 6, 2003).

Figure 3.2 Former FBI Chief's Comments on Counterfeiting (cont.)

(5) There have been recent media accounts reporting a link between the terrorist organization Al Qaeda and the trafficking of counterfeit goods. An investigation, involving several countries, into a shipment of fake goods from Dubai to Copenhagen, Denmark, suggest that Al Qaeda itself may be funding itself by trafficking in counterfeit goods. Danish customs, using sophisticated risk analysis software, examined one of the containers on board and discovered that it contained over one thousand crates full of counterfeit shampoos, creams, cologne and perfume. The goods were ultimately bound for the United Kingdom. The United Kingdom later revealed that the sender of the counterfeit goods was a member of Al Qaeda. This connection was later confirmed by the European Commission's Customs Coordination Office. The intelligence services of three countries Denmark, the United Kingdom and the United States were, according to the same report, involved in investigating the matter. *Al-Qa'idah Trading in Fake Branded Goods,* BBC Monitoring Reports (September 11, 2002); Lenore Taylor, *Big Business Targets Terrorist Pirates,* Australian Financial Review, January 29, 2003,

(6) On January 16, 2003 William Haskell Farmer entered a guilty plea to trafficking in a massive counterfeit clothing operation. (The guilty plea was conditional upon an appeal to the United States Court of Appeals for the Fourth Circuit). According to the United States prosecutor, the scheme involved approximately $7 million in knock off T-shirts and sweatshirts. Farmer sold the shirts to 191 stores throughout the country.

United States Customs agents seized over 300,000 fake items from the Farmer's home and warehouse (the house was a two-story home with a swimming pool and two car garage). Farmer agreed to forfeit over $500,000 in cash and cashier's checks, eight vehicles, (including two Mercedes Benz and a 1998 Corvette), and two cargo trailers.

The cash had been seized in 1998 when Farmer's home was searched. The majority of the money was in $50 and $100 bills. There was $6,000 worth of change in the garage. Clif LeBlanc, *Huge Fake Clothing Ring Cracked, Upstate Man Pleads Guilty to Running $7 Million Scam,* The State (South Carolina), January 18, 2003, at A1; *South Carolina Man Pleads Guilty to Trafficking Clothing with Counterfeit Trademarks*, Department of Justice Press Release, January 16, 2003, *available at:*
http://www.cybercrime.gov/farmerPlea.htm.

(7) Counterfeit operations in Paraguay tri-border region may have been used to raise money to support terrorist operations and

Figure 3.2 Former FBI Chief's Comments on Counterfeiting (cont.)

groups. *Feds Track Counterfeit Goods Sales,* available at: http://abcnews.go.com/wire/US/ap20021024_151.html. (October 24, 2002); Kathleen Millar, *Financing Terror,* U.S. Customs Service Monthly Newsletter, November 2002, available at http://www.customs.gov/custoday/nov2002/index.htm; Larry Rother, *South America Region Under Watch for Signs of Terrorists,* The New York (www.iacc.org) Times, December 15, 2002, at 32; Sebastian Junger, *Terrorism's New Geography,* Vanity Fair, December 2002. The first article cited states:

"Federal authorities have several investigations under way examining evidence suggesting that Hezbollah, Hamas and other terror networks might be selling counterfeit products to pay for their worldwide activities. FBI, Customs Service and other agencies are investigating the sale of stolen or counterfeit computer software, T-shirts and handbags that are suspected of benefiting terrorist networks. Officials said the schemes span the globe from Paraguay to Pakistan. U.S. officials said there is particular concern that a region in South America famous for counterfeit products may have ties to terrorism. The region near the borders of Paraguay, Brazil and Argentina has a large Arab population. Law enforcement officials said they are investigating multimillion-dollar counterfeit software operations based in Ciudad Del Este, in eastern Paraguay, that are believed to have diverted money to Middle Eastern groups with ties to terrorism. Some of the suspects are of Lebanese origin and were arrested by Paraguayan authorities based on information from the U.S. government, the officials said."

(8) A 52-year-old woman was one of four people arrested in November 2001 after being suspected of operating a piracy ring that imported close to $100 million in fake software and computer products from Taiwan. The woman was recently sentenced to nine years in prison and ordered to pay $11 million in restitution to two software companies. *Woman Must Pay $11m in Software,* http://www.cnn.com/2002/TECH/biztech/11/25/counterfeit.software.ap/index.html, November 25, 2002.

(9) According to some media reports, the FBI had compiled strong evidence that the 1993 terrorists financed their activities with counterfeit textile sales from a store on Broadway. James Nurton, *Why Counterfeiting is Not So Harmless,* Managing Intellectual Property, September 2002, at 43; *Feds Track Counterfeit Goods Sales,* at http://abcnews.go.com/wire/US/ap20021024_151.html (October 24, 2002)(noting that testimony before a Senate Judiciary Committee in 1995 confirmed this fact). In 1996, *Business Week*

Figure 3.2 Former FBI Chief's Comments on Counterfeiting (cont.)

reported that that the FBI had investigated the link between counterfeit merchandise sales in New York and the terrorists who bombed the World Trade Center in 1993. Willy Stern, *Why Counterfeit Goods May Kill,* Business Week, September 2, 1996.

(10) According to the private investigator conducting the search, a raid of a souvenir shop in mid-town Manhattan led to the seizure of a suitcase full of counterfeit watches and the discovery of flight manuals for Boeing 767s, some containing handwritten notes in Arabic. A similar raid on a counterfeit handbag shop in New York uncovered faxes relating to the purchase of bridge inspection equipment. Two weeks after the raid on the handbag shop, police in New Jersey were investigating an assault on a Lebanese member of an organized crime syndicate. During a search of the man's apartment, authorities www.iacc.org found fake drivers' licenses and lists of suspected Al Qaeda terrorists including the names of some workers in the handbag shop that had been raided. James Nurton, *Why Counterfeiting is Not So Harmless,* Managing Intellectual Property, September 2002, at 43.

(11) Paramilitary groups in Northern Ireland funded their terrorist activities through the sale of pirate products, including the sale of the Lion King. Kathleen Millar, *Financing Terror,* U.S. Customs Service Monthly Newsletter, November 2002, available at http://www.customs.gov/custoday/nov2002/index.htm; Nick Somerlad, *Two Arrested After Police Find Explosives,* Press Association, December 20, 2000.

(12) In July 2002, three individuals were arrested when police stumbled upon 5,000 fake Rolex watches and Mount Blanc pens and $1 million in cash during a raid of a Flushing (Queens), New York home in connection with a drug operation. Prosecutors stated that the defendants used the sale of counterfeit items to launder drug money. Scott Shifrel, *3 Charged in Money Laundering,* Daily News (New York), July 11, 2002,

(13) Recovered al qaida terrorist training manuals revealed that the organization recommends the sale of fake goods as one means to raise funds to support terrorist operations. John von Radowitz, *Fake Internet Goods (Linked to Terrorists',* Press Association, June 25, 2002. This same article noted that Hezbollah traffics in counterfeit pharmaceuticals. John von Radowitz, *Fake Internet Goods (Linked to Terrorists',* Press Association, June 25, 2002.

(14) The Basque terrorist group ETA in southern Spain is involved in the sale of counterfeit clothes and handbags. John von

Figure 3.2 Former FBI Chief's Comments on Counterfeiting (cont.)

Radowitz, *Fake Internet Goods (Linked to Terrorists',* Press Association, June 25, 2002.

(15) Police in the Chinatown section of New York City uncovered a stash of fakewatches, handbags, sunglasses and wallets worth over $125 million that were hidden in a building that contained secret tunnels, trapdoors and vaults. Ten people were arrested. Erika Martinez & Marsha Kranes, *Knockoffs Knocked Out,* New York Post (May 10, 2002).

(16) In February 2002, John Sankus Jr., 28, of Philadelphia, was sentenced to 46 months in prison leading an international piracy ring responsible for copying and distributing software, games and movies. Sankus headed an international software piracy group called DrinkorDie , which was comprised of about sixty members from numerous countries including the United States, Australia, Norway, Finland and the UK. The group's biggest claim to fame was distributing copies of Windows 95 two weeks before the official release of the operating system. Federal agents conducted raids at Duke University and MIT in connection with DrinkorDie's activities. Some of the computers seized in the operation contained more than one terabyte of hacked software (which is equal to 700,000 floppy disks). Josh White, *Pa. Man Admits Internet Conspiracy,* Washington Post, at B02, (February 28, 2002).

(17) On December 14, 2001, Mark Dipadova (who used three aliases) was sentenced to 24 months in prison and three years of supervised release and ordered to pay over $135,000 in restitution for operating websites through which he sold counterfeit goods. Dipadova and his partner shipped over 10,000 packages, both domestically and internationally and had been sued civilly by trademark holders. At his sentencing hearing, Dipadova admitted to posting a link on one of his websites to an audio recording of a radio interview in which he stated that he was aware that his actions were illegal but that he refused to stop because he was making too much money. *Defendant Who Operated Fakegifts.com Sentenced,* Department of Justice Press release, December 17, 2001, *available at* http://www.cybercrime.gov/DipadovaSent.htm.

(18) In November 2001, US federal authorities made their largest seizure ever of counterfeit computer software in connection with the arrest of the individuals. The seizure of nearly 31,000 copies of phony software was valued at approximately $100 million (US). The software originated in Taiwan and was encased in counterfeit packaging (including holographs and registration codes) and also came with manuals.

Figure 3.2 Former FBI Chief's Comments on Counterfeiting (cont.)

Federal authorities were alerted to the shipment when a member of a criminal syndicate operating between Taiwan and Los Angeles allegedly attempted to bribe an undercover agent who was posing as a U.S. Customs official. Seized in connection with the arrests were a forty foot shipping container containing counterfeit computer software and packaging material, two forty foot containers filled with 85,000 cartons of counterfeit cigarettes (i.e., 17 million cigarettes). A second search warrant executed in connection with the investigation resulted in the seizure of 21 cartons of counterfeit end user license agreements, manuals, bar codes, adhesive labels and registration cards. *Taiwan Fears US Blacklist After Fake Software Haul*, The Strait Times (Singapore), November 19, 2001, at A3; *U. S Customs Seizes $100 Million in Pirated Computer Software, Biggest Case in U.S. History*, Department of Justice Press Release, November 16, 2001, *available at:*
http://www.cybercrime.gov/operationwhitehorse.htm.

(19) The speed and brazenness of Italian counterfeiting groups was demonstrated the summer of 2001 when burglars broke into the headquarters of a prominent Italian luxury goods/apparel producer. An investigation of the incident revealed that the only items missing as a result of the break-in were samples of the designer's 2002 men's spring/summer collection. It is now assumed that counterfeiters stole the samples to copy them before the genuine products made it to market. The sale of fake leather goods alone in Italy is estimated at $1.4 billion. Robert Galbraith, Luxury Groups Battle a Wave of Counterfeit Goods, *The International Herald Tribune*, p. 12 (September 29, 2001).

(20) In November 2001, a Cocoa Florida businessman was convicted of conspiracy to distribute and possession of cocaine and crack cocaine, trafficking in counterfeit merchandise and carjacking. When he was arrested police seized $150,000 in cash and truckloads of counterfeit clothing. John Tuohy, *Testimony from Felons Help Convict Cocoa Man,* Florida Today, (November 27, 2001)

(21) In 1996, the FBI confiscated 100,000 counterfeit T-shirts bearing fake and unauthorized Nike "swoosh" and/or Olympic logos that were intended to be sold at the 1996 summer Olympic games in 1996. The operation generated millions of dollars and was run by the followers of Sheik Omar Abdel Rahman a blind cleric who was sentenced to 240 years in prison for plotting to bomb New York City landmarks. John Mintz & Douglas Farah, *Small Scams Probed for Terror Ties,* Washington Post, August 12, 2002, at A1. Authorities seized three floors worth of illicit merchandise, stacked seven feet high.

Figure 3.2 Former FBI Chief's Comments on Counterfeiting (cont.)

(22) In 1993, law enforcement officials in New York raided a large warehouse in New York and discovered numerous fake handbags. What was unusual was what they found sewn into the lining of the handbags. The ring of drug smugglers would smuggle in the drugs this way, sell the drugs and then sell the bags. Essentially, they used contraband to hide other contraband. George W. Abbott, Jr. and Lee S. Sporn, *Trademark Counterfeiting* § 1.03[B] (2001); S. Rep. 104-177. 104th Cong., 1st Sess. (1995).

Health & Safety Concerns/Dangers

"Perhaps most troubling is the widespread threat counterfeiting poses to public health and safety. Few Americans truly appreciate the significance, scope or consequences for this crime."

Senator Orrin G. Hatch (R-UT) Chairman, Senate Judiciary Committee Press Conference, August 9, 1995

(1) A survey conducted by the Nigerian Institute of Pharmaceutical Research revealed that 80 percent of drugs in the major pharmacy stores in Lagos, Nigeria were fake or counterfeit. *Nigeria Reaffirms Efforts to Eliminate Fake Drugs,* Xinhua General News Service, February 13, 2003.

(2) According to the Shenzhen Evening News (a government owned newspaper), approximately 192,000 people died in China in 2001 because of fake drugs. *China's Killer Headache: Fake Pharmaceuticals,* Washington Post, August 30, 2002. The same article goes onto to state that, since 2001, Johnson & Johnson has established 38 criminal cases against different factories that copied its products in China.

(3) Diet pills imported into Japan (from China) were blamed for at least four deaths and 160 cases of illness. Dozens of people were suffering from liver disorders. *Chinese Diet Pill Casualties Mount,* http://www.cnn.com/2002/WORLD/asiapcf/east/07/21/japan.pills/index.html, July 21, 2002.

(4) According to a federal indictment made public in 2002, U.S. Customs officials seized 59,000 bottles of counterfeit vodka in a Massachusetts warehouse. It had been imported from a former Soviet republic. Thanassis Cambanis, *Fancy Labels, Cheap Vodka Don't Mix,* The Boston Globe, May 2, 2002, at B1. www.iacc.org

(5) In August 2002, Bell Helicopter sued two aircraft maintenance and repair companies for trademark counterfeiting. James E. Swickard (editor), *Bell Helicopter is Suing Two Companies Specializing in Aircraft Maintenance and Repair,* Business &

Figure 3.2 Former FBI Chief's Comments on Counterfeiting (cont.)

Commercial Aviation, Vol. 91, No. 2, p. 33 (Intelligence Section)(August 2002).

(6) In New York it was discovered that a 16-year-old liver transplant recipient had received eight weeks worth of injections of a counterfeit drug (Epogen) to treat his anemia and raise the child's red blood cell count. The treatments, instead of improving the boy's condition, caused excruciating aches and spasms. The vials used for the injections were supposed to contain 40,000 units of the drug, instead the counterfeit version contained only 2,000 units. Other counterfeit lots were found in Texas.

Ridgely Ochs, *Sounding Alarm on Counterfeit Drugs; FDA Investigating Recent of Fake Drug Cases,* New York Newsday, at 6 (June 12, 2002).

(7) Other counterfeit drug cases include a meningitis vaccine made of tap water, birth control pills made of wheat flour, and paracetamol syrup made of industrial solvents. The Engineer, *Fighting the Fakers,* April 26, 2002, at 16; House Report of the Committee on Energy and Commerce, Subcommittee on Oversight and Investigations, *Prescription Drug Diversion and Counterfeiting,* July 10, 1985, at 23 (referring to a scam involving counterfeit birth control pills).

(8) In 2002, a New York County district attorney charged seven people and five companies in the US, China and India with selling counterfeit Viagra over the Internet. Undercover officers purchased over 25,000 pills. Some pills were smuggled into the U.S. in stereo speakers and stuffed toys. One supplier told the agents that he could supply 2.5 million tablets a month. Counterfeits hit market within two weeks. *U.S. Officials Arrest Viagra Counterfeiters,* Scrip, May 22, 2002; Ridgely Ochs, *Sounding Alarm on Counterfeit Drugs; FDA Investigating Recent of Fake Drug Cases,* New York Newsday, (June 12, 2002).

(9) In 2001, illicit vodka containing methyl alcohol killed 60 people in Estonia. The Engineer, *Fighting the Fakers,* (April 26, 2002).

(10) Counterfeit version of the AIDS drug circulated in the US in late 2000; the drug was not effective and caused skin irritations. The Engineer, *Fighting the Fakers,* April 26, 2002, at 16; Jim Shamp, *Glaxo Sends Out Warning About AIDS Drug,* The Herald-Sun, May 14, 2002 (discussing a case of counterfeit labels applied to the wrong type of AIDS drug).

Figure 3.2 Former FBI Chief's Comments on Counterfeiting (cont.)

(11) Seventeen people in the US died between May 1999 and January 2000 after taking a powerful, but counterfeit, antibiotic. The Engineer, *Fighting the Fakers,* at 16 (April 26, 2002).

(12) World Health Organization estimates that counterfeit drugs account for ten percent of all pharmaceuticals. That number can rise to as high as 60% in developing countries. The Engineer, *Fighting the Fakers,* at 16 (April 26, 2002); Phillippe Broussard, *Dangerous Fakes,* World Press Review, v44, n1, p36 (1) (January 1999).

(13) An August 2001 news article reported a host of actions by the Saudi Arabian Ministry of Commerce against distributors attempting to sell potentially unhealthy products. Among the unhealthy products seized were 7,000 bottles of imitation Vaseline and related fake creams found while investigating cosmetic shops. A November 2001 raid at a counterfeit factory in Jeddah resulted in the seizure of 10,000 packets of jelly, 650,000 packets of macaroni, 12,000 bottles of perfume, and 5,000 brake pads. The factory employed 120 workers who were involved in producing fake cardboard cartons, cans and bottles.

(14) Over 100 children died in Nigeria in 1990 after taking cough syrup that was actually antifreeze. Phillippe Broussard, *Dangerous Fakes,* World Press Review, v44, n1, p36 (1) (January 1999).

(15) Counterfeit versions of infant formula were found on the shelves of grocery stores in 16 different states. Marian Burros, *F.D.A. Target: Baby Formula,* N.Y. Times, September 6, 1995; 142 Cong. Rec. 5776 (House). More recently, in 1999, the Food and Drug Administration (FDA) issued a warning regarding counterfeit cans of infant formula for infants allergic to milk protein. The warning came after some of the illicit product had already been purchased. The FDA warning stated that infants who ingested the counterfeit formula could experience fevers, skin rashes or severe allergic reactions. *FDA Warns About Infant Formula Fraudulently Labeled as Nutramigen in Southern California,* HHS NEWS (U.S. Department of Health and Human Services), P99-23, October 8, 1999. *See also Fugitive Who Sold Counterfeit Baby Formula Convicted of Federal Criminal Charges,* Department of Justice (Press Release), August 9, 2002, *available at* http://www.cybercrime/gov/mostafaConvict.htm (discussing the conviction of Mohamad Mostafa on charges involving a conspiracy to sell counterfeit infant formula; the defendant was also in the country illegally and upon indictment in 1995 fled to Canada where he was arrested in 2001).

Figure 3.2   Former FBI Chief's Comments on Counterfeiting (cont.)

(16) One counterfeiter in California filled genuine Coke bottles with his own soda like beverage and offered them for sale as genuine Coca-Cola. *United States v. Petrosian,* 126 F.3d 1232 (9th Cir. 1997).

(17) Counterfeit parts have been discovered in helicopters sold to NATO, in jet engines, bridge joints, and fasteners in areas of nuclear facilities responsible for preventing the meltdown of the reactor itself. H.R. Rep. 104-556 (1996).

(18) In the mid 1990s a major shampoo producer was forced to place newspaper ads in over 25 papers to warn consumers to the presence of fake shampoos that contained unsafe levels of bacteria. Henry Gilgoff, *Counterfeit: Rip-offs of Popular Products Victimize Both Consumers and Manufacturers,* Newsday, August 27, 1995. Fake toothpaste has also found its way into drug stores. *Colgate Warns People Against Fake Toothpaste,* Austin American Statesman, August 12, 1996. www.iacc.org

(19) A Norwegian plane crash in 1989 that killed 55 people resulted, in part, from substandard shear bolts and sleeves of an unknown origin. *55 Killed in Crash of Norwegian Plane, None Aboard Survive as Craft Plunges into Sea Near Denmark,* L.A. Times, September 9, 1989, at 4 (cited and discussed in Robert W. Luedeman, *Flying Underground: The Trade in Bootleg Aircraft Parts,* 62 J. Air L. & Comm. 9396-100 (August/September 1996).

(20) The FAA estimates that 2% of the 26 million airline parts installed each year are counterfeit (that equals 520,000 parts). Billy Stern, *Warning! Bogus Parts Have Turned Up in Commercial Jets. Where's the FAA?,* Business Week, June 10, 1996, at 90.

(21) The operational life of counterfeit bearing seal spacers removed from a United Airlines plane were found to be 600 hours - - the genuine parts had an operational life of 20,000 hours - - the fake parts came complete with fake boxes, labels and paperwork and were only discovered because of a vigilant airline mechanic. In another case, Delta Airlines discovered that an engine mount cone-bolt, (a device which actually fastens the engine to the plane), on one of its planes was actually counterfeit. Billy Stern, *Warning! Bogus Parts Have Turned Up in Commercial Jets. Where's the FAA?* Business Week, June 10, 1996

(22) In 1987, seven children died when the bus they were riding in flipped over. The brakes that were just installed on the bus bore a well-known trademark. Further examination, however, showed they were made of sawdust. *A System Approach to the Counterfeit Problem, Genuine or Bogus: How Can You Tell?,* ASTM Standardization News, April 1990, at 38.

> **Figure 3.2 Former FBI Chief's Comments on Counterfeiting (cont.)**
>
> (23) In a federal case in California the court determined the defendant sold counterfeit helicopter parts that caused several helicopters to crash resulting in injuries and death. S. Rep. No. 98-526 at 4 (1984), *reprinted in* 1984 U.S.C.C.A.N. 3627, 3630-31. (24) One million counterfeit birth control pills caused internal bleeding in women. S. Rep. No. 98-526 at 4 (1984), *reprinted in* 1984 U.S.C.C.A.N. 3627.

TELEMARKETING FRAUD

Telemarketing fraud continues to grow and has been estimated by numerous government agencies to cost $40 billion annually and victimize millions of people. One case in Nevada involved 800,000 victims. The telemarketing industry employs over 3.4 million people, and industry estimates place the total consumer spending through telemarketing at $500 billion per year.

Telemarketing fraud and other fraud by wire matters can be very difficult crimes to investigate. Typically, individuals committing fraud by wire use multiple aliases, telephones, mail drops and business locations. They can change their method of solicitation, product line, and other recognizable traits overnight. Their operations are mobile and their schemes are complex. Criminal intent is often difficult to prove, and the majority of individual losses are under the prospective thresholds set by the prosecuting offices of the United States Attorney or the District Attorney. The elderly population is particularly targeted and susceptible to telemarketers.

Fraud by wire, especially telemarketing fraud, has become an increasingly international crime problem. Telemarketers are moving their operations in response to the law enforcement efforts within the United States. The most egregious fraudulent pitches that are currently being used to victimize American citizens are coming from Canada.

What Is Telemarketing Fraud?

Telemarketing fraud is a term that refers generally to any scheme to defraud in which the persons carrying out the scheme use the telephone as their primary means of communicating with prospective victims and trying to persuade them to send money to the scheme. When it solicits people to buy goods and services, to invest money, or to donate funds to charitable causes, a fraudulent telemarketing fraud operation typically uses numerous false and misleading statements, representations, and promises, for three purposes:

First, to make it appear that the good, service, or charitable cause their telemarketers offer to the public is worth the money that they are asking the consumer to send. Fraudulent telemarketers, by definition, do not want to give consumers fair value for the money they have paid to the telemarketers. Because their object is to maximize their personal profits, even if the consumer suffers substantial financial harm, they will typically adopt one or both of two approaches: to fail to give the consumer anything of value in return for their money; or to provide items of modest value, far below what the consumer had expected the value to be on the basis of the telemarketers' representations. When the item is supposed to be a tangible "gift" or "prize" of substantial value, as in charity schemes or prize-promotion schemes, fraudulent telemarketers will instead provide what they term a "gimme gift." The "diamond watch" that the consumer thought would be worth many hundreds or thousands of dollars, for example, proves to be an inexpensively produced watch with a small diamond chip, for which the fraudulent telemarketer may have paid only $30 to $60.

Second, to obtain immediate payment before the victim can inspect the item of value they expect to receive. Regardless of what good or service a fraudulent telemarketer says he is offering investment items, magazine subscriptions, or office supplies, for example a fraudulent telemarketer will always insist on advance payment by the consumer before the consumer receives that good or service. If consumers were to receive the promised goods or services before payment, and realized that the good or service was of little or no value, most of them would likely cancel the transaction and refuse payment. Fraudulent telemarketers therefore routinely make false and misleading representations to the effect that the consumer must act immediately if he or she is to receive the promised good or service. These representations may suggest that the opportunity being offered is of limited quantity or duration, or that there are others also seeking that opportunity. In addition, fraudulent telemarketers usually persuade the victims to send their money by some means of expedited delivery that allows the telemarketers to receive the victims' payments as quickly as possible. For victims who have checks or money orders, the telemarketers' use nationally advertised courier delivery services, which will deliver victims' checks by the next business day. For victims who have credit cards, the telemarketers obtain merchant accounts at financial institutions, so that the credit-card number can be processed immediately.

Third, to create a aura of legitimacy about their operations, by trying to resemble legitimate telemarketing operations, legitimate businesses, or legitimate government agencies. Magazine-subscription schemes, for example, often tell consumers, "We're just like" a nationally publicized magazine-distribution organization, and in some cases have simply lied to consumers by stating that they are the nationally publicized organization. Telemarketers in "rip-and-tear" schemes or "recovery-room schemes" often falsely impersonate federal agents or other government officials to lend greater credibility to their demands for money.

Another factor that distinguishes fraudulent from legitimate telemarketing operations is "reloading." "Reloading" is a term that refers to the fraudulent telemarketer's practice of recontacting victims, after their initial transactions with the telemarketer, and soliciting them for additional payments. In prize-promotion schemes, for example, victims are often told that they are now eligible for even higher levels and values of prizes, for which they must pay additional (nonexistent) "fees" or "taxes." Because "reload" transactions typically demand increasingly substantial amounts of money from victims, they provide fraudulent telemarketers with their most substantial profits, while causing consumers increasingly large losses that they will never recoup voluntarily from the fraudulent telemarketers.

A third factor that distinguishes fraudulent from legitimate telemarketing operations is the fraudulent telemarketer's general reluctance to contact prospective victims who reside in the state where the telemarketing operation conducts its business. Fraudulent telemarketers recognize that if they contact victims located outside their state, any victims who later realize that they may have been defrauded are likely to be uncertain about which law enforcement agency they should contact with complaints, and less likely to travel directly to the telemarketing operation and confront the telemarketers about their losses.

Although many consumers apparently find it difficult to believe that there are people who will contact them on the telephone and lie and misrepresent facts in order to get their money, the reality is that at any given time, there are at least several hundred fraudulent telemarketing operations some of them employing as many as several dozen people in North America that routinely seek to defraud consumers in the United States and Canada. Moreover, these schemes generally do not choose their victims at random. Fraudulent telemarketers routinely buy "leads" that is, listings of names, addresses, and phone numbers of persons who have been defrauded in previous telemarketing schemes (and typically the amount of their last transaction with a fraudulent telemarketer) from each other and from "lead brokers," companies that engage exclusively in buying and selling fraudulent telemarketers' leads. Although leads are relatively costly to the fraudulent telemarketer as much as $10 or even $100 per lead in some cases they also indicate to the fraudulent telemarketer which consumers are most likely to be persuaded to send substantial amounts of money that will far exceed the cost of the leads.

Firms giving references may provide the names of "touts" or "singers." "Touts" and "singers" are people who praise the telemarketer's services, but who actually are part of the scheme. Telemarketers also sometimes give as a reference an organization with a name similar to the "Better Business Bureau" ("BBB"), but which in reality has nothing to do with a legitimate local BBB.

What Kinds Of Telemarketing Schemes Are Out There?

In one sense, the nature and content of a telemarketing scheme to defraud is limited only by the ingenuity and skill of the scheme's organizers. Fraudulent telemarketers who observe that certain types of business, or certain business trends, are widely publicized in news media will incorporate references to such reports in their solicitations of victims. In practice, most fraudulent telemarketers operate one or more of the following types of schemes: charity schemes, credit-card, credit-repair, and loan schemes, cross-border schemes, Internet-related schemes, investment schemes, lottery schemes, office-supply schemes, "prize-promotion" schemes, "recovery-room" schemes, and "rip-and-tear" schemes.

Charity Schemes

Many people have a laudable desire to help those who are less fortunate by making donations to charitable causes. Fraudulent telemarketers have often exploited that desire, by devising schemes that purport to raise money for worthy causes. At various times, fraudulent telemarketers have falsely claimed, for example, that they were soliciting funds for victims of the Oklahoma City bombing or Mississippi Valley flooding or for anti-drug programs. In one type of charity scheme, known as "badge fraud," fraudulent telemarketers purport to be soliciting funds to support police- or fire department-related causes.

Some of these schemes simply lie outright to would-be donors and give none of their proceeds to charity. Other schemes, to help maintain their aura of legitimacy, will donate a modest amount of their proceeds typically no more than 10 percent to a charitable cause so that they can show some evidence of their "legitimacy" to law- enforcement or regulatory authorities who may have received complaints about the schemes. In one scheme that resulted in successful federal criminal prosecutions, the schemes' organizers tried to enhance their appearance of legitimacy by sending the would-be donors "gimme gifts" and mounted plaques that thanked them for their contributions to a particular "foundation" (which was in fact an organization, run by former fraudulent telemarketers, that did nothing for people in need).

Credit-Card, Credit-Repair, and Loan Schemes

Certain telemarketing schemes are devised to victimize people who have bad credit, or whose income levels may be too low to allow them to amass substantial credit. In many credit-card telemarketing schemes, telemarketers contact prospective victims and represent that they can obtain credit cards even if they have poor credit histories. The victim who pays the fee demanded by the telemarketer usually receives no card, or receives only a credit-card application or some cheaply printed brochures or flyers that discuss credit cards. In a variant of these schemes, the credit card that some consumers are given, after paying the fee to the telemarketer, requires the consumer to pay a company located outside the United States $200 or $300 and limits the consumer's charges on that card to an amount no greater than the amount of money the consumer has paid to the offshore company.

In advance-fee loan schemes, persons with bad credit are promised a loan in return for a fee paid in advance. Victims who pay the fees for the guaranteed loans have their names referred to a "turndown room" that is, an operation, affiliated with the telemarketer, whose sole function is to notify the victims at a later date that their loan applications have been rejected.

Another way that fraudulent telemarketers try to take advantage of people with poor credit histories is by promising to "repair" their credit. Firms that promise that they can remove bankruptcies, judgments, liens, foreclosures and other items from a consumer's credit report, irrespective of the age or accuracy of the information, are misstating the facts. Judgments, paid tax liens, accounts referred for collection or charged off, and records of arrest, indictment, or conviction, may remain on a consumer's report for seven years, while bankruptcies may remain on the report for ten years. Credit reporting agencies are obligated by law to correct mistakes on consumers' reports. People with real errors on their reports can deal directly with the reporting agencies, or obtain assistance from the Federal Trade Commission with their problems. Credit repair agencies cannot generally succeed in eliminating accurate negative information from credit reports, despite the contrary claims of some firms.

Cross-Border Schemes

Cross-border telemarketing schemes consist of telemarketing schemes usually advance-fee loan schemes, investment schemes, lottery schemes, and prize-promotion schemes where the scheme's operators conduct their telemarketing activities in one country and solicit victims in another country. Cross-border telemarketing schemes are appealing to some telemarketers because it further enhances the difficulties for consumers in reporting complaints and for law-enforcement agencies in investigating and prosecuting these schemes. To obtain certain kinds of evidence that they can use in legal proceedings, and to have criminal suspects extradited from foreign countries, law enforcement and regulatory authorities in the United States must use legal procedures that have been established by bilateral treaties with those countries. In some cases, those procedures provide opportunities for the criminal suspects to create substantial delays in legal proceedings by challenging the U.S. authorities' right to the evidence or the extradition of the suspect. A few fraudulent telemarketers have admitted to law enforcement authorities that they believe these delays can last long enough for victim-witnesses to die before they have an opportunity to testify in legal proceedings and receive some restitution of their losses.

Investment and Business-Opportunity Schemes

Since the 1970s, many fraudulent telemarketers have offered a wide variety of spurious investment opportunities to would-be investors. The nature of the purported investments varies largely with what the telemarketers perceive, from widely publicized reports on business matters, to be the trends that less experienced or less sophisticated investors are most likely to consider attractive for high-profit investment. In the 1980s, for example, many telemarketing schemes offered "investments" in rare coins, precious metals, and so-called "strategic metals." In the 1990s, many telemarketing schemes turned to offering "investments" in items as diversified as "investment-grade" gemstones, ostrich farms, and telecommunications technology such as wireless cable systems for television broadcasting.

Where the investment item that the victim purchases is small enough to be held, such as gemstones or rare coins, fraudulent telemarketers often seal the items in a plastic container and ship the sealed container to the victim. The telemarketer also warns the victim not to open the container, as that would void the telemarketer's guarantee on those items. The true purpose of sealing the items in the container is to dissuade the victim from having the items independently appraised, as a genuine appraisal would inform the victim that the real market value of the items is far below what the telemarketer had represented. Where the investment items are too large to be provided directly to the victim, such as oil and gas wells, bars of precious metals, or wireless cable systems, the telemarketers often lie to the victims about the fact that the investment item in fact does not exist or is not yet developed enough to turn a profit.

In a number of investment telemarketing schemes, the operators "reload" their victims by representing that they have prospective buyers who are interested in the investment that the victim has made with the telemarketer, and that the victim must buy more of the same item, or a particular type of item (such as more gemstones), to "round out" their investment portfolio. The victim is later told that the prospective buyer decided not to purchase the victim's investment, leaving the victim with still greater losses and no realistic prospect of recouping those losses.

Business-opportunity schemes are a variant of investment schemes. These prey on people who would like to be in business on their own. Telemarketers frequently promise to set consumers up in business using a formula or method that is supposed to be virtually certain to guarantee success. Many of these businesses involve installing vending machines, toy carousels, computer or video games, pay telephones, and the like. Purchasing such business opportunities can cost many thousands of dollars, but often leaves the consumer with a basement full of products and machines he or she was unable to sell.

A common method of operation is for the telemarketer to take out ads in local newspapers, with an 800 number for interested consumers to call. The ad may or may not make exaggerated earnings claims, like "Earn $100,000 in your spare time." Consumers who call the 800 numbers often hear more about potential earnings, and lots of promises regarding the success of the business. All too often, unfortunately, there is nothing to back up these claims.

A legitimate seller of franchises will provide consumers with detailed information about others who have purchased the franchise, the basis for earnings claims, and other similar information. The list of franchisees provided to the consumer should include at least the 10 franchisees closest to the consumer, if there are 10 franchisees. Consumers should talk to other franchisees to learn about the business. Generally speaking, promises of a lot of money for little effort only describe what the telemarketer will get, not what a consumer will end up with.

Lottery Schemes

Fraudulent telemarketers have often used offers of "investing" in foreign lottery tickets or chances as a vehicle to defraud consumers. Although federal laws forbids the importation, interstate transportation, and foreign transportation of lottery tickets or chances, many fraudulent telemarketers routinely contact people in the United States, through mailings, advertisements, and telephone calls, to solicit their involvement in foreign lotteries such as the "Australian Lottery" or "El Gordo." Victims often begin by paying as little as $5 or $10 for lottery chances. Many of those who do are later contacted by telemarketers who hold themselves out as "experts" in "investing" in lottery chances, and who solicit the victims for larger and larger amounts of money. Law enforcement authorities in the United States and Canada are aware of many instances in which victims have sent thousands, tens of thousands, and even hundreds of thousands of dollars to lottery telemarketers, after hearing repeated promises or guarantees of vast returns.

In reality, the telemarketers invest little or none of the victims' money in the lottery tickets or chances, and keep the money for themselves after paying salaries and other expenses of their fraudulent business. In some instances, where victims had been given certain lottery numbers by the telemarketers, and later learned independently that their numbers had won a real lottery, the victims were told that their winnings had been "invested" in other lottery tickets rather than being paid to them directly.

Magazine-Promotion Schemes

A number of fraudulent telemarketing schemes in recent years have turned to offering magazine subscriptions, in part because of the apparent popularity of several nationally known magazine-promotion businesses that send mailings throughout the United States that advertise their multimillion-dollar prize contests. In a typical fraudulent magazine-promotion scheme, a telemarketer contacts a prospective victim and tells the victim that he or she has won a highly valuable prize or is to be given a highly valuable "gift," and falsely implies that the victim must purchase multiple magazine subscriptions to receive the award or gift. The victim is told the total price for the package of subscriptions, which can range from several hundred to several thousand dollars, but is not told which magazines he or she is to receive when the victim agrees to send money to the telemarketer. Instead, the telemarketer, after receiving the victim's money, sends the victim lists of magazines on which the victim can check off the magazines that he or she wants to order and which the victim then mails back to the telemarketer.

Although magazine-promotion schemes typically claim that they are "just like" the nationally advertised magazine-promotion businesses, consumers should note that there are three critical differences between fraudulent and legitimate magazine-distribution companies:

(1) Advance Disclosure of Prices. In the promotional materials that they mail to consumers, legitimate magazine-promotion companies typically disclose the newsstand price, the discounted price, and the savings to the consumer in advance of any magazine purchase by the consumer. In contrast, fraudulent magazine-subscription schemes do not disclose the newsstand price or the true price per issue that they are charging their victims; to disclose those two prices to the prospective victim would immediately inform the victim that the price is far above even the newsstand price or, in some cases, that the magazine being offered is free and has no subscription price.

(2) Advance Disclosure of Magazine Titles. Legitimate magazine-promotion companies clearly inform consumers of the magazine titles that they can order, before the consumer has to send any money. In contrast, fraudulent magazine-promotion schemes do not disclose these titles in advance; to do so would reveal that many of the most widely circulated and popular magazines are not available through the scheme.

(3) Provision of All Magazines Promised. Legitimate magazine-subscription companies provide all of the magazines that a customer has ordered, and for the full duration of the subscription. In contrast, when they solicit prospective victims, fraudulent telemarketers sometimes telling prospective victims that no one can read dozens of magazines each month represent to victims that their company will donate the magazines to a local hospital or hospice, so that less fortunate people can benefit from the victims' purchase. In reality, fraudulent telemarketers frequently choose not to subscribe to any magazines at all in the victim's name, or submit the victim's subscription for one year rather than two and pocket the remainder of the victim's money.

Office-Supply Schemes

One type of fraudulent telemarketing scheme that is directed specifically at the business community is the office-supply or "toner" scheme. In a typical toner scheme, an employee of the telemarketer first contacts a business under false pretenses to learn the make and model number of the copier used at that business. Within a day or two, a telemarketer then recontacts the business, this time falsely representing himself to be a representative of the copier company whose copier is being used at that business. The telemarketer falsely states that his company is about to increase the price of their toner, but that the company is prepared to offer the business a shipment of toner at the then-current price before the price increase goes into effect. If the business employee who answers the telemarketer's call agrees to have the toner shipped, the business thereafter receives an invoice for the toner without the toner, or receives a shipment of toner with the invoice.

In the latter case, the toner is not only priced far higher per unit than the real copier company charges for its product, but also is mislabeled to leave the impression that it can be used in the type of copier in use at the business. In fact, the toner is usually what is known as "graymarket" toner that is, toner that does not meet the quality specifications and requirements of legitimate copier companies. Businesses who use the graymarket toner often find that it clogs their copiers, requiring them to call their copier company for service. In many cases, businesses do not discover the true extent of the fraud until the copier company's service people repair the copiers and inform the businesses that the toner is not their company's toner and that there was no planned price increase.

Prize-Promotion Schemes

Over the years, law-enforcement and regulatory authorities have observed at least three varieties of telemarketing schemes that purport to offer prizes, awards, or gifts to consumers if the consumers buy certain goods or services or make supposedly charitable donations:

(1) The oldest of these schemes, which still is carried out in some areas of both the United States and Canada, involves a simply false statement to a prospective victim that he or she has won a particular highly valuable item, such as a car. Because the explicit promise of a valuable item that is never delivered provides clear evidence of fraudulent intent, participants in a number of these schemes were successfully prosecuted in the 1980s and 1990s.

(2) More recently, beginning in the late 1980s and early 1990s, some fraudulent telemarketers began conducting so-called "one-in-five" schemes. In a "one-in-five" scheme, the telemarketer contacts a prospective victim and represents that the victim has won one of five (sometimes four or six) valuable prizes. The telemarketer then lists the prizes for the victim. All but one of the promised prizes would in fact have substantial value if awarded (such as a nationally known U.S.-manufacture car, a $3,000 cashier's check, and a $5,000 cashier's

check); the remaining prize, however, was a "gimme gift" such as inexpensive "his and hers diamond watches," plastic dolphin statues, and gold rings. Many telemarketers, in reading the award list to victims, deliberately included the "gimme gift" between two items of much higher real value, to make the victim believe that the "gimme gift's" value was somewhere between the value of the other two items. Although most "one-in-five" schemes invariably gave away only the "gimme gift," the telemarketers typically told victims who asked which prize they would be receiving that they could not give out that information because it would be "collusion" or "bribery." These explanations, while nonsensical, were developed to avoid having to tell prospective victims clearly false information about the prizes' value and the victims' chances of winning the far more valuable items.

(3) A variation on the "one-in-five" scheme is the so-called "mystery pitch" or "integrity pitch" (the latter term being more favored by fraudulent telemarketers). In a "mystery pitch," the telemarketer would tell a prospective victim that he or she had won something of substantial value, but refuse to tell the victim what the prize was because of professed concerns about "collusion" or "bribery." Some telemarketers apparently adopted the "mystery pitch" after seeing that other telemarketers were being successfully prosecuted in "one-in-five" schemes where the prizes were specifically listed for the victims.

In each of these variations of "prize-promotion" schemes, the telemarketers routinely "reload" victims by telling them that they have now qualified for higher levels of prizes, but that they must accordingly pay still more money to the telemarketers to cover the "fees" or "taxes" that the telemarketers claim are due on the prizes.

"Recovery-Room" Schemes

So-called "recovery-room" telemarketing schemes are schemes that often are extensions of other telemarketing schemes. As one or more telemarketing schemes gradually deprive victims of most of their funds, the victims become increasingly desperate to try to recover a portion of their losses, and increasingly concerned about the embarrassment that they would feel if they had to report the true extent of their losses to law enforcement. A telemarketer for a "recovery room" contacts the victim, and invariably claims some affiliation with a government organization or agency that is in a position to help telemarketing victims recover some of their past losses. Some telemarketers have falsely impersonated FBI, IRS, and Customs agents or attorneys in law firms, while others use more nebulous language to suggest a connection to a government agency (such as "I'm working with the court [or the district attorney]") in a particular city.

Because the telemarketers may have worked for the scheme that had previously defrauded the victims, they are well equipped to disclose information about the amounts of the victims' past losses. This in turn gives the telemarketers additional credibility with the victims, who apparently believe that only a legitimate law-enforcement or other government agency could have access to such information. The telemarketers, posing as government officials, then tell victims that they must send a fee to them so that their money can be released by "the court" or otherwise delivered to the victims. This allows the telemarketer to deprive victims of even more money, while simultaneously encouraging the victims to believe that something is being done to protect their interests and causing the victims to postpone the filing of complaints with real law-enforcement or regulatory authorities.

"Rip-and-Tear" Schemes

As law-enforcement and regulatory authorities have become more vigorous in prosecuting fraudulent telemarketing, some fraudulent telemarketers have increasingly engaged in what are known as "rip-and-tear" schemes. What distinguishes a "rip-and-tear" scheme from other telemarketing schemes is simply the methods that the fraudulent telemarketers use to minimize the risks of detection and apprehension of the authorities. Instead of conducting their telemarketing from a single, fixed place of business, "rip-and-tear" telemarketers conduct their calls from various places, such as pay telephones, residences, and hotel rooms. Their contacts with prospective victims who usually are repeat victims of past telemarketing schemes involve explicit promises that the victims have won a valuable prize or is entitled to receive a portion of their past losses.

"Rip-and-tear" schemes often insist that the victims send the required "fees" to commercial mailbox facilities or by electronic wire transfer services, which create far less substantial paper trails than checks or credit cards and which allows the telemarketers to receive the victims' payments in cash. To create further difficulties for law enforcement, "rip-and-tear" telemarketers often hire persons to act as couriers to pick up the payments from the mailbox drop or wire transfer office; if law-enforcement agents pick up the payments and arrest the couriers, the organizers of the scheme are not tied directly to the delivery of the victims' funds. In some instances, law-enforcement authorities have reported that telemarketers appeared to be conducting counter surveillance that is, watching to see whether they were under surveillance at pickup points, and engaging in evasive behavior.

SECURITIES/COMMODITIES FRAUD

The dynamic growth of Wall Street in New York and the Mercantile Exchange in Chicago has led to an unparalleled opportunity for investment and for fraud. Market frauds are committed by a host of players: investors, brokers, shareholders and big-time investment bankers like Ivan Boesky and Michael Milken. Wherever fraud involves large-scale insider trading or a penny stock manipulation, fooling the public is key to the crime.

United States Code, Title 18

§1348. Securities fraud

Whoever knowingly executes, or attempts to execute, a scheme or artifice

(1) To defraud any person in connection with any security of an issuer with a class of securities registered under section 12 of the Securities Exchange Act of 1934 (15 U.S.C. 78l) or that is required to file reports under section 15(d) of the Securities Exchange Act of 1934 (15 U.S.C. 78o(d)); or

(2) To obtain, by means of false or fraudulent pretenses, representations, or promises, any money or property in connection with the purchase or sale of any security of an issuer with a class of securities registered under section 12 of the Securities Exchange Act of 1934 (15 U.S.C. 78l) or that is required to file reports under section 15(d) of the Securities Exchange Act of 1934 (15 U.S.C. 78o(d)); shall be fined under this title, or imprisoned not more than 25 years, or both.

INSURANCE FRAUD

In the United States, about $67 billion is lost every year to fraudulent claims. Diversion of premiums is the most common form of insurance fraud investigated by the FBI. This occurs when an insurance agent, broker or managing general agent fails to send the customer's premiums to the policy underwriter. They just take the money and run.

Another scam involves unlicensed insurance sales. These illegal salesmen collect as much premium income as possible in a short period with no intention of paying customer claims. Their businesses are short-lived and involve high-risk lines of insurance that have significant demand and few legitimate providers.

BANKRUPTCY FRAUD

Bankruptcy laws were put in place to protect businesses and individuals from losing everything they owned in the event of financial failure. Some people duped the bankruptcy courts with fabricated petitions and testimony resulting in unpaid debts and money in their pockets. Bankruptcy fraud costs businesses and taxpayers billions every year.

A wider acceptance of bankruptcy in this country, as well as a changing economic climate, has led to a 500 per cent rise in bankruptcy filings since 1973. About 10 per cent of all bankruptcies involve fraud. In 1995 alone, almost 250 fraudulent bankruptcies were filed every day. Bankruptcy fraud schemes include the hiding of assets, false statements, multiple filings, forged petitions and petition mills that crank out phony information. Two-thirds of all bankruptcy fraud involves hidden assets.

United States Code, Title 18

§151. Definition

As used in this chapter, the term "debtor" means a debtor concerning whom a petition has been filed under title 11.

§153. Concealment of assets; false oaths and claims; bribery

A person who:

(1) Knowingly and fraudulently conceals from a custodian, trustee, marshal, or other officer of the court charged with the control or custody of property, or, in connection with a case under title 11, from creditors or

the United States Trustee, any property belonging to the estate of a debtor;

(2) Knowingly and fraudulently makes a false oath or account in or in relation to any case under title 11;

(3) Knowingly and fraudulently makes a false declaration, certificate, verification, or statement under penalty of perjury as permitted under section 1746 of title 28, in or in relation to any case under title 11;

(4) Knowingly and fraudulently presents any false claim for proof against the estate of a debtor, or uses any such claim in any case under title 11, in a personal capacity or as or through an agent, proxy, or attorney;

(5),1Knowingly and fraudulently receives any material amount of property from a debtor after the filing of a case under title 11, with intent to defeat the provisions of title 11;

(6) Knowingly and fraudulently gives, offers, receives, or attempts to obtain any money or property, remuneration, compensation, reward, advantage, or promise thereof for acting or forbearing to act in any case under title 11;

(7) In a personal capacity or as an agent or officer of any person or corporation, in contemplation of a case under title 11 by or against the person or any other person or corporation, or with intent to defeat the provisions of title 11, knowingly and fraudulently transfers or conceals any of his property or the property of such other person or corporation;

(8) After the filing of a case under title 11 or in contemplation thereof, knowingly and fraudulently conceals, destroys, mutilates, falsifies, or makes a false entry in any recorded information (including books, documents, records, and papers) relating to the property or financial affairs of a debtor; or

(9) After the filing of a case under title 11, knowingly and fraudulently withholds from a custodian, trustee, marshal, or other officer of the court or a United States Trustee entitled to its possession, any recorded information (including books, documents, records, and papers) relating to the property or financial affairs of a debtor, shall be fined under this title, imprisoned not more than 5 years, or both.

Figure 3.3, Sample indictment for Bankruptcy Fraud can be found on the following pages.

When you review this 15 count indictment you will again see how the government presents the facts of the case in terms of the objective of the conspiracy and the overt act in furtherance of the objective. Also note at the end of the indictment the government is asking for a criminal forfeiture of the assets. The document is marked "secret" because the indictment was sealed until the defendants were arrested. The document is now public.

Figure 3.3 Sample Indictment for Bankruptcy Fraud

SECRET

03 JUN 27 PM 2:43

DEPUTY

1	
2	
3	
4	
5	
6	
7	

8   UNITED STATES DISTRICT COURT

9   SOUTHERN DISTRICT OF CALIFORNIA

10   January 2003 Grand Jury **'03 CR ‾1744 J**

11   UNITED STATES OF AMERICA,   )   Criminal Case No. _____

12   Plaintiff,   )   I N D I C T M E N T

13   v.   )   Title 18, U.S.C. , Sec. 371 - Conspiracy;
)   Title 18, U.S.C., Sec. 152 - Bankruptcy

14   TERRY LINN BRUNNING (1),   )   Fraud; Title 18, U.S.C., Sec. 1957 - Money
     SUSAN JENNIFER BRUNNING (2),   )   Laundering, Title 18, U.S.C., Secs. 981(a)(1)(C)

15   )   and 28 U.S.C., Sec. 2461(c) and 18 U.S.C.,
                  Defendants.   )   Sec. 982(a)(1) - Criminal Forfeiture

16   _____)

17   The Grand Jury charges:

18   INTRODUCTORY ALLEGATIONS

19   At all relevant times herein:

20   1.   A bankruptcy case is commenced by the filing of a petition for bankruptcy under Title 11

21 of the United States Code. An individual who files a petition for bankruptcy is known under federal

22 bankruptcy law as a "debtor".

23   2.   Upon the filing of a bankruptcy petition, a debtor is required by law to disclose his

24 interests in all assets, whether in the form of real or personal property, tangible or intangible property,

25 and whether or not the asset is held in the debtor's own name or in the name of another person or entity.

26 The debtor is also required to disclose all liabilities and debts owed to creditors. The assets and the

27 liabilities of the debtor comprise what is called the debtor's bankruptcy estate. The estate is

28 administered by a court appointed-trustee referred to as the "Bankruptcy Court Trustee".

FAD:nlv:San Diego
6/26/03

Figure 3.3 Sample Indictment for Bankruptcy Fraud (cont.)

1　　　　3.　　　A debtor may file a petition for one of several different types of bankruptcy commonly

2　referred to as chapters.　One of these types of bankruptcy is known as "Chapter 7".　A Chapter 7

3　bankruptcy is a liquidation bankruptcy.　A petition filed under Chapter 7 does not allow the debtor to

4　remain in possession of all of the property comprising the bankruptcy estate.　Some of the debtor's

5　assets, such as his home and clothing up to a certain limit, are exempt from the liquidation.　The ultimate

6　goal of a Chapter 7 bankruptcy is to liquidate the debtor's non-exempt assets and pay the proceeds from

7　the liquidation to the debtor's creditors.　The debtor may then be eligible for a discharge of his remaining

8　debts to creditors whose debts were not satisfied by payment of the proceeds from the liquidation.　The

9　disclosure of all assets and liabilities of the debtor is necessary in order to allow the Bankruptcy Court

10　Trustee to liquidate the available assets and pay the outstanding creditors.

11　　　　4.　　　A debtor has certain duties after filing for bankruptcy.　The debtor is required to file

12　promptly a list of creditors, a schedule of assets and liabilities, a schedule of current income and

13　expenses, and a statement of the debtor's financial affairs.　All the property owned or controlled by the

14　debtor must be disclosed in these schedules and in the statement of financial affairs, even if the debtor

15　is uncertain as to whether it is property of the "estate".　These schedules and statement of financial

16　affairs must be signed under penalty of perjury.

17　　　　5.　　　In addition to the filing of a Schedule of Assets and Liabilities and a Statement of

18　Financial Affairs, a debtor is required to attend what is called a 341(a) Meeting of Creditors.　A 341(a)

19　Meeting of Creditors allows the debtor's creditors to examine the debtor under oath as to his financial

20　affairs. In connection with a 341(a) Meeting of Creditors, a debtor is asked to complete a Questionnaire

21　in which he is required to answer certain questions regarding his understanding of the bankruptcy

22　process as well as his financial affairs.　This Questionnaire must be signed under penalty of perjury.

23　　　　6.　　　On or about August 20, 2002, defendants TERRY LINN BRUNNING and SUSAN

24　JENNIFER BRUNNING (also identified as "the BRUNNINGS"), who are husband and wife, filed a

25　petition for Chapter 7 bankruptcy, Case No. 02-08176-B7, in the United States Bankruptcy Court for

26　the Southern District of California.　Prior to August 20, 2002, the BRUNNINGS operated two Postal

27　Annex stores located in San Diego, California.　In addition, TERRY BRUNNING operated a notary

28　public service.

2

Figure 3.3 Sample Indictment for Bankruptcy Fraud (cont.)

<u>Count 1</u>

<u>CONSPIRACY</u>

[18 U.S.C. § 371]

OBJECTS OF THE CONSPIRACY

7.   Beginning on a date unknown to the grand jury, and continuing to and including on or about June 27, 2003, in the Southern District of California, and elsewhere, defendants TERRY LINN BRUNNING and SUSAN JENNIFER BRUNNING, knowingly conspired and agreed with each other, and other persons known and unknown to the grand jury, to commit the following offenses against the United States:

a.   To knowingly and fraudulently conceal assets of the bankruptcy estate in connection with a bankruptcy under Title 11, in violation of Title 18, United States Code, Section 152(1);

b.   To knowingly and fraudulently make and cause to be made false statements under penalty of perjury in and connection with a bankruptcy under Title 11, in violation of Title 18, United States Code, Section 152(3); and

c.   To knowingly and fraudulently make a false claim for proof against the estate of a debtor in connection with a bankruptcy under Title 11, in violation of Title 18, United States Code, Section 152(4).

8.   The purpose of the conspiracy was to enable the BRUNNINGS to discharge their outstanding debts to financial institutions, government agencies, and other third parties, while maintaining control over and access to property of the bankruptcy estate, by means of fraud, concealment and misrepresentations. It was also part of the conspiracy to obtain control over and access to property in the possession of the Bankruptcy Court Trustee.

MEANS OF CONSPIRACY

9.   The objects of the conspiracy were accomplished in substance in the following ways, among others:

a.   Starting in July 2000 and continuing up until August 2002, the BRUNNINGS transferred approximately $1,000,000 from their Postal Annex business account located at Western

3

Figure 3.3 Sample Indictment for Bankruptcy Fraud (cont.)

1   Financial Bank to accounts located at Abbey National Treasury Limited dba Abbey National Offshore,

2   an offshore financial institution located in the Isle of Man, Great Britain. In addition, between March

3   2002 and August 2002, SUSAN BRUNNING transferred $58,000 from her personal checking account

4   located at Union Bank to an account in her name at Lloyds Bank, PLC in London.

5   b.   In or around February 2002, the BRUNNINGS sold their Postal Annex stores

6   in return for approximately $75,000 cash and a promissory note in the amount of $155,000.

7   c.   On or about August 20, 2002, the BRUNNINGS caused a petition for bankruptcy

8   to be filed in the United States Bankruptcy Court for the Southern District of California, Case

9   No. 02-08176-B7, which contained material misrepresentations and failed to disclose the existence of

10 several assets belonging to the bankruptcy estate including offshore financial accounts located at Abbey

11 National Offshore and Lloyds Bank, PLC, a promissory note in the amount of $155,000, a 57-foot

12 sailing yacht named Windsong, a 1990 Jaguar, a 1981 Rolls Royce, and a financial account located at

13 San Diego National Bank .

14   d.   After the filing of the bankruptcy petition, the Bankruptcy Court Trustee

15 discovered the existence of the promissory note which was not listed in the bankruptcy petition. The

16 Bankruptcy Court Trustee then took possession and control of the promissory note and instructed the

17 borrower under the note to make all payments to the Bankruptcy Court Trustee and not the

18 BRUNNINGS.

19   e.   After learning that the Bankruptcy Court Trustee had taken possession and control

20 of the promissory note, the BRUNNINGS created a fictitious claim against the bankrupt estate in the

21 fictitious name of Donna Kerns in an effort to obtain all or part of the proceeds from the sale of the

22 promissory note by the Bankruptcy trustee.

23   f.   On or around October 28, 2002, the BRUNNINGS left the United States on an

24 extended sailing trip to Mexico in their sailing yacht Windsong.

25   g.   In an effort to further conceal assets from the Bankruptcy Court Trustee, in

26 January 2003, the BRUNNINGS attempted to transfer all of the funds located in the offshore financial

27 accounts at Abbey National Offshore in the Isle of Man, Great Britain, to a financial account in their

28 joint names located at Bancomer , S.A., a foreign financial institution located in Mexico.

4

Figure 3.3 Sample Indictment for Bankruptcy Fraud (cont.)

1   h.   After learning that law enforcement authorities in the Isle of Man had obtained

2   a restraint order against the funds in the offshore accounts located at Abbey National Offshore from the

3   High Court of Justice of the Isle of Man, the BRUNNINGS caused false documents to be submitted to

4   the High Court of Justice in order to seek a release of all or part of the funds in those accounts to their

5   financial account at Bancomer, S.A. in Mexico rather than delivering possession to the Bankruptcy Court

6   Trustee.

7   OVERT ACTS

8   10.   In furtherance of the conspiracy and to accomplish its objects, the following overt acts,

9   among others, were committed within the Southern District of California, and elsewhere:

10   a.   On or about July 17, 2000, the BRUNNINGS opened two financial accounts at

11   Abbey National Offshore in their joint names.

12   b.   Between July 17, 2000 and August 1, 2002, the BRUNNINGS transferred

13   approximately $1,000,000 to their Abbey National Offshore accounts from their

14   Postal Annex business account located at Western Financial Bank in San Diego,

15   California.

16   c.   Between December 2001 and March 2002, the BRUNNINGS executed

17   documents transferring the ownership of their Postal Annex stores including a

18   promissory note dated December 11, 2001 in the amount of $155,000.

19   d.   On or about August 20, 2002, TERRY BRUNNING filed a Chapter 7 petition for

20   bankruptcy in the United States Bankruptcy Court for the Southern District of

21   California, Case No. 02-08176-B7 in which he declared under penalty of perjury

22   that the BRUNNINGS had between $0 and $50,000 in assets.

23   e.   On or about October 16, 2002, TERRY BRUNNING submitted a 341(a) Meeting

24   of Creditors Questionnaire in which he stated that he did not have, or has not had

25   in the past, an interest in any offshore account, i.e. accounts outside the borders

26   of the United States.

27   f.   On or about October 27, 2002, TERRY BRUNNING sent a letter to the

28   Bankruptcy Court Trustee in the fictitious name of Donna Kerns in which he

5

Figure 3.3 Sample Indictment for Bankruptcy Fraud (cont.)

1 claimed that Donna Kerns held a claim against the BRUNNINGS' bankruptcy
2 estate.

3 g. On or around October 30, 2002, SUSAN BRUNNING sent a letter to the
4 Bankruptcy Court Trustee in the fictitious name of Donna Kerns in which she
5 claimed that Donna Kerns held a claim against the BRUNNINGS' bankruptcy
6 estate.

7 h. On or before October 30, 2002, TERRY BRUNNING caused a Proof of Claim
8 to be filed in the U.S. Bankruptcy Court for the Southern District of California
9 in the fictitious name of Donna Kerns.

10 i. On a date unknown to the Grand Jury but before January 20, 2003, the
11 BRUNNINGS opened a financial account in their joint names at Bancomer, S.A.
12 located in Jalisco, Mexico.

13 j. On or about January 20, 2003, the BRUNNINGS signed wire transfer instructions
14 instructing Abbey National Offshore to transfer the funds in their account #
15 600108277 at Abbey National Offshore to their bank account #188664-4 at
16 Bancomer, S.A., Jalisco, Mexico.

17 k. On or about April 1, 2003, after learning that law enforcement authorities in the
18 Isle of Man obtained a restraint order against the funds located in their accounts
19 at Abbey National Offshore before the funds could be transferred to Mexico,
20 SUSAN BRUNNING submitted an affidavit to the High Court of Justice of the
21 Isle of Man to support a request to release the funds to the account #188664-4 at
22 Bancomer, S.A. rather than turning over the funds to the Bankruptcy Court
23 Trustee. The affidavit made several misrepresentations in furtherance of the
24 BRUNNINGS' efforts to maintain possession and control over their assets
25 including that SUSAN BRUNNING was separated from TERRY BRUNNING,
26 that they lived separate and apart, and that SUSAN BRUNNING had only seen
27 TERRY BRUNNING on a handful of occasions.

28 //

6

Figure 3.3 Sample Indictment for Bankruptcy Fraud (cont.)

1   1.   On or about April 1, 2003, SUSAN BRUNNING submitted documents to the
2   High Court of Justice of the Isle of Man to support her application to release the
3   funds in the BRUNNINGS' account at Abbey National Offshore Bank. These
4   documents contained forged signatures of two notary publics located in
5   San Diego, California.

6   All in violation of Title 18, United States Code, Section 371.

7   COUNTS 2-9

8   Bankruptcy Fraud - Concealment of Assets

9   [TERRY LINN BRUNNING AND SUSAN JENNIFER BRUNNING]

10   [18 U.S.C. § 152 (1)]

11   11.   The grand jury hereby repeats and realleges paragraphs 1 through 6 and paragraphs 9
12 through 10, as fully set forth herein.

13   12.   On or about August 20, 2002 and continuing to on or about June 27, 2003, defendants
14 TERRY LINN BRUNNING and SUSAN JENNIFER BRUNNING, and others known and unknown to
15 the Grand Jury, knowingly and fraudulently concealed or caused to be concealed from the bankruptcy
16 trustee, the creditors of the BRUNNINGS' bankruptcy estate, and the United States Trustee the
17 following property belonging to the bankruptcy estate in "In re Terry Linn Brunning and Susan Jennifer
18 Brunning", Case No. 02-08176-B7:

19	COUNT	CONCEALED ASSET
20	2	Account # 600108277-HICA located at the Abbey National Offshore Bank in Isle of Man, Great Britain
21, 22	3	Account # 600108277-DEFI located at the Abbey National Offshore Bank in the Isle of Man, Great Britain
23	4	A Vessel named Windsong, Registration # 998688
24	5	1990 Jaguar- License # 2VRN228
25	6	1981 Rolls Royce - License # 3RBT769
26	7	Promissory Note dated December 11, 2001 in the amount of $155,000
27, 28	8	Account # 020604-051737 at Lloyds Bank, PLC

7

Figure 3.3 Sample Indictment for Bankruptcy Fraud (cont.)

1   COUNT   CONCEALED ASSET

2   9   Account # 1820087230 at San Diego National Bank

3   All in violation of Title18, United States Code, Section 152(1).

4   COUNT 10

5   Bankruptcy Fraud-False Declaration

6   [TERRY LINN BRUNNING]

7   [18 U.S.C. § 152 (3)]

8   13.   The grand jury hereby repeats and realleges paragraphs 1 through 6 and paragraphs 9

9   through 10, as fully set forth herein.

10   14.   On or about August 20, 2002, in the Southern District of California, defendant TERRY

11   LINN BRUNNING , knowingly and fraudulently made a false declaration and statement as to a material

12   matter, under penalty of perjury, as defined under Section 1746 of Title 28, United States Code, in and

13   in relation to a case under Title 11 "In re Terry Linn Brunning and Susan Jennifer Brunning", Case

14   No. 02-08176-B7 by submitting a Voluntary Petition in which TERRY LINN BRUNNING falsely stated

15   that the BRUNNINGS' estimated assets were $0-50,000.

16   All in violation of Title 18, United States Code, Section 152(3).

17   COUNT 11

18   Bankruptcy Fraud-False Declaration

19   [TERRY LINN BRUNNING]

20   [18 U.S.C. § 152 (3)]

21   15.   The grand jury hereby repeats and realleges paragraphs 1 through 6 and paragraphs 9

22   through 10, as fully set forth herein.

23   16.   On or about August 20, 2002, in the Southern District of California, defendant TERRY

24   LINN BRUNNING , knowingly and fraudulently made a false declaration and statement as to a material

25   matter, under penalty of perjury, as defined under Section 1746 of Title 28, United States Code, in and

26   in relation to a case under Title 11 "In re Terry Linn Brunning and Susan Jennifer Brunning", Case

27   No. 02-08176-B7 by submitting Schedules of Assets and Liabilities in which TERRY LINN

28   BRUNNING made the following false statements:

8

Figure 3.3 Sample Indictment for Bankruptcy Fraud (cont.)

1   a.   fraudulently omitted to disclose the interests of the BRUNNINGS in offshore

2   financial accounts located at Abbey National Offshore and Lloyds Bank PLC, an account at San Diego

3   National Bank, a sailing yacht, a Jaguar, a Rolls Royce, and a promissory note;

4   b.   falsely stated that the BRUNNINGS had cash on hand of $840 when, in truth and

5   fact, as TERRY LINN BRUNNING well knew, that BRUNNINGS had more than $840 of cash on hand;

6   c.   falsely stated that the BRUNNINGS had no checking, savings or other financial

7   accounts when, in truth and fact, as TERRY LINN BRUNNING well knew, the BRUNNINGS had at

8   least four financial accounts at financial institutions;

9   d.   falsely stated that the BRUNNINGS had no accounts receivable when, in truth

10   and fact, as TERRY LINN BRUNNING well knew, the BRUNNINGS held a promissory note in the

11   amount of $155,000;

12   e.   falsely stated that the BRUNNINGS had no automobiles when, in truth and fact,

13   as TERRY LINN BRUNNING well knew, the BRUNNINGS owned a Jaguar and a Rolls Royce; and

14   f.   falsely stated that the BRUNNINGS had no boats when, in truth and fact, as

15   TERRY LINN BRUNNING well knew, the BRUNNINGS owned a sailing yacht.

16   All in violation of Title 18, United States Code, Section 152(3).

17   COUNT 12

18   Bankruptcy Fraud-False Declaration

19   [TERRY LINN BRUNNING]

20   [18 U.S.C. § 152 (3)]

21   17.   The grand jury hereby repeats and realleges paragraphs 1 through 6 and paragraphs 9

22   through 10, as fully set forth herein.

23   18.   On or about October 16, 2002, in the Southern District of California, defendant TERRY

24   LINN BRUNNING, knowingly and fraudulently made a false declaration and statement as to a material

25   matter, under penalty of perjury, as defined under Section 1746 of Title 28, United States Code, in and

26   in relation to a case under Title 11 "In re Terry Linn Brunning and Susan Jennifer Brunning", Case

27   No. 02-08176-B7 by submitting a 341(a) Meeting of Creditors Questionnaire in which TERRY LINN

28   BRUNNING falsely stated that he did not have, or did not have in the past, any interests in offshore

9

Figure 3.3 Sample Indictment for Bankruptcy Fraud (cont.)

1   accounts, i.e., accounts outside the borders of the United States when, in truth and fact, as TERRY LINN

2   BRUNNING well knew, two offshore accounts existed in which TERRY LINN BRUNNING had an

3   interest.

4   All in violation of Title 18, United States Code, Section 152(3).

5   COUNT 13

6   Bankruptcy Fraud-False Claim

7   [TERRY LINN BRUNNING]

8   [18 U.S.C. § 152(4)]

9   19.   The grand jury hereby repeats and realleges paragraphs 1 through 6 and paragraphs 9

10   through 10, as fully set forth herein.

11   20.   On or before October 30, 2002, in the Southern District of California, defendant TERRY

12   LINN BRUNNING, knowingly and fraudulently presented a false claim for proof against the

13   BRUNNINGS' estate, in and in relation to a case under Title 11 "In re Terry Linn Brunning and Susan

14   Jennifer Brunning", Case No. 02-08176-B7 by preparing, signing, and filing a proof of claim against the

15   BRUNNINGS' estate in the name of Donna Kerns when, in truth and fact, as TERRY LINN

16   BRUNNING well knew, Donna Kerns was a fictitious person and did not have a claim against the

17   BRUNNINGS' estate.

18   All in violation of Title 18, United States Code, Section 152(4).

19   COUNT 14

20   Bankruptcy Fraud-False Account

21   [SUSAN JENNIFER BRUNNING]

22   [18 U.S.C. § 152(2)]

23   21.   The grand jury hereby repeats and realleges paragraphs 1 through 6 and paragraphs 9

24   through 10, as fully set forth herein.

25   22.   On or around October 30, 2002, in the Southern District of California, defendant SUSAN

26   JENNIFER BRUNNING, knowingly and fraudulently made a false account, in and in relation to a case

27   under Title 11 "In re Terry Linn Brunning and Susan Jennifer Brunning", Case No. 02-08176-B7 by

28   preparing, signing, and sending a letter to the Bankruptcy Court Trustee from Donna Kerns in which she

10

Figure 3.3 Sample Indictment for Bankruptcy Fraud (cont.)

1 stated that Donna Kerns held a secured claim against the BRUNNINGS' estate when, in truth and fact,

2 as SUSAN JENNIFER BRUNNING well knew, Donna Kerns was a fictitious person and did not have

3 a claim against the BRUNNINGS' estate.

4 All in violation of Title 18, United States Code, Section 152(2)

5   <u>COUNT 15</u>

6   <u>Money Laundering</u>

7   [TERRY LINN AND SUSAN JENNIFER BRUNNING]

8   [18 U.S.C. § 1957-Engaging In Monetary Transactions
9   in Property Derived from Criminal Activity]

10   23.   The grand jury hereby repeats and realleges paragraphs 1 through 6 and paragraphs 9

11 through 21, as fully set forth herein.

12   24.   On or about January 20, 2003, in the Isle of Man, Great Britain, a place outside the United

13 States, defendants TERRY LINN BRUNNING and SUSAN JENNIFER BRUNNING, who are United

14 States persons (as defined in section 3077 of Title 18 United States Code) did knowingly attempt to

15 engage in a monetary transaction in criminally derived property of a value greater than $10,000 which

16 property was in fact derived from specified unlawful activity, to wit, bankruptcy fraud as charged in

17 Counts 2-14, by preparing, causing the preparation of, and signing wire transfer instructions to Abbey

18 National Offshore requesting that the funds in account # 600108277 DEFI in the amount of

19 $1,000,070.27 be transferred to account # 188664-4 in the names of TERRY and SUSAN BRUNNING

20 at Bancomer, S.A., Jalisco, Mexico.

21 All in violation of Title 18, United States Code, Section 1957

22   <u>CRIMINAL FORFEITURE ALLEGATIONS 1 and 2</u>

23   [TERRY LINN AND SUSAN JENNIFER BRUNNING]

24   [18 U.S.C. § 981 (a)(1)(C) and 28 U.S.C. § 2461(c)]

25   25.   Upon conviction of one or more of the offenses listed in Counts 2-14 of this Indictment,

26 defendants TERRY LINN BRUNNING and SUSAN JENNIFER BRUNNING shall forfeit to the United

27 States pursuant to 18 U.S.C. § 981(a)(1)(C) and 28 U.S.C. § 2461(c) any property constituting or derived

28 //

11

Figure 3.3 Sample Indictment for Bankruptcy Fraud (cont.)

1   from proceeds obtained directly or indirectly as a result of said violations, including but not limited to

2   the following:

3   a.   All funds in Account # 600108277-HICA located at the Abbey National Offshore

4   Bank in Isle of Man, Great Britain;

5   b.   All funds in Account # 600108277-DEFI located at the Abbey National Offshore

6   Bank in the Isle of Man, Great Britain;

7   c.   All funds in Account # 020604-051737 located at Lloyds Bank, PLC, London,

8   England; and

9   c.   One Vessel named Windsong, Registration # 998688;

10 All in violation of Title 18, United States Code, Section 981(a)(1)(C) and Title 28, United States Code,

11 Section 2461(c).

12   [TERRY LINN AND SUSAN JENNIFER BRUNNING]

13   [18 U.S.C. § 982 (a)(1)]

14   26.   Upon conviction of the money laundering offense alleged in Count 15 of this Indictment,

15 defendants TERRY LINN BRUNNING and SUSAN JENNIFER BRUNNING shall forfeit to the United

16 States pursuant to 18 U.S.C. § 982(a)(1), all property, real and personal, involved in such offense, or any

17 property traceable to such property, including but not limited to the following:

18   a.   All funds in Account # 600108277- DEFI located at Abbey National Offshore,

19 Isle of Man, Great Britain.

20 All in violation of Title 18, United States Code, Section 982(a)(1).

21   DATED: June 27, 2003.

22   A TRUE BILL:

23

24   _____
                                                        Foreperson

25 CAROL C. LAM
    United States Attorney

26   I hereby attest and certify on 0/27/03
                                                        That the foregoing document is a full, true and correct
                                                        copy of the original on file in my office and in my legal
27 _____   custody.
    FAITH A. DEVINE   CLERK, U.S. DISTRICT COURT
28 Assistant United States Attorney   SOUTHERN DISTRICT OF CALIFORNIA
                                                        By   Deputy

12

MONEY LAUNDERING

The art of turning dirty money into legitimate funds takes a lot more than a numbered Swiss bank account. Money laundering takes three steps: Placement - get the dirty money into a financial institution; Integration - commingle other money to confuse its origin; and Reintroduction - get the funds back into the economy.

To further insure his success, the money launderer will establish an endless series of shell companies, financial institutions and documents to make tracing the original source that much more difficult. Some schemes are simpler, the violators smuggle the bulk currency out of the country. There is a requirement that financial instruments in excess of $10,000, such as cash or items easily converted to cash, must be reported to Customs officials upon entering the country. Bulk cash can be re-introduced to the United States and declared at the border making the money appear legitimate. Law enforcement now has a burden to prove that the source of that money was illegitimate which is difficult to prove when the source is a foreign country.

INTERNET FRAUD

What Is Internet Fraud?

The term "Internet fraud" refers generally to any type of fraud scheme that uses one or more components of the Internet such as chat rooms, e-mail, message boards, or Web sites to present fraudulent solicitations to prospective victims, to conduct fraudulent transactions, or to transmit the proceeds of fraud to financial institutions or to other connected with the scheme.

If you use the Internet with any frequency, you'll soon see that people and things online tend to move, as the saying goes, on "Internet time." For most people, that phrase simply means that things seem to happen more quickly on the Internet business decisions, information-searching, personal interactions, to name a few and to happen before, during, or after ordinary "bricks-and-mortar" business hours.

Unfortunately, people who engage in fraud often operate in "Internet time" as well. They seek to take advantage of the Internet's unique capabilities for example, by sending e-mail messages worldwide in seconds, or posting Web site information that is readily accessible from anywhere in the world to carry out various types of fraudulent schemes more quickly than was possible with many fraud schemes in the past.

What Are the Major Types of Internet Fraud?

In general, the same types of fraud schemes that have victimized consumers and investors for many years before the creation of the Internet are now appearing online (sometimes with particular refinements that are unique to Internet technology). With the explosive growth of the Internet, and e-commerce in particular, online criminals try to present fraudulent schemes in ways that look, as much as possible, like the goods and services that the vast majority of legitimate e-commerce merchants offer. In the process, they not only cause harm to consumers and investors, but also undermine consumer confidence in legitimate e-commerce and the Internet.

Here are some of the major types of Internet fraud that law enforcement and regulatory authorities and consumer organizations are seeing:

Auction and Retail Schemes Online

According to the Federal Trade Commission and Internet Fraud Watch, fraudulent schemes appearing on online auction sites are the most frequently reported form of Internet fraud. These schemes, and similar schemes for online retail goods, typically purport to offer high-value items ranging from Cartier® watches to computers to collectibles such as Beanie Babies® that are likely to attract many consumers. These schemes induce their victims to send money for the promised items, but then deliver nothing or only an item far less valuable than what was promised (e.g., counterfeit or altered goods).

Business Opportunity/"Work-at-Home" Schemes Online.

Fraudulent schemes often use the Internet to advertise purported business opportunities that will allow individuals to earn thousands of dollars a month in "work-at-home" ventures. These schemes typically require the individuals to pay anywhere from $35 to several hundred dollars or more, but fail to deliver the materials or information that would be needed to make the work-at-home opportunity a potentially viable business.

Identity Theft and Fraud

Some Internet fraud schemes also involve identity theft the wrongful obtaining and using of someone else's personal data in some way that involves fraud or deception, typically for economic gain.

In one federal prosecution, the defendants allegedly obtained the names and Social Security numbers of U.S. military officers from a Web site, and then used more than 100 of those names and numbers to apply via the Internet for credit cards with a Delaware bank.

In another federal prosecution, the defendant allegedly obtained personal data from a federal agency's Web site, and then used the personal data to submit 14 car loan applications online to a Florida bank.

INVESTMENT SCHEMES ONLINE

Market Manipulation Schemes

Enforcement actions by the Securities and Exchange Commission and criminal prosecutions indicate that criminals are using two basic methods for trying to manipulate securities markets for their personal profit. First, in so-called "pump-and-dump" schemes, they typically disseminate false and fraudulent information in an effort to cause dramatic price increases in thinly traded stocks or stocks of shell companies (the "pump"), then immediately sell off their holdings of those stocks (the "dump") to realize substantial profits before the stock price falls back to its usual low level. Any other buyers of the stock who are unaware of the falsity of the information become victims of the scheme once the price falls.

For example, in one federal prosecution in Los Angeles, the defendants allegedly purchased, directly and through another man, a total of 130,000 shares in a bankrupt company, NEI Webworld, Inc., whose assets had been liquidated several months earlier. The defendants then allegedly posted bogus e-mail messages on hundreds of Internet bulletin boards, falsely stating that NEI Webworld was going to be taken over by a wireless telecommunications company. At the time of the defendants' alleged purchases of NEI Webworld stock, the stock was priced between 9 cents and 13 cents a share. Ultimately, in a single morning of trading, NEI Webworld stock rose in 45 minutes from $8 per share to a high of $15 5/16, before falling, within a half-hour, to 25 cents per share. The defendants allegedly realized profits of $362,625.

In another federal prosecution in Los Angeles, a man who worked for a California company, PairGain Technologies, created a bogus Bloomberg news Web site which falsely reported that PairGain was about to be acquired by an Israeli company, and posted fraudulent e-mail messages, containing links to the counterfeit Bloomberg news site, on financial news bulletin boards. On the day that the bogus report was posted on the Internet, PairGain stock rose approximately 30 percent before PairGain issued its own press release stating that the report was false.

Second, in short-selling or "scalping" schemes, the scheme takes a similar approach, by disseminating false or fraudulent information in an effort to cause price decreases in a particular company's stock.

For example, in one recent federal prosecution, a man who described himself as a "day trader" allegedly posted (more than 20 times) a bogus press release falsely stating that a major telecommunications- and Internet-related company, Lucent Technologies, Inc., would not meet its quarterly earnings estimates. The day trader allegedly traded approximately 6,000 shares of Lucent stock the same day that he posted the bogus press release. The false reports allegedly drove the stock's price down 3.6 percent and reduced Lucent's market value by more than $7 billion.

Other Investment Schemes

Other types of fraudulent investment schemes may combine uses of the Internet with traditional mass-marketing technology such as telemarketing to reach large numbers of potential victims.

In a federal prosecution in San Diego, a major fraudulent scheme used the Internet and telemarketing to solicit prospective investors for so-called "general partnerships" involving purported "high-tech" investments, such as an Internet shopping mall and Internet access providers. The scheme allegedly defrauded more than 3,000 victims nationwide of nearly $50 million.

Credit-Card Schemes.

Some Internet fraud schemes, which appear to be variations on the online auction schemes described earlier, involve the use of unlawfully obtained credit card numbers to order goods or services online.

One widely reported and intricate scheme, for example, involves offering consumers high-value consumer items, such as video cameras, at a very attractive price (i.e., below the price set at legitimate e-commerce Web sites). When a potential consumer contacts the "seller," the "seller" promises to ship the consumer the item before the consumer has to pay anything. If the consumer agrees, the "seller" (without the consumer's knowledge) uses that consumer's real name, along with an unlawfully obtained credit card number belonging to another person, to buy the item at a legitimate Web site. Once that Web site ships the item to the consumer, the consumer, believing that the transaction is legitimate, then authorizes his credit card to be billed in favor of the "seller" or sends payment directly to the "seller."

As a result, there are two victims of the scheme: the original e-commerce merchant who shipped the item based on the unlawfully used credit card; and the consumer who sent his money after receiving the item that the "seller" fraudulently ordered from the merchant. In the meantime, the "seller" may have transferred his fraudulent proceeds to bank accounts beyond the effective reach of either the merchant or the consumer.

Other Schemes

Some Web sites on the Internet have purported to offer those who want a "quick divorce" an opportunity to obtain a divorce in the Dominican Republic or other foreign countries for $1,000 or more, without even having to leave the United States. These sites often contain false, misleading, or legally inaccurate information about the process for obtaining such divorces (e.g., that neither spouse has to visit the country in which the divorce is being sought). Typically, people who have sent money to one of these schemes eventually receive false assurances that they are legally divorced. In fact, victims of the scheme have neither received legitimate legal services nor obtained valid divorces. People, who are interested in obtaining a divorce, whether in the United States or elsewhere, should seek a lawyer with whom they can speak personally, and not rely solely on e-mail exchanges or online information.

Prosecution

The Justice Department has begun to bring a number of criminal prosecutions throughout the country against individuals and groups engaging in various types of Internet fraud. Here are some examples of federal criminal prosecutions directed at Internet fraud:

Auction and Retail Schemes Online

- **Oxford, Mississippi** On August 27, 1998, a woman was sentenced in the Northern District of Mississippi to 15 months' imprisonment and $9,432 restitution on fraud charges relating to her conduct of a fraudulent scheme. The scheme involved her use of Web pages and interactive computer locations on the Internet for falsely advertising various computer hardware and software and computer accessories.

- **Philadelphia** On March 2, 2000, three men were criminally charged in the Eastern District of Pennsylvania for their alleged roles in falsely offering the sale of Beanie Babies® on the Internet, and then failing to deliver the orders or sending stolen "Beanie Babies® that generally were of substantially less value than the items ordered.

- **San Diego** On March 6, 2000, a man pleaded guilty in the Southern District of California to mail and wire fraud in connection with his conduct of a fraudulent scheme involving Internet sales of Beanie Babies that he never delivered.

- **Santa Ana, California** On November 1, 1999, a man was sentenced in the Central District of California on mail and credit-card fraud charges to 14 months' imprisonment and $36,000 restitution, for his conduct of an Internet auction fraud that falsely offered digital cameras and laptop computers to consumers.

- **Seattle** On August 6, 1999, a man pleaded guilty in the Western District of Washington to wire fraud in connection with his role in placing on various Web sites false advertisements for computer systems, for which he accepted victims' payments but which he never delivered.

- **West Palm Beach, Florida** On February 12, 1999, a man was sentenced in the Southern District of Florida on wire fraud charges to six months home detention and more than $22,000 restitution, for his conduct of a fraudulent scheme in which he falsely advertised on Internet auction and retail sale Web sites computer components that he purported to have for sale, but did not have or obtain most of the merchandise he advertised.

Business-Opportunity Schemes Online

- **Los Angeles** In November 1999, four individuals were criminally charged in the Central District of California for their roles in conducting a fraudulent scheme, in which they sent out approximately 50 million e-mails that falsely advertised work-at-home opportunities for people but provided few actual opportunities for people who paid the $35 advance fee.

Investment Schemes Online

"Pump-and-dump" schemes, short-selling schemes, Ponzi schemes, and other fraudulent investment schemes have all been subjects of federal prosecution throughout the country.

- **Alexandria, Virginia** In September 1997, a man was sentenced in the Eastern District of Virginia to one year's imprisonment and fined $20,000 on securities fraud conspiracy charges relating to his touting of a stock involved in a "pump and dump" scheme.

- **Brooklyn, New York** In August, 1999, four individuals were indicted in the Eastern District of New York on securities fraud charges for their alleged roles in the fraudulent promotion of eight stocks through misleading Internet Web site and e-mail newsletter profiles.

- **Charlotte, North Carolina** In 1999, two individuals pleaded guilty in the Western District of North Carolina to securities fraud charges for their roles in offering securities in a nonexistent investment bank that purportedly offered, among other things, a "guaranteed" 20 percent return on savings.

- **Cleveland** On March 22, 2000, four people were indicted in the Northern District of Ohio, on charges including conspiracy to commit and committing mail and wire fraud. The defendants allegedly devised and carried out a scheme to defraud "investors" in a "Ponzi" pyramid scheme. A company with which the defendants were affiliated allegedly collected more than $26 million from "investors" without selling any product or service, and paid older investors with the proceeds of the money collected from the newer investors.

- **Los Angeles** On January 4, 2000, two men were indicted in the Central District of California on securities fraud charges for their alleged roles in the NEI Webworld scheme described earlier. In addition, on August 30, 1999, the individual who conducted the PairGain Technologies scheme mentioned earlier was sentenced in the Central District of California to five months' home detention and $93,000 restitution.

- **New York** On August 9, 1999, a man was criminally charged in the Southern District of New York with securities fraud. The man allegedly conducted a scheme to unlawfully inflate the price of stock of a company involved in acquiring retail auto dealerships, by making various false claims that another company (located in the same office suite as the auto dealership company) had developed a cure for HIV infection and AIDS.

Credit Card Fraud

- **Ft. Lauderdale** In November 1997, a former graduate student was sentenced in the Southern District of Florida on wire fraud charges to four months' home detention, for a scheme in which he obtained the names of multiple students from a local university and fraudulently applied for 174 credit cards via the Internet. Because of the quick investigative work by the Postal Inspection Service, no losses were incurred.

- **Wilmington, Delaware** In 2000, three individuals were indicted in the District of Delaware on charges of conspiracy, bank fraud, identity theft, Social Security fraud, and wire fraud, for their alleged roles in the military officers' Social Security number/credit-card fraud scheme described earlier.

Other Types of Internet Fraud

- **Los Angeles** On February 7, 2000, a man was sentenced to 87 months' imprisonment for his role in a scheme that purported to provide immigration assistance to aliens seeking to become residents or citizens of the United States. Using Web sites, newspaper advertisements, recruiters, and word of mouth to offer their services to aliens, the leaders of the scheme typically charged more than $10,000 per client and promised that the client would receive particular immigration documents. In some cases, however, the leaders of the scheme provided their clients with counterfeit or false immigration documents; in other cases, they provided no documents at all, and blamed the government and the legal system for the delay in providing the promised documents.

- **Los Angeles** In November 1999, four men were criminally charged in the Central District of California for their alleged roles in conducting the "work-at-home" scheme described earlier.

WHY USE CONSPIRACY LAWS

Financial cases can be very complex. For that reason they are sometimes difficult for juries to understand. They normally involve two or more people to commit therefore a conspiracy charge can be used to prosecute the violators. Federal conspiracy charges are relatively simple to understand by juries and in combination with wire fraud or mail fraud easy to prove in relation to the more complex financial case.

In a article written by John W. Dean for FindLaw, a web site to locate defense attorneys, he examines why the conspiracy laws should be used to prosecute Enron executives. Dean discussed the Enron case with Alan Baron, the partner in charge of the international powerhouse law firm of Dorsey and Whitney and a former federal prosecutor. Baron suggested that any indictments would include conspiracy, mail fraud and wire fraud. Dean said, "But the federal conspiracy law is relatively simple, and one of the most potent weapons in the federal crime fighting arsenal. And conspiring together seems to be just what Enron officials did when they apparently (and allegedly) approved of shifty accounting procedures, and decided together to engage in dubious transactions, all with the purpose of concealing the company's disastrous finances."

Further he stated, "the beauty of the conspiracy law is that each co-conspirator is held responsible for acts of the other conspirators, even if he or she was totally unaware of these activities in furtherance of the conspiracy. Even more difficult for the conspiracy defendant in is the fact that hearsay evidence, relating to the conspiracy, is admissible." The entire article can be read at writ.findlaw.com/dean/20020816.html. Below are two press releases proving Dean was correct.

Figure 3.4 U.S. Department of Justice Press Release

FOR IMMEDIATE RELEASE THURSDAY, JULY 8, 2002
(202) 514-2XX |TDD (202) 514-1XXX WWW.USDOJ.GOV

FORMER ENRON CHAIRMAN AND CHIEF EXECUTIVE OFFICER KENNETH L. LAY CHARGED WITH CONSPIRACY, FRAUD, FALSE STATEMENTS

Money Laundering Charges Added Against Former CAO Richard Causey

WASHINGTON, D.C. - Deputy Attorney General James B. Comey, Assistant Attorney General Christopher A. Wray of the Criminal Division, FBI Director Robert Mueller, and Enron Task Force Director Andrew Weissmann announced today that a federal grand jury in Houston has indicted former Enron Corp. Chairman and Chief Executive Officer Kenneth L. Lay on charges of conspiracy, securities fraud, wire fraud, bank fraud and making false statements.

A superseding indictment returned by the grand jury in Houston Wednesday, and unsealed today, charges Lay, 62, of Houston, with conspiracy to commit securities fraud, four counts of securities fraud and two counts of wire fraud, one count of bank fraud and three counts of making false statements to a bank. The superseding indictment joins Lay as a defendant in a case pending against former Enron CEO Jeffrey K. Skilling and former Enron Chief Accounting Officer Richard Causey. Causey was originally indicted in January 2004, and Skilling was added to the case in February 2004. The new indictment also adds a money laundering conspiracy count and four counts of money laundering against Causey in connection with fraudulent hedging vehicles, and expands certain factual allegations against Causey in connection with the securities fraud conspiracy. The case is pending before U.S. District Judge Sim Lake in Houston, Texas.

Lay surrendered this morning to FBI agents in Houston and the indictment was unsealed. Lay had an initial appearance this morning before Magistrate Judge Mary Milloy.

"The indictment charges that Lay, Skilling, Causey and others oversaw a massive conspiracy to cook the books at Enron and to

Figure 3.4 U.S. Department of Justice Press Release (cont.)

create the illusion that it was a robust, growing company with limitless potential when, in fact, Enron was an increasingly troubled business kept afloat only by a series of deceptions," said Deputy Attorney General James B. Comey, who heads the President's Corporate Fraud Task Force. "These charges demonstrate the Department's commitment to the rule of law, its commitment to the principle that no one is above the law, and its commitment to unravel even the most complex of fraudulent schemes."

"This indictment alleges that every member of Enron's senior management participated in a criminal conspiracy to commit one of the largest corporate frauds in American history," said Assistant Attorney General Wray. "Kenneth Lay is charged with abusing his powerful position as Chairman of the Board and CEO and repeatedly lying in an effort to cover up the financial collapse that caused devastating harm to millions of Americans. The progress of this investigation shows that the Department of Justice will work tirelessly to hold corporate America to the high standards imposed by federal law."

"The collapse of Enron was devastating to tens of thousands of people and shook the public's confidence in corporate America," said FBI Director Mueller. "The FBI and our partners on the President's Corporate Fraud Task Force responded with a concerted effort to uncover the truth and to bring those responsible to justice. The charges against Ken Lay, Jeffrey Skilling and Richard Causey take us one step closer to restoring the public confidence in our financial markets."

The indictment alleges that at various times between at least 1999 and 2001, Lay, Skilling, Causey and other Enron executives engaged in a wide-ranging scheme to deceive the investing public, the U.S. Securities and Exchange Commission and others about the true performance of Enron's businesses. The alleged scheme was designed to make it appear that Enron was growing at a healthy and predictable rate, consistent with analysts' published expectations, that Enron did not have significant write-offs or debt and was worthy of investment-grade credit rating, that Enron was comprised of a number of successful business units, and that the company had an appropriate cash flow. It had the effect of inflating artificially Enron's stock price, which increased from approximately $30 per share in early 1998 to over $80 per share in January 2001, and artificially stemming the decline of the stock during the first three quarters of 2001.

Figure 3.4 U.S. Department of Justice Press Release (cont.)

The indictment alleges that Lay had a significant profit motive for participating in the scheme. As stated in the indictment, between 1998 and 2001, Lay received approximately $300 million from the sale of Enron stock options and restricted stock, netting over $217 million in profit, and was paid more than $19 million in salary and bonuses. During 2001 alone, Lay received a salary of over $1 million, a bonus of $7 million and $3.6 million in long term incentive payments. Additionally, during the period of August 21 through Oct. 26, 2001, Lay sold 918,104 shares of Enron stock to repay advances totaling $26,025,000 he had received from a line of credit extended to Lay by Enron.

As a part of the alleged scheme, unrealistic and unattainable earnings goals were set for Enron, based on analysts' expectations rather than on actual or reasonably achievable business results. When, as expected within the company, Enron consistently fell short of those goals, Lay, Skilling, Causey and others allegedly orchestrated a series of accounting gimmicks designed to make up the shortfall between actual and predicted results. Enron then announced publicly that it had met or exceeded analysts' expectations when, as Lay, Skilling and Causey allegedly knew, it made its numbers only by engaging in fraud. The indictment also alleges that Lay, Skilling and Causey made false and misleading representations about Enron's finances and business operations to analysts, at press conferences, in SEC filings and elsewhere.

Lay is principally charged for his conduct during the third quarter of 2001. As the indictment alleges, upon Skilling's abrupt departure from Enron in August 2001, Lay resumed his position as CEO of the company, intensified his oversight of Enron's day-to-day operations, and took control as leader of the conspiracy. Starting in August, according to the indictment, Lay was briefed extensively about mounting and undisclosed financial and operational problems, including overvaluation of Enron's assets and business units by several billion dollars. As a result of these and other issues confronting Enron, Lay privately considered a range of potential solutions, including mergers, restructurings, and even divestiture of Enron's pipelines, assets that Lay considered to be the crown jewels of the company. However, the indictment alleges he failed to disclose Enron's problems to the investing public and affirmatively misled the investing public about Enron's financial condition, while falsely claiming that he was disclosing everything that he had learned.

For example, the indictment states that during August 2001, Lay participated in Management Committee meetings at which reports

Figure 3.4 U.S. Department of Justice Press Release (cont.)

were presented showing earnings shortfalls in virtually every Enron business unit, totaling approximately $1 billion. During early September 2001, Lay attended a Management Committee retreat in the Woodlands, Texas, at which the serious problems besetting Enron, including underperforming business units and troubled assets, were further discussed. Among other things, executives discussed the need to take in the third quarter of 2001 at least a $1 billion charge and that Enron had committed an accounting error in the amount of $1.2 billion.

The indictment alleges that throughout the remainder of September 2001, Lay engaged in a series of high-level meetings to discuss the growing financial crisis at Enron and the likely impact on Enron's credit rating. Among other things, Lay knew that the total amount of losses embedded in Enron's assets and business units was, at a minimum, $7 billion. Lay also knew that Enron's auditors had changed their position concerning the accounting treatment of four off-balance sheet vehicles called the Raptors, which required Enron to determine in short order whether an acceptable alternative methodology existed or whether, instead, Enron would have to restate its earnings and admit the error.

Despite knowing these negative facts, on Sept. 26, 2001, in an online forum with thousands of Enron employees, many of whom were investors in Enron stock, Lay allegedly stated that Enron was going to "hit [its] numbers." Lay allegedly created the false impression that his confidence in Enron's stock was such that he had increased his personal ownership of Enron stock in the past two months as a sign of his belief in what he was espousing. As the indictment alleges, during the prior two months, Lay actually purchased $4 million in Enron stock while also selling $24 million in Enron stock through nonpublic transactions.

The indictment states that in the weeks leading up to Enron's third quarter earnings release on Oct. 16, 2001, Lay determined that Enron could not publicly report a loss in excess of $1 billion without triggering negative action by Enron's credit rating agencies. Lay thus artificially capped Enron's losses to that amount. Also during this time, Lay learned that changes to the accounting rules governing goodwill (i.e., the difference between what Enron paid for an entity and the book value of that entity's net assets) would require Enron to

Figure 3.4 U.S. Department of Justice Press Release (cont.)

disclose impairments to certain of its assets, including its interest in Wessex Water, a business located in Bath, England. In order to hide the impact of asset impairment, Lay allegedly claimed, falsely, that Enron was committed to engaging in a "water growth strategy," which would have required Enron to expend between $1 billion and $28 billion in capital investments in the water industry. Lay allegedly knew that Enron had no intention of pursuing such a strategy and did not have the capital to support it.

According to the indictment, on Oct.16, 2001, when Enron announced losses of approximately $1 billion, Lay allegedly sought to minimize the import of the reported losses by falsely describing the losses as "nonrecurring," that is, a one-time or unusual earnings event. Enron also disclosed the same day an approximate $1.2 billion reduction in shareholder equity, which Lay again sought to minimize by falsely attributing it to the unwind of the Raptor vehicles, rather than to an accounting error. According to the indictment, on October 12, Lay misled a representative of a national credit rating agency about the need to take additional write downs and the extent of Enron's goodwill problems. On both October 16 and 23, Lay told the investing public that Enron had determined that its goodwill impairment was up to $200 million. However, he failed to disclose the impact on Enron of an additional goodwill impairment of up to $700 million in connection with Wessex. Also on October 23, Lay allegedly espoused faith in Elektro, a Brazilian power plant which Enron carried on its books as worth in excess of $2 billion. In fact, as Lay allegedly knew, Elektro was overvalued by up to $1 billion. Lay also allegedly distributed materials at the road shows that misleadingly described the value of the international portfolio as $6.5 billion. In reality, as Lay knew, this vastly overstated the true value of the international assets by billions of dollars.

These and other schemes alleged in the indictment quickly unraveled, and on Dec. 2, 2001, Enron filed for bankruptcy, making its stock, which less than a year earlier had been trading at over $80 per share, virtually worthless.

Lay was also charged in four counts with bank fraud and making false statements to three banks arising out of his obtaining and using four personal lines of credit worth over $60 million. Lay allegedly promised the banks that the loans would not be used to purchase stock. As a result of these false representations, the banks extended far greater loans to Lay than they otherwise would. The indictment alleges that in spite of his promises, Lay repeatedly used the lines of credit to buy the stock. The lines of credit were collateralized mainly

Figure 3.4 U.S. Department of Justice Press Release (cont.)

by artificially inflated shares of Enron stock and were repaid with the same. If convicted of all the charges in the indictment, Lay faces a maximum sentence of 175 years in prison and millions of dollars in fines.

Criminal indictments are only charges and not evidence of guilt. A defendant is presumed to be innocent unless and until proven guilty.

The investigation into Enron's collapse is being conducted by the Enron Task Force, a team of federal prosecutors supervised by the Justice Department's Criminal Division and agents from the FBI and the IRS Criminal Investigations Division. The Task Force also has coordinated with and received considerable assistance from the Securities and Exchange Commission. The Enron Task Force is part of President Bush's Corporate Fraud Task Force, created in July 2002 to investigate allegations of fraud and corruption at U.S. corporations.

Thirty-one defendants have been charged to date, including 21 former Enron executives. Eleven defendants have been convicted to date, including former CFO Andrew Fastow and former Treasurer Ben Glisan. To date, the Enron Task Force has restrained more than $161 million in proceeds derived from criminal activity. The Task Force investigation is continuing. # # # 04-470

Figure 3.5 Enron Chief Pleads Guilty

**FOR IMMEDIATE RELEASE JANUARY 14 2004
WWW.USDOJ.GOV (202) 514-2xxx**

FORMER ENRON CHIEF FINANCIAL OFFICER ANDREW FASTOW PLEADS GUILTY TO CONSPIRACY TO COMMIT SECURITIES AND WIRE FRAUD, AGREES TO COOPERATE WITH ENRON INVESTIGATION

Former Assistant Treasurer Lea Fastow Agrees to Plead Guilty
WASHINGTON, D.C. - Deputy Attorney General James B. Comey, Assistant Attorney General Christopher A. Wray of the Criminal Division, Enron Task Force Director Leslie R. Caldwell and FBI Director Robert Mueller announced today that Andrew S. Fastow, the former chief financial officer (CFO) of Enron Corporation, has pleaded guilty to two counts of conspiracy to commit securities and wire fraud and is cooperating with an ongoing criminal investigation into Enron's collapse. Fastow, the

Figure 3.5 Enron Chief Pleads Guilty (cont.)

highest-level defendant to be charged to date in the Enron investigation, entered his plea today before Judge Kenneth Hoyt at U.S. District Court in Houston, Texas.

Under the terms of a plea agreement, Fastow will cooperate fully with the government's investigation, serve a 10-year prison sentence on the two counts to which he's pleading guilty, and forfeit more than $29 million. The remaining 96 criminal charges against Fastow from a May 2003 indictment are pending, and will be dismissed if the government determines that Fastow has cooperated fully and truthfully. In addition, former Enron Assistant Treasurer Lea W. Fastow, Andrew Fastow's wife, has agreed to plead guilty to filing a false joint tax return for 2000, in which she failed to report income from a partnership related to Enron. She is expected to enter the guilty plea before Judge David Hittner at federal court in Houston later today."

As one of the masterminds behind a massive fraud scheme, Andrew Fastow constructed an elaborate wall of deceit - shielding the reality of Enron's failing business from the watchful eye of shareholders and the investing public," said Deputy Attorney General James B. Comey, the head of President Bush's Corporate Fraud Task Force. "Today's plea tears that wall down. Using Mr. Fastow's cooperation, we will continue to tear the wall down by prosecuting each person to which the evidence and the law leads us.'" The Andrew Fastow plea and cooperation agreement opens wide a window into the fraudulent practices of Enron's senior management," stated Assistant Attorney General Christopher A. Wray. "Fastow's prison sentence demonstrates once again that we will uncover fraudulent conduct by corporate officials, and the consequences will be serious. "FBI Director Robert Mueller said, "Today's plea agreements are a significant milestone in an intensive two-year investigation. The FBI and our partners on the Enron Task Force will continue our efforts to uncover the full extent of criminal conduct that contributed to Enron's collapse. Corporate criminals should be on notice that no matter how complex or intricate their schemes, they are going to be held accountable for their actions."

"The forfeiture of more than $29 million in personal assets by the Fastows, a sum only a few Americans will earn in their lifetime, speaks to the magnitude of their criminal activities," stated Internal Revenue Service Commissioner Mark W. Everson. "Our investigation substantiated that the Fastows filed multiple false tax returns, and, through her plea agreement announced today, Mrs. Fastow, an MBA and former Assistant Treasurer at Enron,

Figure 3.5 Enron Chief Pleads Guilty (cont.)

acknowledges the Fastows' willful criminal conduct." Andrew Fastow Pleads Guilty; Agrees to Serve 10 Years in Prison Fastow pleaded guilty to two counts of conspiracy, in violation of 18 U.S.C. § 371. The charges carry a maximum statutory sentence of 10 years in prison, followed by three years of supervised release. As part of his plea agreement, Fastow agreed to serve 10 years in prison and to cooperate fully with the government's ongoing criminal investigation of the collapse of the Enron Corporation. As part of the plea agreement, Fastow admitted that he and other members of Enron's senior management conspired in wide-ranging schemes to fraudulently manipulate Enron's publicly reported financial results. Fastow also admitted participating in schemes to enrich himself at the expense of the company and its shareholders. Specifically, Fastow admitted that he conspired with senior management to cause Enron to enter into improper transactions with the LJM entities, which were under Fastow's control. And he admitted to engaging in self-dealing transactions to enrich himself and others in connection with the so-called Southampton transaction, which involved the $30 million buyout by Enron of an entity called LJM Swap Sub, LP, which Fastow controlled. In engaging in these transactions, Mr. Fastow admitted that he violated his duty of loyalty and honest services to Enron's shareholders. Fastow's sentencing is scheduled for April 19, 2004.Lea Fastow to Plead Guilty; Agrees to Serve Five Months in PrisonLea W. Fastow is scheduled to enter her guilty plea today before Judge David Hittner of the U.S. District Court in the Southern District of Texas. Under the applicable U.S. Sentencing Guidelines, Fastow faces an estimated range of imprisonment of 10 to 16 months. The parties have agreed to recommend to the Court a sentence at the low end of this range, which would allow the Court to impose a "split" sentence of five months incarceration and five months of home confinement as a condition of supervised release. As part of her plea agreement, Fastow admitted that from December 1997 through 2000, she failed to report as income a total of $204,444.34 in proceeds that her family received from an Enron "special purpose entity" known as RADR. Fastow admitted that she knew that this money was derived from RADR and that her husband had been prohibited from investing in RADR. To hide the fact that it was taxable income, the money was disguised as "gifts" to the Fastow family, through checks made payable to Fastow, her husband Andrew and their children. To avoid triggering the law's requirement that gifts in excess of $10,000 to another person be reported to the Internal Revenue Service, most of these checks were made payable in

Figure 3.5 Enron Chief Pleads Guilty (cont.)

amounts of $10,000 or less and in the names of different members of the Fastow family. Although she knew that the payments represented income that should have been reported on their joint federal income tax returns, Fastow concealed the income from the Fastows' accountant and intentionally failed to report the income on their joint federal income tax returns for the years 1997 through 2000. Fastow admitted that she signed these income tax returns under penalty of perjury and caused them to be filed with the Internal Revenue Service. Fastow faces sentencing at a date to be determined. Enron, at one time the seventh-ranked company in the United States with stock trading as high as $80 per share in August 1999, filed for bankruptcy protection on Dec. 2, 2001 and its stock became virtually worthless. The investigation into Enron's collapse is being conducted by the Enron Task Force, a team of federal prosecutors supervised by the Justice Department's Criminal Division and agents from the FBI and the IRS Criminal Investigation Division. The Task Force also has coordinated with an received considerable assistance from the Securities and Exchange Commission. The Enron Task Force is part of President Bush's Corporate Fraud Task Force, created in July 2002 to investigate allegations of fraud and corruption at U.S. corporations. Twenty-six individuals have been charged to date, including 19 former Enron executives. With today's pleas, seven people and Arthur Andersen LLP have been convicted as a result of the ongoing investigation. In addition, the Enron Task Force has restrained more than $93 million in proceeds derived from criminal activity. The Task Force investigation is continuing.

SUMMARY

There are a large variety of financial crimes, but they have greed as common factor. Financial crimes include health care fraud, environmental crimes, fraud against the government, antitrust violations, financial institution fraud, intellectual property crimes, telemarketing fraud, securities/commodities fraud, insurance fraud, and bankruptcy fraud.

DISCUSSION QUESTIONS

1. Discuss who would be the targeted victims of the types of frauds covered in this chapter?
2. What types of evidence would law enforcement likely find when investigating the types of frauds covered in this chapter?

3. Are intellectual property crimes without "real" victims? If not, how does society suffer from these losses, including downloading music from the Internet?

ADDITIONAL READING

Scam School, Chuck Whitlock, paperback, Macmillan, 1997

Vendetta - American Express and the Smearing of Edmond Safra, Bryan Burrough, Hardcover, Harper Collins, 1992

White Paper, The Negative Consequences of International Intellectual Property Theft: Economic Harm, Threats to the Public Health and Safety, and Link to Organized Crime and Terrorists Organizations, International Anti-Counterfeiting Coalition, January, 2005. www.iacc.org/whitepaper.pdf

BIBLIOGRAPHY

Government Accounting Office report on health care fraud, May 1996

International Anti-counterfeiting Coalition (IACC) report, www.iacc.org

United States Department of Justice report on telemarketing fraud

Press release - United States Department of Justice, former Enron Chairman and Chief Executive Officer Kenneth L. Lay charged with conspiracy, fraud, false statements dated July 8, 2002

Press release - United States Department of Justice, former Enron Chief Financial Officer Andrew Fastow pleads guilty to conspiracy to commit securities and wire fraud, agrees to cooperate with Enron investigation dated January 14, 2004

Chapter 4

Crimes Against Persons

OVERVIEW

In this chapter you will examine the crimes against persons including murder, extortion and assault. You will study the famous Patty Hearst kidnapping and her conversion to being a co-conspirator with the SLA. You will read about the elements of the crimes to understand what is needed to prove the violations.

CHAPTER OBJECTIVES

1. Learn what types of crimes are considered crimes against persons.
2. Understand the elements of the various crimes against persons.
3. Know the different conspiracies in the Patty Hearst kidnapping, the one before her joining the conspiracy and after she joined.

Crimes against persons are generally regarded as violent crimes or those with the potential to escalate to violence. The most common types of crimes against persons are armed robbery, murder, assault, sexually related offenses, car jacking and extortion.

HOMICIDE

United States Code, Title 18: §1111. Murder

(a) Murder is the unlawful killing of a human being with malice aforethought. Every murder perpetrated by poison, lying in wait, or any other kind of willful, deliberate, malicious, and premeditated killing; or committed in the perpetration of, or attempt to perpetrate, any arson, escape, murder, kidnapping, treason, espionage, sabotage, aggravated sexual abuse or sexual abuse, burglary, or robbery; or perpetrated from a premeditated design unlawfully and maliciously to effect the death of any human being other than him who is killed, is murder in the first degree. Any other murder is murder in the second degree.

(b) Within the special maritime and territorial jurisdiction of the United States, whoever is guilty of murder in the first degree shall be punished by death or by imprisonment for life; whoever is guilty of murder in the second degree, shall be imprisoned for any term of years or for life.

KIDNAPPING

§115. Influencing, Impeding, or Retaliating Against a Federal Official by Threatening or Injuring a Family Member

(a)(1) Whoever

(A) Assaults, kidnaps, or murders, or attempts or conspires to kidnap or murder, or threatens to assault, kidnap or murder a member of the immediate family of a United States official, a United States judge, a Federal law enforcement officer, or an official whose killing would be a crime under section 1114 of this title; or

(B) Threatens to assault, kidnap, or murder, a United States official, a United States judge, a Federal law enforcement officer, or an official whose killing would be a crime under such section, with intent to impede, intimidate, interfere with such official, judge, or law enforcement officer while engaged in the performance of official duties, or with intent to retaliate against such official, judge, or law enforcement officer on account of the performance of official duties, shall be punished as provided in subsection (b).

(2) Whoever assaults, kidnaps, or murders, or attempts or conspires to kidnap or murder, or threatens to assault, kidnap, or murder, any person who formerly served as a person designated in paragraph (1), or a member of the immediate family of any person who formerly served as a person designated in paragraph (1), with intent to retaliate against such person on account of the performance of official duties during the term of service of such person, shall be punished as provided in subsection (b).

(b)(1) An assault in violation of this section shall be punished as provided in section 111 of this title.

(2) A kidnapping, attempted kidnapping, or conspiracy to kidnap in violation of this section shall be punished as provided in section 1201 of this title for the kidnapping or attempted kidnapping of, or a conspiracy to kidnap, a person described in section 1201(a)(5) of this title.

(3) A murder, attempted murder, or conspiracy to murder in violation of this section shall be punished as provided in sections 1111, 1113, and 1117 of this title.

(4) A threat made in violation of this section shall be punished by a fine under this title or imprisonment for a term of not more than 10 years, or both, except that imprisonment for a threatened assault shall not exceed 6 years.

Figure 4.1 Case Study: The Patty Hearst Kidnapping

The story begins on the evening of February 4, 1974 in Berkeley, California. Peter Benenson was unloading groceries to take inside his residence, when two females and a male confronted him by gunpoint. They demanded the keys to his 1964 Chevy convertible. Benenson was put in the back seat of his car. He was then pistol-whipped, blindfolded, gagged, covered with a blanket and pushed onto the floor of his car. He remained there during the entire kidnapping of Patty Hearst.

While the three co-conspirators acquired the stolen vehicle, two men and a woman were across town preparing to kidnap Patty Hearst,

Figure 4.1 Case Study: The Patty Hearst Kidnapping (cont.)

the daughter of the publishing tycoon, Randolph Hearst. The woman rang the doorbell at the apartment shared by Patty Hearst and her fiancé, Steven Weed. Weed was told by the woman that she had backed into a car in the garage and needed to use a phone. As Weed opened the door, the two-armed men pushed their way into the apartment. Weed was beaten and left on the floor, while Hearst was taken from the apartment to the waiting Chevy convertible and put in the trunk. Hearst's screams attracted the neighbors, but the gunfire from the two men caused a quick retreat into their homes.

The kidnappers only went a couple of blocks and switched vehicles. Benenson was told to keep his head down. The kidnapper left him. The kidnappers took Benenson's key so he walked to the nearby home of his sister. His fear kept him from reporting the crime until he saw the news of the Hearst's kidnapping.

The kidnapping was accomplished by a group of eight known as the Symbionese Liberation Army (SLA), lead by an ex-convict, Donald DeFreeze. The SLA gained notoriety for the November 6, 1973 murder of an Oakland school superintendent. The original motivation for the kidnapping was to use Hearst to trade for the release of two of the group's original members, Joe Remior and Russell Little. They had been arrested for murder. With all publicity from the kidnapping of Hearst, the group quickly realized her value in manipulating the press for their propaganda.

The SLA released a communiqué and describing Hearst as a prisoner of war. The SLA demanded that their messages and communiqués be read on the air, unedited and uncensored in full. The demands were honored when Hearst's father, Randolph Hearst asked his fellow publishers to comply with the request of the SLA. The conversion of Hearst from a captor to a collaborator began. She was keep in a closet and subject to torture, assault, mental cruelty, and sexual intimidation. Eventually, Hearst was made to record a message pleading with her father to meet the demands of the SLA to distribute $70 worth of food to every poor person in California as a gesture of good faith prior to the ransom demands. This calculated

Figure 4.1 Case Study: The Patty Hearst Kidnapping (cont.)

demand was to demonstrate to Patty that her farther cared more about the money than his own daughter. As the SLA predicted, Randolph Hearst released a statement that the demand was impossible to meet. Patty began to give up hope.

As Patty began to weaken, the group changed their treatment towards Hearst. They began to treat her more as a member of the group. She was told that prisoners are given a choice to join the group or die. Patty chose to save to her life and join. The group had her record a statement that she had chosen to join the group to fight for freedom and was given the name of Tania.

On April 15, 1974, the world saw the new Patty Hearst, Tania, when the SLA robbed the San Francisco branch of the Hibernia Bank with automatic weapons. The news was saturated with photos of Hearst holding a weapon and appearing to cover her new friends. Quickly, Attorney General William Saxbe branded Hearst a common criminal.

After the bank robbery, the group moved to a safe house located on West 84th Street, Los Angeles, a predominantly black neighborhood of Watts. DeFreeze would sent his members out in teams of three on practice missions. On May 16, 1974, Patty went on a mission with Bill and Emily Harris. Bill Harris was caught shoplifting outside of a sporting goods store in Los Angeles. Patty fired shots was a parked car that allowed Bill and Emily to escape. They then ditched the car and hijacked another vehicle.

Meanwhile, police investigating the shooting at the sporting goods store found the original vehicle. Inside they found a gun that was registered to Emily Harris and a parking ticket issued at the address of the SLA's 84th Street hideout. After ditching the hijacked vehicles, they purchased an inexpensive vehicle to use and went to a motel in Anaheim. While watching TV they watched as the FBI and the LAPD raided their empty safe house on 84th Street. The hideout burst into flames.

Figure 4.1 Case Study: The Patty Hearst Kidnapping (cont.)

On May 17th, DeFreeze had moved the group to a house located at 1466 East 54th Street. DeFreeze made the mistake of thinking that the neighborhood would not tell police they were there. That evening the police surrounded the residence. The police used bullhorns to demand their surrender. An eight-year-old boy and a visitor left came out of the residence. After 18 announcements the tear gas was fired into the residence. The SLA answered with machine-gun fire. The fight went on for about one hour, and then more tear gas canisters cause the house to catch fire.

All of the members except for Patty, Bill and Emily were dead, who watched the events unfold on their TV. The three left the motel and headed south to Costa Mesa. The three disguised themselves and drove to San Francisco. Upon their arrival in San Francisco, Emily tried to raise support from the radical community, but the group was too hot. Eventually, the three were introduced to a sympathizer named Jack Scott, who ran an underground railroad for political fugitives. Scott agreed to help. He decided that they needed to change locations so they could regroup and make plans.

The three were taken to Manhattan then to a farmhouse on the outskirts of Honesdale, Pennsylvania accompanied by their baby-sitter, Wendy Yoshimura. Yoshimura was from the Bay area and was wanted for federal explosives charges. After some time, the group relocated to Jeffersonville, New York, in the Catskills. The group began working on a book with a ghostwriter hired by Scott. The group then moved back west to Sacramento, California. They were joined by new recruits, Jim Kilgore, Mike Bortin, Seanna and Kathy, Josephine and Steven Soliah. The SLA was back in business.

For their first act, they robbed the Guild Savings and Loan Association in Sacramento. No one made the connection to the SLA. They then robbed the Crocker National Bank in Carmichael, California. Unfortunately, Emily Harris killed a 42 year old mother of four during the robbery. The news called the robbery a SLA style crime. The group decided they needed to move their operation and went back to the Bay area.

Figure 4.1 Case Study: The Patty Hearst Kidnapping (cont.)

While in the Bay area the group succeeded in a series of bombing. Due to fighting among the group, they agreed to live in several safe houses in the San Francisco area. Patty moved into an apartment with Jim Kilgore, Steven Soliah and Wendy Yoshimura.

One day, Walter Scott, brother of Jack Scott, got drunk and walked into the Scranton, Pennsylvania police station to report that Jack Scott, his wife and his parents were hiding Patty Hearst in a Pennsylvania safe house. When the FBI raided the safe house it was empty, but they found the fingerprints of Bill Harris and Wendy Yoshimura. The leads allowed them to put together the connections between Scott, Yoshimua, Hearst, the Harrises, Jim Kilgore, Mike Bortin and the Soliahs. The FBI interviewed the parents of Steven, Kathleen and Josephine Soliah and gained their cooperation to help find their children.

A meeting was eventually arranged for the father to meet his children at a restaurant in the Bay area. He told them the FBI was looking for them. They warned their father not to trust the FBI. The father told the FBI that his children refused to meet with the FBI, but there was one fact he told them that provide the FBI with a starting point to find them. The father told the FBI that they were working as contract painters.

The FBI began checking independent painting jobs in the Bay area and finally located Mike Bortin. Within the hour they had Kathy and Josephine Soliah under surveillance. They were followed to an apartment on Morse Street. The following day the surveillance led them to another apartment on Precita Avenue. The following day the FBI raided the Precita Avenue apartment. The agents arrested Bill and Emily Harris. The FBI then raided the Morse Street apartment where they arrested Wendy Yoshimura and Patty Hearst. Kathy Soliah, Jim Kilgore, Mike Bortin and Josephine Soliah heard of the arrest and went underground.

1. What was the objective of the conspiracy for the eight founding members of the SLA?
2. When did Patty Hearst join the conspiracy?
3. What crimes was Patty Hearst liable for after she joined the conspiracy.
4. Who is liable for the death of the woman in the Crocker National Bank robbery?

EXTORTION

Extortion is the act or practice of wresting anything from a person by force, by threats, or by any undue exercise of power. United States Code, Title 18

§872. Extortion by Officers or Employees of the United States

Whoever, being an officer, or employee of the United States or any department or agency thereof, or representing himself to be or assuming to act as such, under color or pretense of office or employment commits or attempts an act of extortion, shall be fined under this title or imprisoned not more than three years or both; but if the amount so extorted or demanded does not exceed $1,000, he shall be fined under this title or imprisoned not more than one year, or both.

Figure 4.2 News Release - Indictment

07-06-04 David D'Amiano — Indictment — News Release

State Political Party Fundraiser Indicted in Extortion of Piscataway Farm Owner

NEWARK - A New Jersey political fundraiser was indicted today on extortion charges for allegedly demanding and accepting $40,000 in political contributions and cash from a Piscataway farm owner to influence state and county officials to more than double an offer to preserve the farmland, U.S. Attorney Christopher J. Christie announced.

The 11-count Indictment unsealed today describes how the original offer of approximately $3 million to buy the development rights of the Piscataway farmland rose to potentially $7.4 million, following the intervention of fundraiser David D'Amiano, and the involvement of two top state officials and several Middlesex County officials.

Figure 4.2 News Release - Indictment (cont.)

D'Amiano, 45, is a member of a state political party finance committee and the owner of a Carteret recycling and mulch business. D'Amiano will voluntarily surrender today to Special Agents of the FBI and is expected to make an initial appearance this afternoon before a U.S. Magistrate Judge. A news conference with Christie is scheduled for 11:30 a.m. at the U.S. Attorney's Office in Newark.

After D'Amiano had received most of the installments of the $40,000 in extortionate payments in June 2003, D'Amiano began negotiating for more payoffs in connection with another property owned by the farm owner and others in Piscataway, according to the Indictment. Those demanded payments, which were never made, varied from $25,000 in political contributions and $25,000 in cash to as much as $35,000 in contributions and $35,000 in cash. Those payments were allegedly intended by D'Amiano to buy his influence with state, county and local officials to get the township to allow the development of a bank - a use that had been disallowed by the township - on property on Stelton Road in Piscataway.

D'Amiano is also charged with diverting campaign contributions from the state political committee's treasury, with some going into a personal account. (See addendum for specific charges and potential criminal penalties for all counts of the Indictment.)

"The allegations in this Indictment paint a vivid picture of the corrupt and broken political system in New Jersey," Christie said. "The alleged conduct puts on display the belief that some persons in New Jersey still hold - that every action by government is for sale."

D'Amiano had frequent in-person and telephone contacts with at least five state and Middlesex County elected and appointed officials throughout the course of his scheme to extort the cash and political contributions, according to the Indictment. Throughout the period, the farm owner was cooperating with the FBI and recording conversations.

Among those officials described in the Indictment is a high-ranking official identified in the Indictment only as "State Official 1." Others include a subordinate, State Official 2, and an elected county official, identified as County Official 1, who had two subordinate appointed officials beneath him, identified in the Indictment as County Officials 2 and 3.

The Indictment alleges cash payments and political donations solicited and demanded by D'Amiano as follows:

- $10,000 in cash from the farm owner at a Dec. 12, 2002, meeting at D'Amiano's business in Carteret.

Figure 4.2 News Release - Indictment (cont.)

- A $10,000 check payable to the state political party's Victory Fund, post-dated Dec. 23, written on the same day, at the same meeting at D'Amiano's business.
- A $5,000 check to the Victory Fund, written by the farm owner and handed to D'Amiano at D'Amiano's business office on Jan. 28, 2003.
- $5,000 in cash to D'Amiano during a Feb. 19, 2003, meeting with the farm owner and an unidentified co-schemer. Later, D'Amiano is recorded saying that everything was moving forward and that the farm owner would be happy.
- $5,000 check, payable to the Victory Fund, to D'Amiano on May 23, 2003, during a meeting at D'Amiano's office.
- $2,500 in cash accepted by D'Amiano in Piscataway on June 27, 2003
- $2,500 in cash accepted by D'Amiano at D'Amiano's business office, on July 30, 2003

To authenticate political connections D'Amiano said that he had - and to assure the farm owner that D'Amiano and others in state and county government could deliver on the farmland preservation deal - D'Amiano and the cooperating witness agreed upon a code word that the key individuals involved could communicate to him. That word, "Machiavelli," was said by State Official 1 and County Official 3 to the farm owner during face-to-face meetings, according to the Indictment.

For example, at a Feb. 18, 2003, meeting of the finance committee for the state political party, held at an East Brunswick hotel, D'Amiano introduced the farm owner to State Official 1, according to the Indictment. At that meeting, State Official 1 said he understood the problem the farm owner was facing in Piscataway and said the code word. State Official 1 then introduced the farm owner to State Official 2 and asked her to follow up.

D'Amiano repeatedly warned the farm owner to come through with all cash and checks as agreed, or to be prepared to face the financial consequences of not doing so, according to the Indictment.

D'Amiano frequently used veiled references and code to refer to the public officials with whom he was dealing on the farm owner's behalf. Often, D'Amiano would "pat down" the farm owner to be sure he wasn't concealing a recording device, according to the Indictment.

Figure 4.2 News Release - Indictment (cont.)

In one recorded conversation on Nov. 26, 2002, D'Amiano reminded the farm owner that his payment was an "intricate part of everything," and that if the farm owner did not pay, he was "going to get f___d in the end."

On May 21, 2003, after all but $10,000 of the $40,000 in cash payments and political donations had been made, D'Amiano, the farm owner and County Official 2 and County Official 3 met at the Middlesex County Administration Building in New Brunswick to negotiate for farmland preservation, according to the Indictment. At this meeting, County Official 2 observed that the county would be willing to make an offer of $7.4 million for the development rights and would have to come back with a higher appraisal to justify the new offer. (The previous offer to buy the developments rights of the farm was $3 million, made in 2002).

County Official 3 observed, according to the Indictment, that $100,000 an acre for the 74 acres of land was well outside the "edge" of his "envelope" and that it would not be offered if there were not "extraneous circumstances involved."

An Indictment is merely an accusation. All defendants are presumed innocent unless and until proven guilty in court.

Christie credited Special Agents of the FBI, under the direction of Special Agent in Charge Joseph Billy, Jr., in Newark, with developing the case against D'Amiano.

The case is being prosecuted by James Nobile, Chief of the U.S. Attorney's Office Special Prosecutions Division, and Senior Litigation Counsel John Fietkiewicz, of the Special Prosecutions Division.

§873. Blackmail

Whoever, under a threat of informing, or as a consideration for not informing, against any violation of any law of the United States, demands or receives any money or other valuable thing, shall be fined under this title or imprisoned not more than one year, or both.

§874. Kickbacks from Public Works Employees

Whoever, by force, intimidation, or threat of procuring dismissal from employment, or by any other manner whatsoever induces any person employed in the construction, prosecution, completion or repair of any public building, public work, or building or work financed in whole or in part by loans or grants from the United States, to give up any part of the compensation to which he is entitled under his contract of employment, shall be fined under this title or imprisoned not more than five years, or both.

§875. Interstate Communications

(a) Whoever transmits in interstate or foreign commerce any communication containing any demand or request for a ransom or reward for the release of any kidnapped person, shall be fined under this title or imprisoned not more than twenty years, or both.

(b) Whoever, with intent to extort from any person, firm, association, or corporation, any money or other thing of value, transmits in interstate or foreign commerce any communication containing any threat to kidnap any person or any threat to injure the person of another, shall be fined under this title or imprisoned not more than twenty years, or both.

(c) Whoever transmits in interstate or foreign commerce any communication containing any threat to kidnap any person or any threat to injure the person of another, shall be fined under this title or imprisoned not more than five years, or both.

(d) Whoever, with intent to extort from any person, firm, association, or corporation, any money or other thing of value, transmits in interstate or foreign commerce any communication containing any threat to injure the property or reputation of the addressee or of another or the reputation of a deceased person or any threat to accuse the addressee or any other person of a crime, shall be fined under this title or imprisoned not more than two years, or both.

§876. Mailing Threatening Communications

(a) Whoever knowingly deposits in any post office or authorized depository for mail matter, to be sent or delivered by the Postal Service or knowingly causes to be delivered by the Postal Service according to the direction thereon, any communication, with or without a name or designating mark subscribed thereto, addressed to any other person, and containing any demand or request for ransom or reward for the release of any kidnapped person, shall be fined under this title or imprisoned not more than twenty years, or both.

(b) Whoever, with intent to extort from any person any money or other thing of value, so deposits, or causes to be delivered, as aforesaid, any communication containing any threat to kidnap any person or any threat to injure the person of the addressee or of another, shall be fined under this title or imprisoned not more than twenty years, or both.

(c) Whoever knowingly so deposits or causes to be delivered as aforesaid, any communication with or without a name or designating mark subscribed thereto, addressed to any other person and containing any threat to kidnap any person or any threat to injure the person of the addressee or of another, shall be fined under this title or imprisoned not more than five years, or both. If such a communication is addressed to a United States judge, a Federal law enforcement officer, or an official who is covered by section 1114, the individual shall be fined under this title, imprisoned not more than 10 years, or both.

(d) Whoever, with intent to extort from any person any money or other thing of value, knowingly so deposits or causes to be delivered, as aforesaid, any communication, with or without a name or designating mark subscribed thereto, addressed to any other person and containing any threat to injure the property or reputation of the addressee or of another, or the reputation of a deceased person, or any threat to accuse the addressee or any other person of a crime, shall be fined under this title or imprisoned not more than two years, or both. If such a communication is addressed to a United States judge, a Federal law enforcement officer, or an official who is covered by section 1114, the individual shall be fined under this title, imprisoned not more than 10 years, or both. (Amended by P.L. 107273, div. C, title I, subtitle A §11008(d), Nov. 2, 2002, 116 Stat.1818.)

§877. Mailing Threatening Communications from Foreign Country

Whoever knowingly deposits in any post office or authorized depository for mail matter of any foreign country any communication addressed to any person within the United States, for the purpose of having such communication delivered by the post office establishment of such foreign country to the Postal Service and by it delivered to such addressee in the United States, and as a result thereof such communication is delivered by the post office establishment of such foreign country to the Postal Service and by it delivered to the address to which it is directed in the United States, and containing any demand or request for ransom or reward for the release of any kidnapped person, shall be fined under this title or imprisoned not more than twenty years, or both.

Whoever, with intent to extort from any person any money or other thing of value, so deposits as aforesaid, any communication for the purpose aforesaid, containing any threat to kidnap any person or any threat to injure the person of the addressee or of another, shall be fined under this title or imprisoned not more than twenty years, or both.

Whoever knowingly so deposits as aforesaid, any communication, for the purpose aforesaid, containing any threat to kidnap any person or any threat to injure the person of the addressee or of another, shall be fined under this title or imprisoned not more than five years, or both.

Whoever, with intent to extort from any person any money or other thing of value, knowingly so deposits as aforesaid, any communication, for the purpose aforesaid, containing any threat to injure the property or reputation of the addressee or of another, or the reputation of a deceased person, or any threat to accuse the addressee or any other person of a crime, shall be fined under this title or imprisoned not more than two years, or both.

§878. Threats and Extortion Against Foreign Officials, Official Guests, or Internationally Protected Persons

(a) Whoever knowingly and willfully threatens to violate section 112, 1116, or 1201 shall be fined under this title or imprisoned not more than five years, or both, except that imprisonment for a threatened assault shall not exceed three years.

(b) Whoever in connection with any violation of subsection (a) or actual violation of section 112, 1116, or 1201 makes any extortionate demand shall be fined under this title or imprisoned not more than twenty years, or both.

(c) For the purpose of this section "foreign official", "internationally protected person", "national of the United States", and "official guest" shall have the same meanings as those provided in section 1116(a) of this title.

(d) If the victim of an offense under subsection (a) is an internationally protected person outside the United States, the United States may exercise jurisdiction over the offense if (1) the victim is a representative, officer, employee, or agent of the United States, (2) an offender is a national of the United States, or (3) an offender is afterwards found in the United States. As used in this subsection, the United States includes all areas under the jurisdiction of the United States including any of the places within the provisions of sections 5 and 7 of this title and section 46501(2) of title 49.

BANK ROBBERY

Robbery is the taking or attempting to take anything of value from the care, custody, or control of a person or persons by force or threat of force or violence and/or by putting the victim in fear. Bank robbery is robbery at a bank or financial institution. In 2001, a bank robbery occurred every 52 seconds in the United States. Bank robberies accounted for 2.4 percent of all robbery in the United States. The average amount stolen from 1996 to 2001 was $70 million dollars a year. For 2001, the clearance rate for the crime of robbery was only 24.9 percent, but the clearance rate for bank robbery was 57.7 percent, a relatively high rate. Only murder was higher at 62.4 percent.

United States Code, Title 18 §2113. Bank Robbery and Incidental Crimes

(a) Whoever, by force and violence, or by intimidation, takes, or attempts to take, from the person or presence of another, or obtains or attempts to obtain by extortion any property or money or any other thing of value belonging to, or in the care, custody, control, management, or possession of, any bank, credit union, or any savings and loan association; or

Whoever enters or attempts to enter any bank, credit union, or any savings and loan association, or any building used in whole or in part as a bank, credit union, or as a savings and loan association, with intent to commit in such bank, credit union, or in such savings and loan association, or building, or part thereof, so used, any felony affecting such bank, credit union, or such savings and loan association and in violation of any statute of the United States, or any larceny, Shall be fined under this title or imprisoned not more than twenty years, or both.

(b) Whoever takes and carries away, with intent to steal or purloin, any property or money or any other thing of value exceeding $1000 belonging to, or in the care, custody, control, management, or possession of any bank, credit union, or any savings and loan association, shall be fined under this title or imprisoned not more than ten years, or both; or

Whoever takes and carries away, with intent to steal or purloin, any property or money or any other thing of value not exceeding $1,000 belonging to, or in the care, custody, control, management, or possession of any bank, credit union, or any savings and loan association, shall be fined under this title or imprisoned not more than one year, or both.

(c) Whoever receives, possesses, conceals, stores, barters, sells, or disposes of, any property or money or other thing of value which has been taken or stolen from a bank, credit union, or savings and loan association in violation of subsection (b), knowing the same to be property which has been stolen shall be subject to the punishment provided in subsection (b) for the taker.

(d) Whoever, in committing, or in attempting to commit, any offense defined in subsections (a) and (b) of this section, assaults any person, or puts in jeopardy the life of any person by the use of a dangerous weapon or device, shall be fined under this title or imprisoned not more than twentyfive years, or both.

(e) Whoever, in committing any offense defined in this section, or in avoiding or attempting to avoid apprehension for the commission of such offense, or in freeing himself or attempting to free himself from arrest or confinement for such offense, kills any person, or forces any person to accompany him without the consent of such person, shall be imprisoned not less than ten years, or if death results shall be punished by death or life imprisonment.

Figure 4.3 Press Release on Gang Member Sentence for Robbery

GANG MEMBER SENTENCED TO LIFE FOR ARMED BANK ROBBERY

A South Los Angeles gang member was sentenced today pursuant to the federal three strikes law to life without parole in prison for committing an armed bank robbery. Anthony J. Sutton, 31, of Hawthorne, California, was sentenced this afternoon by Senior United States District Court Judge William J. Rea. Sutton was convicted on September 20, 2002, following a two-week trial, on federal charges of conspiracy, armed bank robbery and using a firearm during a crime of violence. Sutton, a member of the 5-Trey Avalon Crips street gang, participated in a January 16, 2002 robbery

> **Figure 4.3 Press Release on Gang Member Sentence for Robbery (cont.)**
>
> at a Bank of America branch at 4400 Tweedy Boulevard in Southgate. The robbery took place after the bank had closed and was facilitated by Suttons's former girlfriend, who was servicing ATM machines inside the closed bank. Sutton and two other gang members were caught fleeing the bank by the Southgate Police Department.
>
> The former girlfriend and the two other robbers have been sentenced to terms ranging from seven to 12 years .The three-strikes information against Sutton asserted that he had previously been convicted of shooting into an inhabited dwelling and armed robbery. Today, Judge Rea found that Sutton had committed these prior serious, violent felonies and sentenced defendant to life imprisonment under the federal three strikes law. The case was investigated by the Southgate Police Department and the Federal Bureau of Investigation.

Figure 4.4, at the end of this chapter is a Special Report on Bank robbery in the United States.

SUMMARY

Conspiracies often include crimes against persons as some of their unlawful acts in furtherance of the object of the conspiracy. All members of the conspiracy at the time of the commission of these crimes against persons are responsible and punishable for those crimes in addition to the charge of conspiracy. These crimes include armed robbery, murder, assault, sexually related offenses, car jacking and extortion.

DISCUSSION QUESTIONS

1. Give an example of a conspiracy where the object of the conspiracy is murder.
2. What are some of the problems of prosecuting a case for conspiracy to commit bank robbery, but they are arrested before the bank is robbed?
3. Should law enforcement always allow the object of the conspiracy to be completed prior to making an arrest?

ADDITIONAL READINGS

True Crime - Mass Murderers, Time - Life, Hardcover, Time - Life Books, 1992

The Other America – Gangs, Gail B. Stewart, Hardcover, Lucent Books, Inc., 1997

Hate Crimes, Tamara L. Roleff (Editor), Hardcover, Greenhaven Press, Inc., 2001

BIBLIOGRAPHY

United States Code Annotated, Title 18

Department of Justice, Bank Robbery Special Report www.claykeck.com

Figure 4.4 Special Report - Bank Robbery in the United States

Special Report
Bank Robbery in the United States

Introduction

According to the Uniform Crime Reporting (UCR) Program, robbery is the taking or attempting to take anything of value from the care, custody, or control of a person or persons by force or threat of force or violence and/or by putting the victim in fear. The focus of this study, bank robbery, is a subtype of robbery targeted at banks. Because of this element of force or the threat of force, bank robbery is highly feared among the population.[1]

Some view robbery in the context of violence; others maintain that robbery offenders come from a subculture of theft.[2] Sometimes it is difficult to separate the two. The UCR Program classifies robbery as a crime against property and includes robbery in its violent crime total.

A bank robbery is indicated when the crime is robbery and the location is a financial institution. UCR-National Instant-Based Reporting System (NIBRS) standards state that the victims in a robbery can be either persons or entities, i.e., businesses, financial institutions, etc., or both.[3] In a bank robbery, the primary victim is the bank itself, but the teller being threatened or injured is also a victim.

A computation of UCR Summary data showed that a bank robbery occurred just under every 52 minutes in 2001, accounting for 2.4 percent of all robbery in the United States.[4] This represented a total loss of approximately $70 million. While this seems like a large amount of money taken, the average amount of money taken in a bank robbery over the period 1996 through 2000, according to NIBRS data is less than $5,000.

The crime of robbery showed a clearance rate of only 24.9 percent in 2001. The clearance for bank robbery was 57.7 percent in 2001.[5] This is a relatively high clearance rate when compared with that of other Part I crimes.* Only murder, at 62.4 percent, has a higher percentage of crimes cleared by arrest.

Even with such a high clearance rate, bank robbery remains prevalent. Bank robbery has been the subject of many studies.[6] Because of the number of incidents, the amount of money taken, and the fear engendered in the public, bank robbery is a serious problem in the United States. Dr. Yoshio Akiyama of the FBI addressed this question in 1983 in the *Crime Indicators System, Fourth Semiannual Briefing on Crime.* That study used a 10-year time series to show the prevalence and characteristics of bank robbery incidents, a profile of offenders, and an analysis of the length of time from the incident until clearance.

The present study will update and extend parts of that earlier study.

Objectives

The general objective of this study is to examine three different criminal justice databases maintained by the FBI. Their similarities and differences are pointed out and discussed with the purpose of producing a fuller picture of bank robbery than that created when using only one of these databases. A further and no less important objective is to provide some assessment of the NIBRS bank robbery data by comparing it with the Bank Crime Statistics database, even though the collection methods, the scope, and content of these databases are different.

To address these objectives, a time series from the Bank Crime Statistics (BCS), collected by the Violent Crimes/Fugitive Unit of the FBI, covering the period 1973 to 2001 was generated and compared to the time series for Summary UCR data and to NIBRS data. NIBRS data on bank robbery incidents used for this analysis is for 1996-2000. Although Summary data have been collected by the FBI since 1930, its comprehensiveness concerning bank robbery is limited. Therefore, only the crime counts and estimates from 1990 through 2001 were examined for comparison to BCS data from the same period.[†]

The study questions in this analysis are designed to compare and contrast the databases on the subject of bank robbery as it is reported to the FBI and are divided into two areas, characteristics of the incident and characteristics of the offender(s).

Further, this study will discuss the general compatibility of the Summary UCR data, the historical BCS database, and bank robbery incidents identified in the NIBRS. By using data from all three of these databases it will be possible to present a fuller picture of the crime of bank robbery in the United States and how it is reported.

Study Question 1— Characteristics of the Incident

The level of analysis here is the incident itself. Variables that describe the incident, such as the number of bank robbery incidents per year, the state, the region, the time of day and day of the week, the violence—deaths, injuries, hostages taken—and the type of weapons used are addressed in question 1.

Study Question 2—Offenders

Question 2 concerns the offender characteristics. What is the age, sex, and race of the offender (or offenders)? What is the average number of offend-

---

* Part I crimes are murder and nonnegligent manslaughter, forcible rape, robbery, aggravated assault, burglary, larceny-theft, motor vehicle theft, and arson. The first seven of these crimes make up the Crime Index. The Modified Crime Index consists of all eight Part I crimes.

† See Data & Methodology Section for a more complete discussion of the databases discussed in this section.

Figure 4.4 Special Report - Bank Robbery in the United States (cont.)

ers per incident? What is the previous bank robbery experience of offenders?

Data and Methodology

Data for the study come from three sources.

The UCR Program's data collections for the years 1990 and 2001. (Summary data)

The UCR Program is a law enforcement initiative that gives an annual depiction of crime in the United States. It is a nationwide cooperative statistical effort of over 17,000 city, county, and state law enforcement agencies that voluntarily report data on crimes that have been reported to them. The FBI has collected Summary data since 1930 with little change in the type of data collected and disseminated. Today, law enforcement agencies active in the UCR Program cover approximately 93.4 percent of the population of the United States.

The UCR's NIBRS data from 1996-2000

The NIBRS is the redesigned, expanded version of the Summary UCR system. NIBRS data differ from Summary data in that the NIBRS contains data on each single incident and arrest. While the Summary data are individual counts of seven Part I crimes, NIBRS collects data on 22 crime categories. Incident, offense, victim, offender, and arrest data are collected on each incident reported by a law enforcement agency. NIBRS is a richer, disaggregated database than the Summary database that can be used to enhance law enforcement and crime research as well as strategic and administrative decision-making. A limited number of agencies began submitting NIBRS data to the FBI's UCR Program in January 1989.

The BCS data collected by the FBI from 1970-2001

In 1934 Congress enacted the Bank Robbery and Incidental Crimes Statute, making it a federal crime to rob any national bank or state member bank of the Federal Reserve System. This statute was expanded to include bank burglary and bank larceny and similar crimes committed against federally-insured savings and loan associations and Federal credit unions. The investigative jurisdiction under this statute has been delegated to the FBI, which today investigates a bank crime concurrently with local law enforcement.[7]

The Violent Crimes/Fugitive Unit of the FBI has collected descriptive data on bank robberies since 1970. This is a database that FBI Special Agents in the 56 field offices use when investigating bank robberies. The variables concern the incident, the solution, the mode of operation, and offender characteristics. Although these data are primarily meant to be used as an investigative tool to clear the particular crime, much of the data contained in the BCS can be used for quantitative research as well. These data can be used alone by the researcher or in concert with other statistical databases, specifically, the NIBRS database, to present a fuller rendering of the bank robbery incident.

The BCS database contains a more comprehensive representation of the U.S. population than the NIBRS database. It also includes several incident-level elements not included in the

Figure 5.1

Number of Bank Robbery Incidents Reported in BCS Database and the Summary UCR, 1990–2001

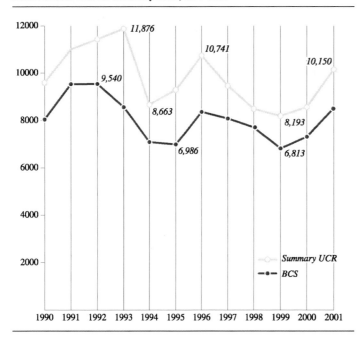

Table 5.1

Number of Bank Robbery Incidents Reported in BCS Database and the Summary UCR, 1990–2001

Year	BCS	Summary UCR
1990	8,042	9,589
1991	9,532	11,004
1992	9,540	11,432
1993	8,561	11,876
1994	7,081	8,663
1995	6,986	9,289
1996	8,362	10,741
1997	8,082	9,461
1998	7,711	8,486
1999	6,813	8,193
2000	7,310	8,565
2001	8,516	10,150

Figure 4.4 Special Report - Bank Robbery in the United States (cont.)

NIBRS. These are institution type, facility type, modus operandi, solution rates (analogous to clearance rates in the UCR Program definitions), types of security devices present in the incident, disguises used by the perpetrator(s), information on hostages that may have been taken, and the contents of any robbery notes.

Since the focus of BCS is a subset of all bank robberies collected by the UCR Program, care must be exercised when BCS statistics show deviations from those of Summary/NIBRS statistics. The definitions in the BCS data differ from those established by the UCR Program. It will be seen, however, that the two sets of statistics show striking similarities.

Methods

Frequency distributions and graphs are used to explore the consistencies and unique aspects of the databases to address the Study Questions.

Findings

Incident characteristics

Although the amount of money taken overall in any given year may seem high, approximately $70 million according to the BCS data for the period 1996 through 2000, the average amount netted from an individual bank robbery is less than $8,000 (BCS). The NIBRS data, covering less population than BCS, indicate an average of less than $5,000 per incident.

BCS reports the amount of money recovered is quite small. Over the period 1996-2000, $469,815,218.10

was reported as being taken and only $94,407,085.90 was recovered. This is only a 20 percent recovery rate.

Number of incidents

Table 5.1 shows the number of bank robbery incidents reported in the Summary UCR Program and in the BCS database of the FBI from 1990 through 2001. Figure 5.1 graphs the same data and makes the pattern easier to see. There was a substantial increase in the early 1990s, followed by an even more substantial decrease in the mid-1990s. Through 1999, the overall trend was down, but beginning in 2000 there was an upturn. The Summary UCR data always shows a greater number of incidents than the BCS database. There are two reasons for this. The first is measurement error, present in any data collection. The second reason may be

Table 5.2

**Number of Bank Robbery Incidents,
NIBRS Data and BCS by State and Region, 2000**

Region, State	BCS robberies 2000	NIBRS robberies 2000	Region, State	BCS robberies 2000	NIBRS robberies 2000
Southern			**Northeastern**		
(South)			**(Northeast)**		
Alabama	77		Connecticut	41	26
Arkansas	18	1	Massachusetts	156	47
DC	12		Maine	4	
Delaware	24		New Hampshire	15	
Florida	559		New Jersey	140	
Georgia	175		New York	304	
Kentucky	66	2	Pennsylvania	339	
Louisiana	87		Rhode Island	13	
Maryland	174		Vermont	13	7
Mississippi	64		**Regional Total**	**1,025**	**80**
North Carolina	288		**Regional %**	**14.18**	**7.70**
Oklahoma	31				
South Carolina	122	164	**Midwestern**		
Tennessee	138	127	**(North central)**		
Texas	342	32	Iowa	50	44
Virginia	149	161	Illinois	181	
West Virginia	17	23	Indiana	137	
Regional Total	**2,343**	**510**	Kansas	49	14
Regional %	**32.41**	**49.04**	Michigan	328	181
			Minnesota	88	
Western			Missouri	96	
(West)			North Dakota	1	1
Alaska	3		Nebraska	47	3
Arizona	184		Ohio	402	89
California	1,291		South Dakota	3	
Colorado	149	79	Wisconsin	115	
Hawaii	37		**Regional Total**	**1,497**	**332**
Idaho	12	16	**Regional %**	**20.71**	**31.92**
Montana	4				
New Mexico	54		**GRAND TOTAL**	**7,289**	**1,040**
Nevada	178				
Oregon	150				
Utah	47	23			
Washington	314				
Wyoming	1				
Regional Total	**2,424**	**118**			
Regional %	**33.53**	**11.35**			

Figure 4.4 Special Report - Bank Robbery in the United States (cont.)

Figure 5.2

Bank Robbery Incidents by Day of the Week, NIBRS Data and BCS, 1996–2000, in percent

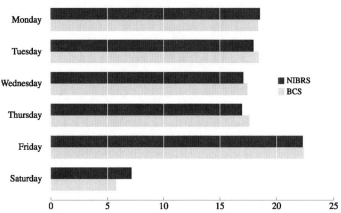

Table 5.3

Bank Robbery Incidents by Day of the Week, NIBRS Data and BCS, 1996–2000 (in percentages)

Day	NIBRS	BCS
Monday	18.53	18.36
Tuesday	17.99	18.46
Wednesday	17.10	17.45
Thursday	16.96	17.59
Friday	22.29	22.37
Saturday	7.13	5.77
Total	100.00	100.00

because of the different, but overlapping, missions of the two databases. The Summary UCR number consists of all bank robbery incidents reported to the Program by local law enforcement. The BCS data includes bank robbery incidents reported to the Violent Crimes/Fugitive Unit of the FBI by the individual FBI field offices. Only in incidents where the FBI has investigative jurisdiction are the field offices required to collect and report data. FBI field offices do not report crime statistics to the UCR Program. Summary UCR data should contain these BCS incidents reported to UCR by the state or local law enforcement entity collaborating with the FBI on the investigation of the incident. Additionally, Summary data include incidents in which the FBI had no jurisdiction and, thus, no role. Therefore, the FBI became involved in the investigation of approximately 85 percent of all bank robbery incidents reported in the United States in 2000.

Although the time series of BCS is considered to reflect bank robbery trends in the Nation, the undulations in the number of bank robberies are also a result of the FBI involvements in the bank robbery investigations. The two time series track each other quite closely as we would expect. When one is moving downward, the other is moving downward as well, and when one turns up, so does the other.

Participation in the NIBRS has been more volatile over the period of the system's existence than either the Summary UCR or BCS participation over this same period of time. With only 17 percent of the U.S. population cov-

Table 5.4

Time of Day of Bank Robbery Incidents, NIBRS Data & BCS, 1996–2000

	NIBRS	NIBRS Percent	BCS	BCS Percent
6 AM - 8:59 AM	87	3.4	1,018	2.66
9 AM - 10:59 AM	711	28.0	10,955	28.65
11 AM - 12:59 PM	518	20.4	8,902	23.28
1 PM - 2:59 PM	502	19.8	8,710	22.78
3 PM - 5:59 PM	601	23.7	7,911	20.69
6 PM - 8 PM	119	4.7	741	1.94
Total	2,538	100.0	38,237	100.00

Figure 5.3

Time of Day of Occurrence of Bank Robbery Incident, NIBRS Data and BCS, 1996–2000, in percent

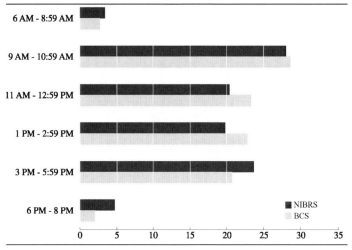

Figure 4.4 Special Report - Bank Robbery in the United States (cont.)

ered in 2000, the NIBRS reported 1,040 bank robberies. Summary UCR data showed approximately 8,565 bank robberies reported to the UCR Program by police agencies. The BCS recorded 7,310 bank robbery incidents with FBI involvement. A comparison of NIBRS data to Summary data to BCS data of this type is not meaningful. The Summary data and BCS data will drown out NIBRS data. However, other comparisons may be more fruitful between NIBRS and BCS data.

Regional breakdown

Table 5.2 shows a regional breakdown for NIBRS and BCS bank robberies in 2000. The UCR Program defines four

Table 5.5

BCS Incidents Involving Shooting

Year	Incidents	Shooting	Percent
1996	8,362	172	2.06
1997	8,082	155	1.92
1998	7,711	159	2.06
1999	6,813	119	1.75
2000	7,310	132	1.81

Table 5.6

BCS Incidents Involving Firearms, 1996–2000

Year	Incidents involving firearms	Percentage of incidents in which firearm used	Incidents involving handguns	Percentage of incidents in which handgun used	Total incidents
1996	2,707	32.37	2,571	30.75	8,362
1997	2,718	33.63	2,539	31.42	8,082
1998	2,505	32.49	2,385	30.93	7,711
1999	2,047	30.05	1,953	28.67	6,813
2000	2,190	29.96	2,105	28.80	7,310
Total	12,167	31.79	11,553	30.18	38,278

Table 5.7

NIBRS Incidents Involving Firearms, 1996–2000

Year	Incidents involving firearms	Percentage of incidents in which firearm used	Incidents involving handguns	Percentage of incidents in which handgun used	Total incidents
1996	127	47.57	109	40.82	267
1997	206	46.29	156	35.06	445
1998	312	50.49	252	40.78	618
1999	312	46.43	238	35.42	672
2000	525	51.12	411	40.02	1,027
Total	1,482	48.93	1,166	38.49	3,029

regions in the United States and calls them Northeastern, Midwestern, Southern, and Western. The BCS also places states into four regions called Northeast, North Central, South, and West. The states in the UCR regions Northeastern, Southern, and Western are placed in the BCS regions Northeast, South, and West, respectively. The BCS region, North Central, contains the states that the UCR Program defines as Midwestern.

The percentages of bank robberies within the regions correspond somewhat between the two databases. Monotonically, they track from a low in the Northeastern, then the Midwestern, or North Central, through the South. The Western, or West region, is the odd one here, with the NIBRS showing it with only 11.3 percent of the bank robberies in 2000, while the BCS shows it with 33.3 percent. These disparities are due to the absence of major cities' participation in the NIBRS. It may also be that even though the Western region contains

13 states, only three of these report NIBRS data. Further, at least two of these three, Idaho and Utah, have small populations and thus would be expected to have fewer bank robberies. Moreover, California alone has more than one-half of the bank robberies in the entire 13-state region reported to BCS. California's 1,291 bank robbery incidents in 2000 are more than twice its closest competitor, Florida, and more than the entire Northeastern region. California drives the numbers in the Western region but is not represented in the NIBRS. On the other hand, 9 of 16 (17 when the District of Columbia is included) states in the Southern [South] region report NIBRS data. Further, 8 of 12 states in the Midwestern [North Central] region are NIBRS states.

Day of the week

Table 5.3 and Figure 5.2 show different presentations of the same data—bank robbery incidents by day of the week. The data are presented as percentages, i.e., the percentage of bank robberies reported in the NIBRS that happen on Sunday, on Monday, etc., and the same for the BCS data. In this way we can begin to make some comparisons between the two databases even though the difference in the absolute number of bank robberies in the two databases is quite high. The striking finding here is how closely the data in the two programs coincide. In both data series, Friday is the day on which most bank robbery incidents occur. Substantively, this may be because Friday has historically been payday for much of the United States and, thus, has required large deliveries of cash to branch banks. This may still be the case even in the modern world of electronic banking with direct deposit of paychecks and bill-paying either as an automatic withdrawal, by posted check, or over the Internet.

The second most prevalent days are Monday and Tuesday. The NIBRS reports a few more incidents on Monday than on Tuesday and BCS reports the opposite. Still, these differences are

Figure 4.4 Special Report - Bank Robbery in the United States (cont.)

negligible and speak well for the integrity of the NIBRS data.

Most bank robberies from 1996 through 2000 happened on workdays, Monday through Friday, with very few occurring on the weekend. The NIBRS reports that workdays accounted for 89.83 percent of bank robbery incidents, while in the BCS the percentage was 93.85 percent for the period.

Time of day

Both the NIBRS data and the BCS data show that the time period during which most bank robberies occur is 9 a.m. until 11 a.m. Table 5.4 and Figure 5.3 present the time of occurrence of bank robberies reported in the NIBRS and BCS from 1996 through 2000 as a percentage of bank robbery incidents reported. The prominent detail presented here is the clear similarity of the two databases on this variable.

Weapons, violence, injury, and other crimes

One obvious reason for an individual to engage in bank robbery is economic where the motive is to obtain money. Another is that because of the low amounts of cash actually stolen per robbery, bank robbers are interested in projecting a persona of violence.[8] Whichever is the case, the threat of violence is always present. Information on weapons used in the commission of a bank robbery, violence, injuries sustained, and other crimes is contained in the NIBRS data as well as the BCS data. The percentage involving an actual shooting reported in BCS is around 2 percent. Table 5.5 shows this percentage over the 1996–2000 period. BCS data displayed in Table 5.6 show that over this period, a firearm was present in about 32 percent of all bank robbery incidents. In almost all of those cases, 30 percent overall, that firearm was a handgun.

Table 5.7 presents NIBRS firearms data. Over the period 1996–2000, NIBRS reports firearms (including handguns) use in 49 percent of the 3,029 bank robbery incidents reported. Handguns were used in 38.5 percent of NIBRS incidents in which a firearm was used over the period.

It may be surprising that only between one-third and one-half of bank robbery incidents involve firearms. The perception one would tend to get from television or the movies is that a bank robber would never attempt a holdup without a firearm—and the more the better.

Table 5.8 holds another surprise. The incidence of violence and injury is very low. NIBRS data show that violence occurred in only 2.34 percent of incidents and BCS shows 4.84 percent over the time period. Given the low

Table 5.8

Percent of Bank Robbery Incidents Involving Violence, Injury, and Other Crimes, NIBRS Data & BCS, 1996–2000

Incidents Involving	NIBRS Incidents	Total NIBRS	Percent*	BCS Incidents	Total BCS	Percent*
Injury	169		5.58	764		2.00
Violence	71		2.34	2151		5.62
Explosives/Explosions	60		1.98	1557		4.07
Kidnapping/Hostages	49		1.62	230		0.60
Assault	19		0.63	1285		3.36
Murder	5		0.17	34		0.09
Total NIBRS Incidents		3,029				
Total BCS Incidents					38,278	

* Will not add to 100% because some incidents involved more than one other crime or weapon.

Figure 5.4

Race of Bank Robbers in Percentage, NIBRS Data and BCS, 1996–2000

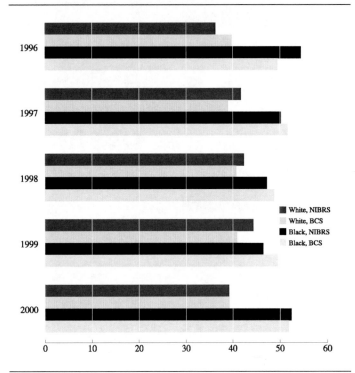

■ White, NIBRS
▢ White, BCS
■ Black, NIBRS
▢ Black, BCS

Figure 4.4 Special Report - Bank Robbery in the United States (cont.)

rates of violence, it should not be unexpected that the injury levels displayed in Table 5.8 are also quite low—5.58 percent for NIBRS data and 2.00 percent for BCS.

Regarding other crimes present in the incident, murder is very low at less than 1.0 percent in both databases, as are kidnapping and hostage-taking. Both NIBRS data and BCS data show that kidnapping/hostage-taking occurs in less than 2.0 percent of reported bank robberies.

Overall, the percentages in the table are close with neither database showing wildly divergent numbers; however, the numbers are so small for the NIBRS that we cannot take total comfort in the only-slight discrepancies the two databases show on these variables.

Offender characteristics

Despite what may be the popular perception, most bank robbery incidents, 79.9 percent in the NIBRS data over the period 1996–2000, were carried out by only one offender. Another

15 percent involved two offenders. Thus, over 95 percent of all the bank robbery incidents reported were attempted by two or fewer offenders.

Race

Bank robbery offenders may not be as many or as varied as one might at first think. Using NIBRS and BCS data, we can analyze their race, and sex, and using NIBRS data we can examine age. Figure 5.4 shows the race of bank robbers from NIBRS data and BCS from 1996 through 2000 as a percentage of all offenders. There are similar patterns evident in the figure. Whites account for between 35 and 45 percent of all offenders in each of the years. Both NIBRS and BCS data bear this out and overall show the same level. Black offenders are responsible for between 45 percent and 55 percent over the period. If we average offenders by race over the 5 years, there is virtually no difference with whites averaging 40.84 percent in the NIBRS data and 39.45 percent in the BCS data. Similarly, the percentage of black offenders in the NIBRS data is very close to that in the BCS at 50.14 percent and 50.26 percent, respectively.

Sex

There is a great disparity between the number of male bank robbery offenders and the number of female offenders in both the NIBRS and the BCS databases. However, there is very little discrepancy when comparing the percentage of male offenders in NIBRS data to that in BCS and when comparing the number of female offenders. Figure 5.5 shows both of these comparisons. Male offenders are shown in dark red (NIBRS) and light red (BCS) and female offenders are shown in either black (NIBRS) or gray (BCS). In both databases, over 95 percent of the offenders are males, and less than 5 percent are females.

The percentage of male offenders in both NIBRS data and BCS is virtually the same. Table 5.9 shows the percentages of offenders that are identified as male in NIBRS data and BCS as well

Table 5.9

Percentage of Offenders in NIBRS Data and BCS, by Sex, 1996–2000

	1996	1997	1998	1999	2000
Male - NIBRS	94.79	94.55	94.66	92.53	92.75
Male - BCS	95.56	94.83	94.41	94.75	93.99
Female - NIBRS	5.21	5.45	5.34	7.47	7.25
Female - BCS	4.44	5.17	5.59	5.25	6.01

Figure 5.5

Sex of Bank Robbers as Percentages, NIBRS Data and BCS, 1996–2000

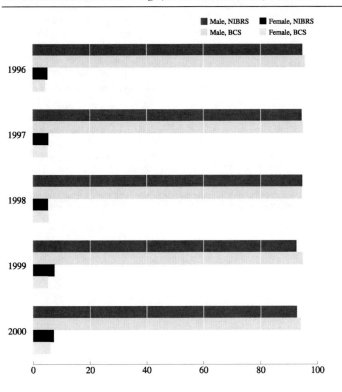

■ Male, NIBRS   ■ Female, NIBRS
■ Male, BCS   ■ Female, BCS

Figure 4.4 Special Report - Bank Robbery in the United States (cont.)

as the percentage identified as females. There is a strong correspondence between the two databases here.

Age

Figure 5.6 displays the age and gender of offenders reported to the NIBRS from 1996–2000. The same information is contained in Table 5.10. Nearly 20 per-cent of all offenders are male, between the ages of 18 and 24. Males, aged 25–29 account for another 14 percent. Summing the two groups, we see that one-third of all bank robbery offenders are between 18 and 29 years of age. This is all the more astonishing because there are 703 offenders contained in the denominator that are either unknown or listed as missing data. If we drop the unknown and missing data from the denominator and recalculate the percent-age, we find that 41.7 percent of bank robbery offenders reported in NIBRS data are 18–29-year-old males.

An examination of only male offenders shows these two age groups account for more then 45 percent of all male bank robbery offenders. Figure 5.6 shows a clear pulse in the late teens and early twenties that damps down in every subsequent age group.

Females show the same general pattern except that the numbers of female bank robbery offenders is much smaller than that of males.

Age, race, and sex are combined and presented in Table 5.11. The same patterns are visible in this table as shown earlier and separately. There are more males than females in every age group. There are more black males than white males in younger age groups and more white males than black in older (>35) age groups. There are more white females than black females. The number of Asian/Pacific Islanders and American Indians/Alaskan Natives are presented but are too small to analyze.

Prior bank robbery convictions

In *Crime Indicators System, Fourth Semiannual Briefing on Crime* (1983), Akiyama discussed the bank robber classifications of "professional" and "amateur." His discussion was based on a previous FBI report from 1977 that divided bank robbers into these cate-

Figure 5.6

Age and Gender of Offender, NIBRS Data, 1996–2000, in percent

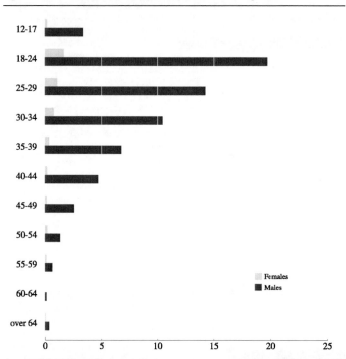

Table 5.10

Age and Gender of Offender, NIBRS Data, 1996–2000

Age	Female	Female %	Male	Male %	Unknown	Unknown %	Missing Values	Missing Values %	Total
12–17	8	0.21	131	3.39	1	0.03		0.00	140
18–24	65	1.68	766	19.80	5	0.13		0.00	836
25–29	42	1.09	554	14.32	7	0.18		0.00	603
30–34	31	0.80	406	10.49	4	0.10		0.00	441
35–39	14	0.36	261	6.75		0.00		0.00	275
40–44	8	0.21	183	4.73	1	0.03		0.00	192
45–49	6	0.16	99	2.56		0.00		0.00	105
50–54	7	0.18	51	1.32	8	0.21		0.00	66
55–59	5	0.13	25	0.65	1	0.03		0.00	31
60–64		0.00	5	0.13		0.00		0.00	5
over 64	2	0.05	14	0.36	1	0.03		0.00	17
Unknown	16	0.41	467	12.07	167	4.32	508	13.13	1,158
Total	204	5.27	2,962	76.56	195	5.04	508	13.13	3,869

Figure 4.4 Special Report - Bank Robbery in the United States (cont.)

gories. A "professional" in this classification scheme is a bank robber with a prior criminal record, despite his or her lack of success as evidenced by his/her incarceration. This professional is a bank robbery specialist. The "amateur" bank robber is a bank robber with no prior record. The amateur is presented as acting almost on a whim. The bank robbery to the amateur is almost a spur-of-the-moment undertaking with the robber engaging in very little planning. This individual robs banks to get the means to fulfill some more fundamental need, such as the need for drugs. Table 5.12 displays BCS data concerning the number and percent of subjects taken into custody for bank robbery who already have a conviction for bank robbery, bank burglary, bank larceny, or bank extortion. From 1996–2000, the average percent of "professional" bank robbers is 20 percent. This was more than the average in the earlier period from 1978–1982. Over that time period the average percent of "professional" bank robbers was 14 percent. This is still a clear indication that the great majority of bank robbers are amateurs and have not been convicted of a bank crime in the past.

Limitations

There are several limitations to this study. Although Summary data have been collected by the FBI since 1930 and cover virtually the entire population of the United States, their comprehensiveness concerning bank robbery is limited. The only information available is the number of bank robberies, the percent of total robberies that that number represents, region of occurrence, bank robberies by population group, month of occurrence, and the amount of money taken in the aggregate. It is not possible to disaggregate Summary data to the individual incident.

Some bank robberies may not be captured in the database because of the Hierarchy Rule that limits reporting of only that crime in the incident that is highest in the "hierarchy" of Part I crimes as defined by the UCR Program. Both murder and rape are higher on this ordering of crimes than robbery. Therefore, if a bank robbery included a murder, the only crime entered into the Summary database is the murder. This would also be the case for a rape occurring within the bank robbery incident. Only the rape would be recorded and the bank robbery would be lost information.

Table 5.11

Age, Race, and Sex of Offender, NIBRS Data, 1996–2000

Sex/Age of Offender	Asian/ Pacific Islander	Black	American Indian/ Alaskan Native	Unknown Race	White	Total
Total Unknown Age, Sex, and Race						508
Female 12–17					8	8
18–24		26			39	65
25–29		22			20	42
30–34		13			18	31
35–39		6			8	14
40–44		2			6	8
45–49		1			5	6
50–54		2			5	7
55–59		1			4	5
over 64		1			1	2
unknown age		5		2	9	16
Total Female		79		2	123	204
Male 12–17		92		2	37	131
18–24	5	465	1	8	287	766
25–29		327		15	212	554
30–34		221		6	179	406
35–39	1	103		3	154	261
40–44		61		1	121	183
45–49		36	1	3	59	99
50–54		15		1	35	51
55–59		9		1	15	25
60–64					5	5
over 64		5			9	14
unknown age	1	262		65	139	467
Total Male	7	1,596	2	105	1,252	2,962
Unknown sex						
12–17					1	1
18–24				5		5
25–29		2		4	1	7
30–34				4		4
40–44				1		1
50–54		1		7		8
55–59				1		1
over 64				1		1
unknown age				163	4	167
Total unknown sex		3		186	6	195

Figure 4.4 Special Report - Bank Robbery in the United States (cont.)

Further, the bank robbery totals are collected on the form entitled Supplement to the Monthly Return of Offenses Known To The Police (Return A), but not on the Return A itself. If the supplement is not submitted, a robbery on the Return A cannot be counted as bank robbery. Thus, it may be the case that some robberies listed on the Return A and, therefore, in *Crime in the United States*, are bank robberies and are not captured in the Summary data.

Even though the NIBRS has distinct benefits as a data source, it is limited in its scope. Currently, agencies from 24 states, representing 17 percent of the U.S. population, participate in the program. These data lack the cross-sectional representation of incidents and cannot be treated as a sample. There are no cities participating that have populations greater than 1 million inhabitants. There are only 11 cities or consolidated counties that contribute NIBRS data whose population is more than 250,000. With this limitation, NIBRS data may not represent the crime experience in the entire United States.

Like the Summary UCR and NIBRS data, the BCS database also has its limitations. Only robberies of banks and financial institutions covered under the Bank Robbery and Incidental Crime Statute and its progeny are included. Further, the NIBRS includes, but BCS does not, specific information on each victim, offender, and arrestee. Finally, BCS is an investigative system; consequently the data are not available for use by the public.

Summary and Conclusions

The objective of depicting bank robbery from the data collected by the FBI has been met. Further, this realization of bank robbery through the use of these data has been an opportunity to compare and contrast elements in the databases—particularly the NIBRS data and the BCS data. These are preliminary findings and require further study.

The presentation of incident characteristics has emphasized the similarity of data submitted to the FBI's NIBRS program by local and state law enforcement to that submitted to the Violent Crimes/Fugitive Unit of the FBI by the separate FBI field offices. Both Summary UCR data and BCS indicate the same trends in the numbers of bank robberies over a 12-year period, 1990–2001.

Further, NIBRS data showing days of the week on which the greatest number of bank robberies occur and the hours during which they are most prevalent are very similar to BCS data, with Friday mornings generally the modal day and time for bank robberies.

In both databases, violence and injury are very low, an unexpected finding since one element of the crime is force or the threat of force. The similarity between the two databases concerning this unanticipated result adds further validation to the quality of NIBRS data.

Evidence of offender race and gender is also quite comparable between the two databases, with the number of whites committing bank robbery reported in NIBRS data very close to the number reported in BCS and the

same for blacks. Reported gender of bank robbers is virtually identical in both databases.

Presenting the age data reported in NIBRS shows that a plurality of bank robberies are committed by offenders between 18 and 30 years of age.

Offenders are clearly amateurs and not bank robbery specialists as evidenced by the low number with previous convictions for a bank crime shown in the BCS statistics. That bank robberies do not involve the meticulously planned caper carried out by a group of highly experienced criminals is further borne out by the significant number of incidents involving only one or two offenders. NIBRS and BCS data show that the money obtained in a bank robbery is low, especially considering the amount of physical risk and the high probability of apprehension involved for the offender.

The money recovered is also not a very high percentage of that stolen. Both databases bear this out. This indicates that Akiyama (1983) was correct in his conclusion that most of these amateur bank robbers committed the crime to fulfill some more immediate need. More research is required, particularly into the aspect of drugs associated with this crime.

These findings are interesting and have significant implications for policymakers. This study and other research, such as which banks are most likely to be robbed, and which are more likely to be robbed more than once, in addition to spatial analyses adding variables such as location of the bank relative to escape routes, entrances to freeways, traffic patterns, location of nearest police station, etc., will allow law enforcement policymakers to develop better, more effective strategies for use in dealing with bank robberies.

The present study is also good news for the NIBRS program. The NIBRS has only 24 states that participate covering 17 percent of the population. Nevertheless, the percentages on

Table 5.12

Prior Bank Robbery Convictions, BCS, 1996–2000

Year	Subjects previously convicted		Subjects not previously convicted		Total	
	Number	Percent	Number	Percent	Number	Percent
1996	1,127	21.04	4,230	78.96	5,357	100.0
1997	917	18.03	4,169	81.97	5,086	100.0
1998	964	19.40	4,005	80.60	4,969	100.0
1999	912	20.75	3,483	79.25	4,395	100.0
2000	957	20.79	3,646	79.21	4,603	100.0
Total	4,877	19.98	19,533	80.02	24,410	100.0

Figure 4.4 Special Report - Bank Robbery in the United States (cont.)

the NIBRS variables examined here clearly accord with the percentages reported in the BCS. This should assure those who do not yet participate in the NIBRS program that they may reap large benefits from becoming a contributor to the Program.

Finally, since 9/11 the government has realized that information-sharing is a powerful tool with which to fight lawlessness. Databases such as those examined here should be examined to derive the maximum information toward this end.

[1] Garofalo, J. 1977. Public Opinion About Crime: The Attitudes of Victims and Nonvictims in Selected Cities. Washington, DC: USGPO.

[2] Wolfgang, M.E. and F. Ferracuti. 1967. The Subculture of Violence. London: Tavistock; Normandeau, A. 1968. "Patterns in Robbery," Criminoligica.

[3] U.S. Department of Justice. Federal Bureau of Investigation. (December 1999). NIBRS, Volume 1: Data Collection Guidelines, Washington D.C.: The Government Printing Office, p. 33.

[4] U.S. Department of Justice. Federal Bureau of Investigation. Crime in the United States, 2001, Washington D.C.: The Government Printing Office.

[5] Bank Crime Statistics Data, 2001.

[6] Baumer, T. and M. Carrington, 1986. The Robbery of Financial Institutions. U.S. Department of Justice; Tavistock; Normandeau, A. 1968. op. cit.; Katz, J. 1991. "The Motivation of the Persistent Robber." In Michael Tonry (Ed.), Crime and Justice: A Review of Research (Vol. 14, pp. 277–306). Chicago: University of Chicago Press.

[7] Crime Indicators System, Fourth Semiannual Briefing on Crime, 1983. Federal Bureau of Investigation.

[8] Katz, J. 1991. op. cit.

Chapter 5

Drugs

OVERVIEW

In this chapter you will examine the most common forms of drugs, Methamphetamine, Cocaine, Marijuana and club drugs. You will read detail briefings on the sources, uses and effects of the drugs. You will study the main geographical areas for drugs including South America, Afghanistan and the Golden Triangle. You will learn about the major criminal organizations and gangs involved in the smuggling and distribution of drugs. Finally, you will look at several case studies in major drug dealers.

CHAPTER OBJECTIVES

1. Be able to identify the major drugs, their forms, and their effects.
2. Know the source countries for the major drugs and how those drugs are smuggled into the United States and distributed.
3. Know the elements of the primary federal drug laws.
4. Know the major international criminal organizations and gangs involved in drug smuggling.
5. Learn how the conspiracy laws are used to disrupt and dismantle drug trafficking organizations.

INTRODUCTION TO DRUG TRAFFICKING

Drug trafficking is the most widespread and lucrative organized crime operation in the United States. In 1986, the President's Commission on Organized Crime estimated that drug trafficking accounts for nearly 40 percent of this country's organized crime activity and generated an annual income estimated to be as high as $110 billion. Title 21 of the United States Code houses the primary drug violations.

§841. Prohibited acts

(a) Unlawful acts. Except as authorized by this subchapter, it shall be unlawful for any person knowingly or intentionally

(1) To manufacture, distribute, or dispense, or possess with intent to manufacture, distribute, or dispense, a controlled substance; or

(2) To create, distribute, or dispense, or possess with intent to distribute or dispense, a counterfeit substance.

§952. Importation of controlled substances

(a) Controlled substances in schedules I or II and narcotic drugs in schedules III, IV, or V; exceptions. It shall be unlawful to import into the customs territory of the United States from any place outside thereof (but within the United States), or to import into the United States from any place outside thereof, any controlled substance in schedule I or II of subchapter I of this chapter, or any narcotic drug in schedule III, IV, or V of subchapter I of this chapter, except that:

(1) Such amounts of crude opium, poppy straw, concentrate of poppy straw, and coca leaves as the Attorney General finds to be necessary to provide for medical, scientific, or other legitimate purposes, and

(2) Such amounts of any controlled substance in schedule I or II or any narcotic drug in schedule III, IV, or V that the Attorney General finds to be necessary to provide for the medical, scientific, or other legitimate needs of the United States

(A) During an emergency in which domestic supplies of such substance or drug are found by the Attorney General to be inadequate,

(B) In any case in which the Attorney General finds that competition among domestic manufacturers of the controlled substance is inadequate and will not be rendered adequate by the registration of additional manufacturers under section 823 of this title, or

(C) In any case in which the Attorney General finds that such controlled substance is in limited quantities exclusively for scientific, analytical, or research uses, may be so imported under such regulations as the Attorney General shall prescribe. No crude opium may be so imported for the purpose of manufacturing heroin or smoking opium.

The Drug Enforcement Administration (DEA) has two intelligence Reports on their web site that present an overview of the evolution of the drug threat and drug trafficking in the United States. As you read the two reports below notice how the conspiracy laws can and must to used to dismantle these drug trafficking organizations.

Figure 5.1 Evolution of Drug Threat

October 2002 Drug Intelligence Brief

INTELLIGENCE DIVISION DRUG ENFORCEMENT ADMINISTRATION

THE EVOLUTION OF THE DRUG THREAT: THE 1980s THROUGH 2002

The illicit drug trade in the United States is affected by numerous factors, including consumer demand, sources of supply, the organizational strengths and adaptability of criminal groups, and the ability of law enforcement and interdiction assets to disrupt or dismantle drug distribution systems. Identifying the most significant drug threats to the United States requires the fusion of current intelligence with a historical perspective to fully assess the dynamics of the illicit drug trade.

This report identifies the most significant changes in the drug threat over the past twenty years, as identified in past issues of the National Narcotics Intelligence Consumers Committee Report (NNICC).

The first part of the report serves as a historical foundation for a current drug threat assessment, and offers a perspective on the dynamics that will affect the drug threats facing the United States in the near future. The second part of the report provides a summary of the most significant factors shaping the distribution of illicit drugs.

The first-level evaluation of the current drug threat assessment was derived from field division assessments, open-source reports, drug abuse indicators, and reports from the El Paso Intelligence

Figure 5.1 Evolution of Drug Threat (cont.)

Center (EPIC) and Joint Interagency Task Force East. The second-level evaluation involved a survey of Drug Enforcement Administration (DEA) field managers who precisely identified the most significant drug problems in the field divisions, and the factors that affected those priorities, such as levels of violence associated with the trade, abuse indicators, and the volume of drugs moved. Rather than a comprehensive study of the drug trade, this report provides a snapshot of a highly dynamic criminal environment, and the challenges facing U.S. intelligence and enforcement agencies.

The 1980s: A Radical Transformation of the Consumer Market

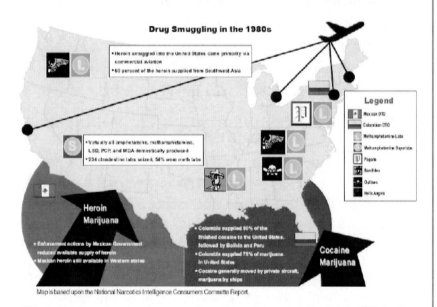

Map is based upon the National Narcotics Intelligence Consumers Committe Report.

The single most important transformation of the U.S. illicit drug market in the 1980s was the rampant growth of cocaine trafficking and abuse. Fed by the perception that the drug was a benign stimulant, cocaine trafficking and abuse radically transformed the illicit drug environment.

The ready supply of cocaine virtually replaced the demand for the synthetic drug, phencyclidine, or PCP. The introduction of crack cocaine, an easily obtained form of smokeable cocaine, increased demand and fueled violent gang wars between rival suppliers.

Although Bolivia and Peru were the largest coca and cocaine base producers, Colombian traffickers dominated the final production of cocaine hydrochloride. Colombian sources supplied at least 50 percent of the cocaine smuggled to the United States, with Colombian distribution organizations firmly entrenched in South Florida. The Caribbean remained the primary cocaine smuggling

Figure 5.1 Evolution of Drug Threat (cont.)

corridor, utilizing maritime and air smuggling routes through The Bahamas.

Southwest Asia was the primary source of heroin to the United States, supplying approximately 60 percent of the U.S. heroin market. Pakistan was the largest and most accessible heroin producer in the region. Opium poppy cultivation in Afghanistan was severely disrupted as a result of the fighting between Soviet forces and the Mujahedeen; however, because interdiction efforts in the country were primarily directed at controlling the flow of weapons to Afghan guerillas, heroin exports continued, albeit at a reduced level. Mexican heroin continued to supply the western United States, although enforcement actions by the Mexican Government severely disrupted heroin sources.

Drug Smuggling in the 1980s

Colombia was the primary source of foreign-produced marijuana in the United States, supplying approximately 80 percent of the marijuana smuggled into the United States. Mexico and Jamaica supplied the balance of the foreign-produced marijuana, with domestic production supplying less than 10 percent of the market. Most of the marijuana from Colombia was smuggled through the Caribbean corridor, using maritime conveyances.

The production and trafficking of synthetic drugs was relatively limited in the 1980s. Domestic clandestine laboratories supplied nearly all of the available synthetic drugs in the United States, with the exception of diverted pharmaceuticals. In 1980, Drug Abuse Warning Network (DAWN) Emergency Room Data identified diazepam (Valium) as the most frequently cited cause for admission. Although the majority of clandestine laboratories in the United States produced methamphetamine, PCP was the only clandestinely produced drug that was identified as a significant problem in DAWN Emergency Room Data. Outlaw Motorcycle Gangs (OMGs), such as the Hells Angels, the Bandidos, the Outlaws, and the Pagans, dominated the production and trafficking of methamphetamine, as well as marijuana distribution. Lysergic acid diethylamide (LSD) made a comeback in the early 1980s; however, its abuse was limited primarily to California and larger urban areas in the East and Midwest.

The 1980s demonstrated the increasing power of drug trafficking organizations to disrupt civil governance of the cocaine-producing regions. The July 1980 coup in Bolivia, led by Garcia Meza and reportedly backed by the "Santa Cruz Cocaine Mafia," severely

Figure 5.1 Evolution of Drug Threat (cont.)

undermined drug control efforts in the country. In 1981, the Colombian paramilitary group M-19 kidnapped Martha Nieves Ochoa, the sister of Medellín cartel head Jorge Luis Ochoa. The cartel responded by organizing a death squad that methodically killed guerillas and their families until Nieves was released. The cartel further directed its squads against journalists and political leaders in an effort to force the repeal of Colombia's extradition treaty with the United States. In one of the more violent acts of the decade, 95 people, including 12 members of the Colombian Supreme Court, were killed when 42 members of M-19 seized the Palace of Justice in Bogota in 1985. In a common cause with the cartel, M-19 demanded the repeal of the extradition treaty.

The 1980s witnessed substantial changes in the law enforcement and security resources directed against drug trafficking. The resources of the Central Intelligence Agency were brought into the counternarcotics mission by Executive Order in 1982. In 1986, National Security Decision Directive 221 articulated the policy that, "The international drug trade threatens the security of the United States by potentially destabilizing democratic allies." United States military assets were formally directed to provide support to the counternarcotic mission under the National Defense Authorization Act of 1989.

The Anti-Drug Abuse Act of 1988 authorized the Director of the Office of National Drug Control

Policy (ONDCP) to designate regions of the United States as "high intensity drug trafficking areas" (HIDTAs). The diversity of the drug trafficking threat was reflected in the geographic diversity of the initial five HIDTAs: the cities of New York, Los Angeles, Miami, and Houston, as well as the Southwest border (all counties along the United States–Mexico border from San Diego to Brownsville, Texas.

1990s: Supply Shifts

During the 1990s, Mexico emerged as the most significant transshipment corridor for illicit drugs smuggled into the United States. Although cocaine continued to move through the Caribbean corridor, increased radar coverage from Aerostats along the Southeast coast deterred the use of aircraft flights directly to the United States. Traffickers thwarted the increased radar surveillance by combining drug airdrops with high-speed boats operating beyond the range of the new systems. The increased law enforcement and military presence in the Caribbean forced traffickers to explore more elaborate smuggling avenues, including the purchase of Soviet cargo

Figure 5.1 Evolution of Drug Threat (cont.)

aircraft; a surplus Soviet diesel submarine; and experimentation with semi-submersible vehicles.

Colombian traffickers increasingly relied upon Mexican and Dominican trafficking organizations to smuggle cocaine shipments to the United States. By the mid-1990s, Colombian organizations started paying Mexican transportation organizations with portions of the smuggled cocaine load, with up to half of the load provided to the transporters. This arrangement reduced the need for large financial transactions, and firmly established Mexico-based drug trafficking organizations as significant illicit drug wholesalers in the United States. The Central American corridor was increasingly used for air and overland cocaine shipments to Mexico. Aircraft were used to move cocaine from Colombia to Northern Mexico. Although smaller, twin-engine aircraft were most often used to smuggle cocaine, larger surplus jet aircraft were also used to transport multiton quantities of cocaine.

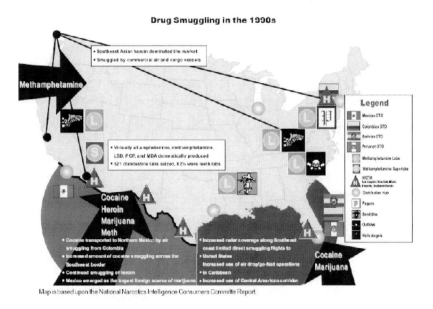

Map is based upon the National Narcotics Intelligence Consumers Committee Report.

Drug Smuggling in the 1990s

Map is based upon the National Narcotics Intelligence Consumers Committee Report.

Drug-related violence continued to undermine government control in South America. Over 150 groups loosely organized in cartels operating out of Medellín and Bogota, dominated the cocaine trade. Colombian insurgent groups such as the Revolutionary Armed Forces of Colombia (FARC) and the Army of National Liberation (ELN) also benefited from the cocaine trade by taxing narcotics

Figure 5.1 Evolution of Drug Threat (cont.)

profits; protecting crops, laboratories, and storage facilities; and occasionally extracting payment in weapons. Insurgent groups also carried out kidnappings and terrorism in support of traffickers' aims.

By 1988, Southeast Asian (SEA) heroin dominated the East Coast heroin market, while Mexican heroin was supplied to users in the Western United States. New York was the primary importation and distribution center for SEA heroin, with San Francisco, Seattle, Los Angeles, and Washington also identified as points of entry. SEA heroin continued to dominate the market throughout the early 1990s, all but replacing Southwest Asian heroin. In 1994, however, a joint Royal Thai Government/DEA endeavor, Operation TIGER TRAP, led to the incarceration in Thailand and extradition to the United States of more than a dozen high-level violators who had played key roles in moving SEA heroin to the United States. These successful actions disrupted long-standing SEA heroin trafficking modus operandi, not only in Asia, but also in the United States.

Expanded opium poppy cultivation and heroin production in Colombia in the early 1990s allowed Colombian traffickers to fill the void created by the decreased flow of SEA heroin to east coast markets. During the mid-to-late 1990s, Colombian heroin traffickers easily undermined the SEA heroin market with a readily available supply of high-quality, low-priced white heroin. They also undercut their competitors' price and used established, effective drug distribution networks to facilitate supply. Since Colombian heroin, often sold on the street with a purity of 90 percent, can be snorted like cocaine, it avoided the stigma of needle usage; thus, Colombian traffickers had a built-in marketing advantage over traffickers from Southeast or Southwest Asia. Throughout the 1990s, Mexico-supplied heroin continued to dominate user preferences in the Western United States.

By 1990, Mexico was the largest supplier of marijuana to the United States. According to the National Household Survey, the number of then current marijuana users (any use within the past 30 days) decreased from 22.5 million in 1979 to 10.2 million in 1990. Despite decreased demand, the profit margin for marijuana not only fueled Mexican trafficking organizations, but also led to an increase in domestic marijuana cultivation, particularly indoor-grow operations producing high-potency marijuana. Synthetic drugs, especially methamphetamine, continued to be primarily produced domestically.

In the early 1990s, high-purity "ice" methamphetamine (80- to 90-percent pure methamphetamine with a crystalline appearance)

Figure 5.1 Evolution of Drug Threat (cont.)

appeared on the West Coast. In addition to domestic production, primarily in California, ice was supplied from laboratories in South Korea and the Philippines.

OMGs dominated the production of methamphetamine through the early 1990s. In the mid-1990s, however, Mexican drug trafficking organizations started large-scale production and trafficking of methamphetamine. The introduction of high-quality, low-priced methamphetamine undercut the monopoly once held by outlaw bikers. Some OMGs, including the Hells Angels, reportedly relied upon Mexico-based sources of supply for their methamphetamine, preferring to avoid the risks associated with the manufacture of the drug. A sharp decrease in the purity of Mexican methamphetamine at the end of the 1990s reportedly pushed OMGs back into drug production.

LSD and PCP remained available throughout the 1990s. In the late 1980s and early 1990s, methylenedioxymethamphetamine (MDMA) also called Ecstasy, gained popularity among young, middle-class college students in limited areas of the United States. Ecstasy use and availability greatly escalated in 1997 when clandestine laboratories, operating in Europe, began exporting significant quantities of MDMA tablets to distributors in the United States.

Drug Threat Assessment 2002

Regional Abuse Patterns

Most DEA field divisions continue to identify cocaine as the primary illicit drug of concern, based upon abuse indicators, the violence associated with the trade, and/or the volume of trafficking through their areas of responsibilities. Heroin remains readily available in major metropolitan areas. Despite the availability of high-purity white heroin, which can be snorted, abuse appears to have stabilized in recent years. Methamphetamine trafficking and abuse dominate the West Coast and much of the Rocky Mountain and Midwest regions of the country. Polydrug trafficking along the Southwest border continues to tax allocated resources, and cocaine remains the drug of choice along the Atlantic seaboard.

Figure 5.1 Evolution of Drug Threat (cont.)

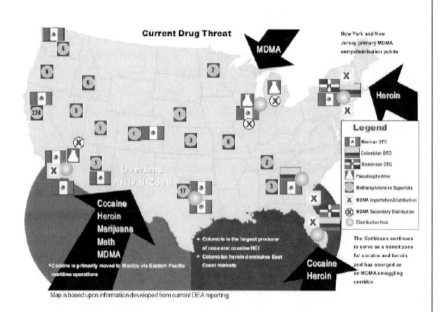

Map is based upon information developed from current DEA reporting.

Smuggling Patterns

The Southwest border remains the most vulnerable region of the United States for border security, followed by the Gulf Coast. Interagency assessments report over 60 percent of the cocaine entering the United States moves across the Southwest border. The U.S. Customs Service identified an increase in the movement of drugs between ports of entry over the last several years, as well as a trend toward smaller drug loads. EPIC reports that traffickers have not changed smuggling methods or routes following the September 11, 2001, terrorist attacks. Although the transportation centers are likely to be located near the border, the command and control centers could operate from nearly any location in the United States. Mobile communications and Internet encryption allow Drug Trafficking Organizations (DTOs) to operate from remote locations.

Availability

The 9-percent decline in cocaine purity over the past 4 years illustrates a vulnerability of cropbased illicit drugs. One possible explanation for the increased use of cutting agents by Colombian DTOs is the expansion of the non-U.S. drug market beyond the traffickers' means to maintain world supplies. Cocaine and heroin production are limited not only by the same factors that affect any agricultural product, but also by the traffickers' abilities to either control production regions or to thwart government crop eradication

Figure 5.1 Evolution of Drug Threat (cont.)

efforts. Supplies of synthetic drugs, such as methamphetamine, MDMA or Ecstasy, PCP, and LSD are not limited by these same factors. The traffickers' capability to quickly move production sites of synthetic drugs presents a significant challenge to law enforcement authorities.

Cocaine

Colombian drug trafficking organizations increasingly rely upon the eastern Pacific Ocean as a trafficking route to move cocaine to the United States. Law enforcement and intelligence community sources estimate that 72 percent of the cocaine shipped to the United States moves through the Central America-Mexico corridor, primarily by maritime conveyance. Fishing vessels and go-fast boats are used to move multiton cocaine loads to Mexico's west coast and Yucatan Peninsula. The loads are subsequently broken down into smaller quantities for movement across the Southwest border. Despite the shift of smuggling operations to the eastern Pacific, the Caribbean corridor remains a crucial smuggling avenue for Colombian cocaine traffickers.

Puerto Rico, the Dominican Republic, and Haiti are the predominant transshipment points for Colombian cocaine transiting the Caribbean.

Traffickers operating from Colombia continue to control wholesale level cocaine distribution throughout the heavily populated northeastern United States and along the eastern seaboard in cities such as Boston, Miami, Newark, New York City, and Philadelphia. There are indications that other drug trafficking organizations, especially Mexican and Dominican groups, are playing a larger role in the distribution of cocaine in collaboration with Colombian organizations. Mexican drug trafficking organizations are increasingly responsible for the transportation of cocaine from the Southwest border to the New York market. Mexico-based trafficking groups in cities such as Chicago, Dallas, Denver, Houston, Los Angeles, Phoenix, San Diego, San Francisco, and Seattle now control the distribution of multiton quantities of cocaine.

Heroin

The Office of National Drug Control Policy's publication, Pulse Check: Mid-Year 2000, reports new heroin users continue to be attracted to high-purity Colombian heroin because it can be snorted

Figure 5.1 Evolution of Drug Threat (cont.)

rather than injected. Reports of Mexico-produced white heroin continue to surface.

Although heroin abuse indicators are stable, the increasing purity of Mexican heroin, as well as ready supplies of high-purity white heroin, may result in geographic "pockets" of overdoses as seen in Chimayo and Espanola, New Mexico, in the late 1990s. The high rate of overdose in these locations served as the initial impetus for Operation TAR PIT, which identified the operations of a Mexico-based heroin distribution organization that operated throughout the western United States and in sections of the Midwest.

Marijuana

Marijuana trafficking is prevalent across the nation, with both domestic and foreign sources of supply. Lax public attitudes regarding marijuana's effects, the high seizure threshold required for federal prosecution, and various state legalization efforts undermine public support of law enforcement endeavors. The Houston Field Division reports that some Mexican DTOs use marijuana as a "cash crop"; the proceeds are used to cover the expenses associated with the trafficking of other drugs. Multiton seizures of marijuana have had a negligible effect on street prices and availability. Moreover, the increased availability of high-quality Sinsemilla and a new generation of marijuana users are threats that cannot be ignored.

Methamphetamine

Methamphetamine, from either foreign or domestic sources, is available in nearly every DEA field division. Large-scale methamphetamine laboratories, located primarily in the western United States, and to a lesser extent in Mexico, provide the majority of the drug. However, even the smaller clandestine laboratories pose a significant public health and safety threat. The majority of the small toxic laboratories are not connected to large-scale drug trafficking organizations.

"Super labs" (laboratories capable of producing in excess of 10 pounds of methamphetamine in one 24-hour production cycle), however, are generally funded and supplied by larger DTOs. An increase in the number of super labs in the Midwest suggests an increased demand for methamphetamine. The increased availability of methamphetamine in urban environments, especially the indications that the drug is occasionally sold in conjunction with, or in place of, club drugs such as MDMA, may usher in a new generation and class of drug abuser. The appearance of Southeast

Figure 5.1 Evolution of Drug Threat (cont.)

Asian methamphetamine tablets in the United States further threatens to introduce the drug as a substitute for, or supplement to, MDMA, although intelligence reporting on this issue suggests the availability of methamphetamine tablets is isolated. Since methamphetamine laboratories can operate in nearly any remote location, either foreign or domestic, identifying production sources poses a substantial challenge for law enforcement assets at the local, state, and federal levels. One response to the growing problem of clandestine laboratories has been the creation of the National Clandestine Laboratory Database maintained by EPIC. Prior to the creation of this database, there was no reliable system capable of obtaining clandestine laboratory seizure information from state or local investigations. EPIC's database provides a valuable instrument for both strategic assessment and a clearinghouse for investigative intelligence.

MDMA

Both field division and epidemiology reports identify club drugs, most notably MDMA, as a significant threat. The increase in domestic MDMA production, although still limited by stringent precursor chemical controls, further illustrates the profitability of this drug. Although the majority of MDMA production takes place in the Netherlands, and to a lesser extent in Belgium, the transferability of the laboratories adds a dynamic to the drug trade that cannot be addressed at this time. Laboratories can be relocated to any nation in the European Union, Eastern Europe, or the former Soviet Union, as long as precursor chemicals can be obtained and transported.

Post-September 11, 2001 Assessment

The September 11, 2001 terrorist attacks on the United States introduced a new set of variables to drug threat assessments: the reallocation of law enforcement, intelligence, and military assets from counternarcotics to counterterrorism reduces available enforcement assets, yet brings a concurrent strengthening of national borders. If history serves as a guide, DTOs will continue to identify and exploit vulnerabilities in order to maintain a steady supply of drugs to the illicit drug market in the United States.

This report was prepared by the DEA Intelligence Division, Office of Domestic Intelligence, Domestic Strategic Unit. This report reflects information received prior to May 2002. Comments and requests for copies are welcome and may be faxed to the Intelligence Production Unit, Intelligence Division, DEA Headquarters, at (202) 307-8XXX clandestine laboratory seizure information from state or local investigations.

Figure 5.2 Drug Trafficking in the U.S.

DRUG TRAFFICKING IN THE UNITED STATES

The Attorney General has determined that publication of this periodical is necessary in the transaction of the public business required by law of the Department of Justice.

This report was prepared by the Domestic Strategic Intelligence Unit (NDAS) of the Office of Domestic Intelligence. Comments and requests for copies are welcome and may be directed to the Intelligence Production Unit, Intelligence Division, DEA Headquarters, at (202) 307-8XXX.

September 2001DEA-01020

Executive Summary

The illegal drug market in the United States is one of the most profitable in the world. As such, it attracts the most ruthless, sophisticated, and aggressive drug traffickers. Drug law enforcement agencies face an enormous challenge in protecting the country's borders. Each year, according to the U.S. Customs Service (USCS), 60 million people enter the United States on more than 675,000 commercial and private flights. Another 6 million come by sea and 370 million by land. In addition, 116 million vehicles cross the land borders with Canada and Mexico. More than 90,000 merchant and passenger ships dock at U.S. ports. These ships carry more than 9 million shipping containers and 400 million tons of cargo. Another 157,000 smaller vessels visit our many coastal towns. Amid this voluminous trade, drug traffickers conceal cocaine, heroin, marijuana, MDMA, and methamphetamine shipments for distribution in U.S. neighborhoods.

Diverse groups traffic and distribute illegal drugs. Criminal groups operating from South America smuggle cocaine and heroin into the United States via a variety of routes, including land routes through Mexico, maritime routes along Mexico's east and west coasts, sea routes through the Caribbean, and international air corridors. Furthermore, criminal groups operating from neighboring Mexico smuggle cocaine, heroin, methamphetamine, amphetamine, and marijuana into the United States. These criminal groups have smuggled heroin and marijuana across the Southwest Border and distributed them throughout the United States since the 1970s. Reporting suggests that, in addition to distributing cocaine and methamphetamine in the West and Midwest, these Mexico-based groups now are attempting to expand the distribution of those drugs into eastern U.S. markets.

Figure 5.2 Drug Trafficking in the U.S. (cont.)

The use of the drug 3, 4-methylenedioxymethamphetamine (MDMA), also known on the street as Ecstasy, has increased at an alarming rate in the United States over the last several years. Israeli and Russian drug trafficking syndicates and Western Europe-based drug traffickers are the principal traffickers of MDMA worldwide. MDMA, primarily manufactured clandestinely in Western Europe, is smuggled into the United States by couriers via commercial airlines, as well as through the use of express package carriers. Finally, criminal groups based in Southeast and Southwest Asia smuggle heroin into the United States. Using New York City as a major distribution hub, these criminal groups move heroin up and down the eastern seaboard and into the Midwest.

Besides these criminal groups based abroad, domestic organizations cultivate, produce, manufacture, or distribute illegal drugs such as marijuana, methamphetamine, phencyclidine (PCP), and lysergic acid diethyamide (LSD). By growing high-potency Sinsemilla, domestic cannabis growers provide marijuana that easily competes with other illegal drugs. With demand for methamphetamine remaining high, especially in the West and Midwest, so, too, does the number of illicit laboratories that supply methamphetamine to a growing number of addicts. Additionally, a small number of chemists manufacture LSD that is subsequently distributed primarily to high school and college students throughout the United States.

COCAINE

Cocaine trafficking and abuse continue to threaten the health and safety of American citizens. According to drug abuse indicators, the abuse of both powder and crack cocaine have stabilized, albeit at high levels. The trafficking, distribution, and abuse of cocaine and crack cocaine have spread from urban environments to smaller cities and suburban areas of the country, bringing a commensurate increase in violence and criminal activity. The level of violence associated with cocaine trafficking today, however, does not compare to the rampant violence of the 1980s when the crack epidemic was at its worst.

Trafficking by Colombian and Mexican Organizations

The U.S./Mexico border is the primary point of entry for cocaine shipments being smuggled into the United States. According to a recent interagency intelligence assessment, approximately 65 percent of the cocaine smuggled into the United States crosses the Southwest border. Cocaine is readily available in nearly all major cities in the United States. Organized crime groups operating in Colombia

Figure 5.2 Drug Trafficking in the U.S. (cont.)

control the worldwide supply of cocaine. These organizations use a sophisticated infrastructure to move cocaine by land, sea, and air into the United States. In the United States, these Colombia-based groups operate cocaine distribution and drug money laundering networks comprising a vast infrastructure of multiple cells functioning in many major metropolitan areas. Each cell performs a specific function within the organization, e.g., transportation, local distribution, or money movement. Key managers in Colombia continue to oversee the overall operation.

Over the past decade, the Colombia-based drug groups have allowed Mexico-based trafficking organizations to play an increasing role in the U.S. cocaine trade. Throughout most of the 1980s, the criminals in Colombia used the drug smugglers in Mexico to transport cocaine shipments across the Southwest border into the United States. After successfully smuggling the drugs across the border, the Mexican transporters transferred the drugs back to the Colombian groups operating in the United States. However, the seizure of nearly 21 metric tons of cocaine in 1989 led to a new arrangement between transportation organizations operating from Mexico and the organized crime groups operating from Colombia. This new arrangement radically changed the role and sphere of influence of the Mexico-based trafficking organizations in the U.S. cocaine trade. By the mid-1990s, Mexico-based transportation groups were receiving up to half the cocaine shipment they smuggled for the Colombia-based groups in exchange for their services. Both sides realized that this strategy eliminated the vulnerabilities and complex logistics associated with large cash transactions. The Colombia-based groups also realized that relinquishing part of each cocaine shipment to their associates operating from Mexico ceded a share of the wholesale cocaine market in the United States.

Today, traffickers operating from Colombia continue to control wholesale-level cocaine distribution throughout the heavily populated northeastern United States and along the eastern seaboard in cities such as Boston, Miami, Newark, New York, and Philadelphia. There are indications, however, that other drug trafficking organizations are playing a larger role in the distribution of cocaine in conjunction with the Colombian organizations. Dominican drug trafficking organizations have traditionally been responsible for the street-level distribution of cocaine. The DEA Philadelphia Field Division reports that the primary sources of supply for cocaine in the city are Colombian and Dominican organizations, which are capable of moving multi-kilogram quantities. The DEA

Figure 5.2 Drug Trafficking in the U.S. (cont.)

Boston Field Division reports that Dominican traffickers are expanding their roles in cocaine distribution, and have been instrumental in obtaining multi-kilogram quantities of cocaine for distribution in New England. In New York City, Colombian, Dominican, and Mexican drug trafficking organizations distribute multi-kilogram quantities of cocaine. Furthermore, Mexican drug trafficking organizations are increasingly responsible for the transportation of cocaine from the Southwest border to the New York market.

Traffickers operating from Mexico, however, now control wholesale cocaine distribution throughout the western and midwestern United States. The distribution of multi-ton quantities of cocaine, once dominated by the Colombia-based drug groups, is now controlled by Mexico-based trafficking groups in cities such as Chicago, Dallas, Denver, Houston, Los Angeles, Phoenix, San Diego, San Francisco, and Seattle. In the early 1990s, when the organized crime groups from Mexico were expanding their roles as cocaine transporters and wholesale-level distributors, most of their U.S.-based command and control operations were in southern California. Today, Chicago is also a key command and control center for their cocaine operations. Currently, these traffickers control cocaine shipments from the time they are smuggled across the border until they are distributed to markets across the country.

The role of Mexico-based trafficking organizations is continuing to evolve. Recent reports suggest that some major international criminals in Colombia are continuing to distance themselves from day-to-day wholesale-level cocaine distribution in the United States by turning this task over, at least occasionally, to the organizations operating from Mexico. Likely motivations for this change include the non-retroactive extradition law enacted by the Colombian National Assembly in December 1997. Accordingly, Colombian traffickers now face the prospect of extradition for overt acts committed on or after the date (December 17, 1997) that the extradition amendment went into effect. By distancing themselves from overt acts in the United States, Colombian drug lords hope to minimize the threat that the United States will gather sufficient evidence to support an extradition request. This shift does not mean to suggest that traffickers operating from Colombia will abandon the U.S. cocaine market *en masse*. Emerging drug lords who do not face the difficulties in micro-managing operations, as do the jailed Cali criminal leaders have little reason to forego the profits generated by the wholesale U.S. cocaine market.

Figure 5.2 Drug Trafficking in the U.S. (cont.)

Colombian drug trafficking organizations have increasingly relied upon the eastern Pacific Ocean as a trafficking route to move cocaine to the United States. Law enforcement and intelligence community sources estimate that 65 percent of the cocaine shipped to the United States moves through the Central America-Mexico corridor, primarily by vessels operating in the eastern Pacific. Colombian traffickers utilize fishing vessels to transport bulk shipments of cocaine from Colombia to the west coast of Mexico and, to a lesser extent, the Yucatan Peninsula. The cocaine is off-loaded to go-fast vessels for the final shipment to the Mexican coast. The loads are subsequently broken down into smaller quantities to be moved across the Southwest border.

However, cocaine continues to be transported through the Caribbean; Puerto Rico, the Dominican Republic, and Haiti are the predominant transshipment points for Colombian cocaine transiting the Caribbean. Because of lawlessness and deteriorating economic conditions, Haiti is becoming a growing transshipment point for Colombian cocaine destined for eastern U.S. markets. Haitian drug traffickers, utilizing maritime shipments to transport cocaine to South Florida, are becoming a major threat. Law enforcement reporting indicates that Jamaica is an increasingly significant transshipment point for cocaine destined for the United States since it is located midway between South America and the United States. Cocaine is primarily smuggled into Jamaica by maritime methods, and the cocaine transshipped through Jamaica often is destined for the Canadian, European, and U.S. markets. Cocaine destined for the United States is usually smuggled from Jamaica to the Bahamas aboard go-fast boats. The cocaine is subsequently smuggled to the Florida coast using go-fast boats, pleasure craft, and fishing vessels.

Crack Cocaine Trafficking

Crack, the inexpensive, smokable form of cocaine, continues to be distributed and used in most major cities. While cocaine use in the United States has declined over the past decade, the rate of use in recent years has stabilized at high levels. Crack cocaine usage, which initially drove these rates, has similarly stabilized, and shows some indications of declining although it also remains at a high level. Street gangs, such as the Crips and the Bloods, and criminal groups of ethnic Dominicans, Puerto Ricans, and Jamaicans dominate the retail market for crack cocaine nationwide. The directed expansion of these gangs to smaller U.S. cities and rural areas, as well as a growth in street gangs that imitate their urban counterparts, resulted in an

Figure 5.2 Drug Trafficking in the U.S. (cont.)

increase in the number of homicides, armed robberies, and assaults as gang members used physical violence to maintain their drug distribution monopolies.

Prices and Purity

Cocaine prices in 2000 remained low and stable, suggesting a steady supply to the United States. Nationwide, wholesale cocaine prices ranged from $12,000 to $35,000 per kilogram. In most major metropolitan areas, however, the price of a kilogram of cocaine ranged from $13,000 to $25,000. Average purity for cocaine at the gram, ounce, and kilogram levels remained stable at high levels. In 2000, the average purity of a kilogram of cocaine was 75 percent. Typically, cocaine HCl is converted into crack cocaine, or "rock," within the United States by the secondary wholesaler or retailer. Crack cocaine is often packaged in vials, glassine bags, and film canisters. The size of a crack rock can vary, but generally ranges from 1/10 to 1/2 gram. Rocks can sell for as low as $3 to as high as $50, but prices generally range from $10 to $20.

Seizures

According to the Federal-wide Drug Seizure System (FDSS), U.S. federal authorities seized nearly 103 metric tons of cocaine in 2000 compared to 135 metric tons in 1999. According to a recent interagency intelligence assessment, cocaine production has not declined. The decline in cocaine seizures is primarily attributed to the decrease in the size of the average load transiting the Southwest border and an increase in the number of drug loads moving between ports of entry.

HEROIN

Heroin is readily available in many U.S. cities as evidenced by the unprecedented high level of average retail, or street-level, purity. Criminals in four foreign source areas produce the heroin available in the United States: South America (Colombia), Southeast Asia (principally Burma), Mexico, and Southwest Asia/Middle East (principally Afghanistan). While virtually all heroin produced in Mexico and South America is destined for the U.S. market, each of the four source areas has dominated the U.S. market at some point over the past 30 years. Over the past decade, the United States has experienced a dramatic shift in the heroin market from the domination of Southeast Asian heroin to a dominance of the wholesale and retail markets by South American heroin, especially in the East. In the West, by contrast, "black tar" and, to a lesser extent,

Figure 5.2 Drug Trafficking in the U.S. (cont.)

brown powdered heroin from Mexico have been, and continue to be, the predominant available form.

The increased availability of high-purity heroin, which can effectively be snorted, has given rise to a new, younger user population. While avoiding the stigma of needle use, this user group is ingesting larger quantities of the drug and, according to drug treatment specialists, progressing more quickly toward addiction.

South American Heroin

The availability of South American (SA) heroin, produced in Colombia, has increased dramatically in the United States since 1993. SA heroin is available in the metropolitan areas of the Northeast and along the East Coast. Independent traffickers typically smuggle SA heroin into the United States via couriers traveling aboard commercial airlines, with each courier usually carrying from 500 grams to 1 kilogram of heroin per trip. These traffickers increased their influence in the lucrative northeastern heroin market, which has the largest demand in the United States, by pursuing an aggressive marketing strategy. They distributed high-quality heroin (of purity frequently above 90 percent), undercut the price of their competition, and used their long-standing, effective drug distribution networks. Investigations also indicate the spread of SA heroin to smaller U.S. cities.

Since the mid-1990s, Colombian heroin traffickers have diversified their methods of operation. Couriers still come into Miami, New York City, San Juan, and other U.S. cities on direct commercial flights from Colombia. Increasingly, however, Colombian traffickers are smuggling heroin from Colombia into the United States through such countries as Costa Rica, the Dominican Republic, Ecuador, Panama, Mexico, Argentina, and Venezuela.

In response to increased drug law enforcement presence at eastern ports of entry, some SA heroin traffickers have sought alternative routes. Recent seizures reflect the use of Mexico to smuggle SA heroin into the United States. In February 2001, for example, two separate seizures of suspected SA heroin, totaling 4.9 kilograms, were made at the airport in Tijuana, Mexico. Also, in late 2000, the DEA Houston Field Division reported two seizures of suspected SA heroin. Nearly 2 kilograms were seized at a bus terminal in Houston from a Colombian female who was traveling from San Antonio to New York City. In the other instance, four Venezuelans, in possession of 1.4 kilograms of heroin, were arrested at a local hotel.

Figure 5.2 Drug Trafficking in the U.S. (cont.)

More recently, Colombian heroin traffickers are using commercial maritime methods to move larger amounts of their drug into the United States. Some of the past maritime heroin shipments have been intermixed with larger shipments of cocaine, and some have been transported via cruise ships. Larger shipments of heroin are now being smuggled via containerized cargo, as evidenced by the May 16, 2001, seizure of 54 kilograms of SA heroin in New York. The heroin, packaged in 1.5-pound bricks, was secreted in false bottoms of 1,400 25-pound boxes of frozen plantains. This seizure represents the largest seizure of SA heroin to date in the United States.

Within the United States, ethnic Dominican criminal groups have played a significant role in retail-level heroin distribution in northeastern markets for at least the past two decades. During the 1990s, Dominican groups secured their role in the heroin trade by selling high-purity SA heroin. Currently, Dominican groups dominate retail heroin markets in northeastern cities such as New York City, Boston, and Philadelphia. New York City is the primary base of operation for ethnic Dominican groups. Colombian distribution networks at the wholesale level deal directly with Dominican trafficking groups responsible for retail sales.

Mexican Heroin

Mexican heroin has been a threat to the United States for decades. It is produced, smuggled, and distributed by polydrug trafficking groups, many of which have been in operation for more than 20 years. Nearly all of the heroin produced in Mexico is destined for distribution in the United States. Organized crime groups operating from Mexico produce, smuggle, and distribute the black tar heroin sold in the western United States. Traditionally, trafficking groups operating from Mexico evaded interdiction efforts by smuggling heroin to the U.S. market as they received orders from customers. By keeping quantities small, traffickers hoped to minimize the risk of losing a significant quantity of heroin in a single seizure. Even large polydrug Mexican organizations, which smuggle multi-ton quantities of cocaine and marijuana, generally limited smuggling of Mexican heroin into the United States to kilogram and smaller amounts. Nevertheless, trafficking organizations were capable of regularly smuggling significant quantities of heroin into the United States.

Although illegal immigrants and migrant workers frequently smuggle heroin across the U.S./Mexico border in 1- to 3- kilogram amounts for the major trafficking groups, seizures indicate that larger

Figure 5.2 Drug Trafficking in the U.S. (cont.)

loads are being moved across the border, primarily in privately owned vehicles. Once the heroin reaches the United States, traffickers rely upon well-entrenched polydrug smuggling and distribution networks to deliver their product to the market, principally in the metropolitan areas of the midwestern, southwestern, and western United States with sizable Mexican immigrant populations.

Indicative of larger shipments of Mexican heroin being smuggled into the United States are a series of recent seizures along the Southwest border. In January 2001, the USCS in Del Rio, Texas, seized 42 kilograms of black tar heroin. In December 2000, the USCS seized 27 kilograms of black tar heroin at the Laredo port of entry. Texas has not been the only border state where large amounts of black tar heroin were seized. In October 2000, 46 kilograms of black tar heroin were seized in Arizona at the San Luis port of entry. This seizure ranks as one of the largest ever made along the Southwest border.

Although recent DEA cases have involved Mexican black tar heroin trafficking groups east of the Mississippi River, there has been no successful, long-term penetration of the East Coast markets by organizations selling Mexico-produced heroin.

Southeast Asian Heroin

High-purity Southeast Asian (SEA) heroin dominated the market in the United States during the late 1980s and early 1990s. Over the past few years, however, all indicators point to a decrease in SEA heroin available domestically. Significant investigations led to the incarceration in Thailand and extradition to the United States of more than a dozen high-level violators who played key roles in moving SEA heroin shipments to the United States. SEA heroin trafficking links run from independent brokers and shippers in Asia through overseas Chinese criminal populations to ethnic Chinese criminal wholesale distributors in the United States. In the United States, ethnic Chinese criminals rely upon local criminal organizations for the distribution of SEA heroin. Despite the recent decline in the trafficking of SEA heroin in the United States, Chinese criminal groups remain the most sophisticated heroin trafficking organizations in the world.

SEA heroin shipments destined for U.S. markets may transit through China, Japan, Malaysia, the Philippines, Singapore, Taiwan, or South Korea. Largely independent U.S.-based ethnic Chinese traffickers control distribution within the United States, principally in

Figure 5.2 Drug Trafficking in the U.S. (cont.)

the Northeast and along the East Coast. During the late 1990s, Vancouver, British Columbia, emerged as a key operational headquarters for ethnic Chinese criminal elements. These criminal groups were enmeshed with North American gangs of Asian descent in transporting SEA heroin to the United States, mainly to the East Coast. A DEA New York Field Division investigation led to the seizure, in January 2001, of 57 kilograms of SEA heroin from a container ship docked at the port in Elizabeth, New Jersey.

Trafficking groups composed of West African criminals also smuggle SEA heroin to the United States. Nigerian criminals have been most active in U.S. cities and areas with well-established Nigerian populations, such as Atlanta, Baltimore, Houston, Dallas, New York City, Newark, Chicago, and Washington, D.C. Over the past several years, Chicago has become a hub for heroin trafficking controlled by Nigerian criminals who primarily deal in SEA heroin.

Southwest Asian Heroin

While a large portion of Southwest Asian (SWA) heroin is consumed in Western Europe, Pakistan, and Iran, traffickers operating from Middle Eastern locations smuggle SWA heroin to ethnic enclaves in the United States. Criminal groups composed of ethnic Lebanese, Pakistanis, Turks, and Afghans are all involved in supplying the drug to U.S.-based groups for retail distribution. SWA heroin traffickers and wholesale distributors generally have been consistently cautious, rarely conducting heroin business with persons not of Southwest Asian or Middle Eastern ethnicity. Therefore, the ethnic aspect of SWA heroin importation and distribution has made SWA heroin more prevalent in areas with large Southwest Asian populations.

West African traffickers, who primarily smuggled SEA heroin to the United States in the 1990s, now also deal in SWA heroin. In a particularly noteworthy seizure of approximately 24 kilograms of heroin in New York in May 2000, 90 percent of the seized heroin consisted of SWA heroin, and the remaining 10 percent was SEA. While unusual, a shipment containing the two types of heroin is not unexpected. For the last two years, West African traffickers, based in Bangkok who normally deal in SEA heroin, have been sending couriers to Pakistan to buy the cheaper Afghanistan-produced SWA heroin. Heroin in Pakistan ranges from $1,000 to $2,000 a kilogram, while in Bangkok the West Africans must pay between $10,000 and $12,000 for a kilogram.

Figure 5.2 Drug Trafficking in the U.S. (cont.)

Purity

On the street, heroin purity and price often reflect the drug's availability. High purities and low prices, for example, indicate that heroin supplies are readily available. DEA's Domestic Monitor Program (DMP), a retail heroin purchase program, tracks urban street-level heroin purity and price. The most recent data available show that, in 1999, the nationwide average purity for retail heroin from all sources was 38.2 percent. This number is significantly higher than the average of 7 percent reported two decades ago and higher than the 26 percent recorded in 1991. The significant rise in average purity corresponds to the increased availability of high-purity SA heroin, particularly in the northeastern United States.

Moreover, the DMP indicated that the retail purity of SA heroin was the highest for any source, averaging 51.2 percent in 1999. SWA heroin followed with a 44.0 percent average. SEA heroin averaged 41.9 percent at the retail level and Mexican heroin averaged 27.3 percent, a drop from 33.5 percent in 1998. Heroin purity at the street level generally remained highest in the northeastern United States, where most of the nation's user population lives. In 1999, Philadelphia recorded the DMP's highest heroin purity average of 72.0 percent. Over the last several years, Philadelphia has ranked consistently at or near the top in DMP retail heroin purity levels. In addition, New York City continues to be one of the major importation and distribution centers for SA and SEA heroin.

Prices

Nationwide, in 2000, SA heroin ranged from $50,000 to $200,000 per kilogram. SEA and SWA heroin ranged in price from $40,000 to $190,000 per kilogram. Wholesale-level prices for Mexican heroin were the lowest of any type, ranging from $13,200 to $175,000 per kilogram. The wide range in kilogram prices reflects variables such as buyer/seller relationships, quantities purchased, purchase frequencies, purity, and transportation costs.

Seizures

FDSS statistics indicate that U.S. federal law enforcement authorities seized 1,575 kilograms of heroin in 2000, compared to 1,149 kilograms in 1999.

METHAMPHETAMINE

Domestic methamphetamine production, trafficking, and abuse are concentrated in the western, southwestern, and midwestern

Figure 5.2 Drug Trafficking in the U.S. (cont.)

United States. Methamphetamine is also increasingly available in portions of the South, especially Georgia and Florida. Clandestine laboratories in California and Mexico are the primary sources of supply for methamphetamine available in the United States.

Over the last decade, the methamphetamine trafficking and abuse situation in the United States changed dramatically. In 1994, ethnic Mexican drug trafficking organizations operating "super labs" (laboratories capable of producing in excess of 10 pounds of methamphetamine in one 24-hour production cycle) based in Mexico and in California began to take control of the production and distribution of methamphetamine domestically. Independent laboratory operators, including outlaw motorcycle gangs, previously maintained control of methamphetamine production and distribution within the United States, and continue to operate today on a lesser scale. The entrée of ethnic Mexican traffickers into the methamphetamine trade in the mid-1990s resulted in a significant increase in the supply of the drug. Mexican criminal organizations, based in Mexico and California, provided high-purity, low-cost methamphetamine originally to cities in the Midwest and West with Mexican populations.

In 2000, of the 6,394 clandestine methamphetamine laboratories seized and reported to the National Clandestine Laboratory Database at the El Paso Intelligence Center (EPIC), only 126 were super labs. In the first 5 months of fiscal year (FY) 2001, Mexican law enforcement and military officials seized 15 clandestine methamphetamine laboratories of unknown production capacity. Twelve of the FY 2001 seizures occurred in the border cities of Tijuana and Mexicali in the State of Baja California Norte. Due to the proximity of these laboratories to the United States, it is believed that the majority of the methamphetamine was bound for the United States.

The primary points of entry into the United States for methamphetamine produced in Mexico have traditionally been California ports of entry, particularly San Ysidro. Although a great amount of methamphetamine still transits this area, ports of entry in South Texas are experiencing significant increases in smuggling activity. The most common method of transporting methamphetamine is within concealed compartments in passenger vehicles.

The supply of methamphetamine in the United States also stems from multiple small-scale laboratories, often operated by independent cooks who obtain the ingredients necessary for

Figure 5.2 Drug Trafficking in the U.S. (cont.)

manufacture from retail and convenience stores. Methamphetamine produced in these "mom-and-pop" laboratories is generally for personal use or limited distribution. A clandestine laboratory operator can use relatively common items, such as mason jars, coffee filters, hot plates, pressure cookers, pillowcases, plastic tubing, and gas cans to substitute for sophisticated laboratory equipment. The growing use of the Internet, which provides access to methamphetamine "recipes," coupled with increased demand for high-purity product, has resulted in a dramatic increase in the number of mom-and-pop laboratories throughout the United States. The number of clandestine methamphetamine laboratories seized nationwide by DEA increased from 263 in 1994 to 1,815 in 2000, a 590-percent increase. In addition, state and local police agencies seized almost 4,600 clandestine laboratories in the United States during 2000.

The vast majority of meth- amphetamine precursor chemicals diverted to clandestine laboratories in the United States are dosage-form pseudoephedrine or ephedrine drug products. They are usually purchased from U.S. manufacturers and distributors who sell case quantities of the tablets. Ultimately, the tablets are destined for California where they are manufactured into multiple pounds of methamphetamine. The finished methamphetamine is then distributed throughout the United States through preexisting smuggling methods to the traffickers.

Because of law enforcement attention and strong state precursor control laws in California, traffickers have now diversified to pseudoephedrine suppliers nationwide, buying at relatively lower prices in other parts of the country and trafficking the product to California, where the black market price can bring up to $5,000 per pound of product.

Nationwide networks of suppliers, working together, also now provide ton quantities of pseudoephedrine tablet products to the market in California and to distributors in other states. The latter divert the product to local methamphetamine laboratories. Small-scale lab operators commonly buy over-the-counter pseudoephedrine products in small amounts from legitimate retailers. Recent reporting indicates that Canadian companies have also been implicated in supplying U.S. laboratories because of minimal chemical controls in Canada. In April 2001, the USCS seized approximately 10,700 kilograms of pseudoephedrine from a tractor-trailer attempting to enter the United States from Canada at the Ambassador Bridge in Detroit, Michigan. It is estimated that this

Figure 5.2 Drug Trafficking in the U.S. (cont.)

pseudoephedrine had the potential to produce between 2,300 and 2,600 kilograms of methamphetamine.

In addition, the use of methylsulfonylmethane (MSM) has been encountered as a "cut" in meth- amphetamine produced primarily by Mexican organizations. Legitimately used as a dietary supplement for horses and humans, MSM is readily available at feed and livestock stores, as well as health and nutrition stores. The addition of MSM can be used to add volume to the finished methamphetamine, thus increasing the profit. Increases in the use of MSM may be a signal of difficulty in obtaining precursors, or a simple marketing method to meet demand while increasing profit.

The crystalline form of methamphetamine, known as "ice," "glass," or "crystal," is gaining popularity. Converted from powder by criminal elements in Southeast Asia, Mexico, and the United States, ice traditionally was used in Hawaii and southern California. More recently, its use has spread along the West Coast and Southwest border areas.

The importation of meth- amphetamine tablets from Southeast Asia, primarily via the mail system, is increasing. Produced mainly by the United Wa State Army, the largest heroin and methamphetamine trafficking group in Burma, the tablets, which weigh approximately 90 milligrams (mg), typically contain 25 to 30 mg of methamphetamine, and 45 to 65 mg of caffeine. Although it is believed that the tablets are trafficked primarily by ethnic Thais or Laotians for use in the Asian community, it is likely that larger amounts will be smuggled into the United States as demand increases outside that community.

Purity

Until 1999, the meth- amphetamine problem was increasing at an alarming rate. International chemical control efforts reduced the supply of those chemicals needed to produce high-quality methamphetamine. As a result, the national purity level for methamphetamine has decreased dramatically. The average purity of methamphetamine exhibits seized by DEA dropped from 71.9 percent in 1994 to 30.7 percent in 1999. The average purity of methamphetamine exhibits seized by DEA in 2000 rose slightly to 35.3 percent.

Prices

Methamphetamine prices vary throughout different regions of the United States. At the distribution level, prices range from $3,500 per

---

Figure 5.2 Drug Trafficking in the U.S. (cont.)

pound in parts of California and Texas to $21,000 per pound in southeastern and northeastern regions of the country. Retail prices range from $400 to $3,000 per ounce.

Seizures

According to the FDSS, U.S. federal authorities seized a total of 3,163 kilograms of methamphetamine in 2000 compared to 2,776 kilograms in 1999.

In 2000, authorities seized 301,697 SEA methamphetamine tablets in U.S. Postal Service facilities in Oakland, Los Angeles, and Honolulu. This represents a 656-percent increase from the 1999 seizure total of 39,917.

MARIJUANA

Marijuana is the most widely abused and readily available illicit drug in the United States, with an estimated 11.5 million current users. At least one-third of the U.S. population has used marijuana sometime in their lives. The drug is considered a "gateway" to the world of illicit drug abuse. Relaxed public perception of harm, popularization by the media and by groups advocating legalization, along with the trend of smoking marijuana-filled cigars known as "blunts," contribute to the nationwide resurgence in marijuana's popularity.

The Internet also contributes to marijuana's popularity. Websites exist that provide information and links extolling the virtues of marijuana. These sites provide forums for user group discussions, post documents and messages for public discussions, and advocate the "legal" sale of marijuana. Several web sites advertising the sale of marijuana and providing instructions on home grows have also been identified.

Marijuana smuggled into the United States, whether grown in Mexico or transshipped from other Latin American source areas, accounts for most of the marijuana available in the United States. Marijuana produced in Mexico remains the most widely available. Moreover, high-potency marijuana enters the U.S. drug market from Canada. The availability of marijuana from Southeast Asia generally is limited to the West Coast. U.S. drug law enforcement reporting also suggests increased availability of domestically grown marijuana.

Figure 5.2 Drug Trafficking in the U.S. (cont.)

Domestic Marijuana

According to 2000 Domestic Cannabis Eradication/Suppression Program (DCE/SP) statistics, the five leading states for indoor growing activity were California, Florida, Oregon, Washington, and Wisconsin. DCE/SP statistics indicate that the major outdoor growing states in 2000 were California, Hawaii, Kentucky, and Tennessee; these states accounted for approximately three-quarters of the total of eradicated outdoor cultivated plants.

Mexican Marijuana

Organized crime groups operating from Mexico have smuggled marijuana into the United States since the early 1970s. These groups maintain extensive networks of associates, often related through familial or regional ties to associates living in the United States, where they control polydrug smuggling and wholesale distribution from hub cities to retail markets throughout the United States.

Groups operating from Mexico employ a variety of transportation and concealment methods to smuggle marijuana into the United States. Most of the marijuana smuggled into the United States is concealed in vehicles often in false compartments or hidden in shipments of legitimate agricultural or industrial products. Marijuana also is smuggled across the border by rail, horse, raft, and backpack. Shipments of 20 kilograms or less are smuggled by pedestrians who enter the United States at border checkpoints and by backpackers who, alone or in groups ("mule trains"), cross the border at more remote locations. Jamaican organizations also appear to be involved in dispatching Mexican marijuana via parcel carriers.

Organized crime groups operating from Mexico conceal marijuana in an array of vehicles, including commercial vehicles, private automobiles, pickup trucks, vans, mobile homes, and horse trailers, driven through border ports of entry. Larger shipments ranging up to multi-thousand kilograms are usually smuggled in tractor-trailers, such as the 6.9 metric tons of marijuana seized on April 3, 2001, by USCS officials from a tractor-trailer at the Otay Mesa, California, port of entry. The marijuana packages had been wrapped in cellophane, coated with mustard, grease, and motor oil, and commingled in a load of television sets.

Besides overland smuggling, drug traffickers use ocean vessels to move Mexican marijuana up the coast of Mexico to U.S. ports, drop-off sites along the U.S. coast, or to rendezvous points with other boats bound for the United States.

Figure 5.2 Drug Trafficking in the U.S. (cont.)

Law enforcement authorities in southern California indicate that marijuana is transferred from mother ships in international waters to Mexican fishing vessels. The smaller vessels then deliver the marijuana to overland smugglers on the Mexican Baja California Peninsula. From there, the marijuana is generally moved to border transit points and then carried to the Los Angeles metropolitan area for distribution to eastern markets.

Canadian Marijuana

Canada is becoming a source country for indoor-grown, high-potency (15 to 25 percent THC) marijuana destined for the United States. Canadian law enforcement intelligence indicates that marijuana traffickers there are increasingly cultivating cannabis indoors. Such indoor-grow operations have become an enormous and lucrative illicit industry, producing a potent form of marijuana that has come to be known as "BC Bud." Canadian officials estimate that cannabis cultivation in British Columbia is a billion-dollar industry, and that traffickers smuggle a significant portion of the Canadian harvest into the United States.

Prices and Potency (THC Content)

Prices for commercial-grade marijuana have remained relatively stable over the past decade, ranging from approximately $400 to $1,000 per pound in U.S. Southwest border areas to between $700 to $2000 per pound in the Midwest and northeastern United States. The national price range for Sinsemilla, a higher quality marijuana usually grown domestically, is between $900 and $6,000 per pound. BC Bud sells for between $1,500 and $2,000 per pound in Vancouver; but when smuggled into the United States, it sells for between $5,000 and $8,000 per pound in major metropolitan areas.

During the past two decades, marijuana potency has increased. According to the University of Mississippi's 2000 Marijuana Potency Monitoring Project (MPMP), commercial-grade marijuana THC levels rose from under 2 percent in the late 1970s and early 1980s to 6.07 percent in 2000. The MPMP reports that Sinsemilla potency also increased, rising from 6 percent in the late 1970s and 1980s to 13.20 percent in 2000.

Seizures

According to the FDSS, U.S. federal authorities seized 1,222 metric tons of marijuana in 2000 compared to 1,094 metric tons in 1999.

Figure 5.2 Drug Trafficking in the U.S. (cont.)

MDMA

Commonly referred to as Ecstasy, XTC, Clarity, or Essence, 3, 4-methylenedioxymethamphetamine (MDMA) is a synthetic psychoactive drug possessing stimulant and mild hallucinogenic properties. In the early 1990s, MDMA became increasingly popular among European youth. However, it is within the last five years that MDMA use in the United States has increased at an alarming rate.

MDMA is popular among middle-class adolescents and young adults. MDMA is increasingly becoming an abuse problem because many users view it as nonaddictive and benign. MDMA is sold primarily at legitimate nightclubs and bars, at underground nightclubs sometimes called "acid houses," or at all-night parties known as "raves."

MDMA tablets range in weight from 150 to 350 mg and contain between 70 to 120 mg of MDMA. The profit margin associated with MDMA trafficking is significant. It costs as little as 25 to 50 cents to manufacture an MDMA tablet in Europe, but the street value of that same …insert ch 05 fig 5.2 image 17 MDMA tablet can be as high as $40, with a tablet typically selling for between $20 and $30.

Although the vast majority of MDMA consumed domestically is produced in Europe, a limited number of MDMA laboratories operate in the United States. Law enforcement seized 7 clandestine MDMA laboratories in the United States in 2000 compared to 19 seized in 1999. It should be noted that these laboratories were primarily capable of limited drug production. While recipes for the clandestine production of MDMA can be found on the Internet, acquiring the necessary precursor chemicals in the United States is difficult.

MDMA is manufactured clandestinely in Western Europe, particularly in the Netherlands and Belgium. Much of the MDMA is manufactured in the southeast section of the Netherlands near Maastricht. Despite the Dutch Government's efforts to curtail MDMA trafficking, the Netherlands remains a primary source country for the drug. International MDMA traffickers based in the Netherlands and Belgium, and a significant number of U.S.-based traffickers who coordinate MDMA shipments to major metropolitan areas of the United States often use Montreal and Toronto as transit points. In December 2000, the Royal Canadian Mounted Police (RCMP) seized approximately 150,000 MDMA tablets in Toronto that had been shipped via DHL from Brussels, Belgium, by an Israeli MDMA trafficking organization. The shipment was destined for distributors in the United States.

Figure 5.2 Drug Trafficking in the U.S. (cont.)

Due to the availability of precursor chemicals in Canada, a number of MDMA laboratories have been discovered operating near metropolitan areas such as Vancouver, Toronto, and Montreal. Such laboratories continue to supply U.S.-based MDMA trafficking organizations. According to the RCMP, the total potential yield of MDMA from laboratories uncovered in Canada since 1999 is in excess of 10 million tablets.

Another emerging trend is the use of Mexico as a transit zone for MDMA entering the United States. During 2000, several seizures were reported in or destined for Mexico. In September 2000, Dutch authorities seized a 1.25 million-tablet shipment of MDMA destined for Mexico. Previously, in April 2000, a shipment of 200,000 MDMA tablets was seized at the airport in Mexico City. The MDMA was discovered in an air cargo shipment manifested as aircraft parts sent from the Netherlands and destined for the United States.

USCS statistics show a dramatic increase in seizures of MDMA tablets. In FY 1997, approximately 400,000 MDMA tablets were seized compared to approximately 9.3 million tablets seized in FY 2000. On July 22, 2000, approximately 2.1 million tablets were seized in Los Angeles. To date, this is the largest seizure of MDMA tablets in the United States.

LSD

Lysergic acid diethylamide (LSD) remains available in retail quantities in virtually every state. LSD production reportedly is centered on the West Coast, particularly in San Francisco, northern California, the Pacific Northwest, and recently the Midwest. Since the 1960s, LSD has been manufactured illegally within the United States. LSD production is a time-consuming and complex procedure. Several chemical recipes for synthesizing LSD are on the Internet, but clandestine production requires a high degree of chemical expertise. Chemists maintain tight control at the production level, but do not necessarily participate in the distribution of the drug. These chemists usually sell the crystal LSD product to one or two trusted associates, insulating themselves from the wholesale distributors.

Few LSD laboratories have ever been seized in the United States because of infrequent and irregular production cycles. In 2000, DEA seized one LSD laboratory that was located in a converted missile silo in Kansas. LSD is produced in crystal form that is converted to liquid and distributed primarily in the form of squares of blotter paper saturated with the liquid. To a lesser extent, LSD is sold as a liquid, contained in breath mint bottles and vials; in gelatin tab form

Figure 5.2 Drug Trafficking in the U.S. (cont.)

("window panes") of varying colors; and in pill form known as "microdots."

Distribution of LSD is unique within the drug culture. A proliferation of mail order sales has created a marketplace where the sellers are virtually unknown to the buyers, giving the highest-level traffickers considerable insulation from drug law enforcement operations. The vast majority of users are middle-class adolescents and young adults attracted by its low prices. Rock concerts continue to be favorite distribution sites for LSD traffickers; however, distribution at raves throughout the United States is becoming more popular. Contacts made at raves and concerts are used to establish future transactions and shipments of larger quantities of LSD.

Phencyclidine (PCP), a clandestinely manufactured hallucinogen commonly used in conjunction with marijuana, causes users to feel detached from their surroundings and, in some cases, paranoid and violent. PCP production is centered in the greater Los Angeles metropolitan area. During the late 1980s and early 1990s, the widespread availability and use of crack cocaine displaced demand for PCP. More recently, however, reporting suggests that PCP abuse is increasing slightly in many cities, as some crack addicts return to the use of this drug. DEA reporting indicates that PCP is being encountered with greater frequency along the Southwest border, particularly in Texas.

Since 2000, four major seizures of PCP have occurred in Sierra Blanca, Texas, alone: approximately 6 kilograms of PCP were seized on April 21, 2000; 2 kilograms seized on December 12, 2000; 1,773 dosage units of liquid PCP seized on June 11, 2001; and 33 kilograms of liquid PCP on July 31, 2001. DEA, state, and local authorities also seized two PCP laboratories in 1999 and two in 2000.

FLUNITRAZEPAM

Flunitrazepam is sold under the trade name Rohypnol, from which the street name "Rophy" is derived. Other street names include "circles," "Mexican valium," "roofies," and "R-2." Flunitrazepam is a depressant used in the treatment of short-term insomnia and as a hypnotic sedative and pre-anesthetic medication.

Flunitrazepam is manufactured worldwide, particularly in Europe and Latin America, where it is sold legally by prescription. This drug is neither manufactured nor approved for medical use in the United States. Distributors in Texas allegedly travel to Mexico to obtain the drug. In addition, Colombian sources of supply smuggle Flunitrazepam into South Florida via international mail services and/or couriers using commercial airlines.

Figure 5.2 Drug Trafficking in the U.S. (cont.)

According to law enforcement officials in south Florida, Flunitrazepam is routinely referred to as a "club drug," since it is popular in local nightclubs. It is also referred to as the "date rape drug," characteristically causing the victim to experience short-term memory loss after ingestion. It is ingested orally, frequently in conjunction with alcohol or other drugs. High school and college students are the most frequent users of Flunitrazepam, commonly using it as an "alcohol extender." Young people also have the misconception that Flunitrazepam is unadulterated, and, therefore, "safe" because of pre-sealed bubble packaging.

GHB/GBL

GHB (gamma hydroxybutyrate), a central nervous system depressant, was banned by the FDA in 1990. On February 18, 2000, President William J. Clinton signed the Hillory J. Farias and Samantha Reid Date-Rape Prohibition Act of 2000. This legislation makes GHB a Schedule I drug under the Controlled Substance Act (CSA).

GHB generates feelings of euphoria and intoxication. It is often combined in a carbonated, alcohol, or health food drink, and is reportedly popular among adolescents and young adults attending raves and nightclubs. At lower doses, GHB causes drowsiness, nausea, and visual disturbances. At higher dosages, unconsciousness, seizures, severe respiratory depression, and coma can occur.

GHB has been used in the commission of sexual assaults because it renders the victim incapable of resisting, and may cause memory problems that could complicate case prosecution. GHB recipes are accessible over the Internet; the drug is simple to manufacture, and can be made in a bathtub or even a Pyrex baking dish. DEA, along with state and local law enforcement agencies, seized 17 GHB laboratories in 2000, 10 of which were located in California.

GBL (gamma butyrolactone), an analog of GHB, is also abused. GBL is a chemical used in many industrial cleaners and it also has been marketed as a health supplement. GBL is synthesized by the body to produce GHB. One 55-gallon drum yields 240,000 capfuls of GBL. One capful sells for $8.00, potentially yielding 1.9 million dollars per 55-gallon drum.

STEROIDS

The Anabolic Steroid Control Act was passed by Congress in the fall of 1990 and became effective on February 21, 1991. The Steroid Act classified 27 steroids as Schedule III substances under the CSA.

Figure 5.2 Drug Trafficking in the U.S. (cont.)

Street prices of anabolic steroids have increased substantially as a result.

Fitness clubs have been, and continue to be, the primary distribution centers of steroids, since bodybuilders and weight lifters comprise a predominant portion of the user population. Once viewed as a problem strictly associated with professional athletes, a recent survey of students indicates increased steroid use among boys in the 8th and 10th grades. The percentage of 8th grade boys reporting past-year use of steroids increased from 1.6 percent in 1998 to 2.5 percent in 1999, and from 1.9 percent to 2.8 percent among 10th grade boys.

Anabolic steroids are illicitly smuggled from Mexico and European countries to the United States. Recent DEA reporting indicates that Russian and Romanian nationals are significant traffickers of steroids and are responsible for substantial shipments of steroids entering the United States. The lack of international control over foreign sources of supply, however, makes it impossible to attack the trafficking at its source.

MARIJUANA

Marijuana has long been the most extensively available and commonly abused illicit drug throughout the United States. In 2001, the most recent year for which statistics are available, approximately 21 million of an estimated 28.4 million past-year illicit drug users (aged 12 and older) reported marijuana use in the past year. These figures increased significantly from 2000 when 18.6 million of an estimated 24.5-million past-year illicit drug users reported past-year marijuana use. Use of marijuana often occurs sequentially or concurrently with the use of other illicit drugs.

Most of the foreign-produced marijuana in the United States originates in, or transits through, Mexico before being smuggled across the U.S. - Mexican border. Mexican drug trafficking organizations, with extensive networks within the United States, control the transportation of marijuana that is both smuggled through, and between, Ports of Entry along the U.S. Southwest border.

Reporting indicates that Mexican and other Hispanic drug trafficking organizations are the dominant wholesale distributors of most foreign-produced marijuana in the United States. Many of these organizations also distribute cocaine, methamphetamine, and heroin. Mexican organizations are deepening their involvement in domestic cannabis cultivation. Reportedly, Mexico-based drug trafficking organizations supply workers, or otherwise control cannabis cultivation, at sites in California, including those on Forest Service lands, and at sites in Arkansas, Idaho, Oregon, Utah, and Washington. The cultivation of cannabis within the United States affords Mexican drug trafficking organizations two identifiable advantages: domestic cultivation diminishes the risk of law enforcement detection, as the necessity of smuggling marijuana across the border into the Unites States is eliminated while domestic cultivation increases profit margins by growing and selling marijuana closer to market.

Home Grows

Most of the marijuana that is sold and used in the United States is smuggled in from Mexico. Some of the production comes from home grow operations. The marijuana plants are grown in remote locations or potted and grown indoors. The advantage to growing indoors in a year round controlled environment to increase production. Law enforcement agencies look for unusually high utilities bills when investigating suspected home grow operations. The five leading states for home grows in the United States are California, Florida, Oregon, Washington and Wisconsin. Canada is a source country for high-potency marijuana known as "BC Bud."

METHAMPHETAMINE

Commonly referred to on the street as speed, meth, ice, crystal, or glass, methamphetamine is a synthetically produced central nervous system stimulant that produces effects similar to cocaine. It metabolizes much slower than cocaine therefore it has longer lasting effects. It produces effects including increased alertness and euphoria, as well as increases in heart rate, blood pressure, respiration, and body temperature. Agitation, tremors, hypertension, memory loss, hallucinations, psychotic episodes, paranoid delusions, and violent behavior can result from chronic abuse.

Powder methamphetamine, known as crystal methamphetamine is the most common form in the United States. Ice, also known as glass, is similar in appearance to rock candy, crushed ice, or broken glass. Ice is a very pure form of methamphetamine and is more addictive than the other forms. The pill form of methamphetamine is popular is Asia and is just getting to the United States.

In the 1980s to the mid-1990s, Power Meth was made and sold by outlaw motorcycle gangs such as the Hells Angels, the Bandidos, the Outlaws and the Pagans. Since the mid-1990s, Mexican criminal groups have dominated the market. Meth is made in clandestine laboratories located in Mexico and California and distributed throughout the United States. The laboratories can be small mom and pop operations or "super labs" that can produce ten pounds or more of methamphetamine in a 24-hour period. Power Meth is distributed in the West, Midwest, Northwest and portions of the South.

Historically, criminal groups from South Korea, Taiwan, or China supplied Ice to Guam, Hawaii, and parts of California. In the United States the distribution, sale, and consumption of Ice in the Los Angeles area have been centered in the Asian community. In the mid-1990s, the same Mexican criminal groups trafficking in power meth also produced and sold Ice and at a price significantly less than rival Asian trafficking groups. The increase availability of Ice has lead to wider distribution and use. Ice can now be found in Ohio, Florida, New York, and Virginia.

Figure 5.3 U.S. Department of Justice Press Release

News Release FOR IMMEDIATE RELEASE April 15, 2003

Over 65 Arrested in International Methamphetamine Investigation

Law Enforcement Officials Announce Victory From left to right:

John Clark, Bureau of Immigration and Customs Enforcement (ICE); Raf Souccar, RCMP; David B. Palmer, IRS; and Roger Guevara, the Chief of Operations at the DEA.

Today, the Drug Enforcement Administration (DEA) and the Royal Canadian Mounted Police (RCMP) announced the arrests of over 65 individuals in ten cities throughout the United States and Canada. The arrests are the result of an 18month international investigation targeting the illegal importation of pseudoephedrine, an essential chemical used in methamphetamine production.

This investigation, dubbed Operation Northern Star, employed a comprehensive top to bottom strategy targeting the entire methamphetamine trafficking process, including the suppliers of precursor chemicals, chemical brokers, transporters, manufacturers, distributors, and the money launderers who helped conceal their

Figure 5.3 U.S. Department of Justice Press Release (cont.)

criminal proceeds. Arrests occurred in: Detroit; Chicago; Los Angeles; Riverside, California; New York; Cincinnati; Gulfport, Mississippi; Montreal; Quebec; Vancouver, British Colombia; and Ottawa, Ontario.

As part of this investigation, agents targeted 6 executives from 3 Canadian chemical companies: G.C. Medical Products, Formulex, and Frega, Inc. The executives arrested today have all sold bulk quantities of pseudoephedrine to methamphetamine manufacturers in the United States. They did so with the full knowledge that their sales were intended for the illegal production of the highly addictive and dangerous drug methamphetamine.

"Methamphetamine is a devastating, addictive drug that destroys human dignity, tears apart families, and disrupts the peace and security of our communities," said Assistant Attorney General Michael Chertoff of the Criminal Division. "We believe that Operation Northern Star has disrupted a major pseudoephedrine pipeline from Canada and sent a clear message to pharmaceutical companies there and elsewhere that they will be held criminally responsible for dispensing their products in the United States for illegal use."

Roger Guevara, DEA's Chief of Operations, said, "Operation Northern Star sends a message to people at all stages of meth production that the community of nations is becoming far less tolerant of executives who are willing to destroy other people's lives so they can line their own pockets."

Raf Souccar, RCMP

"Today, you have witnessed the power of integrated policing. As criminal organizations do not respect borders, it takes true cooperation between law enforcement in our respective countries to bring transnational criminal organizations to justice," said Superintendent Raf Souccar of the RCMP. "We have done this and we will continue to do this as the DEA and the RCMP are committed to working together to enforce the law to its fullest extent."

Operation Northern Star is the fourth in a series of investigations targeting the illegal diversion and importation of pseudoephedrine. Pseudoephedrine is a regulated chemical commonly found in over the counter sinus medications but also diverted and used in producing methamphetamine. Prior investigations regarding illegal use of pseudoephedrine were Operations Mountain Express I, II, and III.

Figure 5.3 U.S. Department of Justice Press Release (cont.)

Operations Mountain Express I and II targeted the domestic diversion of pseudoephedrine, primarily by individuals and companies registered by DEA to handle controlled substances and chemicals. With the success of these investigations and enhanced regulatory oversight by DEA, methamphetamine producers began to find it increasingly difficult to obtain sufficient quantities of pseudoephedrine domestically. As a result, they turned to Canada where pseudoephedrine was readily available in bulk quantities. In response, Operation Mountain Express III was initiated to address the importation of Canadian pseudoephedrine. In January 2002, Mountain Express III concluded with the arrest of over 100 defendants.

Thereafter, further investigation revealed that other pseudoephedrine brokers had stepped in to fill the void created by the Mountain Express III arrests. Investigators and analysts also determined that several Canadian pharmaceutical companies were continuing to export huge quantities of pseudoephedrine with knowledge or in deliberate ignorance of the fact that the ultimate consumers were methamphetamine producers in the United States. Operation Northern Star was initiated to address these developments.

During the course of Operation Northern Star, pseudoephedrine brokers identified in Chicago, Cincinnati, Detroit, and Los Angeles arranged for bulk pseudoephedrine shipments from Canada, most of which entered the U.S. through Detroit, Michigan in tractortrailer trucks often hidden beneath "cover loads" of legitimate products like bottled water and bubble gum.

In some instances these brokers, many of whom are of Middle Eastern origin, had direct contact with Canadian pharmaceutical company officials. One company, Frega, Inc. is charged criminally in Detroit for its role in supplying bulk quantities of pseudoephedrine to brokers in Cincinnati and Chicago. Approximately 14,000 pounds (108 million tablets) of pseudoephedrine originating from Frega, Inc. was seized during this investigation. This pseudoephedrine, believed to be destined for meth labs in the western United States, would yield approximately 9,000 pounds of methamphetamine with a street value of between $36 and $144 million.

According to court documents and DEA statistics, trafficking in pseudoephedrine is a lucrative business. One box of Canadian pseudoephedrine containing 80,000 60mg tablets can be purchased in Canada for approximately $900 U.S. currency. After going through two to three brokers, that box of pseudoephedrine would be sold to

> ### Figure 5.3 U.S. Department of Justice Press Release (cont.)
>
> meth manufacturers in California for $18,000 to $20,000. The New York indictment charges that some of these pseudoephedrine brokers were assisted in laundering their drug proceeds by two individuals who transferred the proceeds through bank accounts in the Middle East using a form of the ancient "Hawala" money transfer system.
>
> The DEA and the RCMP were assisted in this investigation by numerous state and local departments and the following federal agencies: the Bureau of Immigration and Customs Enforcement (ICE), the Federal Bureau of Investigation (FBI), the Internal Revenue Service (IRS), the National Drug Intelligence Center (NDIC), and the Financial Crimes Enforcement Network (FinCEN).
>
> Operation Northern Star was coordinated by a joint law enforcement program called the Special Operations Division which is comprised of agents and analysts from the DEA, FBI, ICE, IRS, and NDIC and attorneys from the Department of Justice's Criminal Division.
>
> Michael J. Garcia, Assistant Secretary Designee of the Bureau of Immigration and Customs Enforcement, said, "Operation Northern Star represents a great example of crossborder cooperation. Thanks to the joint efforts of U.S. and Canadian authorities, methamphetamine lab operators in this country have been denied a huge source of precursor chemicals. This case should have significant impact on the ability of meth traffickers to make and sell their deadly product."
>
> David B. Palmer, Chief of Criminal Investigation for the Internal Revenue Service, stressed the importance of IRS participation in Operation Northern Star by saying, "For the IRS, the link between where the money comes from, who gets it, when it is received, and where it is stored or deposited can provide proof of criminal activity."

COCAINE

Crack and Cocaine

Cocaine is a powerfully addictive drug of abuse. Once having tried cocaine, an individual cannot predict or control the extent to which he or she will continue to use the drug.

The major routes of administration of cocaine are sniffing or snorting, injecting, and smoking (including free-base and crack cocaine). Snorting is the process of inhaling cocaine powder through the nose where it is absorbed into the bloodstream through the nasal tissues.

Injecting is the act of using a needle to release the drug directly into the bloodstream. Smoking involves inhaling cocaine vapor or smoke into the lungs where absorption into the bloodstream is as rapid as by injection.

"Crack" is the street name given to cocaine that has been processed from cocaine hydrochloride to a free base for smoking. Rather than requiring the more volatile method of processing cocaine using ether, crack cocaine is processed with ammonia or sodium bicarbonate (baking soda) and water and heated to remove the hydrochloride, thus producing a form of cocaine that can be smoked. The term "crack" refers to the crackling sound heard when the mixture is smoked (heated), presumably from the sodium bicarbonate.

There is great risk whether cocaine is ingested by inhalation (snorting), injection, or smoking. It appears that compulsive cocaine use may develop even more rapidly if the substance is smoked rather than snorted. Smoking allows extremely high doses of cocaine to reach the brain very quickly and brings an intense and immediate high. The injecting drug user is at risk for transmitting or acquiring HIV infection/AIDS if needles or other injection equipment is shared. Cocaine is a strong central nervous system stimulant that interferes with the reabsorption process of dopamine, a chemical messenger associated with pleasure and movement. Dopamine is released as part of the brain's reward system and is involved in the high that characterizes cocaine consumption.

Physical effects of cocaine use include constricted peripheral blood vessels, dilated pupils, and increased temperature, heart rate, and blood pressure. The duration of cocaine's immediate euphoric effects, which include hyper-stimulation, reduced fatigue, and mental clarity, depends on the route of administration, the faster the absorption, the more intense the high. On the other hand, the faster the absorption, the shorter the duration of action. The high from snorting may last 15 to 30 minutes, while that from smoking may last 5 to 10 minutes. Increased use can reduce the period of stimulation.

Some users of cocaine report feelings of restlessness, irritability, and anxiety. An appreciable tolerance to the high may be developed, and many addicts report that they seek but fail to achieve as much pleasure as they did from their first exposure. Scientific evidence suggests that the powerful neuropsychological reinforcing property of cocaine is responsible for an individual's continued use, despite harmful physical and social consequences. In rare instances, sudden death can occur on the first use of cocaine or unexpectedly thereafter. However, there is no way to determine who is prone to sudden death.

High doses of cocaine and/or prolonged use can trigger paranoia. Smoking crack cocaine can produce a particularly aggressive paranoid behavior in users. When addicted individuals stop using cocaine, they often become depressed. This also may lead to further cocaine use to alleviate depression. Prolonged cocaine snorting can result in ulceration of the mucous membrane of the nose and can damage the nasal septum enough to cause it to collapse. Cocaine-related deaths are often a result of cardiac arrest or seizures followed by respiratory arrest.

Figure 5.4 U.S. Department of Justice Press Release

News Release FOR IMMEDIATE RELEASE June 9, 2003

**FIRST MAINE MET DEPLOYMENT
RESULTS IN 26 ARRESTS**

New England Field Division SAC Mark R. Trouville and Lewiston Maine Police Chief Bill Welch announcing the successful culmination of the first MET deployment in Maine Which resulted in 26 arrests.

JUN 9 Lewiston, ME Mark R. Trouville, Special Agent in Charge of the Drug Enforcement Administration in New England; Bill Welch, Chief of the Lewiston Maine Police Department; Richard Small, Chief of the Auburn Maine Police Department; Roy McKinney, Director of the Maine Drug Enforcement Agency; and Paula Silsby, United States Attorney announced today the arrest of 26 individuals for cocaine and crack cocaine violations.

These twenty-six defendants are facing a variety of charges including the distribution of cocaine and the distribution of crack cocaine. Approximately (kilogram of crack cocaine was seized during this investigation as well as approximately (kilogram of powder cocaine. A facet of this investigation resulted in the identification and arrest of four defendants whose organization distributed significant amounts of powder cocaine in Lewiston. Arrested were:

William BRYANT, 33 of Lewiston;

Michael GILBERT, 30 of So Paris ;

Carlos Alfredo HUERTAS , 30 of Miami, FL; and

Figure 5.4 U.S. Department of Justice Press Release

Michael RODRIGUEZ, 59 of Miami, FL

BRYANT and GILBERT were charged last month with conspiracy both to distribute 500 grams or more of powder cocaine and to possess that amount of drug with intent to distribute.

HUERTAS and RODRIGUEZ were also charged last month with conspiracy both to distribute an unspecified amount of powder cocaine and to possess powder cocaine with intent to distribute. Both are currently detained in Florida awaiting removal to Maine.

Undercover DEA agents traveled from Lewiston to Miami where they met with the sources of supply and negotiated for multi-kilograms of cocaine.

"The individuals who believe trafficking in drugs is a viable occupation in Maine have just been given notice, " said DEA Special Agent in Charge Trouville. "Trafficking these poisons into our neighborhoods is an unconscionable act and one that will not be tolerated. Today here in Lewiston, the power of cooperative law enforcement has been demonstrated. Through the hard work of all these agencies there are now fewer purveyors of destruction on the streets of Maine."

The DEA Mobile Enforcement Team had been deployed in the Lewiston Maine area since February 2003 at the invitation of Chief Welch and Chief Small. This is the first MET deployment in Maine and more arrests are anticipated.

"Thanks to the efforts of this special team, there are fewer drug traffickers on the streets of central Maine this afternoon," Silsby said. "These arrests demonstrate a continuing federal commitment to work cooperatively with state and local enforcement to help make Lewiston/Auburn and all Maine communities free from illegal drugs."

CLUB DRUGS

"Club Drugs" is a general term for a number of illicit drugs, primarily synthetic, that are most commonly encountered at nightclubs and "raves." The drugs include MDMA, ketamine, GHB, GBL, Rohypnol, LSD, PCP, methamphetamine, and, to a lesser extent, psilocybin mushrooms. The drugs have gained popularity primarily due to the false perception that they are not as harmful, nor as addictive, as mainstream drugs such as cocaine and heroin.

The dangers associated with this emerging drug market are that drug quality may vary significantly, and customers are often unaware that drug substitutions may occur when suppliers are unable to provide the drug currently in demand. This has been a problem with MDMA in some markets across the United States because "look-alike" substances, such as paramethoxyamphetamine (PMA) and dextromethorphan (DXM), are sold as MDMA. In addition, in a small percentage of cases, MDMA tablets have been found to contain other substances such as ketamine, PCP, caffeine, ephedrine, or methamphetamine. Since club drug users usually do not have a steady distribution network on which to depend, they unwittingly risk taking dangerous combinations of drugs. Not only can this lead to a greater risk of a drug overdose, the lack of knowledge regarding what drug was ingested can complicate the task of emergency medical response personnel.

INTERNATIONAL CARTELS

Columbian Cartels

The Columbian cartels are a group of drug dealers that come from the same city. The two best-known cartels are the Cali and Medellin cartels. The Medellin cartel was supposedly formed in 1978 when Carlos Lehder, a young marijuana smuggler, purchased a large portion of Normans Cay, a small island off the coast of the Bahamas. Lehder convinced the other kingpins to begin using airplanes to bring larger loads of cocaine into the United States using his property in the Bahamas as a refueling point. Prior to that, the loads were smuggled into the United States in luggage. The Medellin cartel was known for its violence which eventually leads to the destruction of the cartel. The cartel waged a war against the Columbian government in the late 1980s after one of its cocaine factories was raided and burned. Rodriguez Gacha was gunned down by the Colombian police, Jorge, Juan David and Fabio Ochoa turned themselves into the Colombian government in the early 1990s in exchange for a lenient prison terms. Pablo Escobar was hunted and killed by the Colombian police with help from the Cali cartel.

Cali Cartel

The Rodriguez Orejuela brothers and Santacruz Londono made up the Cali cartel. They were subtler than the Medellin cartel. In addition to their smuggling activities they reinvested their profits into legitimate businesses. They also began to expand their cocaine smuggling venture to Europe and Asia. They invested heavily in political protection. The cartel leaders were arrested in the mid-1990s and are currently serving 10 to 15 year prison terms. Some believe this was an arrangement with the Colombian government and they are still running their business empire from their prison cells.

OTHER CRIMINAL ORGANIZATIONS INVOLVED IN DRUGS

Chinese Organizations

Triads

The best organized and a significant threat in Asian heroin trafficking. The Triad was a secret society formed in the 17th century as a resistance group. Beginning about 1911, the group began in trafficking opiates. After the collapse of the Nationalist government in 1949, the group fled China to seek refuge in Hong Kong and Taiwan. In 1989, the Department of Justice estimated that the Triad had 100,000 members in 50 Triads in Hong Kong.

The Triads have rigid chain of command. After the leader is a deputy and under him are two assistants. One assistant is the ceremonial officer and the other handles recruiting. Below them are the hit men and enforcers who have direct control of some operational Triad groups. At the same levels are the general administrators who handle liaisons between Triads and other groups. The remainder of the organization is the soldiers.

The Triads get revenue through gambling and drugs. They are involved in opium products at the wholesale level. They do not normally get involved in street level sales.

Tongs

During the 1840s and 1850s, California experienced a large influx of Chinese immigrants. Resentment by whites caused the Chinese to form a fraternal society to protect members. The Chinese worked as manual laborers on railroads and in gold mines. Tong gangs at the railroad construction camps began to form. The gangs spread to large urban areas such as San Francisco and New York where they gained control of the gambling and opium trade in the Chinese community.

The Tongs never expanded beyond the Chinese community because of a language barrier, historical background and differences in culture.

Japanese Yakuza

The Japanese Yakuza may be the largest organized crime group in the world with more than 110,000 members belonging to some 2,500 gangs. The Yakuza was formed during the 16th and 17th centuries by dissident Samurai warriors. After World War II, the Yakuza's prospered in the black market then made a dramatic change in their business. They began to get involved in prostitution, drug trafficking and racketeering. They used their profits to infiltrate legitimate businesses in entertainment, sports, and labor unions. They were known for their willingness to use brutal enforcement tactics.

The group acts as an exporter of illegal goods to and from the United States and Japan and vise-versa. The group is said to control 80% of all cargo on the docks of Japan, and is known to smuggle amphetamines and firearms from the United States to Japan. The group has used its profits to invest in legitimate businesses in Hawaii, Los Angeles, Las Vegas, Denver and San Francisco.

Jamaican Posses

The Jamaican gangs began appearing in the United States in the mid-1980s, mainly on the east coast. They are estimated to have a U.S. membership of about 100,000 with the majority of its members convicted felons and illegal aliens. They are known for their street violence.

They are heavily involved in the crack cocaine industry and marijuana smuggling. They obtain their cocaine from the Columbians or Cubans. They are a vertically integrated organizations handling their own importation, wholesale, distribution, and money laundering to maximize their profits.

Jamaican grown marijuana is known for its high concentration of THC, which is why it is in high demand. It is estimated that about 14% of the marijuana that is smuggled into the United States comes from Jamaica. The Jamaicans smoke and drink in a concoction known as "green tea."

It is estimated that there are 30 posses operating in the United States, with thousands of members. They operate in Jamaican neighborhoods and their names correspond to the names of each of the neighborhoods in which they operate. The posses maintain close ties.

Afghanistan

Prior to the U.S. invasion of Afghanistan in 2001, the Islamic State of Afghanistan was and still is a major source country for the cultivation, processing and trafficking of opiate and cannabis products, producing approximately 70 per cent of the world's illicit opium. Afghanistan was 90 percent controlled by the Taliban, a fundamentalist Islamic group. A loose coalition of opposition forces, referred to as the Northern Alliance, maintains control of portions of northern Afghanistan.

Afghanistan produces morphine base, heroin and hashish. Morphine base is produced for drug traffickers based in Turkey. The Heroin and Hashish are trafficked worldwide. The precursor chemicals needed in the production process, mainly acetylating agent for heroin processing, are smuggled in from Pakistan, India, the Central Asian Republics, China and Europe. After the invasion of Afghanistan by the U.S., the trafficking is controlled by local "warlords."

Golden Triangle

The Golden Triangle consists of Burma, Thailand and Laos. Mexican heroin production decreased in the late 1970s due to enforcement, eradication and poor weather conditions. At the same time, production of heroin in Southeast Asia accelerated dramatically. By 1976, the golden Triangle supplied more than a third of the heroin consumed in the United States.

Burma produces about 90 per cent of the opium from the Golden Triangle. About two-thirds of this crop is produced in the northeast area of the country, where the Burmese Communist Party (BCP) and the Shan United Army (SUA) share control. The BCP and the SUA levy taxes and fees from the traffickers in exchange for protection of their illicit enterprises.

The crops are taken by horse and donkey to refineries along the Thailand-Burma border for conversion to heroin and heroin base transport the opium and morphine base produced in northeastern Burma. The finished products are shipped across the border into various towns in North Thailand and down to Bangkok for further distribution to international markets.

CASE STUDIES

Manuel Noriega

 In December 1989, soldiers from Operation Just Cause, the U.S. invasion of Panama, kicked opened the door of General Manuel Noriega's office to arrest him. Instead of finding General Noriega they found a good deal of cash, pornographic materials, a collection of porcelain frogs and a framed picture of Adolf Hitler.

On January 3, 1990, General Noriega surrendered to American authorities from his refuge in the Papal Nuncio. After his arrest, he was flown to Florida. On July 10, 1992, General Noriega was sentenced to 40 years without parole in a federal prison for eight counts of drug smuggling, conspiracy and racketeering.

The case against General Noriega began in 1985 when a light plane containing a shipment of smuggled cocaine made a forced landing on a Florida highway, nearly hitting a DEA agent's car. That pilot became a confidential informant and revealed the identity of the plane's owner, a Panamanian named Floyd Carlton. Carlton, a Noriega henchman, was apprehended and also turned informant. That led to the case against General Noriega.

General Noriega was a CIA operative since the 1970s. This allowed Noriega to operate safely. Noriega was involved with the U.S. involvement in Central America during the 1980s. Guns to arm the counter-revolutionaries against Nicaragua's Sandinista government were flown south on airplanes owned by CIA companies. Cocaine was the return cargo bound for the United States from Columbia.

Columbia Cartels-Pablo Escobar

Pablo Escobar was born in 1949 the son of a peasant framer and a schoolteacher in Medellin, Columbia. He was expelled from school and began a career as a thief in Medellin. He got his start in cocaine delivering cocoa paste from the Andean Mountains to the laboratories in Medellin.

Eventually, Escobar moved up to a drug smuggler using planes carrying small amounts to limit his financial exposure in case of detection by law enforcement agencies. By the age of 30, Escobar had made enough money from smuggling cocaine in the United States that he purchased the Hacienda Napoles for $63 million, his own helicopter, a private zoo and thousands of acres throughout Colombia.

Approximately 1981, Escobar formed a loose business arrangement with his biggest competition, the three Ochoa brothers. This new partnership became known as the Medellin cartel. They began to combine cocaine from all four organizations in each load to minimize their loss to seizures. The group was soon running five flights a week into the United States and Escobar personally was making a million dollars a day. With this Escobar invested millions back into Columbia. He purchased a soccer field and sponsored a soccer team, set up social programs for poor people, hired poor people to do construction, hired poor people to run some of his businesses, and hired teachers for the local schools. His generosity provided him with a power base among the people of Columbia.

In 1982, Escobar ran in the Congressional election and was elected as a substitute congressman. Senior congress member Rodrigo Lara Bonilla fought to have Escobar removed from the Congress. Under pressure Escobar stepped down in 1984. Bonilla was assassinated in retaliation for his comments.

During Escobar's reign he was one of the most ruthless and violent criminals in the history of Columbia. His violent acts lead to a new word, Narco-Terrorism. Among his most violent acts are the killing of newspaper reporters who wrote articles against him, a bombing outside the police headquarters which killed 63 and wounded 600, and the killing of three presidential candidates in Columbia including one aboard an Avianca jet in 1989.

All this violence created immense pressure for the Columbian government to take actions, and Escobar struck a deal with the government to build his own prison for a term of five years after which he would be set free with a law degree. His prison was known as la Catedral had a Jacuzzi, a discotheque, a spacious living room. He had visitors come and go as he pleased. On one occasion, Escobar had three men executed inside the compound. After the new president heard about this, he dispatched the military to arrest Escobar and send him to a normal prison.

Escobar learned of this plan to put him in a normal prison and escaped prior to his arrest. Escobar's whereabouts was learned by pinpointing his location during a call he made to his son. On December 2, 1993, Escobar was killed in a gunfight.

The Pizza Connection

During the late 1970s and early 1980s member of La Cosa Nostra in the United States allegedly cooperated with the Sicialina Mafia in a drug trafficking conspiracy, which resulted in the importation of heroin worth over $1.6 billion into the United States. In April of 1984, 38 individuals were indicted on charges related to the trafficking operation, popularly known as the "Pizza Connection."

The Bonanno crime family ran the Pizza Connection. Camine Galante was the leader of the Bonanno crime family. Salvatore Catalano served has his capo in 1976 after Catalano arranged for the murder of Pietro Licata. The neighborhood where the Bonanno family operated saw a large influx of Sicilians in the mid-1970s. In 1979, Galante was murdered. That cleared the way for Catalano to take over the Bonanno crime family. Catalano was born in Sicily in 1941 and was favored by the Sicilians in the neighborhood. Catalano made a deal with the Sicilians to supply heroin to be distributed through a chain of pizza parlors. The Sicilians needed a partner they could trust and understand and Catalano was that person. The heroin came from the Golden Triangle via Italy. Around 1980, again Philip Rastelli took over the reigns of the Bonanno crime family after his release from jail. This left Catalano more time to concentrate on the heroin business.

Direct evidence of the existence of the network was first obtained in 1980 when couriers were observed transferring enormous amounts of cash through investment houses and banks in New York. One of the couriers for this laundering operation was Franco Della Torre, a Swiss resident. In March 1982, Della Torre deposited slightly more than $1 million in $5, $10 and $20 bills in an account at the Manhattan office of Merrill Lynch Pierce Fenner and Smith. Torre made four additional cash deposits totaling $3.9 million in the same account in late March and mid-April 1982.

Torrre would request that security personnel accompany him from his hotel to Merrill Lynch offices. After several such deposits, it was decided by Merrill Lynch it would be better to escort Della Torre directly to Bankers Trust, where Merrill Lynch maintained accounts. Torre refused to enter the money room at Bankers Trust because of the presence of surveillance cameras. Merrill Lynch New York became suspicious and contacted the account managers in Zurich, Switzerland who assured them the account was in order, however, Merrill Lynch decided to close the account.

Torre then moved his account to E.F. Hutton and Company and over the next two years, his heroin networked laundered $25.4 million.

SUMMARY

Conspiracy laws are especially useful in the prosecution of drug organizations. As drug organizations vertically integrate their organizations to include manufacturing, transportation, and distribution of their products the conspiracy laws are used to disrupt and dismantle the entire organization. The drug industry requires many people to operate and the conspiracy laws allows for the prosecution of all involved. It also enables the organizers to be charged for the actual crimes from which they isolate themselves.

DISCUSSION QUESTIONS

1. Prepare an organizational chart for a drug organization that manufactures, transports and distributes cocaine.
2. What is the drugs organization in your geographical area, i.e. Chinese, Jamaican posses?
3. What are the most common drugs in your geographical area? If those drugs come from outside your geographical area, what is the most likely route that they take from the source?

ADDITIONAL READING

Ecstasy and Other Designer Drug Dangers, Myra Weatherly, Hardcover, Enslow Publishers, Inc, 2000

Inhalant Drug Dangers, Judy Monroe, Handcover, Enslow Publishers, Inc. 1999

Facts on the Crack and Cocaine Epidemic, Clint Twist, Franklin Watts, 1989

BIBLIOGRAPHY

United States Code Annotated, Title 21

Department of Justice, Drug Enforcement Administration, www.dea.gov and www.drugabuse.gov

Chapter 6

Terrorism

CHAPTER OVERVIEW

In this chapter you will look at the definition of terrorism, its history, terrorism in both the international and domestic areas, the motivation of terrorist organizations, currents trends in terrorism and current threats.

CHAPTER OBJECTIVES

1. Be able to define terrorism.
2. Know the history of terrorism.
3. Understand some of the key laws used to fight terrorism.
4. Know the currents trends of terrorism including suicide bombers and chemical, biological, radiological and nuclear devices (CBRN).
5. Know about some of the current threats including Al Qaeda, Hezballah and Hamas.

DEFINITION OF TERRORISM

Terrorism is the systematic use of terror or unpredictable violence against governments, publics, or individuals to attain a political objective. Terrorism has been used by political organizations with both rightist and leftist objectives, by nationalistic and ethnic groups, by revolutionaries, and by the armies and secret police of governments themselves.

Terrorism is defined in the U.S. by the Code of Federal Regulations as: "the unlawful use of force and violence against persons or property to intimidate or coerce a government, the civilian population, or any segment thereof, in furtherance of political or social objectives."

HISTORY OF TERRORISM

While it is impossible to definitively ascertain when it was first used, that which we today call terrorism traces its roots back at least some 2,000 years. Moreover, today's terrorism has, in some respects come full circle, with many of its contemporary practitioners motivated by religious convictions something, which drove many of their earliest predecessors. It has also, in the generally accepted usage of the word, often possessed a political dimension.

Among the earliest such examples were the Sicari and the Zealots, Jewish groups active during the Roman occupation of the first century Middle East. The favored weapon of the Sicari was the sica (the short dagger which gave them their name, which literally means "dagger men"), which they used these to murder those (mainly Jews) they deemed apostate and thus selected for execution. The Zealots, who generally targeted Romans and Greeks, give us the modern term Zealot, one translation of which is "a fanatical partisan." Such killings usually took place in daylight and in front of witnesses, with the perpetrators using such acts to send a message to the Roman authorities and those Jews who collaborated with them a tactic that would also be used by subsequent generations of what would become known as terrorists.

Adherents of other religions also resorted to methods, which might today be termed terrorism, such as the Assassins an 11th century offshoot of a Shia Muslim sect known as the Ismailis. Like the Zealots-Sicari, the Assassins were also given to stabbing their victims (generally politicians or clerics who refused to adopt the purified version of Islam they were forcibly spreading) in broad daylight. The Assassins whose name gave us the modern term but literally meant "hashish-eater" a reference to the ritualistic drug-taking they were (perhaps falsely) rumored to indulge in prior to undertaking missions also used their actions to send a message. Often, the Assassins' deeds were carried out at religious sites on holy days a tactic intended to publicize their cause and incite others to it. Like many religiously inspired terrorists today, they also viewed their deaths on such operations as sacrificial and a guarantor that they would enter paradise.

Sacrifice was also a central element of the killings carried out by the Thugees (who bequeathed us the word "thug") an Indian religious cult who ritually strangled their victims (usually travelers chosen at random) as an offering to the Hindu goddess of terror and destruction, Kali. In this case, the intent was to terrify the victim (a vital consideration in the Thugee ritual) rather than influence any external audience.

Active from the seventh until the mid-19th centuries, the Thugees are reputed to be responsible for as many as 1 million murders. They were perhaps the last example of religiously inspired terrorism until the phenomenon reemerged a little over 20 years ago.

The English word "terrorism" comes from the regime de la terreur that prevailed in France from 1793-1794. Originally an instrument of the state, the regime was designed to consolidate the power of the newly installed revolutionary government, protecting it from elements considered "subversive." Always value-laden, terrorism was, initially, a positive term. The French revolutionary leader, Maximilien Robespierre, viewed it as vital if the new French Republic was to survive its infancy, proclaiming in 1794 that: "Terror is nothing other than justice, prompt, severe, inflexible; it is therefore an emanation of virtue; it is not so much a special principle as it is a consequence of the general principle of democracy applied to our country's most urgent needs."

Under such justification, some 40,000 people were executed by guillotine a fate Robespierre and his top lieutenants would themselves suffer when later that same year, his announcement of a new list of subversives led to a counter-inquisition by some in the Revolutionary government who feared their names might be on the latest roll of "traitors." Before long, the Revolution devoured itself in an orgy of paranoiac bloodletting. Meanwhile, terrorism itself began taking on the negative connotations it carries today.

The newly defined notions of nationalism and citizenship, which both caused and were a result of the French Revolution, also saw the emergence of a new predominantly secular terrorism. The appearance of political ideologies such as Marxism also created a fertile sense of unrest at the existing order, with terrorism offering a means for change. The Italian revolutionary Carlo Pisacane's theory of the "propaganda of the deed", which recognized the utility of terrorism to deliver a message to an audience other than the target and draw attention and support to a cause, typified this new form of terrorism.

Pisacane's thesis, which was not in itself new and would probably have been recognizable to the Zealots-Sicari and the Assassins, was first put into practice by the Narodnaya Volya (NV). A Russian Populist group (whose name translates as the People's Will) formed in 1878 to oppose the Tsarist regime. The group's most famous deed, the assassination of Alexander II on March 1, 1881, also effectively sealed their fate by incurring the full wrath of the Tsarist regime. Unlike most other terrorist groups, the NV went to great lengths to avoid "innocent" deaths, carefully choosing their targets usually state officials who symbolized the regime and often compromising operations rather than causing what would today be termed "collateral damage."

The NV's actions inspired radicals elsewhere. Anarchist terrorist groups were particularly enamored of the example set by the Russian Populists (although not, it must be noted, their keenness to avoid casualties among bystanders). Nationalist groups such as those in Ireland and the Balkans adopted terrorism as a means towards their desired ends. As the 19th century gave way to the 20th, terrorists attacks were carried out as far a field as India, Japan, and the Ottoman empire, with two U.S. presidents and a succession of other world leaders victims of assassination by various anarchists and other malcontents often affiliated to groups but operating without their explicit knowledge or support.

As with Europe, terrorism arrived on America's shores before the 20th century. Not only were Anarchists active in America throughout the 1880s, but the country's recent Civil War had seen acts deserving of the name committed on both sides as well as the formation of the Ku Klux Klan to fight the Reconstruction effort which followed.

Long before the outbreak of Word War I in Europe in 1914, what would later be termed state-sponsored terrorism had already started to manifest. For instance, many officials in the Serbian government and military were involved (albeit unofficially) in supporting, training and arming the various Balkan groups which were active prior to the assassination of the Archduke Franz Ferdinand on June 28, 1914 in Sarajevo (an act carried out by an activist from one such group, the "Young Bosnians" and credited with setting in progress the chain of events which led to the war itself. Similarly, the IMRO (Macedonian Revolutionary Organization) survived largely "because it became for all intents and purposes a tool of the Bulgarian government, and was used mainly against Yugoslavia and well as against domestic enemies. As such examples illustrate, state-sponsored terrorism is not a new phenomenon.

The 1930s saw a fresh wave of political assassinations deserving of the word terrorism. This led to proposals at the League of Nations for conventions to prevent and punish terrorism as well as the establishment of an international criminal court (neither of which came to ought as they were overshadowed by the events which eventually led to World War II). Despite this, during the interwar years, terrorism increasingly referred to the oppressive measures imposed by various totalitarian regimes, most notably those in Nazi Germany, Fascist Italy and Stalinist Russia. More recently, other governments, such as those military dictatorships, which ruled some South American countries in recent years, or the current regime in Zimbabwe, have also been open to charges of using such methods as a tool of state. Such considerations notwithstanding, some commentators argue that 'such usages are generally termed terror in order to distinguish that phenomenon from "terrorism," which is understood to be violence committed by non-state entities."

By contrast, the preponderance of non-state groups in the terrorism that emerged in the wake of World War II is less debatable. The immediate focus for such activity mainly shifted from Europe itself to that continent's various colonies. Across the Middle East Asia and Africa, nascent nationalist movements resisted European attempts to resume colonial business as usual after the defeat of the Axis powers. That the colonialists had been so recently expelled from or subjugated in their overseas empires by the Japanese provided psychological succor to such indigenous uprisings by dispelling the myth of European invincibility.

Often, these nationalist and anti-colonial groups conducted guerilla warfare, which differed from terrorism mainly in that it tended towards larger bodies of "irregulars" operating along more military lines than their terrorist cousins, and often in the open from a defined geographical area over which they held sway. Such was the case in China and Indochina, where such forces conducted insurgencies against the Kuomintang regime and the French colonial government respectively. Elsewhere, such as with the fight against French rule in Algeria, these campaigns were fought in both rural and urban areas and by terrorist and guerilla means.

Still other such struggles like those in Kenya, Malaysia, Cyprus and Palestine (all involving the British who, along with the French, bore the brunt of this new wave of terrorism a corollary of their large pre-war empires) were fought by groups who can more readily be described as terrorist. These groups quickly learned to exploit the burgeoning globalization of the world's media. Moreover, in some cases (such as in Algeria, Cyprus, Kenya and Israel) terrorism arguably helped such organizations in the successful realization of their goals. As such these nationalist and anti-colonial groups are of note in any wider understanding of terrorism.

Through the 1960s and 1970s, the numbers of those groups that might be described as terrorist swelled to include not only nationalists, but also those motivated by ethnic and ideological considerations. The former included groups such as the Palestinian Liberation Organization (and its many affiliates), the Basque ETA, and the Provisional Irish Republican Army, while the latter comprised organizations such as the Red Army Faction (in what was then West Germany) and the Italian Red Brigades. As with the emergence of modern terrorism almost a century earlier, the United States was not immune from this latest wave, although there the identity-crisis-driven motivations of the white middle-class Weathermen starkly contrasted with the ghetto-bred malcontent of the Black Panther movement.

Like their anti-colonialist predecessors of the immediate post-war era, many of the terrorist groups of this period readily appreciated and adopted methods that would allow them to publicize their goals and accomplishments internationally. Forerunners in this were the Palestinian groups who pioneered the hijacking of a chief symbol and mean of the new age of globalization the jet airliner as a mode of operation and publicity. One such group, Black September, staged what was (until the attacks on America of September 11, 2001) perhaps the greatest terrorist publicity coup then seen, with the seizure and murder of 11 Israeli athletes at the 1972 Olympic Games. Such incidents resulted in the Palestinian groups providing the inspiration (and in some cases mentorship and training) for many of the new generation of terrorists' organizations.

Many of these organizations have today declined or ceased to exist altogether, while others, such as the Palestinian, Northern Irish and Spanish Basque groups, motivated by more enduring causes, remain active today although some now have made moves towards political rather than terrorist methods. Meanwhile, by the mid-1980s, state-sponsored terrorism reemerged, the catalyst for the series of attacks against American and other Western targets in the Middle East. Countries such as Iran, Iraq, Libya and Syria came to the fore as the principle such sponsors of terrorism. Falling into a related category were those countries, such as North Korea, who directly participated in covert acts of what could be described as terrorism.

Such state-sponsored terrorism remains a concern of the international community today (especially its Western constituents), although it has been somewhat overshadowed in recent times by the re-emergence of the religiously inspired terrorist. The latest manifestation of this trend began in 1979, when the revolution that transformed Iran into an Islamic republic led it to use and support terrorism as a means of propagating its ideals beyond its own border. Before long, the trend had spread beyond Iran to places as far a field as Japan and the United States, and beyond Islam to ever major world religion as well as many minor cults. From the Sarin attack on the Tokyo subway by the Aum Shinrikyo in 1995 to the Oklahoma bombing the same year, religion was again added to the complex mix of motivations that led to acts of terrorism. The al Qaeda attacks of September 11, 2001, brought home to the world, and most particularly the United States, just how dangerous this latest mutation of terrorism is.

TERRORISM LAWS

§2332. Criminal penalties

(a) Homicide. Whoever kills a national of the United States, while such national is outside the United States, shall

(1) If the killing is murder (as defined in section 1111(a)), be fined under this title, punished by death or imprisonment for any term of years or for life, or both;

(2) If the killing is a voluntary manslaughter as defined in section 1112(a) of this title, be fined under this title or imprisoned not more than ten years, or both; and

(3) If the killing is an involuntary manslaughter as defined in section 1112(a) of this title, be fined under this title or imprisoned not more than three years, or both.

(b) Attempt or conspiracy with respect to homicide. Whoever outside the United States attempts to kill, or engages in a conspiracy to kill, a national of the United States shall

(1) In the case of an attempt to commit a killing that is a murder as defined in this chapter, be fined under this title or imprisoned not more than 20 years, or both; and

(2) In the case of a conspiracy by two or more persons to commit a killing that is a murder as defined in section 1111(a) of this title, if one or more of such persons do any overt act to effect the object of the conspiracy, be fined under this title or imprisoned for any term of years or for life, or both so fined and so imprisoned.

(c) Other conduct. Whoever outside the United States engages in physical violence

(1) With intent to cause serious bodily injury to a national of the United States; or

(2) With the result that serious bodily injury is caused to a national of the United States; shall be fined under this title or imprisoned not more than ten years, or both.

(d) Limitation on prosecution. No prosecution for any offense described in this section shall be undertaken by the United States except on written certification of the Attorney General or the highest ranking subordinate of the Attorney General with responsibility for criminal prosecutions that, in the judgment of the certifying official, such offense was intended to coerce, intimidate, or retaliate against a government or a civilian population.

§2332a. Use of Certain Weapons of Mass Destruction

(a) Offense against a national of the United States or within the United States. A person who, without lawful authority, uses, threatens, or attempts or conspires to use, a weapon of mass destruction (other than a chemical weapon as that term is defined in section 229F)

(1) Against a national of the United States while such national is outside of the United States;

(2) Against any person within the United States, and the results of such use affect interstate or foreign commerce or, in the case of a threat, attempt, or conspiracy, would have affected interstate or foreign commerce; or

(3) Against any property that is owned, leased or used by the United States or by any department or agency of the United States, whether the property is within or outside of the United States, shall be imprisoned for any term of years or for life, and if death results, shall be punished by death or imprisoned for any term of years or for life.

(b) Offense by national of the United States outside of the United States. Any national of the United States who, without lawful authority, uses, or threatens, attempts, or conspires to use, a weapon of mass destruction (other than a chemical weapon (as that term is defined in section 229F)) outside of the United States shall be imprisoned for any term of years or for life, and if death results, shall be punished by death, or by imprisonment for any term of years or for life.

§2332b. Acts of Terrorism Transcending National Boundaries

(a) Prohibited acts.

(1) Offenses. Whoever, involving conduct transcending national boundaries and in a circumstance described in subsection (b)

(A) Kills, kidnaps, maims, commits an assault resulting in serious bodily injury, or assaults with a dangerous weapon any person within the United States; or

(B) Creates a substantial risk of serious bodily injury to any other person by destroying or damaging any structure, conveyance, or other real or personal property within the United States or by attempting or conspiring to destroy or damage any structure, conveyance, or other real or personal property within the United States; in violation of the laws of any State, or the United States, shall be punished as prescribed in subsection (c).

(2) Treatment of threats, attempts and conspiracies. Whoever threatens to commit an offense under paragraph (1), or attempts or conspires to do so, shall be punished under subsection (c).

(b) Jurisdictional bases.

(1) Circumstances. The circumstances referred to in subsection (a) are

(A) The mail or any facility of interstate or foreign commerce is used in furtherance of the offense;

(B) The offense obstructs, delays, or affects interstate or foreign commerce, or would have so obstructed, delayed, or affected interstate or foreign commerce if the offense had been consummated;

(C) The victim, or intended victim, is the United States Government, a member of the uniformed services, or any official, officer, employee, or agent of the legislative, executive, or judicial branches, or of any department or agency, of the United States;

(D) The structure, conveyance, or other real or personal property is, in whole or in part, owned, possessed, or leased to the United States, or any department or agency of the United States;

(E) The offense is committed in the territorial sea (including the airspace above and the seabed and subsoil below, and artificial islands and fixed structures erected thereon) of the United States; or

(F) The offense is committed within the special maritime and territorial jurisdiction of the United States.

(2) Coconspirators and accessories after the fact.

Jurisdiction shall exist over all principals and coconspirators of an offense under this section, and accessories after the fact to any offense under this section, if at least one of the circumstances described in subparagraphs (A) through (F) of paragraph (1) is applicable to at least one offender.

§2332d. Financial Transactions

(a) Offense. Except as provided in regulations issued by the Secretary of the Treasury, in consultation with the Secretary of State, whoever, being a United States person, knowing or having reasonable cause to know that a country is designated under section 6(j) of the Export Administration Act of 1979 (50 U.S.C. App. 2405) as a country supporting international terrorism, engages in a financial transaction with the government of that country, shall be fined under this title, imprisoned for not more than 10 years, or both.

§2332f. Bombings of Places of Public Use, Government Facilities, Public Transportation Systems and Infrastructure Facilities

(a) Offense.

(1) In general. Whoever unlawfully delivers, places, discharges, or detonates an explosive or other lethal device in, into, or against a place of public use, a state or government facility, a public transportation system, or an infrastructure facility

(A) With the intent to cause death or serious bodily injury, or

(B) With the intent to cause extensive destruction of such a place, facility, or system, where such destruction results in or is likely to result in major economic loss, shall be punished as prescribed in subsection (c).

(2) Attempts and conspiracies. Whoever attempts or conspires to commit an offense under paragraph (1) shall be punished as prescribed in subsection (c).

§2339. Harboring or Concealing Terrorists

(a) Whoever harbors or conceals any person who he knows, or has reasonable grounds to believe, has committed, or is about to commit, an offense under section 32 (relating to destruction of aircraft or aircraft facilities), section 175 (relating to biological weapons), section 229 (relating to chemical weapons), section 831 (relating to nuclear materials), paragraph (2) or (3) of section 844(f) (relating to arson and bombing of government property risking or causing injury or death), section 1366(a) (relating to the destruction of an energy facility), section 2280 (relating to violence against maritime navigation), section 2332a (relating to weapons of mass destruction), or section 2332b (relating to acts of terrorism transcending national boundaries) of this title, section

236(a) (relating to sabotage of nuclear facilities or fuel) of the Atomic Energy Act of 1954 (42 U.S.C. 2284(a)), or section 46502 (relating to aircraft piracy) of title 49, shall be fined under this title or imprisoned not more than ten years, or both.

§2339A. Providing Material Support to Terrorists

(a) Offense. Whoever provides material support or resources or conceals or disguises the nature, location, source, or ownership of material support or resources, knowing or intending that they are to be used in preparation for, or in carrying out, a violation of section 32, 37, 81, 175, 229, 351, 831, 842(m) or (n), 844(f) or (i), 930(c), 956, 1114, 1116, 1203, 1361, 1362, 1363, 1366, 1751, 1992, 1993, 2155, 2156, 2280, 2281, 2332, 2332a, 2332b, 2332f or 2340A of this title, section 236 of the Atomic Energy Act of 1954 (42 U.S.C. 2284), or section 46502 or 60123(b) of title 49, or in preparation for, or in carrying out, the concealment of an escape from the commission of any such violation, or attempts or conspires to do such an act, shall be fined under this title, imprisoned not more than 15 years, or both, and, if the death of any person results, shall be imprisoned for any term of years or for life. A violation of this section may be prosecuted in any Federal judicial district in which the underlying offense was committed, or in any other Federal judicial district as provided by law.

§2339B. Providing Material Support or Resources to Designated Foreign Terrorist Organizations

(a) Prohibited activities.

(1) Unlawful conduct. Whoever, within the United States or subject to the jurisdiction of the United States, knowingly provides material support or resources to a foreign terrorist organization, or attempts or conspires to do so, shall be fined under this title or imprisoned not more than 15 years, or both, and, if the death of any person results, shall be imprisoned for any term of years or for life.

INTERNATIONAL TERRORISM

According to the FBI, international terrorism involves violent acts dangerous to human life that are a violation of the criminal laws of the United States or any state, or that would be a criminal violation if committed with the jurisdiction of the United States or any state. These acts appear to be intended to intimidate or coerce a civilian population, influence the policy of a government by intimidation or coercion, or affect the conduct of a government by assassination or kidnapping. International terrorist acts occur outside the United States or transcend national boundaries in terms of the means by which they are accomplished, the person they appear intended to coerce or intimidate, or the locale in which the perpetration operates or seek asylum. Groups such as al Qaeda, Hamas and the Hezbollah are examples of international terrorist organizations.

DOMESTIC TERRORISM

According to the FBI, domestic terrorism is the unlawful use, or threatened use, of force or violence by a group or individual based and operating entirely within the United States or its territories without foreign direction committed against persons or property to intimidate or coerce a government, the civilian population, or any segment thereof, in furtherance of political or social objectives. The Ku Klux Klan is an example of a domestic terrorist organization.

MOTIVATION OF TERRORIST

The terrorists are motivated by political and religious reasons and use criminal acts to further their goals. Al Qaeda believes its terrorist acts are part of a religious war to eliminate the Westerners and other outsiders from their lands and control. The radical Muslims despise our way of life. They believe their society has been corrupted by our ways.

Terrorism itself is a criminal act, but they commit many criminal acts to further cause such as murder, kidnapping, extortion, and drug dealing. The Drug Enforcement Administration published a study in September 2002 relating to their drug business.

Figure 6.1 Drug Intelligence Brief

Drugs and Terrorism: A New Perspective
SEPTEMBER 2002

Introduction

Prior to September 11, 2001, drug trafficking and terrorist activities were usually addressed by the law enforcement community as separate issues. In the wake of the terrorist attacks in New York City, Washington, DC, and Pennsylvania, the public now perceives these two criminal activities as intertwined. For the Drug Enforcement Administration (DEA), investigating the link between drugs and terrorism has taken on renewed importance.

Throughout history, various aspects of the criminal world have been linked together, such as drug traffickers with connections to illegal gambling, prostitution, and arms dealing. Perhaps the most recognizable illustration of this linkage is the expansion of the Italian Mafia in the United States during the early 20th century. The links between various aspects of the criminal world are evident because those who use illicit activities to further or fund their lifestyle, cause, or well-being often interact with others involved in various illicit activities. For example, organizations that launder money for drug traffickers also launder money for arms traffickers, terrorists, etc. The link between drugs and terrorism is not a new phenomenon.

Globalization has made the world a smaller place, changing the face of both legitimate and illegitimate enterprise. Criminals, by exploiting advances in technology, finance, communications, and transportation in pursuit of their illegal endeavors, have become criminal entrepreneurs. Perhaps the most alarming aspect of this "entrepreneurial" style of crime is the intricate manner in which drugs and terrorism may be intermingled. Since September 11th , the public's image of terrorism is magnified. Not only is the proliferation of illegal drugs perceived as a danger, but also the proceeds from drugs are among the sources for funding for other criminal activities, including terrorism.

Narco-Terrorism

The nexus between drugs and violence is not new; in fact, it is as old as drug abuse itself. The mind-altering strength of drugs has always had the power to create violence, but there is another kind of connection between drugs and violence the use of drug trafficking to fund the violence perpetrated by terrorist groups.[1]

Within the context of current world events, narco-terrorism is difficult to define. Historically, DEA has defined narco-terrorism in

Figure 6.1 Drug Intelligence Brief (cont.)

terms of Pablo Escobar, the classic cocaine trafficker who used terrorist tactics against noncombatants to further his political agenda and to protect his drug trade. Today, however, governments find themselves faced with classic terrorist groups that participate in, or otherwise receive funds from, drug trafficking to further their agenda. In this respect, are narco-terrorists actual drug traffickers who use terrorism against civilians to advance their agenda? Or are narco-terrorists first and foremost terrorists who happen to use drug money to further their cause? Perhaps, the correct answer is that narco-terrorism may apply in both situations.

DEA defines a narco-terrorist organization as "an organized group that is complicit in the activities of drug trafficking in order to further, or fund, premeditated, politically motivated violence perpetrated against noncombatant targets with the intention to influence (that is, influence a government or group of people)."

The Pablo Escobar Example

One of the most infamous "narco-terrorists" was Pablo Escobar. As leader of the Medellin cocaine cartel in Colombia, he became one of the wealthiest and most feared men in the world. At the height of his success, Escobar was listed in Forbes Magazine among the world's wealthiest men. While on the surface, he was nothing more than a street thug who became successful by trafficking in cocaine, Escobar had political aspirations and strove to project the appearance of legitimacy, claiming his wealth was the result of real estate investments. He eventually ran for Congress and campaigned for foreign policy changes that would prohibit the extradition of Colombian citizens to the United States.

Escobar had a penchant for violence. He wreaked havoc on Colombia while attempting to persuade the government to change its extradition policy. Due to the numerous assassinations of politicians, presidential candidates, Supreme Court justices, police officers, and civilians, as well as a number of bombings culminating in the bombing of an Avianca commercial airliner in 1989, Escobar

Figure 6.1 Drug Intelligence Brief (cont.)

enraged both Colombia and the world. These actions resulted in a massive manhunt and his death in 1993.

Escobar was a drug trafficker who used drug-related violence and terrorism to further his own political, personal, and financial goals. Moreover, he funded his terrorist activities with the money obtained from his drug trafficking endeavors. He was the classic narco-terrorist; his cause was simply himself.

Terrorist organizations use a number of sources to garner funds for their activities, such as petty crimes, kidnap-for-ransom, charities, sympathizers, front companies, and drug trafficking. Most of the known terrorist organizations use several of these methods to collect funding, while preferring particular methods to others. Drug trafficking is among the most profitable sources. According to the Office of National Drug Control Policy (ONDCP), Americans alone spend an estimated $64 billion on illegal drugs annually.

Drug trafficking has always been a profitable means for criminal organizations to further or fund their activities. The complicity of terrorist groups in drug trafficking varies from group to group and region to region. In the broadest sense, some terrorist groups may be involved in all aspects of the drug trade, from cultivation, production, transportation, and wholesale distribution to money laundering. These groups may also provide security for drug traffickers transporting their product through territory controlled by terrorist organizations or their supporters. Finally, in some cases, terrorist groups or their supporters may require a "tax" to be paid on illicit products, or passage through controlled territory. No matter which form it takes, or the level of involvement in drug trafficking, many terrorist groups are using drug money to fund their activities and perpetrate violence against governments and people around the world.

Afghanistan Under the Taliban

As in the case of formerly Taliban-controlled Afghanistan, narco-terrorism was not limited to terrorist organizations. Afghanistan is a major source country for the cultivation, processing, and trafficking of opiates, producing over 70 percent of the world's supply of illicit opium in 2000. Because of the country's decimation by decades of warfare, illicit

Figure 6.1 Drug Intelligence Brief (cont.)

drugs have become a major source of income. The Taliban's Afghanistan would be an example of a state primarily funded by illicit opium production. Through this drug income, the Taliban were able to support and protect Osama bin Laden and the al Qaeda organization. As in this case, drugs and terrorism frequently share a common ground of geography, money, and violence.

Narco-Terrorism Versus Drug-Related Violence

When looking at the connection between drugs and violence, it is important to differentiate between drug-related violence and narco-terrorism. By definition, terrorism is premeditated, politically motivated violence perpetrated against noncombatant targets. With drug-related violence, we see financially motivated violence perpetrated against those who interfere with or cross the path of a drug trafficking organization. While we see drug-related violence on a daily basis on the streets of major cities, narco-terrorism is, in many cases, less visible. Drug-related violence permeates society at all levels and is visible at every stage of the drug trade, from domestic violence to turf warfare between rival drug trafficking gangs or groups.[2] With narco-terrorism, the acts of terror are clearly evident, but the funding source is often well-disguised.

Evolution of Narco-Terrorism

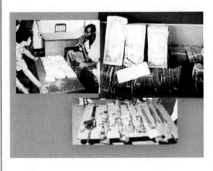

Any region, in which illegal drugs are cultivated, transported, distributed, or consumed, is susceptible to narco-terrorism. Throughout the world, insurgent groups, revolutionary groups, and ideological or spiritual groups, who use violence to promote their political mission may use drug proceeds to fund acts of terror in furtherance of their ideology. Leadership, cultural, political, and economic change may affect the ideology or mission of a group. Internal divisions and splinter groups may result, each seeking to pursue their goals via different avenues, be they legitimate political activity, perpetuation of violence, or criminal activity, such as drug trafficking.

History has shown that narco-terrorist organizations fall into different categories. One category includes politically motivated groups that use drug proceeds to support their terrorist activities; activities that will confer legitimacy upon them within the state.

Figure 6.1 Drug Intelligence Brief (cont.)

These groups usually call for a ceasefire with the government or take measures to establish a legal political party whereby their political goals are realized through nonviolent, legal means. Groups that fall into this category are generally viewed with skepticism by the state. An example of a group in this category is the Kurdistan Worker's Party (PKK).

Another category consists of groups that continually pursue their ideological goals while participating in aspects of the drug trade; for example, the Revolutionary Armed Forces of Colombia (Fuerzas Armadas Revolucionarias de Colombia or FARC).

There are notable examples of narco-terrorist groups in almost every corner of the world. Many insurgent and extremist groups are suspected of drug trafficking involvement, such as Hezbollah and the Islamic Resistance Movement (HAMAS) in the tri-border region of Paraguay, Argentina, and Brazil; Sendero Luminoso (the Shining Path) in Peru; and the Basque Fatherland and Liberty (ETA) in Spain. The level of involvement in drug trafficking by actual narco-terrorist groups and the evolution of the groups and their purposes are often very different.

Kurdistan Worker's Party

The PKK in Turkey was founded in 1974. Developed as a revolutionary socialist organization, the goal of the PKK is to establish an independent nation of Kurdistan. In 1984, the PKK began to use violence against Turkish security forces, gradually escalating the level of violence to include civilians. In the early 1990s, the group added urban terrorism to their repertoire of violent activities.

The PKK, considered a terrorist organization by most Western Governments, is represented in Kurdish immigrant communities throughout the world and is particularly prevalent in Europe.

The PKK is known to benefit from drug trafficking, but the extent of their involvement is often debated. The Government of Turkey consistently reports that the PKK, as an organization, is responsible for much of the illicit drug processing and trafficking in Turkey. Turkish press reports state that the PKK produces 60 tons of heroin per year and receives an estimated income of US$40 million each year from drug trafficking proceeds. According to historic DEA

Figure 6.1 Drug Intelligence Brief (cont.)

reporting, the PKK may receive funding from a number of illicit means, including kidnap-for-ransom and drugs.

Reporting from the early 1990s indicated that several large drug trafficking families were supporters or sympathizers of the PKK, and that direct funds from their trafficking organizations were provided to the PKK to buy supplies. However, recent changes in the structure of the organization, due in part to the group's founder declaring a peace initiative in 1999, have led elements of the PKK to strive for legitimacy and possible involvement in Turkey's political process.

Revolutionary Armed Forces of Colombia

The FARC is one of Colombia's major insurgent groups. The FARC is a pro-Communist group that wants to replace the current Colombian Government with a leftist, anti-U.S. regime. The FARC emerged in 1964 as the military wing of the Colombian Communist Party, with the goal of overthrowing the government and the ruling class of Colombia. The FARC is the largest, best-trained and equipped, and most effective insurgent group in Colombia. Over the past two decades, the FARC has controlled large areas of Colombia's eastern lowlands and rain forest, which are the primary coca cultivation and cocaine processing regions in the country.

The FARC is an economically self-sufficient organization, supporting its mission through kidnappings, extortion, bank robberies, and the drug trade. Some FARC fronts are promoting coca cultivation, managing cocaine processing, selling drugs for cash, and negotiating arms deals with international drug trafficking organizations to support their broad based weapons procurement program.

Recent DEA reporting indicates that some FARC units in southern Colombia are directly involved in drug trafficking activities, including controlling local cocaine base markets and selling cocaine to international smuggling organizations. At least one FARC front—the 16th Front—has served as a cocaine source of supply for one international drug trafficking organization.

In March 2002, the United States announced its indictment of several FARC members. This case marks the first time that members

Figure 6.1 Drug Intelligence Brief (cont.)

of a known terrorist organization have been indicted in the United States for their drug trafficking activities, including selling cocaine in exchange for currency, weapons, and equipment.

Despite the differences between the PKK and the FARC, both were initially motivated to take action in furtherance of their ideological goals—the desire for independent homelands or political thought. The drug trade and terrorist activities were the means through which these groups furthered their missions. Changes in leadership, politics, and economics affected the varying outcomes; that is, movement toward political legitimacy for the PKK, and pursuit of an ideological mission through engagement in the drug trade by the FARC.

International Efforts Against Narco-Terrorism

There are three crucial elements to attacking narco-terrorism: law enforcement efforts, intelligence gathering, and international cooperation. Many terrorist groups rarely act within the borders of one state, but tend to have a more global view in regard to their activities and fundraising. This means that combating narco-terrorism requires a global network of law enforcement and intelligence officials tackling this issue wherever it appears. It is the cooperation at all levels of law enforcement and intelligence organizations that will prevent atrocities such as those financed by drug money in South America, Southwest Asia, and the rest of the world.

Several international measures have been taken over the years to combat terrorism. According to the U.S. Department of State, there are 12 major multilateral conventions and protocols on combating terrorism.[3] International efforts to combat narco-terrorism are focusing on asset seizure and control of all funding sources used by terrorist organizations. In 1999, the International Convention for the Suppression of the Financing of Terrorism was adopted. It required signatories "to take steps to prevent and counteract the financing of terrorists, whether directly or indirectly, through groups claiming to have charitable, social or cultural goals or which also engage in such illicit activities as drug trafficking or gun running." Under this convention, signatories also were required to hold those who finance terrorism to be criminally, civilly, or administratively responsible for their acts.

In response to the incidents of September 11, 2001, the international community is expanding their efforts to control and extinguish financing that supports terrorism. On September 28, 2001,

Figure 6.1 Drug Intelligence Brief (cont.)

the United Nations Security Council unanimously adopted an anti-terrorism resolution that called for the suppression of terrorist group financing, and improved international cooperation against terrorists. The resolution, identified as Resolution 1373 (2001), requires all states to prevent and abolish the financing of terrorism, and to criminalize the willful collection and distribution of funds for such acts. Furthermore, the resolution created a committee to monitor the implementation of the guidelines set forth in this resolution. The Security Council noted, "the close connection between international terrorism and transnational organized crime, illicit drugs, money-laundering, illegal arms-trafficking, and illegal movement of nuclear, chemical, biological and other potentially deadly materials, emphasizes the need to enhance coordination of efforts on national, sub-regional, regional and international levels to strengthen a global response to this serious challenge and threat to international security."

Conclusion

The events of September 11th brought new focus to an old problem, narco-terrorism. These events have forever changed the world and demonstrate the vulnerability to acts of terrorism of even the most powerful nation. In attempting to combat this threat, the link between drugs and terrorism came to the fore. Whether it is a state, such as formerly Taliban controlled Afghanistan, or a narco-terrorist organization, such as the FARC, the nexus between drugs and terrorism is evident.

Nations throughout the world are aligning to combat this scourge on international society. The War on Terror and the War on Drugs are linked, with agencies throughout the United States and internationally working together as a force-multiplier in an effort to dismantle narco-terrorist organizations. Efforts to stop the funding of these groups have focused on drugs and the drug money used to perpetuate violence throughout the world. International cooperative efforts between law enforcement authorities and intelligence organizations is crucial to eliminating terrorist funding, reducing the drug flow, and preventing another September 11th.

Endnotes

1. According to Chapter 22 of the U.S. Code (USC), terrorism is the premeditated, politically motivated violence perpetrated against noncombatant targets by sub-national groups or clandestine agents. International terrorism involves citizens, or

Figure 6.1 Drug Intelligence Brief (cont.)

territory, of more than one country. A terrorist group is any group practicing, or that has significant sub-groups that practice, international terrorism.

2. According to the DEA Briefing Book, "one-quarter to one-half of all incidents of domestic violence are drug related".

CURRENT TRENDS

The 20th century witnessed great changes in the use and practice of terrorism. Terrorism became the hallmark of a number of political movements stretching from the extreme right to the extreme left of the political spectrum. Technological advances such as automatic weapons and compact, electrically detonated explosives gave terrorists a new mobility and lethality.

Terrorism has most commonly become identified, however, with individuals or groups attempting to destabilize or overthrow existing political institutions. Terrorism has been used by one or both sides in anticolonial conflicts (Ireland and the United Kingdom, Algeria and France, Vietnam and France/United States), in disputes between different national groups over possession of a contested homeland (Palestinians and Israel), in conflicts between different religious denominations (Catholics and Protestants in Northern Ireland), and in internal conflicts between revolutionary forces and established governments (Malaysia, Indonesia, the Philippines, Iran, Nicaragua, El Salvador, Argentina).

Terrorism's public impact has been greatly magnified by the use of modern communications media. Any act of violence is certain to attract television coverage, which brings the event directly into millions of homes and exposes viewers to the terrorists' demands, grievances, or political goals. Modern terrorism differs from that of the past because its victims are frequently innocent civilians who are picked at random or who merely happen into terrorist situations. Many groups of terrorists in Europe hark back to the anarchists of the 19th century in their isolation from the political mainstream and the unrealistic nature of their goals. Lacking a base of popular support, extremists substitute violent acts for legitimate political activities. Such acts include kidnappings, assassinations, skyjackings, bombings, and hijackings.

The Baader-Meinhof gang of West Germany, the Japanese Red Army, Italy's Red Brigades, the Puerto Rican FALN, al-Fatah and other Palestinian organizations, the Shining Path of Peru, and France's Direct Action were among the most prominent terrorist groups of the later 20th century.

Since the attacks of September 2001, in the United States at least, terrorism has largely been equated to the threat posed by al Qaeda a threat inflamed not only by the spectacular and deadly nature of the September 11 attacks themselves, but by the fear that future strikes might be even more deadly and employ weapons of mass destruction.

Whatever global threat may be posed by al Qaeda and its franchisees, the U.S. view of terrorism nonetheless remains, to a degree, largely egocentric despite the current administration's rhetoric concerning a so-called "Global War Against Terrorism." This is far from unique. Despite the implications that al Qaeda actually intends to wage a global insurgency, the citizens of countries such as Colombia or Northern Ireland (to name but two of those long faced with terrorism) are likely more preoccupied with when and where the next FARC or Real Irish Republican Army attack will occur rather than where the next al Qaeda strike will fall.

As such considerations indicate, terrorism goes beyond al Qaeda, which it not only predates but will also outlive. Given this, if terrorism is to be countered most effectively, any understanding of it must go beyond the threat currently posed by that particular organization. Without such a broad-based approach, not only will terrorism be unsolvable but it also risks becoming unmanageable.

Figure 6.2 Terrorism Statistics

Total International Terrorist Attacks, 1982-2003

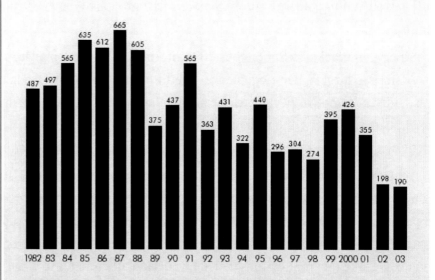

In past years, serious violence by Palestinians against other Palestinians in the occupied territories was included in the database of worldwide international terrorist incidents because Palestinians are considered stateless people. This resulted in such incidents being treated differently from intraethnic violence in other parts of the world. In 1989, as a result of further review of the nature of intra-Palestinian violence, such violence stopped being included in the US Government's statistical database on international terrorism. The figures shown above for the years 1984 through 1988 have been revised to exclude intra-Palestinian violence, thus making the database consistent.

Investigations into terrorist incidents sometimes yield evidence that necessitates a change in the information previously held true (such as whether the incident fits the definition of international terrorism, which group or state sponsor was responsible, or the number of victims killed or injured). As as result of these adjustments, the statistics given in this report may vary slightly from numbers cited in previous reports.

Figure 6.2 Terrorism Statistics (cont.)

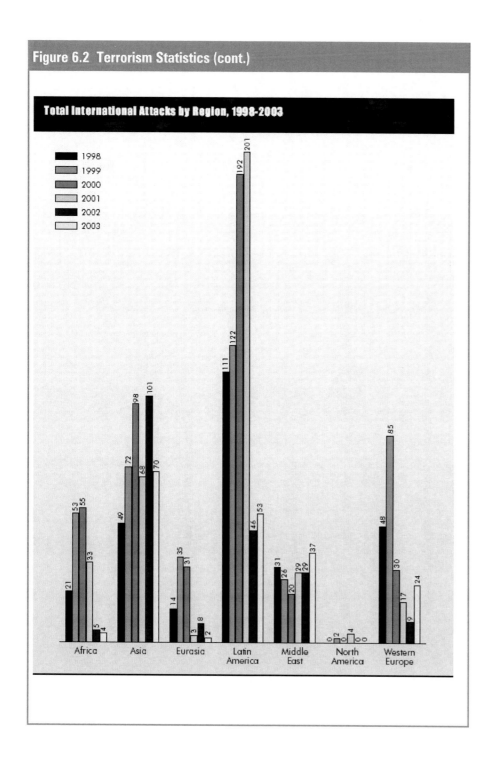

Total International Attacks by Region, 1998-2003

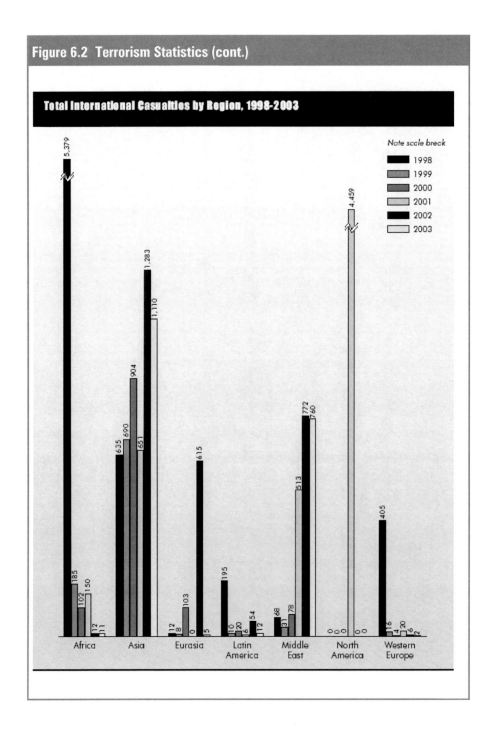

Figure 6.2 Terrorism Statistics (cont.)

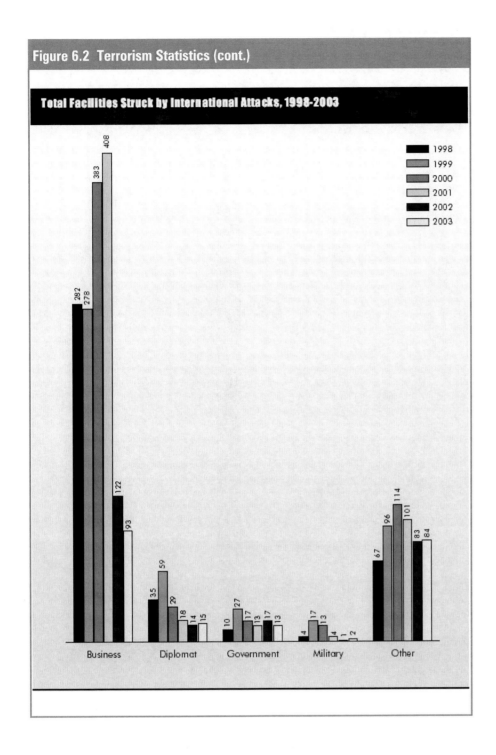

Figure 6.2 Terrorism Statistics (cont.)

Total Facilities Struck by International Attacks, 1998-2003

Legend:
- 1998
- 1999
- 2000
- 2001
- 2002
- 2003

Business: 282, 278, 383, 408, 122, 93
Diplomat: 35, 59, 29, 18, 14, 15
Government: 10, 27, 17, 13, 17, 13
Military: 4, 17, 13, 4, 1, 2
Other: 67, 96, 114, 101, 83, 84

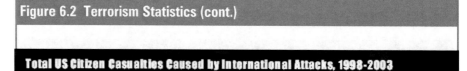

Figure 6.2 Terrorism Statistics (cont.)

Total US Citizen Casualties Caused by International Attacks, 1998-2003

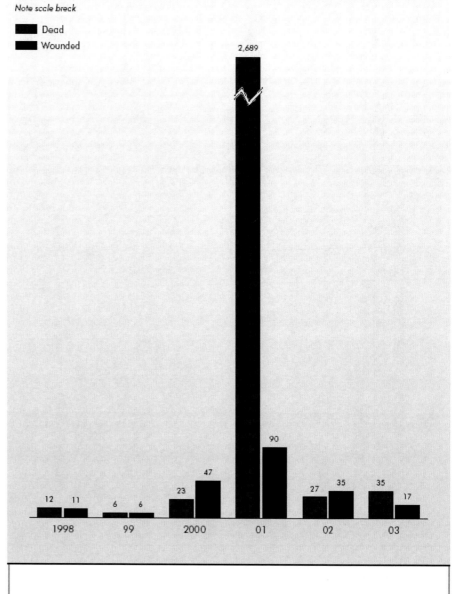

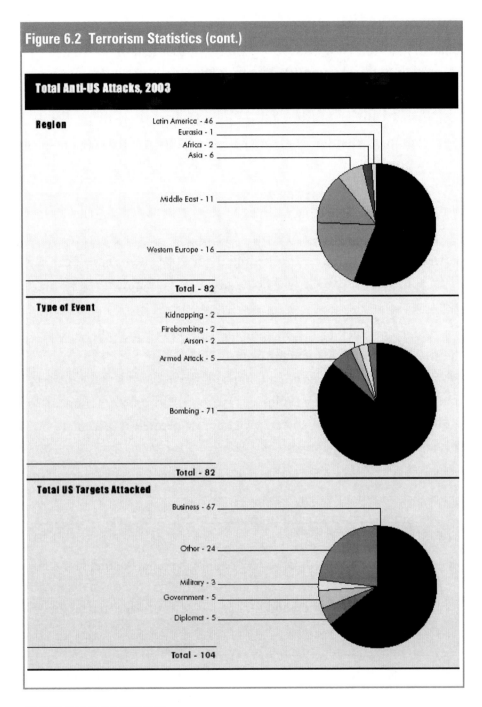

Figure 6.2 Terrorism Statistics (cont.)

SUICIDE BOMBERS

Suicide attacks have been carried out in Israel since 1993 and continued sporadically until 1999. Since the beginning of so-called "al-Aqsa Intifada," the Palestinian terrorist organizations, this time assisted by the Palestinian Authority, have once again begun perpetrating suicide bombings against the Israeli civilian population. Between October 2000 and July 2001, there were 18 suicide bombings in the disputed territories and in Israel. The two leading terrorist organizations perpetrating this type of attack are Hamas and The Islamic Jihad in Palestine. It was these organizations that first imported this type of attack into Israel in the 1990's. Activists from these two groups, who were deported from Israel to Lebanon, received in addition to spiritual motivation, military instruction from Hezballah and the Iranian "Revolutionary Guards" who provided hospitality for them in Lebanon. These organizations still receive assistance from Hezballah in the perpetration of terror attacks in general and suicide bombings in particular.

In general, suicide terror attacks in Israel are no different from those carried out worldwide. As of the middle of 2001, there have been well over 300 suicide attacks carried out in 14 countries by 17 terror organizations.

A suicide attack is an "operational method in which the very act of the attack is dependent upon the death of the perpetrator." The terrorist is fully aware that if he does not kill himself, the planned attack will not be implemented. Activating explosives worn or carried by the terrorist in the form of a portable explosive charge, or planted in a vehicle he is driving carries out the attack.

Suicide attacks are attractive to terrorist organizations, as they offer them a variety of advantages:

- Suicide attacks result in many casualties and cause extensive damage.
- Suicide attacks attract wide media coverage. A suicide attack is a newsworthy event for the media as it indicates a display of great determination and inclination for self-sacrifice on the part of the terrorists.

Although a suicide attack is a very primitive and simple attack, the use of suicide tactics guarantees that the attack will be carried out at the most appropriate time and place with regard to the circumstances at the target location. This guarantees the maximum number of casualties (in contrast to the use of technical means such as a time bomb or even a remote controlled explosive charge). In this regard the suicide bomber is no more than a sophisticated bomb a carrier that brings the explosive device to the right location and detonates it at the right time.

In a suicide attack, as soon as the terrorist has set off on his mission his success is virtually guaranteed. It is extremely difficult to counter suicide attacks once the terrorist is on his way to the target; even if the security forces do succeed in stopping him before he reaches the intended target, he can still activate the charge and cause damage. (Thus the need for accurate intelligence concerning the plans of the terrorist organizations is crucial).

Planning and executing the escape route after a terror attack has occurred is usually one of the most complicated and problematic stages of any terrorist attack. Suicide attacks require no escape plan.

Since the perpetrator is killed during the course of the suicide attack, there is no fear of him being caught afterwards, being interrogated by the security forces and passing on information liable to endanger other activists.

Suicide attacks are considered attractive by groups of religious and nationalistic fanatics who regard them as a kind of "Holy War" and a divine command. The phenomenon has seen a growing popularity especially among Islamist fundamentalist terror groups. Here we will focus on the Hamas; an organization that has carried out a number of suicide attacks against Israeli buses, markets and other civilian targets.

For Hamas, the perpetrator of the suicide attack is not considered either by himself or by other activists to have committed suicide. He is rather perceived to be a 'shahid" a martyr who fell in the process of fulfilling a religious command, the "Jihad" or "Holy War." Suicide attacks may provide the shahid and his families with substantial rewards: The majority of the shahids come from a low social status background. The shahid improves his social status after their death as well as that of his families.

The family of the shahid is showered with honor and praise, and receives financial rewards for the attack. In addition to the religious mission and the family rewards, the shahid also receives some personal benefits (according to his belief), including:

- Eternal life in paradise,
- The permission to see the face of Allah,
- And the loving kindness of 72 young virgins who will serve him in heaven.
- The shahid also earns a privilege to promise a life in heaven to 70 of his relatives.

Again, focusing on suicide attacks carried out by Hamas against Israeli targets, we can see a number of common characteristics of the shahid, which serve as a basic profile of the suicide bomber. These include:

- Young, usually from18 to 27 years of age,
- Usually not married, unemployed and from a poor family.
- Usually the shahid completed high school,
- Most were devoted students in the Islamic fundamentalist education centers in Gaza and in the West Bank directed and financed by Hamas.
- Some of the shahids arrested by Israel in the past have expressed the desire to avenge the death or injury of a relative or a close friend at the hands of Israel.

The reason for committing a suicide attack for most of the shahids is therefore first and foremost religious fanaticism combined with nationalist extremism, and a wish for revenge, but not personal despair.

Usually a shahid does not volunteer for his missions. His Islamic religious teacher at the mosques and Islamic education centers in Gaza and the West Bank may select the shahid. Usually the most devoted students are selected after a close examination by the teachers and over a long time of acquaintance. Sometimes the planner or the initiator of the attack on the basis of previous acquaintance picks the Shahid.

After the potential shahid is selected, he usually participates in long training sessions in order to test his attitudes and performance under pressure and in life-threatening situations. Only the trainees who are both willing and cool-headed are permitted to move on to the next stage.

Subsequently the shahid usually "disappears" from his home without farewell, while he begins several days of intensive training in order to understand all operational aspects of his mission and learn how to deal with the explosive device. At this time the shahid also undergoes a process of physical and mental purification.

Some of the terrorists who were trained to be shahids testified that at this stage they were taken to a graveyard and told to lie down inside one of the graves for several hours in order to overcome the fear of death.

On the last day before the attack the shahid is well trained, brain washed, and willing and able to execute the suicide attack. At his point he writes a will, in which he asks his family not to mourn him, because he did not die but rather was transformed to another life in which he will be with Allah. Also, he records a propaganda videocassette in which he is disguised (usually by wearing an IDF uniform or typical Israeli clothes and shaving his beard), he says a special prayer, and together with his collaborators he drives to the target area.

The shahid usually transports the explosive in a vehicle, sometimes even by bicycle or cart. Alternately the device is hidden in a bag or in a military vest under a coat.

Standard explosives run to about 3-15 kilograms of TNT or homemade explosives. In order to increase the damage small chunks of iron or a large quantity of nails are often packed around the explosives. The detonator is of a very simple design, which allows the perpetrator to activate the explosives at the proper time even when under pressure.

WEAPONS OF MASS DESTRUCTION/CHEMICAL, BIOLOGICAL, RADIOLOGICAL AND NUCLEAR DEVICES (CBRN)

Chemical and Biological

A wide range of potentially deadly chemical and biological (CB) agents including various insecticides, industrial chemicals and potent toxins such as ricin may be relatively easy to produce or otherwise acquire. Some deadly pathogens can be obtained through the mail from scientific supply houses; in other cases it is possible to harvest them from nature or to "grow your own" with relatively unsophisticated equipment and limited expertise. It may also be possible to steal deadly agents from civilian research facilities or military stockpiles, as reportedly has occurred in the case of chemical weapons, at least in the former Soviet Union. Nor is it inconceivable that a state sponsor of terrorism would be willing deliberately to provide terrorists with CB weapons or materials, if it could convince itself of "plausible deniability" while using a surrogate group to inflict a devastating blow on an enemy.

The effective dissemination of CB agents may be more difficult than their manufacture. For example, the popular scenario involving poisoning the water supply of a major metropolitan area does not appear very feasible, given the large quantities of agent that would be required and the various filtering or purification measures usually in place. It is also true that the lethality of some types of highly toxic agents depends crucially on the type of exposure; and that some of the deadliest agents, while perhaps suitable for individual assassinations, may not easily be adapted for use in a mass-casualty attack. The open-air release of an agent may be crucially affected by unpredictable or difficult-to-predict meteorological conditions, while even the release of an agent in a confined space may be subject to the vagaries of individual doses and air circulation patterns. Nevertheless, credible scenarios can be devised that, assuming optimal meteorological conditions and the most effective means of dispersal possible, could result in staggering numbers of fatalities, ranging well into the thousands for chemical agents and into the hundreds of thousands for biological.

The use of chemical weapons offers many advantages to terrorists. These include the limited capacity of detecting such weapons, the relatively low cost required developing them, their frightening image and psychological effect on the population, and potential damage. Terrorists thrive on the shock factor of their activities, and chemical warfare exhibits a high degree of immediate shock factor. Therefore, the use of chemical weapons might enhance many terrorist groups" images and provides extra incentive to the ambition to wreak mass-scale casualties and havoc.

Biological weapons are more destructive than chemical weapons, including nerve gas. Under certain circumstances, biological weapons can be as devastating as nuclear ones, a few military-grade, efficiently disseminated kilograms of anthrax can kill as many people as a Hiroshima-size nuclear attack. A terrorist group might choose to biological weapons because of their extreme destructive potential is concentrated in a relatively small and difficult to trace package, with virtually no detectable sensor signature. Because of the agent's incubation period, the perpetrators might be gone before anyone knew that an attack had been made. Finally, biological agents, unlike ballistic missiles, lend themselves to clandestine dissemination.

Chemical Agents

Terrorists have considered a wide range of toxic chemicals for attacks. Typical plots focus on poisoning foods or spreading the agent on surfaces to poison via skin contact, but some also includes broader dissemination techniques.

Cyanides

Terrorists have considered using a number of toxic cyanide compounds.

Sodium or potassium cyanides are whitetopale yellow salts that can be easily used to poison food or drinks. Cyanide salts can be disseminated as a contact poison when mixed with chemicals that enhance skin penetration, but may be detected since most people will notice if they touch wet or greasy surfaces contaminated with the mixture.

Hydrogen cyanide (HCN) and cyanogen chloride (ClCN) are colorless to pale yellow liquids that will turn into a gas near room temperature. HCN has a characteristic odor of bitter almonds, and ClCN has an acrid choking odor and causes burning pain in the victim's eyes. These signs may provide enough warning to enable evacuation or ventilation of the attack site before the agent reaches a lethal concentration.

Both HCN and ClCN need to be released at a high concentration only practical in an enclosed area to be effective, therefore, leaving the area or ventilating will significantly reduce the agent's lethality.

Exposure to cyanide may produce nausea, vomiting, palpitations, confusion, hyperventilation, anxiety, and vertigo that may progress to agitation, stupor, coma, and death. At high doses, cyanides cause immediate collapse. Medical treatments are available, but they need to be used immediately for severely exposed victims.

Mustard Agent

Mustard is a blister agent that poses a contact and vapor hazard. Its color ranges from clear to dark brown depending on purity, and it has characteristic garlic like odor. Mustard is a viscous liquid at room temperature.

Mustard is not commercially available, but its synthesis does not require significant expertise if a step-by-step procedure with diagrams is available.

Initial skin contact with mustard causes mild skin irritation, which develops into more severe yellow fluidfilled blisters. Inhalation of mustard damages the lungs, causes difficulty breathing, and death by suffocation in severe cases due to water in the lungs. For both skin contact and inhalation, symptoms appear within six to 24 hours. There are only limited medical treatments available for victims of mustard agent poisoning.

Nerve Agents

Sarin, tabun, and VX are highly toxic military agents that disrupt a victim's nervous system by blocking the transmission of nerve signals.

These agents are not commercially available, and their synthesis requires significant chemical expertise.

Exposure to nerve agents causes pinpoint pupils, salivation, and convulsions that can lead to death. Medical treatments are available, but they need to be used immediately for severely exposed victims. Toxic Industrial Chemicals

There are a wide range of toxic industrial chemicals that while not as toxic as cyanide, mustard, or nerve agents can be used in much larger quantities to compensate for their lower toxicity.

Chlorine and phosgene are industrial chemicals that are transported in shipments by road and rail. Rupturing the container can easily disseminate these gases. The effects of chlorine and phosgene are similar to those of mustard agent.

Organophosphate pesticides such as parathion are in the same chemical class as nerve agents. Although these pesticides are much less toxic, their effects and medical treatments are the same as for military grade nerve agents.

Biological Agents

Anthrax

Bacillus anthracis, the bacterium that causes anthrax, is capable of causing mass casualties. Symptoms usually appear within one to six days after exposure and include fever, malaise, fatigue, and shortness of breath. The disease is usually fatal unless antibiotic treatment is started within hours of inhaling anthrax spores; however, it is not contagious. Few people are vaccinated against anthrax.

Anthrax can be disseminated in an aerosol or used to contaminate food and water.

Cutaneous anthrax can be caused by skin contact with B. anthracis. This form of the disease, which is easily treated with antibiotics, is rarely fatal.

Botulinum toxin

Botulinum toxin is produced by the bacterium Clostridium botulinum, which occurs naturally in the soil. Crude but viable methods to produce small quantities of this lethal toxins have been found in terrorist training manuals.

Symptoms usually occur 24 to 36 hours after exposure, but onset of illness may take several days if the toxin is present in low doses. They include vomiting, abdominal pain, muscular weakness, and visual disturbance.

Botulinum toxin would be effective in smallscale poisonings or aerosol attacks in enclosed spaces, such as movie theaters. The toxin molecule is likely too large to penetrate intact skin.

Ricin

Ricin is a plant toxin that is 30 times more potent than the nerve agent VX by weight and is readily obtainable by extraction from common castor beans. There is no treatment for ricin poisoning after it has entered the bloodstream. Victims start to show symptoms within hours to days after exposure, depending on the dosage and route of administration.

Terrorists have looked at delivering ricin in foods and as a contact poison, although we have no scientific data to indicate that ricin can penetrate intact skin.

Ricin will remain stable in foods as long as they are not heated, and it will have few indicators because it does not have a strong taste and is offwhite in color.

Radiological and Nuclear Devices

Radiological Dispersal Devices (RDD)

In general, CB agents are considered to be cheaper and easier to produce or otherwise acquire than would be nuclear weapons. Nevertheless, the seizure in recent years of special nuclear materials on the black market in Europe, albeit in quantities insufficient to construct a nuclear explosive device, has lent new credibility to the threat of nuclear terrorism as well. The experts appear to disagree on whether a small group of technicians such as might be brought together by one of today's terrorist groups would be able to overcome the engineering difficulties of constructing a nuclear explosive device. Theft of an intact nuclear weapons is not considered very likely, given the stringent security measures in place in most of the nuclear-weapons states, although political instability and socio-economic decay in some of them, including the former Soviet Union, must remain of some concern. Tactical nuclear weapons, whose security features may be more vulnerable to tampering, are of greater concern than strategic nuclear weapons in this regard.

Of greatest concern from the viewpoint of a potential nuclear explosive capability may be the security of weapons-usable fissile material held in research institutes, naval fuel depots, and other similar nuclear facilities, especially in the former Soviet Union. However, a more likely threat of nuclear terrorism would be the radiological one, that is, the dispersal of radioactive substances to contaminate air or water, or to render unusable a particular area or facility. Radioactive materials that could be used for such contamination are available from a wide range of relatively non-secure facilities, including hospitals, medical and research laboratories, universities, waste dumps, and so forth.

An RDD is a conventional bomb not a yield producing nuclear device. RDDs are designed to disperse radioactive material to cause destruction, contamination, and injury from the radiation produced by the material. An RDD can be almost any size, defined only by the amount of radioactive material and explosives.

A passive RDD is a system in which unshielded radioactive material is dispersed or placed manually at the target.

An explosive RDD often called a "dirty bomb" is any system that uses the explosive force of detonation to disperse radioactive material. A simple explosive RDD consisting of a leadshielded container commonly called a "pig" and a kilogram of explosive attached could easily fit into a backpack.

An atmospheric RDD is any system in which radioactive material is converted into a form that is easily transported by air currents.

Use of an RDD by terrorists could result in health, environmental, and economic effects as well as political and social effects. It will cause fear, injury, and possibly lead to levels of contamination requiring costly and time consuming cleanup efforts.

A variety of radioactive materials are commonly available and could be used in an RDD, including Cesium137, Strontium90, and Cobalt60. Hospitals, universities, factories, construction companies, and laboratories are possible sources for these radioactive materials.

Improvised Nuclear Device (IND)

An IND is intended to cause a yield producing nuclear explosion. An IND could consist of diverted nuclear weapon components, a modified nuclear weapon, or indigenous designed device.

INDs can be categorized into two types: implosion and gun assembled. Unlike RDDs that can be made with almost any radioactive material, INDs require fissile material, highly enriched uranium or plutonium, to produce nuclear yield.

CURRENT THREATS

 ## Al Qaeda

The origins of al Qaeda are rooted in the Afghan resistance to the Soviet invasion from 1979 to 1989. Believing that the war with the Soviets was a holy battle between Islam and the infidel, Usama bin Laden, the son of a wealthy Saudi contractor, traveled to Afghanistan to aid the fight. At the time, Afghanistan lacked both the infrastructure and manpower for a protracted war. Bin Laden paid for their transportation and training, he imported specialists in guerilla warfare and other professional, while Afghan local leaders contributed land and resources.

Anywhere from 20,000 to 60,000 people, most of who were not native Afghans, received training and combat experience in Afghanistan. In 1988, bin Laden, broke with his ally to form al Qaeda (The Base) and carry on his jihad on a worldwide scale.

With the withdrawal of the Soviet Union from Afghanistan, bin Laden returned to Saudi Arabia to combat what he saw as an infidel Saudi government. Further angered by the U.S. presence in Saudi Arabia accompanying the Gulf War, bin Laden became even more outspoken in his ant-regime rhetoric. With his immediate family and a bank of followers, he moved to Sudan. His Saudi citizenship was revoked in 1994 for his opposition to the Saudi government. In Sudan, bin Laden established businesses, paved roads, built an airport, and created training camps to supply out-of-work mujahedin with jobs. In 1996, as Sudanese relations with the United States improved, the government of Sudan asked bin Laden to depart. He then returned to Afghanistan where he established his ties with the Taliban movement, followed by training camps and a terrorist infrastructure. This infrastructure supported a number of plots against the United States and its citizens.

Current goal is to establish a pan-Islamic Caliphate throughout the word by working with allied Islamic extremist groups to overthrow regimes it deems: non-Islamic and expelling Westerners and non-Muslims from Muslim countries, particularly Saudi Arabia. Issued statement under banner of "the World Islamic Front for Jihad Against the Jews and Crusaders" in February 1998, saying it was the duty of all Muslims to kill U.S. citizens, civilian or military, and their allies everywhere. Merged with Egyptian Islamic Jihad in June 2001. It was designated a Foreign Terrorist Organizations in October 1999.

In 2003, al Qaida carried out the assault and bombing on May 12th of three expatriate housing complexes in Riyadh, Saudi Arabia, that killed 20 and injured 139. They assisted in carrying out the bombings on May 16th in Casablanca, Morocco, of a Jewish center, restaurant, nightclub, and hotel that killed 41 and injured 101. Probably supported the bombing of the J.W. Marriott Hotel in Jakarta, Indonesia, on August 5th that killed 17 and injured 137. They were responsible for the assault and bombing on November 9th of a housing complex in Riyadh, Saudi Arabia that killed 17 and injured 100. They conducted the bombings of two synagogues in Istanbul, Turkey, on November 15th that killed 23 and injured 200 and the bombings in Istanbul of the British Consulate and HSBC Bank on November 20th that resulted in 27 dead and 455 injured. They have been involved in some attacks in Afghanistan and Iraq.

Other attacks include the September 11, 2001 attack on the World Trade Center that killed approximately 3,000 people. The October 12, 2000 attack on the USS Cole that killed 17 and injured another 39. The August 1998 attack of the U.S. Embassies in Nairobi, Kenya and Dar es Salaam, Tanzania that killed at least 301 individuals and injured more than 5,000. They attempted to kill Pope John Paul II and President Clinton.

Al Qaida probably has several thousand members and associates. The arrest of senior level al Qaida operatives has interrupted some terrorist plots. They serve as a focal point or umbrella organization for a worldwide network that includes many Sunni Islamic extremist groups.

Al Qaida was based in Afghanistan until coalition forces removed the Taliban from power in late 2001. Al Qaida has dispersed in small groups across South Asia, Southeast Asia, and the Middle East and probably will attempt to carry out future attacks against U.S. interest.

Al Qaida maintains moneymaking front businesses, solicits donations from like-minded supporters, and illicitly siphons funds from donations to Muslim charitable organizations. U.S. and international efforts to block al Qaida funding have hampered the group's ability to obtain money.

Hamas

Hamas was originally designated as a Foreign Terrorist Organization October 8, 1997. Hamas is a radical Islamic Palestinian organization that initially sought to expel Jews and the state of Israel from Israel/Palestine, and to establish an Islamic Palestinian state based on Islamic law. These goals appear to have been moderated somewhat in recent years, however, with indications that the group would likely accept a favorable Israeli-Palestinian agreement.

Hamas split off from the Palestinian Muslim Brotherhood organization in 1987, taking a much more militant line than its parent organization in terms of both Israel and the establishment of an Islamic state in Israel/Palestine. The group maintains both a social services wing that reportedly runs "clinics, kindergartens, orphanages, colleges, summer camps and even sports clubs," and a terrorist wing that carries out attacks against Israeli military and civilian targets. It social services wing has been very popular and important among Palestinians. Hamas carried out scores of bombings and has been among the most vigorous participants in the first and second Palestinian uprisings against Israel. The group has opposed the Middle East peace process and has positioned itself as a challenger to the Palestinian Authority in the Gaza Strip, which it criticizes for making concessions to Israel and for corrupt and ineffective government.

Since 1994, the primary terrorist tactic of Hamas has been suicide bombings. Hamas bombers have not generally fit the expected profile, sometimes including older men and people with relatively well paying jobs and families. The group also employed car bombings, mortar attacks, and assassinations. Hamas operates in the West Bank and Gaza Strip but is strongest in the latter. The group also has presences in Syria, Lebanon, and the Gulf States.

The number of official members is unknown. According to some estimates, the group has tens of thousands of supporters and sympathizers for its uncompromising anti-Israel position and its attacks against Israel, its opposition to corruption in the Palestinian Authority, and its network of social services.

Hamas reportedly receives some aid from Iran but apparently derives most of its financing from Palestinian expatriates around the world, private sympathizers in Arab states, and legitimate businesses in Palestinian controlled areas. Hamas is known to acquire money from charities operating in the West, reportedly including: The Palestinian Relief Development Fund (U.K.); the Holy Land Foundation (U.S.); Al Aqsa Foundation (Germany, Holland and Belgium); and Comite de Bienfaisance et Solidartie avec la Palestine (France).

Figure 6.3 U.S. Department of Justice Press Release

FOR IMMEDIATE RELEASE TUESDAY JULY 27 2004
WWW.USDOJ.GOV

HOLY LAND FOUNDATION, LEADERS, ACCUSED OF PROVIDING MATERIAL SUPPORT TO HAMAS TERRORIST ORGANIZATION

WASHINGTON, D.C. - Attorney General John Ashcroft, FBI Executive Assistant Director John Pistole, Homeland Assistant Secretary for Immigration and Customs Enforcement Michael J. Garcia, and IRS Commissioner Mark Everson announced today that the Holy Land Foundation and seven of its leaders were indicted on Monday by a federal grand jury in Dallas, Texas on charges of providing material support to HAMAS, a designated foreign terrorist organization.

The indictment, which was unsealed earlier today, alleges the Holy Land Foundation for Relief and Development ("HLF"), of Dallas, Texas, was an organization created by, among others,

Figure 6.3 U.S. Department of Justice Press Release (cont.)

defendants Shukri Abu-Baker, Mohammed El-Mezain, and Ghassan Elashi to provide financial and material support to the HAMAS movement. It is also alleged that, since 1995, HLF and its members have illegally sent $12.4 million to support HAMAS and its goal of creating an Islamic Palestinian state by eliminating the State of Israel through violent jihad. In addition to the charges of providing material support to a foreign terrorist organization, the 42-count indictment also charges the defendants with engaging in prohibited financial transactions with a Specially Designated Global Terrorist, money laundering, conspiracy and filing false tax returns. The indictment also seeks the forfeiture of $12.4 million in HAMAS assets.

"To those who exploit good hearts to secretly fund violence and murder, this prosecution sends a clear message: There is no distinction between those who carry out terrorist attacks and those who knowingly finance terrorist attacks," said Attorney General John Ashcroft. "The United States will ensure that both terrorists and their financiers meet the same, certain justice."

As the U.S. Government began to scrutinize individuals and entities in the United States who were raising funds for terrorist groups in the mid-1990s, the indictment alleges that the Holy Land Foundation intentionally cloaked their financial support for HAMAS behind the mantle of charitable exercise. The indictment alleges that the Foundation and the defendants provided financial support to the families of HAMAS martyrs, detainees, and activists knowing and intending that such assistance would support HAMAS" terrorist infrastructure. In screening potential aid recipients and in providing funds, the defendants allegedly distinguished between needy Palestinian families generally, and those Palestinian families who had a relative "martyred" or jailed as a result of terror activities. In some cases, the defendants allegedly targeted financial aid specifically for families related to well-known HAMAS terrorists who had been killed or jailed by the Israelis. In this manner, the defendants effectively rewarded past, and encouraged future, suicide bombings and terrorist activities on behalf of HAMAS. Since 1995, when it first became illegal to provide financial support to HAMAS, the Holy Land has allegedly provided over $12,400,000 in funding to HAMAS through various HAMAS affiliated committees and organizations located in Palestinian-controlled areas and elsewhere.

The defendants are charged with violating the prohibition against providing "material support and resources" to a foreign terrorist organization. The "material support statute," as it is commonly

Figure 6.3 U.S. Department of Justice Press Release (cont.)

referred to, was enacted in 1996 as part of the Antiterrorism and Effective Death Penalty Act, and has become one of our most effective weapons in the government's war on terrorist financing. The defendants are also charged with violating the International Emergency Economic Powers Act ("IIEPA"), which prohibits transactions that the Executive Branch has determined to be inimical to the national security of the United States, including transactions with HAMAS; as well as with money laundering and tax evasion.

HLF is alleged to have been so concerned about investigators uncovering the group's intentions that the defendants followed a manual entitled "The Foundations Policies and Procedures." The HLF followed security procedures outlined in the manual to include, as referenced in the indictment: hiring a security company to search the HLF for listening devices; ordering defendant Haitham Maghawri to take training on advanced methods in the detection of wiretaps; shredding documents after board meetings; and maintaining incriminating documents in off-site locations.

Besides the organization itself, the other defendants charged are: Shukri Abu Baker, the Secretary and Chief Executive Officer; Mohammed El-Mezain, the Director of Endowments; Ghassan Elashi, the Chairman of the Board; Haitham Maghawri, the Executive Director; Akram Mishal, the projects and grants director; Mufid Abdulqater, one of the HLF's top fundraisers; and Abdulraham Odeh, the HLF's New Jersey representative. Shurkri Abu Baker, Mohammed El-Mezain, Ghassan Elashi, Mufid Abdulqater and Abdulraham Odeh were arrested this morning. Haitham Maghawri and Akram Mishal are not in the United States and are considered to be fugitives from justice.

Today's charges are the result of a three-year investigation by the Joint Terrorism Task Force, involving agents from federal, state, and local agencies including: the FBI, IRS, BICE, Department of State, Secret Service, U.S. Army CID, the Texas Department of Public Safety, and the police departments of Dallas, Plano, Garland, and Richardson, Texas. The case is being prosecuted by the United States Attorney's Office in Dallas, Texas, along with the Counterterrorism Section of the United States Department of Justice.

The details contained in the indictment are accusations and the defendants are presumed to be innocent unless and until proven guilty in a court of law.

Hezballah

Hezballah was originally designated as a Foreign Terrorist Organization October 8, 1997. According to its manifestos, Hezballah is dedicated to the liberation of Jerusalem, the destruction of Israel, and the ultimate establishment of an Islamic state in Lebanon.

Established in 1982 by Lebanese Shiite clerics and ideologically inspired by the Iranian revolution, Hezballah was formed in response to the Israeli invasion of Lebanon. The group was the principal supporter of anti-Western and anti-American terrorism in the 1980s and is directed by its Majlis al-Shura or Consultative Council. Since 1992, Hezballah has participated in Lebanon's political system and currently holds 12 seats, with its allies, in parliament. Other terrorist activities include the highjacking of TWA flight 847 in 1985; the detention of 18 American hostages in Lebanon throughout the 1980s and 1990s, the bombing of Israel's Embassy in Argentine in March 1992, and the bombing of the Argentine-Jewish Mutual Association in Bueno Aries in July 1994. During its 15year military insurgency campaign against Israeli and Israeli-aligned forces in Southern Lebanon, Hezballah carried out rocket attacks that killed Israeli civilians.

Hezballah has engaged in kidnapping, bombings, and highjackings, as well as rocket strikes against Israeli settlements and the firing of surface-to-air missiles at Israeli jets.

Hezballah has been implicated in or is known to have carried out the truck bombings of the U.S. Embassy in Beirut in April 1983, the U.S. Marine barracks in Beirut in October 1983, and the U.S. Embassy Annex in Beirut in September 1984. Hezballah claimed responsibility for an April 1984 bombing that killed 18 U.S. service members in Torrejon, Spain.

Hezballah operates in the southern suburbs of Beirut, the Bekaa valley, and southern Lebanon. It has established cells in Europe, Africa, South America, North America, and Asia. The group is believed to have two to five thousand supporters and a few hundred terrorist operatives.

Iran supports Hezballah with financial, political, and organizational aid, while Syria provides diplomatic, political, and logistic support.

SUMMARY

Terrorism is one of the greatest threats to our country today, but their roots go back more than 2,000 years. Terrorism comes not only from outside the United States, but also from within our own borders. Terrorism does not take the most sophisticated technology or hundreds of people. The bomb that destroyed the Federal Building in Oklahoma City was not complicated and the airplanes that destroyed the World Trade Center were not meant to be weapons. However, we are vulnerable to many types of terrorist weapons such as suicide bombers, and chemical, biological, radiological and nuclear devices (CBRN).

DISCUSSION QUESTIONS

1. Who are the groups that are our greatest threat and what are their motives?
2. Where would terrorist get the materials to make a dirty bomb?
3. Describe some of the biological agents, their advantages and disadvantages from the terrorist perceptive.

ADDITIONAL READINGS

Nuclear Terrorism, Graham Allison, Hardcover, Times Books, Henry Holt and Co., LLC, 2004

Terrorism - Opposing Viewpoints, Hardcover, Greenhaven Press, 2000

BIBLIOGRAPHY

CRS Report for Congress, Foreign Terrorist Organizations dated February 6, 2004

Center for Defense Information, www.cdi.org

International Policy Institute for Counter-Terrorism (ICT), www.ict.org.il

The United Nations, Report on Chemical, Biological, Radiological and Nuclear Terrorism dated December 18, 1999

Canadian Security Intelligence, www.csis-scrs.org

Office of the Coordinator for Counterterrorism, Patterns of Global Terrorism dated April 29, 2004 United States Department of Justice, Drug Enforcement Administration, Drugs and Terrorism: A New Perspective dated September 2002

Chapter 7

Investigative Techniques

OVERVIEW

In this chapter you will study a variety of investigative techniques used to develop criminal cases involving conspiracies. Those techniques include undercover agents, sources of information, electronic surveillance, physical surveillance, grand juries, confidential informants, intelligence gathering and use of search warrants.

CHAPTER OBJECTIVES

1. Know the difference between an undercover agent, a confidential informant, and a contracted informant.
2. Know the advantages and disadvantages of using an undercover agent, a confidential informant, and a contracted informant.
3. Know the different types of electronic surveillance, their uses, and the legal ramifications of each.
4. Learn about physical surveillance.
5. Under the function of a Grand Jury and how it can be used to further an investigation.
6. Learn about the different types of intelligence and how they can be used in an investigation.
7. Know what level of proof is needed to obtain a search warrant and study an actual search warrant and an affidavit for a search warrant.

UNDERCOVER AGENTS

An undercover agent is a law enforcement officer who assumes the role of someone else for the purpose of obtaining information or to gather evidence of a crime. Undercover assignments can be casual, short term or long term. Casual undercover can just be going into a business location posing as a customer to engage the counter person in a conversation to learn about the business or an employee. Short-term assignments can be assignments such as the purchase of narcotics from a drug dealer. These assignments are usually sporadic and intermingled with telephone calls and meetings. Long-term assignments involve the law enforcement officer assuming a full time life style to suit the assignment. This means cutting off all contact with friends and family for long periods of time.

Except for casual undercover assignments, most agencies have stringent requirements before their officers are allowed to work undercover. The requirements usually include formal training and a psychological evaluation. Then they are allowed to work undercover under the supervision of an experienced undercover agent. While they are working undercover, they meet with a coordinator from time to time for reevaluation.

The undercover agent is the best for court purposes. They are trained observers who make contemporaneous notes for their reports for court purposes. They do not have credibility problems when they testify in court as others might. The case agent knows the information he is getting from the undercover agent is truthful, unlike information from confidential informants and contracted informants that needs to be substantiated. This means the undercover agent is able to obtain admissions that can be introduced in court.

There are disadvantages to using an undercover agent. Primarily, it is an officer safety issue. There are times when you cannot provide coverage for the undercover agent, particularly on long term assignments. You cannot always plant an electronic listening device on the undercover agents for fear of him being searched. Even when you are able to cover him during meeting, you may not be able to respond quickly enough to guaranty his safety. You can lose surveillance of him during the undercover assignment leaving him unprotected.

Another disadvantage on long-term assignments is the psychological impact it can have on your undercover agent. Undercover agents have been forced to engage in alcohol, drugs and sex while on assignment. The stress of working undercover can be enormous and has caused agents to cross line from law enforcement officer to the role they are assuming. This can have a negative impact on their marriage or family life creating more problems.

It is difficult for an undercover agent to get access to the criminals. This can be overcome by an introduction by a confidential informant or a source of information.

The undercover agent must be careful not to participate in criminal activity. If he is forced to participate in a criminal act it must be reported to the proper authority as soon as possible. A determination will then be made to terminate the undercover assignment or attempt to continue.

An undercover agent has a responsibility to protect to protect the life of individuals if he becomes aware of information that their life may be in jeopardy, such as a "hit" on a person. This can be accomplished without comprising the undercover. The law enforcement agency may just tell the person they believe they may be the subject of a contract for murder scheme.

CONFIDENTIAL INFORMANTS

Confidential informants (CI) or contracted informants are the lifeblood of law enforcement. CIs can make your career and they can break your career. By the very nature of what they are and what they do, CIs have to be criminals or associated with criminals. That is the primary problem with a CI, when they take the witness stand they lack credibility. Their motive is brought into question. CIs are normally recruited when they commit a crime and want a reduced sentence or need money. Defense attorneys easily attack both of these motivations.

In order to overcome the credibility issue of an informant a number of investigative techniques can be used. Surveillance can be use to corroborate the presence of the CI at meetings or locations. Law enforcement officers can record telephone conversations between the CI and the targets. If the CI is trusted by the target and not likely to be searched an electronic listening device can be placed on the CI and monitored and recorded by law enforcement officers. Sometimes an undercover agent can be inserted into the organization by having the CI vouch for the undercover agent. You must be very careful when you have a CI vouch for an undercover agent because the identity of your undercover agent is with an untrusted source.

ELECTRONIC SURVEILLANCE

One of the more difficult tasks for an investigator in a conspiracy case is to show an agreement to the objective of the conspiracy and a connection between the co-conspirators. If you don't have an undercover agent in the organization, then electronic surveillance is how you can prove the conspiracy exists and corroborate a confidential informant. The jury loves to hear about crimes directly from the mouths of the defendants. That is what a wiretap can do for you or a recorded conversation between the co-conspirators and a confidential informant.

Electronic surveillance is communication interception; obtaining evidence of communications; and video surveillance. Two statutes cover communication interception and obtaining evidence of communications, Title III of the Omnibus Crime Control and Safe Streets Act of 1968 and the Electronic Communications Privacy Act of 1986. The statutes are codified as follows:

- 18 U.S.C. Section 2510-2522 - Interception of Communications (Title III)
- 18 U.S.C. Section 2701 - 2711 - Stored Wire and Electronic Communications and Transactional Records Access
- 18 U.S. C. Section 3121 - 3127 - Pen Registers and Trap and Trace Devices

In addition to the above statues there are restrictions on the interception of communications imposed by the Constitution. The statutory and Constitutional restrictions are imposed on the activities of all individuals, public and private.

Wiretaps

A wiretap is the interception of oral or wire communications. It can mean agents intercepting calls made to and from a land line or a cell phone. It can also mean the intercept of fax transmissions over telephone lines. Wiretaps are only allowed for certain predicate offenses. The following are some of the predicate offenses:

a. 18 U.S.C. § 115 - Retaliation Against Federal Official;

b. 18 U.S.C. § 201 - Bribery of Public Officials;

c. 18 U.S.C. § 659 - Theft from Interstate Shipment;

d. 18 U.S.C. §§ 1956, 1957 - Money Laundering and Certain Monetary Transactions;

e. 18 U.S.C. § 1963 - Racketeer Influenced and Corrupt Organizations;

f. 18 U.S.C. §§ 2251-2260 - Sexual Exploitation of Children;

g. 18 U.S.C. § 2332d - Financial Transactions with Certain Governments

h. 22 U.S.C. § 2778 - Arms Export Control Act;

i. 31 U.S.C. § 5322 - Monetary Reporting Requirements;

j. Any offense involving the importation of narcotic drugs, marijuana or other dangerous drugs, punishable under any law of the United States;

k. Any conspiracy to commit any of the foregoing offenses;

l. The location of any fugitive from justice from any (predicate offenses.

A federal judge approves authorizations for interception of wire or oral communications. The Attorney General, Deputy Attorney General, Associate Attorney General, any Assistant Attorney General or acting Deputy Assistant Attorney General in the Criminal Division, must approve the application for authorizations for an interception of wire or oral communications.

The case agent works with a local assistant United States attorney to prepare an affidavit. The affidavit must have a full and complete statement of the facts that identifies the subjects, list the alleged offenses, describes the facility or location, and establish probable cause that the targets are using the targeted telephone or location for the criminal activity. The agent must show in the affidavit the necessity to use electronic surveillance. He must show what other investigative techniques were tried and failed, why other investigative techniques are unlikely to succeed or why they are too dangerous to employ. It is not necessary to try all other techniques first, just articulate why they were considered and rejected.

The authorization orders may not exceed 30 days. Extensions may be continuously granted for periods not to exceed 30 days. Extension requests contain the same information as in the original affidavit plus the results for the prior 30 days to show the telephone is still being used for criminal activity.

Digital Number Recorders (DNR)

A pen register is any device or process that records or decodes dialing, routing, addressing or signaling information transmitted by a communication instrument or facility. A trap and trace device is a device or process, which captures the incoming electronic impulses, which identify the originating number or other information reasonably likely to identify the source of the communication. This is different from a wiretap that intercepts the conversation. These devices identify the incoming and outgoing information that will identify the source of the calls or the identity of the person receiving the call.

Obtaining an authorization for a pen register or trap and trace device is easy and routine for most investigations. Any assistant United States attorney can make an application to any court of competent jurisdiction that includes federal judges and magistrate judges, and circuit judges. The standard for obtaining an authorization is that the information likely to be obtained is relevant to an ongoing criminal investigation. The standard is lower than a wiretap because it has been determined that a person does not have a reasonable expectation of privacy of the numbers they dial. The order of authorization is for a period not to exceed 60 days, with possible extensions of 60 days. These orders are sealed by the court to prevent disclosure.

The value of these devices is to prove a connection between parties. These connections can usually be tied to an event to show participant or command and control over operations. They are used to identify additional co-conspirators in a conspiracy. These connections when linked to physical surveillance are evidence to establish an agreement to commit criminal acts.

In most cases, subpoenaing the information from the telephone company can get the informant you would get from a pen register. It will delay your receipt of the information, but there is no cost to the agency. A pen register can cost thousands of dollars.

Consensual Monitoring

Consensual monitoring is done by wiring a person or a location with a recording device or a transmitting device or both or by placing a recording devise on a telephone to record the conversation. The person who consents to the monitoring is the undercover agent or a confidential informant who is participating in the conversation. It only takes the consent of one of the parties to the conversation to record the conversation.

No court order is necessary for consensual monitoring. The case agent prepares an agency form with the information of who is likely to be monitored, the criminal violations being investigative, the length of time being requested, the identity of the consenting party, the method of recording and the reason for the recording. The reasons given can include one or all of the following reasons, to collect evidence of a criminal violation, avoid an entrapment defense, and in the case of a transmitting device to protect the undercover agent or confidential informant. That is why sometimes two devices are used, one a small recorder that provides high quality recordings for court purposes and a second device so that the cover team will know if the undercover agent or confidential informant is in trouble. For telephone conversations of course only recording devices are needed.

Defense attorneys hate to hear their own client's voices acknowledging participation in a criminal act, but the juries love it.

Global Positioning Systems (GPS)

A device that uses the GPS technology determines the location of that device by triangulating the position from two or more satellites. The use of these devices is not regulated by T III, however, they are subject to Fourth Amendment principles of unreasonable searches without warrants. These devices are installed on vehicles and their position is constantly being transmitted. An agent can sit in his office on his computer and watch where his subject is going. The program records every movement in a log with time and location.

These devices are expensive and they are hard wired to the vehicle, or they are attached to the vehicle with magnets. The magnet's connection can fall off the vehicle and are powered by a battery so the time the device will work is limited. Recently, some agencies have purchased inexpensive GPS cell phones to use and have rigged magnetic cases to attach them to vehicles.

GPS devices are excellent investigative tools, but remember that they are subject to Fourth Amendment principles. This means that if whatever the device is attached to enters an area with a reasonable expectation of privacy such as a private residence, a search warrant is required to use the device. This also holds true if the device is installed on the inside of the vehicle where there is a reasonable expectation of privacy.

Radio Transmissions

The following radio transmissions do not require any authorizations for interceptions:

- Broadcast radio and television not scrambled or encoded
- Amateur (Ham), CB, general mobile radio transmissions not scrambled or encoded
- Marine, Aeronautical transmissions
- General mobile radio service (Taxi cabs, etc.)
- Fire, Police, Military transmissions that are readily accessible to the general public and are not encoded or encrypted
- Television, Science satellite transmissions that are readily accessible to the general public and are not encoded or encrypted
- Civil Defense that are readily accessible to the general public and are not encoded or encrypted
- Private land mobile (business radios, etc.) that are readily accessible to the general public and are not encoded or encrypted
- Family radio service that are readily accessible to the general public and are not encoded or encrypted

As you can see by the above list, if a transmission is encoded or encrypted there is a reasonable expectation of privacy.

Video Surveillance

The requirement for video surveillance is determined by whether the camera is located in an area where there is a reasonable expectation of privacy, whether there is the consent of one party or if it is in a public area with no reasonable expectation of privacy.

Where there is a reasonable expectation of privacy the procedure is the same as the wiretap. In addition, there must be an order of authorization for each camera installed. Where the video is combined with audio, an authorization for the wiretap is also necessary, however, the same affidavit to establish the probable cause can be used in both applications. The above guidelines are used by the Department of Justice, but not all Federal Circuits are in agreement on all the requirements needed for video surveillance. For that reason, the Department of Justice takes the most conservative position.

PHYSICAL SURVEILLANCE

Physical surveillance can be a simple act of just walking into a public building to observe a person to a complex coordinated plan to include electronic surveillance, ground surveillance, and air surveillance. Surveillance can be moving or fix.

In the Multicore case that you studied in an earlier chapter, valuable information was obtained when an agent followed the suspect into the United Parcel store and observed the name of the sender on the shipping documents. From that information, agents were able to trace the shipments to Singapore then to Iran.

In international controlled deliveries (ICD) performed at the Port of Entries, the agents, posing as an inspector, will place a GPS device under the vehicle using magnets while appearing to be performing a routine inspection. An agent in the office monitors that device. The agents then set up their surveillance to pick up the vehicle as soon as it exits the inspection area. The vehicle's license plate and description are radioed to all the surveillance units. A helicopter or high wing airplane such as a Cessna is launched and waiting near the Port of Entry. As the vehicle exists the Port of Entry, the first unit makes a positive identification of the vehicle by license plate. The surveillance units then radio the air unit and give the exact location and description of the vehicles around the target vehicle. They make sure that the air unit is watching the correct vehicle. Once the air unit has a positive make on the target vehicle the ground units follow in a loose manner. If the traffic becomes heavy, the surveillance units will close in to maintain a tighter tail. This continues until the target vehicle reaches its final destination.

In a moving surveillance the key is not to let the target know he is being followed. Rotating vehicles in a leapfrog manner does this. If the target makes a right turn, you might have the follow vehicle stay straight and let the second vehicle take up the "eye" position. The former "eye" position vehicle then moves to the back. The agents use different types of vehicles such as sedan, coupes, trucks and SUVs. The colors are bland and do not have any identifying marks such as bumper stickers, so they do not stick out. Most of the surveillance vehicles are equipped with switches to make either of the front headlights appear to be out.

Fix surveillance have a different set of problems. You don't have to worry about losing the target, but not being "burned" is the biggest hurdle. First, the target is surveyed for a potential site to conduct the surveillance. Is the target in a neighborhood where everyone knows each other, a retail business area, or an industrial park? Is there an advantage point on a hill or a nearby building where you can set up surveillance? Once you conduct a site survey you can select an appropriate method to conduct the surveillance.

Video cameras are the best method to do a fixed surveillance. It's not only difficult or near possible to spot, but if you record the video it is excellent evidence. Video cameras can be set up on utility poles such as telephone or electric poles. The government has boxes built to look like the boxes you see every day on the poles, but these have a camera inside. Vehicles are equipped with hidden cameras that can be parked anywhere. The vehicle usually transmits the video signal to a van in a nearby location that records and monitors the signal. For short-term surveillance, helicopters are equipped with cameras with high power lens, recorders and monitors.

SURVEILLANCE AND CONSPIRACIES

Electronic surveillance and physical surveillance can tie together people, places and acts. When used in conjunction with other investigative techniques an investigator starts to build evidence of relationships by connecting activities with people. Using video to document these relationships is a valuable piece of evidence that can be presented to a jury. Many times surveillance videos have caught the violators in the actual criminal act. Surveillance has caught drug smugglers driving up to a house, opening the trunk and taking out packages of narcotics. When the agents execute a search warrant and they seize the narcotics, they are able to show with the video that the packages being taken out of the vehicle looked the same as the packages that were seized in the house that contained the narcotics.

GRAND JURY

The Fifth Amendment states, "…no person shall be held to answer for a capital or otherwise infamous crime unless on a presentment or indictment of a grand jury." The government cannot bring a person to trial for a felony unless a grand jury returns an indictment or that person waives his right.

Grand juries consist of 16 to 23 members. The grand jury generally sits for a period of 18 months, but may be extended up to 6 more months. A member of a grand jury must be a citizen of the United States, at least 18 years old and has resided in the judicial district for at least one year. A member cannot be a convicted felon, unless his civil rights have been restored by a pardon or amnesty. A member cannot have a felony charge pending against him. Members must be able to read and write English. Members may not be incapable of serving due to a mental or physical condition.

In the grand jury the government must show probable cause that the person to be indicted committed the crime. Probable cause means more likely than not. The government is normally the only person presenting evidence to the grand jury. For that reason, it is not that difficult to get the grand jury to believe that the person committed the crime. If the grand jury does agree that the person most likely committed the crime they return a "True Bill."

In addition to hearing cases, the grand jury has broad investigative powers to determine if a federal crime has been committed and who committed it. This function is another valuable investigative technique for investigators. First, the grand jury can compel any person to appear before it and give testimony and produce documents. Grand jury subpoenas are used to obtain documents that cannot be obtained through administrative subpoenas, more about this in the next chapter. Second, witnesses can be compelled to appear before the grand jury to give testimony. Of course, witnesses can invoke their Fifth Amendment right against self-incrimination. If that happens, the agents might start looking for evidence on the witness for the crime or have the government attorney consider limited immunity to force the witness' testimony. By bringing witnesses before the grand jury, the government has "locked" in their testimony under oath. This is helpful in some conspiracy cases where cooperating co-conspirators can be called before the grand jury. If the witness changes their story, they risk being charged with perjury. In addition, the grand jury testimony can be used to impeach the witness if they do change their testimony during the trial, giving the government a chance to rehabilitate their witness or save their case.

SOURCES OF INFORMATION (SOI)

A source of information is a person who is willing to provide information or intelligence that will guide or other wise assist in the investigation, but they are not willing to testify. The basic types of sources of information are those that provide information not readily available without legal service and those who provide information on criminal acts.

Some sources of information work for companies that have information you may need quickly or information you will not use in any reports or legal proceedings. This might be a connection at the local gas and electric company, the telephone company, a government agency such as the Central Intelligence Agency, a real estate agent, a title company, a storage company or any other business. If the information later becomes necessary for your case, you can obtain the information with an administrative subpoena or a grand jury subpoena, but you will already know what it will show. Information received from intelligence agencies can never be subpoenaed, but must be developed by parallel construction. The investigator knows where to look for the information and must find the information from a third party to protect the source and method. These types of sources of information are motivated out of a desire to help law enforcement and are not providing the information for money.

The sources of information that are connected to criminals and provide information are usually motivated by money. The difference between a source of information who will not testify and a confidential informant who will testify is that confidential informant was caught and is trying for a reduced sentence or they are a professional confidential informant who does this for a living to earn money and who carefully selects his targets. The investigator in his reports must protect the source of information that is providing the information. The investigator must be careful in writing his reports not to provide information that could have only come from the source of information. These reports may be subject to discovery by the defense.

If possible it is best to use the source of information to guide you in the right direction. For example, if the source provides you with the license plate of a vehicle entering the United States with a smuggled load of narcotics, you can use this information without letting the violators know. In these cases, the inspectors are requested to do a "block inspection" on the vehicle and the five vehicles in front of the target vehicle and the five vehicles behind the target vehicle. The vehicles are lead to the secondary area where they all open their trunks and hoods, then the narcotic dogs are run on the vehicles. The inspectors are not told about the information you have on the target vehicle, but they suspect it when the agents show up requesting the block inspection. To the violator, it appears as if he just had bad luck and was caught.

INTELLIGENCE

Most agencies have full time professional intelligence research specialists who are trained to find and analyzed data and information. There are two types of intelligence for law enforcement, strategic and tactical/operational. Tactical/operational intelligence provides information that can be used at the street level to make cases, such as other vehicles owned by the same person who is involved in smuggling narcotics. Strategic intelligence is trend analysis and overviews, such as a shift in narcotic smuggling from Texas to California.

Another important duty performed by the intelligence research specialist or the investigator is the linking of people, events and evidence in a logical manner that shows the relationship of the people, events and evidence to each other in the furtherance of the objective of the conspiracy. In many cases, it is the intelligence research specialist who takes all the raw information and connects the dots for the case agent. They are looking for commonalities. This information is put on charts using software packages such as Analysis Notebook. The charts are usually event driven or time driven. In an event driven linking chart, various overt acts show the relationship of individual acts to the organizers. Charts are also help in finding holes in cases that need further investigation.

Figure 7.1 Medi-Cal Fraud and Money Laundering

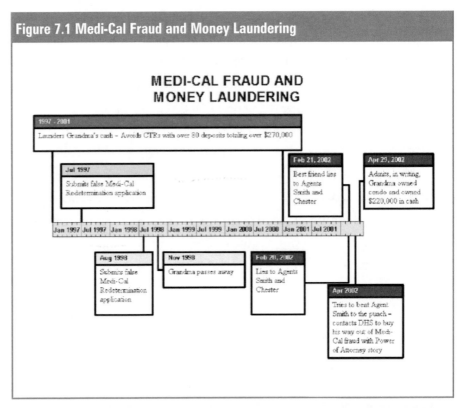

Figure 7.2 Medi-Cal Fraud and Money Laundering 1997-2001

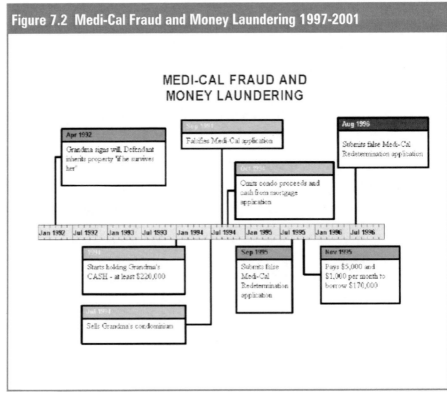

Intelligence Research Specialists have access to public and private databases. They use public databases like Choicepoint, Dun and Bradstreet, and Lexis/Nexis. These databases provide public information on people and companies including real estates owned, any licenses (e.g. insurance agent), neighbors, addresses, and bankruptcies. They also have access to agency databases and criminal justice databases.

The Intelligence Research Specialists are the one who collect the information from the pen registers and trap and trace devices. That information is put into a software package for analysis such as Penlink. The software will sort the information and put it in a databases and chart for easy analysis.

SEARCH WARRANTS

A Search Warrant is a court authorized instrument allowing the named law enforcement officer to enter a defined location to search for evidence of a crime. Federal judges, magistrate judges, or judges of state courts of record within the district where the property sought is located can issue a search warrant. The search warrant is applied for by filing an affidavit for a search warrant. In the affidavit the officer must show probably cause that a crime has been committed and evidence of that crime is located at the premises to be searched. If the judge finds that probable cause exists they will issue a search warrant.

The search warrant must describe in detail the area to be searched and the things to be seized. In the description of the place to be searched, the officer must give as many details as possible so that a person not familiar with the area would be able to find the place to be searched with little chance of confusion or mistake. Sometimes photos are attached to the search warrant.

Describing the items to be seized may include items that are generally found where the search is going to be located such as business records keep in the normal course of business, notes, financial records, telephone records and bank statements.

Below you will find an actual application and affidavit for search warrant and a search warrant for the Multicore case that you studied in an earlier chapter. In the application and affidavit for search warrant notice how Special Agent Wendy Duarte described the place to be searched in detail. In the affidavit in support of application for search warrant, Special Agent Duarte starts out by describing her duties, her training and experience. She then goes on to explain some of the laws being violated to set the groundwork for the criminal acts. She then explains the case in the chronological order of events. Each of the events is a building block to a conclusion for the judge that a crime has been committed and where the evidence of that crime is located. She then explains to the judge how based on her training and experience and the experiences of other agents what business records are normally keep in committing these types of violations. She talks about computer data using "canned" language and finally ends with a conclusion using more "canned" language. Finally she attaches to the affidavit a list of items to be seized that is mostly "canned" language, but is customized for the circumstance of each warrant.

The search warrant itself is issued against the property to be searched. The search warrant is to Special Agent Wendy J. Duarte and any authorized officer of the United States. The search warrant lists the property to be searched in great detail, describing the street address, the style, size and construction of the property and other unique identifying information. The search warrant commands the agent to search the property on or before December 14, 2000. The warrant was issued December 6, 2000. The maximum time that the judge could have given the agents to execute the search warrant is 10 days. The search warrant tells the agents that the property can only be searched between the hours of 6:00 a.m. and 6:00 p.m., and if the property be found there to seize same, leaving a copy of the warrant and receipt for the property taken, and prepare a written inventory of the property seized and return the warrant to a United States Magistrate Judge as required by law. The second page of the search warrant is the return that is completed and signed when returned to the judge along with an inventory of what was seized. Attached to the search warrant and incorporated by reference is the same attachment "A" listing the items to be seized that was in the application and affidavit for search warrant.

An interesting note is that search warrants issued for drugs violations of Title 21, United States Code can be served anytime day or night. Even though the search warrant is addressed to federal law enforcement officers, the courts have held that any other federal or local officer may accompany them, and anyone participating in the warrant execution may lawfully seize evidence.

The reasons for searching for items like documents are two fold. First this type of evidence helps prove the violation with financial records or records showing residency or dominion and control. Second it allows searching the entire house where you may find other contraband. If a search warrant is issued to search for an elephant you cannot legally look in a drawer where an elephant cannot fit.

Figure 7.3 Sample Search Warrant

United States District Court
— *EASTERN DISTRICT OF CALIFORNIA* —

In the Matter of the Search of   COPY   SEARCH WARRANT

Garage #26
Jasmine Garden Apartments   CASE NUMBER:
800 New Stine Road   SW-F 00-3210
Bakersfield, California 93309

TO: Special Agent Wendy J. Duarte and any Authorized Officer of the United States:

Affidavit having been made before me by Special Agent Wendy J. Duarte, who has reason to believe that on the premises described as

Garage # 26 within the Jasmine Garden Apartment Complex, 800 New Stine Road, Bakersfield, California 93309. The garage is beige stucco with brown wooden trim. It is located in a building composing garage units 22 to 26. The door to the garage is white and has the number "26" on the face of the door.

in the Eastern District of California, there is now concealed a certain person or property, described in Attachment A, which is incorporated by reference herein.

I am satisfied that the affidavit and any recorded testimony establish probable cause to believe that the person or property so described is now concealed on the premises above-described and establish grounds for the issuance of this warrant.

YOU ARE HEREBY COMMANDED to search on or before ___December 14, 2000___
                                                            Date (Not to Exceed 10 days)

the person or place named above for the property specified, serving this warrant and making the search between 6:00 a.m and 6:00 p.m., and if the property be found there to seize same, leaving a copy of this warrant and receipt for the property taken, and prepare a written inventory of the property seized and return this warrant to a United States Magistrate Judge as required by law.

December 6, 2000 at ____11:20 a.m____   at Fresno, California.
             Date and Time Issued

_____
Honorable Lawrence J. O'Neill
United States Magistrate Judge

Figure 7.3 Sample Search Warrant (cont.)

RETURN

Date Warrant Received	Date and Time Executed	Copy of Warrant and Receipt for Items Left with

Inventory Made in the Presence of

Inventory of Person or Property Taken Pursuant to the Warrant

CERTIFICATION

I swear that this inventory is a true and detailed account of the person or property taken by me on the warrant.

_____

Subscribed, sworn to, and returned before me this ____ day of _____ , 2000.

_____
UNITED STATES MAGISTRATE JUDGE

Figure 7.3 Sample Search Warrant (cont.)

ATTACHMENT "A"

ITEMS TO BE SEIZED:

The following evidence of violations of 22 U.S.C. § 2778 (Arms Export Control Act), 50 U.S.C. App. § 2410 (Export Administration Act), 18 U.S.C. § 1956(a)(2)(A) (Money Laundering), and 18 U.S.C. § 371 (Conspiracy):

A.   Defense articles; that is, items on the United States Munitions List;

B.   Goods or technology subject to export control;

C.   Cash, checks, money orders, or other financially negotiable instruments available to purchase defense articles, or goods or technology subject to export control;

D.   The following records and documents, referencing or related to Multicore Ltd or Rowland Diesel, for the period January 1, 1996, to the present:

1.   Business records of Multicore Ltd, and of Rowland Diesel, including requests for quotes, quotes, correspondence, memoranda, e-mails, notes, daily calendars, invoices, purchase orders, shipping documents, receipts, airway bills, facsimiles, telexes, delivery records, inventory documents, sales records, export licenses and contracts;

2.   Specifications for, and descriptions of, defense articles, and goods and technology subject to export control;

3.   Certificates of conformance;

4.   Applications for export licenses, and regulations and statutes related to United States export license requirements;

5.   Banking statements, returned checks, check registers, checkbooks, deposit slips, withdrawal slips, cashier's checks, money orders, wire transfers, currency transaction reports, credit card statements, and credit card receipts;

6.   Documents and effects that show residency, or dominion and control, of the place to be searched as described in Attachment A, including keys, receipts, bills, canceled checks, mail envelopes, rental agreements, telephone records, utility bills, internet/cable provider statements and receipts;

Figure 7.3 Sample Search Warrant (cont.)

7.   Records of domestic and international travel, including airplane, hotel, gasoline, rental vehicles expenses, and travel itineraries.

D.   As used above, the terms "records and documents" includes records, documents, programs, applications or materials created, modified or stored in any form, including

E.   In searching for data capable of being read, stored or interpreted by a computer, law enforcement personnel executing this search warrant will employ the following procedure:

1.   Upon securing the premises, law enforcement personnel trained in searching and seizing computer data (the "computer personnel") will make an initial review of any computer equipment and storage devices to determine whether these items can be searched on-site in a reasonable amount of time and without jeopardizing the ability to preserve the data.

2.   If the computer equipment and storage devices cannot be searched on-site, and it has been determined that the items are not instrumentalities or fruits of the offense stated above, do not contain contraband, and are not otherwise illegally possessed, then the computer personnel will determine whether it is practical to copy the data during the execution of the search in a reasonable amount of time without jeopardizing the ability to preserve the data.

3.   If the computer personnel determine it is not practical to perform an on-site search or make an on-site copy of the data, then the computer equipment and storage devices will be seized and transported to an appropriate law enforcement laboratory for review. The computer equipment and storage devices will be reviewed by appropriately trained personnel in order to extract and seize any data that falls within the list of items to be seized set forth herein.

4.   If law enforcement personnel determine, either on-site or during a subsequent off-site search, t hat any computer equipment, storage device or data (a) is an instrumentality of the offense stated above, meaning that is was designed or intended for use of, or is being or has been used, as the means of committing the offense; (b) contains any contraband, such as counterfeit or stolen software, child pornography, national security information, or unauthorized access devices such as stolen credit card numbers; (c) is the fruits of criminal activity; or (d) is otherwise criminally possessed, the

Figure 7.3 Sample Search Warrant (cont.)

property shall be seized and not returned pursuant to Federal Rule of Criminal Procedure 41(b).

5.   Any data that is encrypted and unreadable will not be returned unless law enforcement personnel have determined that the data is not (a) an instrumentality of the offense, (b) a fruit of the criminal activity, (c) contraband, (d) otherwise unlawfully possessed, or (e) evidence of the offense specified above.

6.   In searching the data, the computer personnel will examine all of the data contained in the computer equipment and storage devices to view their precise contents and determine whether the data falls within the items to be seized as set forth herein. In addition, the computer personnel will search for and attempt to recover "deleted," "hidden" or encrypted data to determine whether the data falls within the list of items to be seized as set forth herein.

7.   If the computer personnel determine that the computer equipment and storage devices are no longer necessary to retrieve and preserve the data, and the items are not subject to seizure pursuant to Federal Rule of Criminal Procedure 41(b), the government will return these items within a reasonable period of time not to exceed 60 days from the date of seizure.

8.   In order to search for data that is capable of being read or interpreted by a computer, law enforcement personnel will need to seize and search the following items, subject to the procedures set forth above:

    a.   Any computer equipment and storage device capable of being used to commit, further or store evidence of the offenses listed above;

    b.   Any computer equipment used to facilitate the transmission, creation, display, encoding or storage of data, including word processing equipment, modems, docking stations, monitors, printers, plotters, encryption devices, and optical scanners;

    c.   Any magnetic, electronic or optical storage device capable of storing data, such as floppy disks, hard disks, tapes, CD-ROMs, CD-R, CD-RWs, DVDs, optical disks, printer or memory buffers, smart cards, PC cards, memory calculators, electronic dialers, electronic notebooks, and personal digital assistants;

Figure 7.3 Sample Search Warrant (cont.)

    d.   Any documentation, operating logs and reference manuals regarding the operation of the computer equipment, storage devices or software;

    e.   Any applications, utility programs, compilers, interpreters, and other software used to facilitate direct or indirect communication with the computer hardware, storage devices or data to be searched;

    f.   Any physical keys, encryption devices, dongles and similar physical items that are necessary to gain access to the computer equipment, storage devices or data; and

    g.   Any passwords, password files, test keys, encryption codes or other information necessary to access the computer equipment, storage devices or data.

F.   If a safe is found on the premises, searching agents will attempt to open it at the scene in order to search it for the items specified above. In the event that the safe is locked and agents are unable to open it on the scene, they will remove the safe from the premises to a site where it may be opened. The safe and any items outside the scope of the items described above will be returned to the premises to be searched within five business days.

Figure 7.4 Sample Search Warrant #2

United States District Court

EASTERN DISTRICT OF CALIFORNIA

In the Matter of the Search of

Apartment #6
Jasmine Garden Apartments
800 New Stine Road
Bakersfield, California 93309

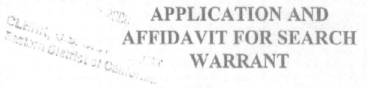

APPLICATION AND AFFIDAVIT FOR SEARCH WARRANT

CASE NUMBER: 00SW 3209

I, the undersigned affiant, being duly sworn, state that the following is true and correct to the best of my knowledge and belief. I am a Special Agent of the United States Department of Treasury, United States Customs Service, and have reason to believe that on the premises described as

A two-story apartment, apartment #6, located within the Jasmine Garden Apartment Complex, 800 New Stine Road, Bakersfield, California 93309. The apartment is a two-story apartment with beige stucco and brown wood shingle roofing. The door to the apartment is white in color with the number "6" on the face of the door. A brown wooden patio fence approximately 5 feet in height encloses the entry to the door. The apartment faces Belle Terrace in a southeasterly direction.

in the Eastern District of California, there is now concealed certain property, described in Attachment A which is incorporated by reference herein, which constitutes evidence, fruits, or instrumentalities of crimes in violation of 22 U.S.C. § 2778, 50 U.S.C. § 2410, 18 U.S.C. § 1956(a)(2), and 18 U.S.C. § 371.

The facts to support the issuance of a search warrant are contained in the attached Affidavit, a Statement of Probable Cause, incorporated by reference herein.

_____
Special Agent Wendy J. Duarte
United States Customs Service

Sworn to before me, and subscribed in my presence at Fresno, California

this _6th_ *day of* _December_ _____, 2000, at _11:20 a.m._.

_____
Honorable Lawrence J. O'Neill
United States Magistrate Judge

Figure 7.4 Sample Search Warrant #2 (cont.)

**AFFIDAVIT IN SUPPORT OF APPLICATION FOR
SEARCH WARRANT**

PAUL L. SEAVE
United States Attorney
JOHN J. SCIORTINO
Assistant U.S. Attorney
3654 Federal Building
1130 0 Street
Fresno, California 93721
Telephone: (559) 487-5172

UNITED STATES DISTRICT COURT

EASTERN DISTRICT OF CALIFORNIA

I, Wendy Duarte, state as follows:

1.   I am a Special Agent of the United States Department of Treasury, United States Customs

Service. I have been employed in this capacity since July, 1997. I am currently assigned to the

Strategic Investigations Group at the Special Agent in Charge (SAIC), in San Diego, California.

As part of my training I attended the Federal Law Enforcement Training Center (FLETC), Glynco,

Georgia for approximately four months. At FLETC, I was trained in, among other things, criminal

investigations, financial investigation techniques, and strategic investigations. I also attended an

advanced Strategic Investigations Course coordinated by the U.S. Customs Service.

2.   As a Federal law enforcement officer I have participated in and directed numerous criminal

investigations involving, among other things, the illegal importation and exportation of technology

items into and out of the United States. I have also participated in the execution of numerous

search warrants in connection with the above investigations.

3.   I have had training and experience in the methods utilized to import and export materials

contrary to United States laws. During my tenure in law enforcement, I have functioned in a

1

Figure 7.4 Sample Search Warrant #2 (cont.)

variety of capacities which include, but are not limited to, the following: a case agent who, among

other things, conducts undercover activities and supervises confidential informants; a surveillance

agent who observes and records the movements of individuals who traffic in drugs or other illicit

contraband, and those suspected of trafficking in illicit contraband; an interviewer of witnesses,

cooperating individuals, and informants regarding these illegal activities.

4.   In preparing this affidavit, I have conferred with other Agents who are experienced in the

area of enforcing federal laws relating to the illegal exportation of defense articles and technology,

including the Arms Export Control Act (AECA) and the Export Administration Act (EAA). The

opinions below are shared by them. Furthermore, the information contained in this Affidavit is

based on my own observations and information obtained from other law enforcement personnel

involved in the investigation.

5.   Under the Arms Export Control Act (22 U.S.C. §2778) the President is authorized to

control the export of "defense articles." The President is authorized to designate those items, which

shall be considered to be "defense articles" and to promulgate regulations. The items so designated

shall constitute the United States Munitions List. If an article is covered by the U.S. Munitions

List, the U.S. Department of State, Office of Defense Trade Controls (ODTC) regulates its exports.

The ODTC develops and updates the regulations, known as the International Traffic in Arms

Regulations (ITAR).

6.   Under the provisions of AECA, individuals or organizations must register with the Office

of the Defense Trade Controls, U.S. Department of State and apply for an export license to export

defense articles. It is a felony to willfully violate the provisions of the Arms Export Control Act.

This includes the requirement that those in the business of exporting defense articles or the

business of brokering activities with respect to exporting defense articles must register, and obtain

a license before exporting defense articles.

2

Figure 7.4 Sample Search Warrant #2 (cont.)

7.   Under the Export Administration Act (50 U.S.C. App. §§2401-20) the exportation of goods

and technology is controlled by the Department of Commerce, Office of Export Enforcement,

through the issuance of export licenses for goods or technology included in the "Control List"

maintained by the Secretary of Commerce. It is a felony to willfully violate, or conspire, or attempt

to violate any provision of the Act. This includes the possession of goods or technology on the

Control List with intent to export in violation of export controls, and the possession of goods or

technology on the Control List knowing or having reason to believe the goods would be so

exported. 50 U.S.C. § 2410(b)(3).

ILLEGAL EXPORT INVESTIGATION

8.   In February 1999, United States Customs Service Agent and Defense Criminal Investigative

Service began investigating the illegal exporting activities of MULTICORE LTD.

9.   On February 10, 1999, a U.S. Customs source informed Agents that MULTICORE LTD.,

800 New Stine Road, Suite 6, Bakersfield, California, 93309, requested pricing information for

licensable military aircraft parts specific to the Northrop-Grumman F-14 fighter aircraft. The

request concerned pricing information specific to Part No. A51B9019-13, NSN 5330-037-9822,

identified as a seal assembly. The request was signed, PAMELA FUNG, MULTICORE LTD., 800

New Stine Road, #6, Bakersfield, California 93309.

10.   On March 26, 1999, Richard Gurrell, Logistics Specialist, Northrop-Grumman, Product

Support Divisions, St. Augustine, Florida, advised that Part No. A51B9019-13, National Stock

Number (NSN) 5330-01-037-9822, is an air intake duct seal assembly specific to the F-14 Tomcat

aircraft fighter and has no commercial application. Consequently, a license is required to export

it.

11.   A Dun and Bradstreet Report disclosed that MULTICORE LTD. is headquarted in London,

England at 1a Dorset Street, W1H 3FD London, and has a branch office located at 800 New Stine

Figure 7.4 Sample Search Warrant #2 (cont.)

Road, Suite 6, Bakersfield, California. The shareholders for MULTICORE LTD, London are listed as Soroosh HOMAYOUNI and Mahboubeh Eshraghi. The report reflects that MULTICORE LTD is an industrial equipment overhauler with 60% of its sales devoted to European community countries.

12.   A review of the Treasury Enforcement Communications System (TECS) disclosed that MULTICORE LTD has been the subject of approximately 7 prior U.S. Customs investigations regarding suspected illegal exports of military equipment. In 1987, Soroosh HOMAYOUNI, owner of MULTICORE LTD was arrested and convicted of violating the Arms Export Control Act, (22 U.S.C. 2778) that is, unlawfully, willfully and knowingly attempting to export from the United States two Klystron B Amplifiers.

13.   On July 7, 1999, a review of records at the Office of the Clerk, City of Bakersfield, California, revealed that no business tax certificate has been issued to MULTICORE LTD, 800 New Stine Road, Suite 6, Bakersfield, California, 93309. On July 7, 1999, a review of records at the Office of the County Clerk, Kern County, Bakersfield, California, disclosed no Fictitious Business Name Index report identifiable with MULTICORE LTD, 800 New Stine Road, Suite 6, Bakersfield, California, 93309.

14.   Contact with the U.S. Postal Service disclosed the identity of the mail recipients at 800 New Stine Road, Suite 6, Bakersfield, California to be "John Ryan" and "Saeed HOMAYOUNI." Mail was also delivered in the name of MULTICORE LTD.

15.   A review of County property records revealed 800 New Stine Road, Suite 6, Bakersfield, California, to be within the Jasmine Gardens Apartment Complex.

16.   On June 2, 1999, the U.S. Customs source referenced above received a purchase order from MULTICORE LTD requesting 10 half-quick couplings, part #A51H9182-1 for $585.00. The RFQ requested that the parts be shipped COD to MULTICORE LTD, 800 New Stine Road, Suite 6,

4

Figure 7.4 Sample Search Warrant #2 (cont.)

Bakersfield, California, 93309. The purchase order was sent by "Peter Harris" and signed by "P. Harris."

17.   On June 9, 1999, the U.S. Customs source contacted "Peter Harris" at (661) 832-5490 and negotiated a price of $610 apiece for the half quick couplings. Later that date, the order was shipped COD via UPS to 800 New Stine Road, Suite 6, Bakersfield, California, 93309 and billed to the same address. On June 14, 1999, the package was picked up at the Bakersfield UPS facility by an individual who signed the name "Sid Hamilton" and provided a check in the amount of $6130.31.

18.   Howard S. Cohen, F-14 Integrated Logistics Systems Project Engineer, Northrop-Grumman Linthicum, Maryland, advised that part #A51H9182-1, NSN 4730-00-009-0371 was specific to the F-14 Fighter Aircraft. Mr. Cohen indicated that the part has no commercial application. Consequently, a license is required to export it.

19.   On June 24, 1999, information was received from the U.S. Department of State, Office of Defense Trade Controls which disclosed that MULTICORE LTD is not registered with the U. S. Department of State to export and that no export license or export license application was on file in the name MULTICORE LTD. It was also confirmed that a quick release coupling, part #A51H9182-1, NSN 4730-00-009-0371, requires a U.S. Department of State license for export.

20.   On June 24, 1999, the U.S. Department of Commerce advised that no export licenses had been issued to MULTICORE LTD.

21.   On March 24, 1999, a Grand Jury Subpoena was served on Pacific Bell Telephone Company requesting subscriber information and tolls on (661) 832-5490 and (661) 833-8549. The return revealed that MULTICORE LTD and Saeed HOMAYOUNI are the subscribers to each number.

5

Figure 7.4 Sample Search Warrant #2 (cont.)

22.   On June 21, 1999, a grand jury subpoena was served on MCI World Com requesting long

distance toll records on (661) 832-5490 and (661) 833-8549. The documents revealed that

incoming calls to both numbers were being forwarded to London, England. Incoming calls to

telephone no. (661) 832-5490 were being forwarded to 441719355499 and incoming calls to

telephone no. (661) 833-8549 were being forwarded to 441712243209. Telephone toll analysis

showed outgoing calls from (661) 832-5490 to the United Kingdom, Canada, Germany,

Switzerland and Iran.

23.   On July 19, 1999, a grand jury subpoena was served on Pacific Bell Telephone Company

for subscriber information and toll records for (661) 836-2788, another telephone line at 800 New

Stine Road, #6, Bakersfield, California. The return revealed Saeed HOMAYOUNI is the subscriber

to (661) 836-2788. Telephone toll analysis of HOMAYOUNI's telephone showed calls placed to

the United Kingdom, Canada, Germany, Switzerland and Iran. The toll analysis also revealed calls

placed to several Southern California numbers on a daily basis.

24.   On June 21, 1999, a grand jury subpoena was served on UPS for records pertaining to

shipments and/or deliveries to MULTICORE LTD, 800 New Stine Road, Suite 6, Bakersfield,

California, 93309. The return revealed from July 1998 to July, 1999, approximately 99 packages

were delivered to MULTICORE LTD, 800 New Stine Road, Suite 6, Bakersfield, California,

93309. The value of the cash on delivery (COD) packages totaled $114,950. The UPS records

reflect the vast majority of the packages received were from organizations, which specialize in

aerospace technology and defense articles.

25.   July 7, 1999, Robert Ely, UPS driver, Bakersfield, California, was interviewed by agents

concerning the deliveries made at 800 New Stine Road, Suite 6, Bakersfield, California. Ely

identified an individual known as "Sid Hamilton" residing at the aforementioned address who

receives packages for MULTICORE LTD. Ely identified Hamilton as the party who would

6

Figure 7.4 Sample Search Warrant #2 (cont.)

provide payment for the deliveries in the form of a MULTICORE LTD company check. Ely indicated that on one occasion he asked Hamilton about the contents of the numerous packages delivered. Hamilton replied "aircraft parts." Ely identified Saeed HOMAYOUNI from a photo lineup to be the person he knows as "Sid Hamilton."

26.   On July 7, 1999, Geneva T. Hawkins, UPS, Counter Clerk, Bakersfield, California, was interviewed by Agents concerning the deliveries to MULTICORE LTD, 800 New Stine Road, Suite 6, Bakersfield, California. Hawkins identified Saeed Homayouni from a California Driver's License photograph as the person she knows as "Sid Hamilton." Hawkins indicated that Hamilton would pick up packages at the UPS facility and would pay with a MULTICORE LTD. company check. Hawkins advised that Hamilton had picked up packages on multiple occasions in the past year.

27.   On June 30, July 27, 1999, October 29, 1999, February 8, 2000, May 5, 2000 and August 2, 2000, grand jury subpoenas were served on Bank of America requesting records pertaining to MULTICORE LTD, Saeed HOMAOUNI or Soroosh HOMAYOUNI. The subpoena returns disclosed a business account in the name of MULTICORE LTD, with Saeed HOMAYOUNI and Soroosh HOMAYOUNI as signators on Bank of America account No. 00336-37940. The records disclosed approximately 399 payments in support of MULTICORE LTD's business operations. The majority of disbursements from the bank account were made to aerospace and military parts brokers. The disbursements totaled approximately $2,259,495.80. The return also showed approximately $2,218,671.26 in deposits made to account no. 00336-37940.

28.   An examination of banking records further revealed that payments had been made to Brimhall Mini Storage, 7830 Brimhall Road, Bakersfield, California, 93309.

29.   A grand jury subpoena was issued on October 6, 1999, to Brimhall Mini Storage, for a listing of renters of storage units within the facility. The return disclosed that Saeed

Figure 7.4 Sample Search Warrant #2 (cont.)

HOMAYOUNI rents storage unit B-48.   A review of the access entry logs indicated that

1   HOMAYOUNI entered the facility approximately 38 times from February 28, 1999 to October 22,

2   1999.   A review of Bank of America records on February 24, 2000, disclosed that HOMAYOUNI

3   rented an additional storage unit identified as unit B-45.

4

5   30.   On July 19, 1999, a grand jury subpoena was served on Airborne Express requesting

6   shipping and delivery documents for MULTICORE LTD, 800 New Stine Road, Suite 6,

7   Bakersfield, California, 93309. The subpoena return disclosed that Airborne Express had been

8   utilized on 12 occasions by MULTICORE LTD. A review of the documents disclosed that on June

9   30, 1998, Rowland Diesel Parts, 1330 E. Vista Way, Suite 7, Vista, California, 92084, had sent a

10 shipment to MULTICORE LTD, C/O All Cargo Express, #03-02A Crocodile House, 3 UBI Ave

11 3, Singapore 408857. The Airborne Express shipment with tracking no 383919620 identified the

12

13 contents as a windshield panel valued at $1,965. The sender was identified as "Joe Barry" with

14 telephone number (760) 639-2649. The shipment originated from the Fresno Airborne Express

15 Station, Fresno, California. It was later determined that "Joe Barry" is an alias of Saeed

16 HOMAYOUNI, and the Vista, California, address is an answering service.

17

18 31.   In July 22, 1999, agents met with Special Agent Juventino Martin, U.S. Department of

19 Commerce, to discuss an ongoing investigation that had identified MULTICORE LTD, London,

20 as a buyer for 20 Litton Magnatron Tubes valued at approximately $300,000. Special Agent

21 Martin advised that a grand jury in the Northern District of Illinois had issued a grand jury

22 subpoena to Richardson's Electronics for shipping documents. A review of the returned documents

23

24   identified invoices for three separate shipments for Magnatron Tubes that were shipped from

25 Richardson's Electronics to MULTICORE LTD, Bakersfield, California.

26 32.   On August 19, 1999, information was received from the U.S. Department of State, Office

27 of Defense Trade Controls which determined that part no. L4940 CFA, Magnatron Tube, requires

28

8

Figure 7.4 Sample Search Warrant #2 (cont.)

a U.S. Department of State license to be exported. The U.S. Department of State also revealed that the magnatron tube is used as a component on the Hawk Missile Defense System.

33.   On December 8, 1999, a surveillance was conducted in the area of 800 New Stine Road, Suite 6, Bakersfield, California. Agents observed Saeed HOMAYOUNI leave his residence with packages and proceed to Mail Boxes, Etc., 8200 Stockdale Highway, Suite M-10, Bakersfield, California. Special Agent Lori Giannantonio entered Mail Boxes, Etc., and observed HOMAYOUNI provide a package to the shipping clerk and heard the clerk advising HOMAYOUNI that the shipping costs $239.00. On the same day at approximately 2:50 p.m. Agents observed HOMAYOUNI entering Mail Boxes, Etc., 7850 White Lane, Suite E, Bakersfield, carrying a package. At approximately 2:55 p.m., HOMAYOUNI exited the Mail Boxes, Etc. without the package and returned to his apartment.

34.   On December 8, 1999, Agents proceeded to the Bakersfield Airport, UPS Courier Plane and observed an international air package with tracking no. 4609 105 332 –2 with the shipper identified as Rowland Diesel Parts, 1330 East Vista Way, #7, Vista, California, 92084 being shipped to M&E Diesel, C/O All Cargo Express, No.9, Airline Road, #02-14, Cargo Agents Building D, Singapore, 819475. The international waybill identified the sender as "Joe Barry", telephone number (760) 639-2649. The waybill description indicated that the contents of the package were "electricals" with a declared value of $1870. A review of the shipping manifest disclosed that the package originated from Mail Boxes, Etc., 8200 Stockdale Highway, Suite M-10, Bakersfield, California.

35.   On December 9, 1999, an Special Agent David Pinchetti, observed Saeed HOMAYOUNI exit his apartment with trash bags and deposited the bags into a trash dumpster. Special Agent Lori Giannantonio retrieved the trash bags from the dumpster. The contents were examined and revealed to be packaging material and wrapping material from Imaging and Sensing Technology Corp., 300 Westinghouse Circle, Horseheads, New York, 14845-2256. The contents also contained

9

Figure 7.4 Sample Search Warrant #2 (cont.)

an invoice from Imaging and Sensing Technology Corp., identifying the components as electron

tubes with part no. NY10137P43. A warning label was included on the invoice, which stated

"diversion contrary to U.S. law prohibited."

36.   On February 2, 2000, Jeff Taylor, CRT Marketing, Electro-Optical Department Imaging

and Sensing Technology was contacted and advised that Part Number NY10137P43, NSN 5960-

01-015-7330, is a cathode ray tube. Taylor also stated that this part is utilized on the F-4 Phantom

aircraft and is for military application only. He added that this part would require a State

Department license to be exported.

37.   A license determination was sent to the Department of State for Part Number NY10137P43,

NSN 5960-01-015-7330. On March 7, 2000 information was received from the Office of Defense

Trade Controls, Department of State that this part requires a State Department license to be

exported.

38.   On December 9, 1999, at approximately 3:10 p.m. after Agent Giannantonio retrieved trash

bags, HOMAYOUNI was observed by Special Agent Sam Medigovich entering the Mail Boxes,

Etc., 8250 Stockdale Highway, Bakersfield, California. Agent Medigovich entered the Mail Boxes,

Etc., and observed HOMAYOUNI preparing shipping documents for shipping a package. Agent

Medigovich observed HOMAYOUNI exit the Mail Boxes, Etc., and return to his apartment.

39.   Later this same date, Agents proceeded to the UPS facility and reviewed paperwork for

international shipments. An examination disclosed UPS waybill, tracking no. 4609 105 330 4

which indicated the shipper as Rowland Diesel Parts, 1330 East Vista Way, #7, Vista, California,

92084. The name of the sender, as indicated on the document, was "Joe Barry", telephone number

(760) 639-2649. The package was being shipped to M&E Diesel, C/O All Cargo Express, No. 9,

Airline Road, #02-14, Cargo Agents Building D, Singapore, 819475. The waybill description

indicated that "electricals" were contained within the box with a value of $1920. A review of the

Figure 7.4 Sample Search Warrant #2 (cont.)

shipping manifest disclosed that the package originated from Mail Boxes, Etc., 8250 Stockdale Highway, Suite M-10, Bakersfield, California.

40.   On February 2, 2000, a review of the records at the Office of Business Licenses, City Hall, Vista, California, for any business license filed for Rowland Diesel Parts, 1330 E. Vista Way, #7, Vista, California, 92084. The reviewed disclosed no records filed by Rowland Diesel Parts for business operations within the City of Vista, California. On the same date, records of the County of San Diego, Fictitious Business Names, were queried for Rowland Diesel Parts, 1330 Vista Way, #7, Vista, California, 92084, with negative results. A check of 1330 E. Vista Way, #7, Vista, California, disclosed an answering service known as "Precise Communications."

41.   On April 11, 2000, agents observed a female, dark hair, dark eyes, approximately 5' 5" to 5' 7", 120 pounds, white clothing, exit 800 New Stine Road, #6, Bakersfield, California, 93309, at approximately 6:45 p.m. The female walked south on New Stine Road. At approximately 8:00 p.m. she returned to 800 New Stine Road, #6, Bakersfield, California, 93309 and entered the apartment. At approximately 10:00 p.m. she was observed in the upstairs window of the second floor room.

42.   On April 13, 2000, a check of the TECS revealed an I-94 listed to a Yew Leng FUNG, DOB 04/05/61, Passport #A8082807, entering the country on British Airways, from London/Heathrow International Airport. She entered the United States on February 25, 2000 on a B2 Visa and was cleared to stay until 8/23/00. She listed her U.S. address as 800 New Stine Road, Bakersfield, California, on the I-94.

43.   On April 25, 2000, agents observed a UPS delivery at approximately 11:00 a.m. to 800 New Stine Road, #6, Bakersfield, California, 93309. The delivery was accepted by Yew Leng FUNG.

11

Figure 7.4 Sample Search Warrant #2 (cont.)

44.   On same date, Robert Ely, UPS driver, advised agents that sometime after the first of the new year, an Asian female, 5'6", 120 pounds, dark hair, started accepting deliveries at 800 New Stine Road, #6, Bakersfield, California 93309. She signed for the packages with the surname of FUNG and paid for the deliveries with MULTICORE LTD checks. Ely observed FUNG completing the amount of the check and the payee (vendor). He advised that the delivery that had taken place earlier this same date had been shipped by Avionics Industries Inc., 7214 N.W. 50 Street, Miami, Florida, 33166. Ely stated that on one occasion in March, he delivered several large packages to FUNG at 800 New Stine Road, #6, Bakersfield, California. FUNG requested that he drive the delivery truck to a garage located within the Jasmine Garden Apartments at 800 New Stine Road, Bakersfield, California. After FUNG opened the garage door, Ely placed the packages in the garage and in the process noticed several large crates within the garage. This garage is believed to be garage number 26 in the Jasmine Garden Apartment complex. The garage is in a beige stucco building with brown trim, containing 5 garages (numbered 22-26). Garage number 26 has a white door and the number 26 on the face of the door.

45.   On April 25, 2000, a review of the records at Brimhall Mini Storage, 7820 Brimhall Road, Bakersfield, California, identified Saeed HOMAYOUNI as renting Unit B45 and B48. A review of the daily sign-in logs revealed that during the month of January, 2000, HOMAYOUNI entered unit B-48 approximately 15 times. During the month of February, 2000, HOMAYOUNI entered unit B-48 approximately 17 times, the last of which was on February 22. FUNG entered units B-45/B-48 approximately 11 times in March and three times in April.

46.   On April 26, 2000, agents observed UPS deliver five large boxes to 800 New Stine Road, #6, Bakersfield, California. The packages were accepted by FUNG.

Figure 7.4 Sample Search Warrant #2 (cont.)

47.   On April 26, 2000, agents interviewed Mary Alford, Manager, Jasmine Garden Apartments, 800 New Stine Road, #6, Bakersfield, California 93309. Alford told agents that Saeed HOMAYOUNI was in London for three months and that a female would be staying in his apartment. Alford verified that Saeed HOMAYOUNI occupied garage number 26 in the Jasmine Garden Apartment complex, and has since June of 1999. Alford stated that she observed Saeed HOMAYOUNI on a couple of occasions with a u-haul trailer that he pulled behind an older model silver Mercedes, which was parked in the rear of the complex. Alford stated that on several occasions she accepted packages for Saeed HOMAYOUNI/MULTICORE LTD when he was not available. Alford also observed the female standing outside of garage number 26 with the door open.

48.   A check of California Department of Motor Vehicles disclosed the Mercedes Benz, California license 2AWF958, VIN 12313012019575, is registered to Saeed HOMAYOUNI, 800 New Stine Road, #6, Bakersfield, California.

49.   On May 9, 2000, a grand jury subpoena was served on Mackenzie Aircraft, 2505 Commerce Way, Vista, California 92083. A review of the records revealed that on May 28, 1999, Mackenzie received an invoice from Peter HARRIS, MULTICORE LTD requesting part number 080-021-001, NSN: 1560-01-042-6351, identified as a cable assembly. On June 1, 1999, the part was shipped to 800 New Stine Road, #6, Bakersfield, California, 93309, via UPS COD with tracking #1Z8E99720342940663.

50.   On May 10, Edward De Marco, Field Service Engineer, Parker-Hannifin, Parker Electronic Systems Division (PESD), 300 Marcus Boulevard, Smithtown, New York 11787, was telephonically interviewed concerning the applications of part number 080-021-001. DeMarco advised that part number 080-021-001 is a harness assembly for a fuel indication system for the F-14 fighter aircraft that is currently in use by the U.S. Navy and Iran.

13

Figure 7.4 Sample Search Warrant #2 (cont.)

51.   On May 10 and 12, 2000, Sol Desimone, Contracts Manager, Contracts Department, Parker-Hannifin, Parker Electronic Systems Division (PESD), 300 Marcus Boulevard, Smithtown, New York 11787 was telephonically interviewed concerning the licensing requirements for part number 080-021-001, the F-14 fuel indication system harness. Desimone advised that part number 080-021-001 would require a U.S. State Department license to be exported.

52.   On May 11, 2000, John and Judy Saffel, Resident Managers, Brimhall Storage (BS), 7830 Brimhall Road, Bakersfield, California, 93308, were interviewed concerning the activities of Saeed HOMAYOUNI. John Saffel advised that HOMAYOUNI rented storage space B-48 on July 8, 1999, and obtained a second storage unit identified as B-45 on October 8, 1999. After reviewing the records of BS, Saffel advised that HOMAYOUNI rented the two units in his own name but pays for them with a check from MULTICORE LTD. John Saffel has observed on several occasions freight trucks arrive and offload boxes for HOMAYOUNI. Judy Saffel advised that the storage units were half full of cardboard boxes and some plastic containers. Both Saffels identified an Asian woman, using the surname of FUNG, as a person seen entering the storage units on numerous occasions. On one occasion FUNG told the Saffels that she was there taking inventory.

53.   On May 11, 2000 a surveillance was conducted at 800 New Stine Road, #6, Bakersfield, California, 83309. FUNG was seen leaving the apartment with a white bag tied at the top and walking in the direction of the trash dumpster located across the parking lot. The white bag was later recovered from the dumpster. Found in the white bag was a note asking to have "bearings" shipped. The note was signed "Peter" and dated May 5, 2000. On the opposite side of the paper, another note was written to "Peter" letting him know the bearings were shipped earlier that day. Also found in the white bag were two labels from Kaydon Corporation,

14

Figure 7.4 Sample Search Warrant #2 (cont.)

stating "Reali-Slim Ball Bearing" with KG200AHO written on the bottom of the label.

54.   On May 23, 2000, agents observed Saeed HOMAYOUNI and Yew FUNG proceed to COMP USA, 3001 California Avenue, Bakersfield, California, 93309 and purchase a computer system.

55.   On May 25, 2000, SA Kevin Keating observed Saeed HOMAYOUNI and Yew Leng FUNG loading approximately eight boxes into HOMAYOUNI's white Volkswagen Jetta. Agents followed FUNG to the Brimhall Mini Storage facility and observed her at Unit B-48. Agents noticed that approximately ½ to ¾ of the unit was full of crates and boxes.

56.   A check of California Department of Motor Vehicles disclosed the Volkswagen Jetta, California license 3LFX477, VIN 3VWRC81H0SM027083 is registered to Saeed HOMAYOUNI, 800 New Stine Road, #6, Bakersfield, California.

57.   On August 8, 2000, a subpoena was served on Patrick Lee, Vice President of Lee Air Company, Inc., requesting business records pertaining to any transactions between Lee Air and **MULTICORE LTD.** Mr. Lee described Lee Air Company as a family-owned business which specializes in aerospace components and approximately 85 percent of the business is related to military components. Lee advised that his business is conducted through the utilization of Lee Air Company facsimile lines and detailed the following procedure: customers will fax an RFQ to Lee Air; Lee reviews the RFQ and provides pricing information and availability information and will then fax this response back to the identified return fax number. If a customer wants to procure the part, the purchase order will be faxed to Lee Air and the order will be shipped out via UPS with an invoice. Lee advised that he requires COD payments with customers that he is unfamiliar with, or do not have a credit history pertaining to procurements. After reviewing the records of Lee Air Company, it was determined that from November, 1998, to August, 2000, Lee Air Company had received 35 RFQ's for aerospace components from **MULTICORE**

Figure 7.4 Sample Search Warrant #2 (cont.)

LTD, the last one (**MULTICORE's** reference: ANAH/3F04/10) being received on August 1,

2000. Records also revealed that from the period of March 1999 to August, 2000, nine

purchase orders from **MULTICORE LTD** were filled by from Lee Air company.

58. · The purchase order received by Lee Air, dated July 31, 2000, from MULTICORE LTD,

identifies part #571617-1, NSN 1660-00-006-7982 as an "impeller" manufactured by

Honeywell International, Inc. The purchase order was for 40 units at $3,000 per unit for a total

purchase order of $120,000, including shipping and insurance. The parts were shipped COD

via UPS to **MULTICORE LTD,** 800 New Stine Road, #6, Bakersfield, California 93308.

Within the shipment was an invoice that included a warning statement, "If the material

supplied/quoted herewith is to be exported or delivered to a representative of a foreign country

or company, you may be required to first obtain appropriate license (s) from either the U.S.

State Department or the U.S. Department of Commerce." The parts were shipped on August 3,

2000, in three separate packages with tracking numbers #1Z9199847241141287,

#1Z9199847241053275, and #1Z9199847241958691. Information obtained from UPS

indicates that on August 4, 21000, the packages were signed for and received by a

"HAMILTON" at the UPS facility in Bakersfield, California. Lee believes that he received a

verbal request from **MULTICORE LTD** for availability and pricing information for part

#571617-1, NSN: 1660-00-006-7982 (an impeller). Later, MULTICORE LTD purchased 40

impellers at $3,000 each for a total purchase price of $120,000.

59.   On August 9, 2000, Duane Huff, Honeywell International, customer Service

(Engineering), advised that part #571617-1, NSN 1660-00-006-7982 is an impeller which was

specifically designed for use on the F-14A Tomcat Fighter Aircraft. Part #571617-1 is a

component utilized for the cooling turbine on the F-14A air cycle system which controls the

cabin pressure of the cockpit and regulates cooling of the electronics. Huff indicated that the

16

Figure 7.4 Sample Search Warrant #2 (cont.)

part was specifically designed for the F-14A and has no commercial application. Huff advised

1   that this part requires a State Department license to be exported.

2   60.   On August 10, 2000, George Rao, Honeywell International, Export Compliance Office,

3   Washington D.C., advised that a Department of State export license is required for part

4   #571617-1, NSN 1660-00-006-7982. Rao advised that the U.S. Navy and the Iranian Air Force

5

6   are the only two organizations that fly the F-14 in the world. Rao advised, "If somebody is

7   trying to export this item, they are smugglers and should be arrested."

8   61.   Further analysis disclosed that on August 7, 2000, a purchase order was received by Lee

9   Air from **MULTICORE LTD** via facsimile for part #40-619-1, NSN 1630-00-197-6899,

10 identified as a sensor, with a unit price of $300.00 and a total price of $900. The purchase

11 order also requested part #180820-7, NSN 1680-00-003-1454, identified as a control assembly,

12

13 with a unit price of $500 and a total price of $500. The purchase order identified two separate

14 quotation numbers that were sent to **MULTICORE LTD** from Lee Air Company Inc. The

15 first quotation was sent via facsimile on January 5, 1999, requesting pricing on part #180820-7,

16

17 NSN 1680-00-003-1454 identified as a control assembly. The second quotation was sent to

18 MULTICORE LTD from Lee Air Company Inc. via facsimile on August 2, 2000, requesting

19 pricing for part #40-619-1, NSN 1630-00-197-6899 identified as a sensor. Part # 40-619-1,

20 NSN 1630-00-197-6899 and part #180820-7, NSN 1680-00-003-1454 were scheduled to be

21 shipped on August 8, 2000.

22 62.   On August 9, 2000, Patrice Davis, Hydro-Aire, Burbank, California, advised that part

23

24 #40-619-1, NSN 1630-00-197-6899, is a wheel speed sensor for an installation kit which is

25 utilized on the F-4 Fighter Aircraft. Davis indicated that the item would require an export

26 license to be exported.

27 63.   On August 10, 2000, Sandra Brooks, Program Administrator, Curtis Wright Flight

28

17

Figure 7.4 Sample Search Warrant #2 (cont.)

Systems Inc., North Carolina, advised that part #180820-7, NSN 1680-00-003-1454, is a component utilized on the shaft assembly that controls the flaps/slats drive system on the F-14 Tomcat Fighter Aircraft. Brooks advised that the aforementioned part would require an export license issued by the Department of State.

64.   On September 21, 2000, at approximately 7:00 p.m., Justin Ingram, UPS, notified affiant regarding a shipment made by JOE BARRY, dba ROWLAND DIESEL, 1330 E. Vista Way, #7, Vista California, 92084. On September 22, 2000, SA David Pinchetti and affiant retrieved the package from UPS. Shipping records disclosed the package was being shipped to M&E Diesel C/O All Cargo Express, No.9 Airline Road, #02-14, Cargo Agents Building D, Singapore, 819475 with tracking number 45974007274. The UPS waybill identified the package contents as "Electrical" and were valued at $1,800. A commercial invoice filed with the UPS waybill identified the contents as 10 motors valued at $180 each. Examination of the contents disclosed ten direct current (DC) motors packaged separately in small boxes. No invoices or shipping instructions were found in the package. Review of the parts revealed no part numbers or manufacturing labels. Found on the sides of the parts was a glue like substance where a label may have been affixed. It is your affiant's belief that lack of shipping documentation and the removal of all identifiable information is a sanitation method to thwart U.S. Customs in the identification of such parts.

65.   On September 26, 2000, Derek Keegan, Director of Marketing, Globe Motors Inc., Daton, Ohio, advised that the direct current (DC) motor appeared to be a Globe Motors produced DC motor of the LL or MM class. He advised that such DC motors have applications in military, aerospace and industrial uses. He further indicated that the export of such a motor to such countries as India, South Korea would require a U.S. Department of State export license. He indicated that there were other countries where as a minimum a U.S. Department of

18

Figure 7.4 Sample Search Warrant #2 (cont.)

Commerce export license would be required. Keegan advised that he was aware of Globe

Motor customers in Singapore but could not articulate why one of those customers would have

a requirement for such a part. He indicated that such aerospace applications for such a part

range from military helicopter use to missile applications. He advised that the part has been

utilized in commercial applications such as industrial welding and deep sea submersible

vehicles.

66.   On October 6, 2000, during a surveillance operation, HOMAYOUNI was seen throwing

trash into the apartment complex dumpster. The trash was retrieved and the contents are as

follows:

A. 3 separate facsimile transmissions which contain a matrix work sheet of

purchases and instructions of the parts to be shipped, number of each item to

be shipped and how to package each item. Each item is identified by

Supplier Name, Qty, P/N, Desc, Order No., Box, #PriceUnit $Price Total.

B. An invoice, #73481077 from Avnet Electronics Mktg., dated 08-08-00 with

Customer PO#ANH/3DRA-ORD-1. The invoice shows Multicore LTD, 800

New Stine Road, Suite 6, Bakersfield, California 93309, as the company

responsible for the bill and where the items should be shipped. On 08-08-00

10 of Part #5A1426 were ordered, three were shipped and 7 were on back

order. A second invoice, #73696899 was found, same billing and shipping

information, and PO#, identifying the same part number ordered and 7

shipped.

C. Four sheets of paper with the following information; 1. "Aerolex

Engineering 14-61402-1 Seal Qty:5;" 2. "Aerolex Engineering Inc. 2-

70465-1 Handle Emergency Qty:5;" 3. "Aerolex Engineering 14-50706-11

19

Figure 7.4 Sample Search Warrant #2 (cont.)

Tube Qty:2;" 4. "Avial PN:7511945 Filter Element Qty:10."

D. A FedEx COD shipping document with tracking #790860376648 from Aerolex Engineering Corp 5318 E 2nd St, Ste 155, Long Beach, California to Multicore Ltd, 800 New Stine Rd Suite 6, Bakersfield, California. The document shows the delivery was made on July 12, 2000.

E. Four more sheets of paper were found and identified as, 1. "Aerolex Engineering 14-40410-2 Lock Assy S/N 6992-217 Qty:1;" 2. "Aerolex Engineering 14-61104-1 Amplifier S/N: 115, 116, 117, 118, 119 Qty: 5;" 3. "Aerolex Engineering 855CF1 Pitot Static Tube S/N 30342 Qty: 1;." 4. "Connector Distr. Corp. P.N.:PC-211-E49 Desc: Connector Qty: 2;" Also found was a parts slip from Connector Distribution Corporation, 2985 E. Harcourt Street Rancho Dominguez, California, 90221, for Part No. PC-211-E49, W.O. 93116, Quantity 2.

F. Part of a package with a partial shipping label attached from Peerless Aerospace, referencing Order # ANH/3A41/ORD-1. This order number matches the information found on one of the facsimiles requesting Peerless Aerospace, Part #HL18PB-8-4, Order No. ANH/3A41/ORD-1 to be shipped with specific instructions.

G. One plastic bag with a company sticker identifying "AVIALL" which contained an item manufactured and or sold by Aviall.

H. A UPS delivery notice showing attempted delivery October 2, of a COD package sent by Quality Aviation in the amount of $13,738.00.

I. An attempted delivery notice from FedEx on August 24, 2000 with tracking #425951610122 sent by Bage Industries. The package was sent COD in the

Figure 7.4 Sample Search Warrant #2 (cont.)

amount of $211.62.

67.   Also during the October 6, 2000, surveillance operation, Senior Special Agent Clark

Settles witnessed Saeed HOMAYOUNI, transport boxes from his apartment, Number 6, located

at the Jasmine Garden apartments, to his garage, Number #26, located at the Jasmine Garden

apartments. SA Settles also witnessed Saeed HOMAYOUNI load his white Jetta on two

occasions this same date removing boxes from his apartment, placing them in the white Jetta

and then driving to the Brimhall Storage Facility. Once at the facility, Saeed HOMAYOUNI

unloaded the boxes into Unit 45. Later in the afternoon, Saeed HOMAYOUNI loaded boxes

from his apartment into his white Jetta and proceeded to the Brimhall Storage Facility where he

unloaded the boxes into Unit 45.

68.   On October 9, 2000, through surveillance it was determined that Saeed HOMAYOUNI

visited Mail Boxes Etc., 8200 Stockdale Highway, Bakersfield, for the purpose of sending a

package via Fed Ex to Singapore. Later this same date, Agents went to the Fed Ex Bakersfield

Facility and retrieved a package with tracking # 812402251852 sent by Joe Barry, dba Rowland

Diesel Parts, 1330 E. Vista Way #7, Vista, California, 92084. The package was addressed to

M&E Diesel C/O All Cargo Express, No. 9 Airline Rd #02-14, Cargo Agents Building D,

Singapore, 819475. The contents were identified as 5 seals valued at $5.00 each, 6 filters valued

at $50.00 each, 7 bolts valued at $2.00 each, 10 bolts valued at $3.00 each, 2 connectors valued

at $60.00 each and 5 handles valued at $120.00 for a total value of $1,189.00. An examination

of the package contents disclosed three boxes labeled A, B and C. No invoices were found.

Box A: Contained four items numbered 1, 2, 3, 4; Item #1 - 5 rubber seals I

dentified by part number 14-61402; Item #2 - 6 filters identified by part

number 7511945; Item #3 - 7 bolts, identified by number PBF 51B464;

Item #4 - 10 bolts identified by number PBF 51B464.

21

Figure 7.4 Sample Search Warrant #2 (cont.)

Box B: Contained 2 connectors identified by part number 14-50706-11.

Box C: Contained 5 yellow handles with a pull cord identified by numbers 6823, 2-70465-1 and No. 18229.

69.   It is affiant's belief that the papers retrieved from the trash on October 6, 2000, identifying Aerolex Engineering, part number 14-61402-1 identified as a seal, part number 2-70465-1 identified as a handle emergency, and part number 14-50706-11 identified as a tube are an exact match to the parts found in Box A, item #2, Box C and Box B respectively.

70.   On October 10, 2000, Bruce Rice, Northrop-Grumman, Logistics Specialist, was contacted regarding part # 14-61402-1 identified as rubber seals; part # 7511945 identified as filters; part #PBF51B464 identified as bolts and part #14-50706-11 identified as connectors. Rice identified all four parts as associated with the F-5 Tiger Military Aircraft and indicated that part numbers beginning with "14" were specifically associated with the F-5 Program. He indicated that the aforementioned parts could be traced back to Northrop-Grumman specification number 78623. He further advised that if Northrop-Grumman were exporting such parts to Singapore a U.S. Department of State export license would be required to cover the transaction.

71.   On October 11 and 18, 2000, Alan Jones, Export Compliance, Northrop-Grumman, was contacted regarding part numbers 14-61402-1 identified as a rubber seal, part number 7511945 identified as a filter, part PBF 51B464 identified as a bolt, part number 14-50706-11 identified as a connector, part number 768 23-2 70465-1 #18229 identified as a handle with a pull cord and part number NAS1435-K2 identified as a clip. Jones indicated that all the items are identifiable with the F-5 Tiger Program and are utilized on this aircraft. Jones relayed that the clips and bolts could be used on other aircraft, however, Northrop-Grumman would consider the items as covered under the ITAR and found on the U.S. Munitions List, therefore would

22

Figure 7.4 Sample Search Warrant #2 (cont.)

require a U.S. Department of State license to be exported.

72.   On November 2, 2000, through surveillance it was determined that Saeed HOMAYOUNI visited Mail Boxes Etc., 8200 Stockdale Highway, Bakersfield, for the purpose of sending a package via UPS to Singapore. Later this same date, Agents went to the UPS Bakersfield Facility and retrieved a package with tracking #45974007309 sent by Joe Barry, dba Rowland Diesel Parts, 1330 E. Vista Way #7, Vista, Califonria, 92084. The package was addressed to M&E Diesel C/O All Cargo Express, No. 9 Airline Rd #02-14, Cargo Agents Building D, Singapore, 819475. The contents were identified as 10 lamps valued at 20.00 each, 5 bearing sleeves valued at 25.00 each, 10 valves valued at 65.00 each, 3 screws valued at 5.00 each, and two actuator kits valued at 60.00 each for a total value of $1110.00. An examination of the package contents disclosed five packages labeled Item 1, Item 2, Item 3, Item 4, and Item 5. A copy of the airway bill was enclosed. The package labeled Item 1 contained 10 bulbs (identified by part number CM8-109). The package labeled Item 2 bearing sleeves, contained five sleeves individually wrapped. The package labeled Item 3 contained 9 check valves (identified by part number 2C5820). The package labeled Item 4 contained three aluminum bolts (identified by part number 32-32255-11). The package labeled Item 5 contained one check valve (identified by part number 2C5820) and two actuator kits (identified by part 140121-1).

BUSINESS RECORDS:

73.   Based upon my training and experience and information related to me by agents and others experienced in investigating conspiracies to illegally export defense articles and technology subject to export control, individuals involved in this illegal activity often maintain records and documents that relate to, or otherwise evidence their illicit activities in order to keep track of the ordering, purchasing, storage, distribution and transportation of the illegal items. The records and documents

23

Figure 7.4 Sample Search Warrant #2 (cont.)

include requests for quotes, quotes, correspondence, memoranda, e-mails, notes, daily calendars, invoices, purchase orders, shipping documents, receipts, airway bills, facsimiles, telexes, delivery records, inventory documents, sales records, export licenses and contracts.

74.   Affiant believes, based on the investigation described above, that MULTICORE LTD and ROWLAND DIESEL are conducting no legitimate business. Rather, they are front organizations used to acquire and ship overseas, contrary to law, defense articles and other goods and technology subject to export control. All business records that reference or relate to these entities, therefore, would be evidence of the criminal violations referenced herein.

COMPUTER DATA:

75.   Based upon my training, experience and information related to me by agents and others involved in the forensic examination of computers, I know that computer data can be stored on a variety of systems and storage devices including hard disk drives, floppy disks, compact disks, magnetic tapes and memory chips. I also know that during the search of the premises it is not always possible to search computer equipment and storage devices for data for a number of reasons, including the following:

　　a. Searching computer systems is a highly technical process which requires specific expertise and specialized equipment. There are so many types of computer hardware and software in use today that it is impossible to bring to the search site all of the necessary technical manuals and specialized equipment necessary to conduct a thorough search. In addition, it may also be necessary to consult with compuer personnel who have specific expertise in the type of computer, software application or operating system that is being searched.

　　b. Searching computer systems requires the use of precise, scientific procedures which are designed to maintain the integrity of the evidence and to recover "hidden," erased,

24

Figure 7.4 Sample Search Warrant #2 (cont.)

compressed, encrypted or password-protected data. Computer hardware and storage devices may contain "boobytraps" that destroy or alter data if certain procedures are not scrupulously followed. Since computer data is particularly vulnerable to inadvertent or intentional modification or destruction, a controlled environment, such as a law enforcement laboratory, is essential to conduct a complete and accurate analysis of the equipment and storage devices from which the data will be extracted.

c. The volume of data stored on many computer systems and storage devices will typically be so large that it will be highly impractical to search for data during the execution of the physical search of the premises. A single megabyte of storage space is the equivalent of 500 double-spaced pages of text. A single gigabyte of storage space, or 1,000 megabytes, is the equivalent of 500,000 double-spaced pages of text. Storage devices capable of storing fifteen gigabytes of data are now commonplace in desktop computers. Consequently, each non-networked, desktop computer found during a search can easily contain the equivalent of 7.5 million pages of data, which, if printed out, would completely fill a 10' x 12' x 10' room to the ceiling.

d. Computer users can attempt to conceal data within computer equipment and storage devices through a number of methods, including the use of innocuous or misleading filenames and extensions. For example, files with the extension ".jpg" often are image files; however, a user can easily change the extension to ".txt" to conceal the image and make it appear that the file contains text. Computer users can also attempt to conceal data by using encryption, which means that a password or device, such as a "dongle" or "keycard", is necessary to decrypt the data into a readable form. In addition, computer users can conceal data within another seemingly unrelated and innocuous file in a process called "steganography." For example, by using steganography a computer

25

Figure 7.4 Sample Search Warrant #2 (cont.)

user can conceal text in an image file which cannot be viewed when the image file is opened. Therefore, a substantial amount of time is necessary to extract and sort through data that is concealed or encrypted to determine whether it is evidence, contraband or instrumentalities of a crime.

CUSTODY OF EVIDENCE:

76.   I respecfully request permission to maintain evidence seized pursuant to this search warrant at the offices of the participating investigative agencies in the Southern District of California, where the investigation is based.

CONCLUSION:

77.   Based on the facts set forth herein, and on my experience and training in investigating cases involving violations of federal law, I submit there is probable cause to believe that the evidence of violations of 22 U.S.C. § 2778 (Arms Export control Act), 50 U.S.C. App. § 2410 (Export Administration Act), 18 U.S.C. § 1956 (a) (2) (Money Laundering), and 18 U.S.C. § 371 (Conspiracy) specified in Attachment "A" will be found at the premises to be searched.

I declare under penalty of perjury under the laws of the United States that the foregoing is true and correct.

Wendy J. Duarte, Special Agent
U.S. Customs Service

Subscribed to and sworn before me

This 6th day of ___Dec___, 2000.

United States Magistrate Judge

26

Figure 7.4 Sample Search Warrant #2 (cont.)

ATTACHMENT "A"

ITEMS TO BE SEIZED:

The following evidence of violations of 22 U.S.C. § 2778 (Arms Export Control Act), 50 U.S.C. App. § 2410 (Export Administration Act), 18 U.S.C. § 1956(a)(2)(A) (Money Laundering), and 18 U.S.C. § 371 (Conspiracy):

A.   Defense articles; that is, items on the United States Munitions List;

B.   Goods or technology subject to export control;

C.   Cash, checks, money orders, or other financially negotiable instruments available to purchase defense articles, or goods or technology subject to export control;

D.   The following records and documents, referencing or related to Multicore Ltd or Rowland Diesel, for the period January 1, 1996, to the present:

    1.   Business records of Multicore Ltd, and of Rowland Diesel, including requests for quotes, quotes, correspondence, memoranda, e-mails, notes, daily calendars, invoices, purchase orders, shipping documents, receipts, airway bills, facsimiles, telexes, delivery records, inventory documents, sales records, export licenses and contracts;

    2.   Specifications for, and descriptions of, defense articles, and goods and technology subject to export control;

    3.   Certificates of conformance;

    4.   Applications for export licenses, and regulations and statutes related to United States export license requirements;

    5.   Banking statements, returned checks, check registers, checkbooks, deposit slips, withdrawal slips, cashier's checks, money orders, wire transfers, currency transaction reports, credit card statements, and credit card receipts;

    6.   Documents and effects that show residency, or dominion and control, of the place to be searched as described in Attachment A, including keys, receipts, bills, canceled checks, mail envelopes, rental agreements, telephone records, utility bills, internet/cable provider statements and receipts;

Figure 7.4 Sample Search Warrant #2 (cont.)

      7.   Records of domestic and international travel, including airplane, hotel, gasoline, rental vehicles expenses, and travel itineraries.

   D.   As used above, the terms "records and documents" includes records, documents, programs, applications or materials created, modified or stored in any form, including

   E.   In searching for data capable of being read, stored or interpreted by a computer, law enforcement personnel executing this search warrant will employ the following procedure:

      1.   Upon securing the premises, law enforcement personnel trained in searching and seizing computer data (the "computer personnel") will make an initial review of any computer equipment and storage devices to determine whether these items can be searched on-site in a reasonable amount of time and without jeopardizing the ability to preserve the data.

      2.   If the computer equipment and storage devices cannot be searched on-site, and it has been determined that the items are not instrumentalities or fruits of the offense stated above, do not contain contraband, and are not otherwise illegally possessed, then the computer personnel will determine whether it is practical to copy the data during the execution of the search in a reasonable amount of time without jeopardizing the ability to preserve the data.

      3.   If the computer personnel determine it is not practical to perform an on-site search or make an on-site copy of the data, then the computer equipment and storage devices will be seized and transported to an appropriate law enforcement laboratory for review. The computer equipment and storage devices will be reviewed by appropriately trained personnel in order to extract and seize any data that falls within the list of items to be seized set forth herein.

      4.   If law enforcement personnel determine, either on-site or during a subsequent off-site search, t hat any computer equipment, storage device or data (a) is an instrumentality of the offense stated above, meaning that is was designed or intended for use of, or is being or has been used, as the means of committing the offense; (b) contains any contraband, such as counterfeit or stolen software, child pornography, national security information, or unauthorized access devices such as stolen credit card numbers; (c) is the fruits of criminal activity; or (d) is otherwise criminally possessed, the

Figure 7.4 Sample Search Warrant #2 (cont.)

property shall be seized and not returned pursuant to Federal Rule of Criminal Procedure 41(b).

5. Any data that is encrypted and unreadable will not be returned unless law enforcement personnel have determined that the data is not (a) an instrumentality of the offense, (b) a fruit of the criminal activity, (c) contraband, (d) otherwise unlawfully possessed, or (e) evidence of the offense specified above.

6. In searching the data, the computer personnel will examine all of the data contained in the computer equipment and storage devices to view their precise contents and determine whether the data falls within the items to be seized as set forth herein. In addition, the computer personnel will search for and attempt to recover "deleted," "hidden" or encrypted data to determine whether the data falls within the list of items to be seized as set forth herein.

7. If the computer personnel determine that the computer equipment and storage devices are no longer necessary to retrieve and preserve the data, and the items are not subject to seizure pursuant to Federal Rule of Criminal Procedure 41(b), the government will return these items within a reasonable period of time not to exceed 60 days from the date of seizure.

8. In order to search for data that is capable of being read or interpreted by a computer, law enforcement personnel will need to seize and search the following items, subject to the procedures set forth above:

    a. Any computer equipment and storage device capable of being used to commit, further or store evidence of the offenses listed above;

    b. Any computer equipment used to facilitate the transmission, creation, display, encoding or storage of data, including word processing equipment, modems, docking stations, monitors, printers, plotters, encryption devices, and optical scanners;

    c. Any magnetic, electronic or optical storage device capable of storing data, such as floppy disks, hard disks, tapes, CD-ROMs, CD-R, CD-RWs, DVDs, optical disks, printer or memory buffers, smart cards, PC cards, memory calculators, electronic dialers, electronic notebooks, and personal digital assistants;

Figure 7.4 Sample Search Warrant #2 (cont.)

    d.   Any documentation, operating logs and reference manuals regarding the operation of the computer equipment, storage devices or software;

    e.   Any applications, utility programs, compilers, interpreters, and other software used to facilitate direct or indirect communication with the computer hardware, storage devices or data to be searched;

    f.   Any physical keys, encryption devices, dongles and similar physical items that are necessary to gain access to the computer equipment, storage devices or data; and

    g.   Any passwords, password files, test keys, encryption codes or other information necessary to access the computer equipment, storage devices or data.

F.   If a safe is found on the premises, searching agents will attempt to open it at the scene in order to search it for the items specified above. In the event that the safe is locked and agents are unable to open it on the scene, they will remove the safe from the premises to a site where it may be opened. The safe and any items outside the scope of the items described above will be returned to the premises to be searched within five business days.

Consent Searches

If you do not have probable cause to obtain a search warrant, do not overlook the possibility of getting the suspect to agree to a consent search. It has always amazed me why people allow law enforcement officers to search their houses, belongings and vehicles when they know it contains contraband, but it happens. You must be in a position to show that the person understood that they were not under duress when they allowed you to conduct the search. Most agencies have a consent form they have the person sign. Be sure they can read and write and understand what they are signing. Have a witness and if possible videotape the consent.

Figure 7.5 Sample Consent to Search Computer Equipment Form

DHS/ICE San Diego

Department of Homeland Security
Immigration and Customs Enforcement

CONSENT TO SEARCH COMPUTER EQUIPMENT / ELECTRONIC DATA

I, _____ hereby authorize

_____, who has identified himself as a law enforcement officer, and any other person(s), including but not limited to a computer forensic examiner he may designate to assist him, to remove, take possession of and /or conduct a complete search of the following computer system, electronic data storage device, computer data storage diskettes or CD-ROMs, or any other electronic equipment capable of storing, retrieving, and / or accessing data or necessary to assist in the accessing of said electronic data.

I further authorize the law enforcement officer(s) to copy, print and keep any document or data found on the computer equipment described above that is contraband or evidence of any crime.

I give this consent to search freely and voluntarily without fear, threat, coercion or promises of any kind and with full knowledge of my constitutional right to refuse to give my consent for the removal and / or search of the aforementioned equipment / data, which I hereby waive. I am also aware that if I wished to exercise this right at any time during the seizure and or search of the equipment / data, it would be respected.

This consent to search is given by me this _____ day of _____,

_____, at _____ am/pm.

Witness: _____   Name Printed: _____

Signed: _____   Signed: _____

Agency /Address: _____   Address: _____

_____   _____

     Phone: _____

Witness: _____

Signed: _____

Agency /Address: _____

_____

SUMMARY

Criminal investigators have a number of investigative techniques available to them. For conspiracy investigations, electronic surveillance is probably the most important. Remember that the agreement is an essential element to the crime of conspiracy. Wiretaps enable investigators to listen in on the conversations of the suspects. However, getting the evidence to obtain a wiretap requires using other investigative techniques. Confidential informants, trash runs, DNRs, surveillance, and other techniques are necessary prior, during and sometimes after wiretaps. Using undercover agents provides the government with a credible witness, but safety is an issue.

DISCUSSION QUESTIONS

1. Take the organizational chart you did for the drug organization in Chapter 5 and discuss what investigative techniques you would use and in what order to disrupt and dismantle the organization.

2. How would go about recruiting confidential informants and sources of information?

3. If you were a juror, how would you evaluate the testimony of a confidential informant?

ADDITIONAL READINGS

The Informant, Kurt Eichenwald, Hardcover, Broadway Books, 2000

Department of Justice, United States Attorney's Manual, www.usdoj.gov/usao/eousa/foia_reading_room, Title, Section 9.7, Electronic Surveillance

Department of Justice, United States Attorney's Manual, www.usdoj.gov/usao/eousa/foia_reading_room, Title, Section 9.13, Obtaining Evidence

BIBLIOGRAPHY

United States Customs Service, Law Course for Custom Officers

Chapter 8

Evidence

CHAPTER OVERVIEW

In this chapter you will learn about different types of evidence such as documentary evidence, electronic evidence and physical evidence. You will examine in detail the different types of evidence and what tools are available for law enforcement officers to legally obtain the different types of evidence.

CHAPTER OBJECTIVES

1. Know the definition of documentary evidence.
2. Know the different types of documentary evidence available to help prove a case.
3. Know the definition of electronic evidence.
4. Know the different types of electronic evidence.
5. Know the definition of physical evidence.
6. Know the different types of physical evidence and how they can help prove your case.
7. Know what legal tools are available to law enforcement officers to legally obtain evidence and the pros and cons of some of the tools.

INTRODUCTION

Evidence is the foundation for building a criminal case. It is the burden of the government to prove beyond a reasonable doubt that the person on trial committed the crime for which they stand trial. The court will examine the evidence and the defense counsel for its relevancy and that it is legally admissible. Prior to trial a defendant will receive all the evidence that the government intends to enter in the trial through a process known as discovery. The defense attorney will examine the evidence and how it was obtained. The defense's best chance to obtain an acquittal is to have the damaging evidence thrown out so that it never gets introduced at trial. The first place the defense attorney is likely to look is at the search warrant or search warrants in the case. The problem for the defense is that all the warrants have been examined and authorized by a judge that the government did have the probable cause necessary to obtain the warrant. A search conducted under a warrant is presumed to be lawful and the defendant has the burden of proving it was illegal. The defense will look for misconduct by the government or its informants. The defense will look at the documentary, electronic and physical evidence in the application and affidavit for search warrant to be sure the informant was legally obtained. So it is important that the investigators know how to legally obtain the evidence they need.

OBTAINING EVIDENCE

There are a number of ways to obtain evidence. Someone can just give you evidence that they have or control. A person who was defrauded by someone can turn over to you any documents they have for the transactions for which they were defrauded. You can obtain a search warrant as was discussed in Chapter 7 and seize the evidence. You can collect evidence at a crime scene. Most of the documentary evidence you will need will be controlled by a business and they will not turn over information on their customers without the legal obligation to do so.

The two types of subpoenas available to law enforcement officers are administrative and grand jury. An administrative subpoena is a subpoena authorized by state or federal regulations. A number of federal agencies have the authority to require the production of records and the testimony of persons for specific federal laws. The former United States Customs Service, now part of the new Department of Homeland Security, has administrative subpoenas for export cases, drug cases and customs violations. Those subpoenas are authorized to be issued by any assistant special agent in charge or higher on behalf of the Commissioner of Customs.

A federal grand jury subpoena can be issued for any records. The Grand Jury can compel the production of records and the testimony of any person. An assistant United States attorney who will appear before the grand jury and tell them why the information is needed will request the subpoena. This is a routine matter. When the records are received, the grand jury will be told. Grand Jury subpoenas can only be used prior to an indictment. Once an indictment has been issued, the court must issue a trial subpoena.

The question is which subpoena would you use and why? Administrative subpoenas are preferred to grand jury subpoenas. First, they are easier to obtain. The agent simply completes the subpoena and gives it to his supervisor to have it signed by the designated agency person. Any issues can be addressed quickly. The second and more important reason is that grand jury information is secret and under the Federal Rules for Criminal Procedures, rule 6(e), the grand jury must be advised and authorize each person who will have access to the information. Therefore, it is difficult to share the information with other investigators or law enforcement officials from other agencies or even with people within your own agency. Some cases have both a civil and criminal parallel investigation being conducted at the same time. Evidence obtained via a grand jury subpoena cannot be used in the civil side, unless it is become public through a trial. Information obtained via an administrative subpoena can be used in both the civil and criminal cases, saving both time and money. There are some things that can only be obtained by a grand jury subpoena such as a credit report. Normally, banks will require grand jury subpoenas for financial information.

Figure 8.1 Sample Subpoena

CUSTOMS CONTROLLED SUBSTANCES ENFORCEMENT SUBPOENA

1 To (Name, Address, City, State, Zip)	DEPARTMENT OF THE TREASURY United States Customs Service **S U B P O E N A** TO APPEAR AND/OR PRODUCE RECORDS

By the service of this subpoena upon you, YOU ARE HEREBY REQUIRED TO:

(a) ☐ APPEAR before the Customs Special Agent named in Block 2 below at the place, date, and time indicated to testify and give information.

(b) ☒ PRODUCE the records (including statements, declarations, other documents, and tangible things), indicated in Block 3 below, before the Customs Officer named in Block 2 at the place, date and time indicated.

Your testimony and/or the production of the indicated records is required in connection with an investigation or inquiry concerning the enforcement of Section 545, Title 18, U.S. Code (relating to the smuggling of goods into the United States), with respect to any controlled substance.

Failure to comply with this subpoena will render you liable to proceedings in a U.S. District Court to enforce compliance with this subpoena as well as other sanctions.

2 (a) Name, title, address, and telephone number of Customs Special Agent before whom you are to appear US Customs Service 185 West F Street, Suite 600 San Diego, California 92101 TEL: FAX: 619.	(b) Date: January 30, 2002 (c) Time: 1:00 p.m.

3 RECORDS REQUIRED TO BE PRODUCED FOR INSPECTION:

Pursuant to an Official Investigation being conducted by the United States Customs Service, it is directed that your company furnish all subscriber, credit and service information, or any reseller/portability information for the following numberto include phone tolls for the time frame of November 1, 2001 until present.

You are requested not to disclose this subpoena for an indefinite period of time. Any such disclosure will impede this investigation and thereby interfere with the enforcement of Federal law.

Issued under authority of 21 U.S.C. 967, Public Law 97-258, Section 1 as amended.

4 Name of person authorized to serve subpoena **Special Agent** or any other Customs Special Agent	5 Date Of Issue January 30, 2002
	COMMISSIONER OF CUSTOMS BY *(Signature)*
If you have any questions regarding this subpoena, contact the Customs officer identified in Block 2.	6 Name, title, address, and telephone number of person issuing this subpoena **Special Agent in Charge** **U.S. CUSTOMS SERVICE** 185 West F street, Suite 600 San Diego, CA 92101 TEL: 619.744.4600

CUSTOMS FORM 389 (10/01)

Figure 8.1 Sample Subpoena (cont.)

CERTIFICATE OF SERVICE AND ACKNOWLEDGEMENT OF RECEIPT

A. CERTIFICATE OF SERVICE OF SUBPOENA

I certify that I serviced the subpoena on the front of this form as follows:

☐ I delivered a copy of the subpoena to the person to whom it was directed as follows:

Address of Location

Date:

Time:

☐ (For corporations, partnerships, and incorporated associations which may be sued under a common name)

I delivered a copy of the subpoena to an officer, managing or general agent, or agent authorized to accept service of process as follows:

Person to who subpoena was delivered:

Name:

Title:

Address or Location

Date:

Time:

Signature

Title

Date

X

B. ACKNOWLEDGEMENT OF RECEIPT

I acknowledge receipt of a copy of the subpoena on the front of this form.

Signature

Title

Date

Time

X

Customs Form 389 (Back) (10/01)

Figure 8.2 Sample Grand Jury Subpoena (cont.)

United States District Court

SOUTHERN ·DISTRICT OF· CALIFORNIA

TO:

Custodian of Records

Ref. No. 00-139

SUBPOENA TO TESTIFY BEFORE GRAND JURY

SUBPOENA FOR:

☐ PERSON ☑ DOCUMENTS OR OBJECT(S)

YOU ARE HEREBY COMMANDED to appear and testify before the Grand Jury of the United States District Court at the place, date, and time specified below.

PLACE	ROOM
Federal Office Building 880 Front Street San Diego, California 92101-8893	Grand Jury Room Room 5251
	DATE AND TIME December 19, 2000 9:00 a.m. GJ 00-1

YOU ARE ALSO COMMANDED to bring with you the following document(s) or object(s):*

PLEASE SEE ATTACHMENT "A"

Should you require any assistance regarding this subpoena, please contact Special Agent   at (619)744·   at (858) 569-

IMPORTANT: PLEASE NOTE WE CANNOT REIMBURSE YOU FOR ANY EXPENSES INCURRED IN PROVIDING THESE RECORDS. PLEASE REFER TO THE ATTACHED NOTICE.

You are requested NOT TO DISCLOSE this information for an INDEFINITE period of time. Any such disclosure would impede the investigation being conducted.

☐ *Please see additional information on reverse*

This subpoena shall remain in effect until you are granted leave to depart by the court or by an officer acting on behalf of the court.

CLERK ROBERTA WESTDAL	Date
(BY) DEPUTY CLERK	December 14, 2000

This subpoena is issued upon application of the United States of America

NAME, ADDRESS AND PHONE NUMBER OF ASSISTANT U.S. ATTORNEY

U.S. Department of Justice 880 Front Street, Room 6293 San Diego, California 92101-8893 Telephone: (619) 557-

*If not applicable, enter "none."

To be used in lieu of AO110

FORM OBD-227 Revised April 1997

Figure 8.2 Sample Grand Jury Subpoena (cont.)

ATTACHMENT "A"

Any and all records in your possession or under your control that reflect any sales or requests for quotes to
r any other   ication, domestic or
international, for the period of January , 1997 to the present.

The records should include but are not limited to the following:

1. Quote sheets and quote documentation, sales documents, sales orders, invoices, shipping documents, shipping receipts, and bills of lading pertaining to any sales and shipments to

2. Any specifications, product descriptions, catalog material or engineering specifications concerning products sold to

3. Correspondence notes of memoranda, memos, telephone conversation notes, internal company correspondence, concerning any Sales or quotes to

Figure 8.2 Sample Grand Jury Subpoena (cont.)

N O T I C E

Pursuant to the Right to Financial Privacy Act, Title 12, United States Code, Section 3415, financial institutions may be reimbursed for necessary costs actually incurred, effective October 1, 1979. The following are defined as financial institutions:

1. banks
2. trust companies
3. savings and loan or building and loan companies
4. credit unions
5. consumer loan companies
6. industrial loan companies
7. homestead associations
8. credit card issuers

The Federal Reserve Board has established the following guidelines:

1. Search and Processing Costs - May be billed at the rate of $11.00 per hour for Clerical/Technical employees and $17.00 per hour for Manager/Supervisory employees, for time spent locating and retrieving documents, reproducing documents, or packaging and preparing documents for shipment. Computer time and necessary supplies may also be billed if itemized separately.

2. Reproduction Costs - May be billed at the following rates:

Photocopying: $ .25 cents per page
Paper copies of microfiche: $ .25 cents per frame
Duplicate microfiche: $ .50 cents per microfiche
Computer diskette: $5.00 per diskette

3. Transportation Costs - May bill for direct costs incurred to transport employees to locate and retrieve material required. May also bill for direct costs incurred in transporting material to location required by legal process.

An itemized bill or invoice must be furnished to the United States Attorney in order to receive reimbursement. However, reimbursement may be made only in connection with the following types of financial records: checking, savings, share, loan or credit card account records pertaining to accounts of individuals or partnerships of five or fewer partners. Reimbursement cannot be made for records relating to accounts of:

1. Corporations
2. Large partnerships (6 or more partners)
3. Associations
4. Trusts
5. Government agencies
6. Other legal entities

You may refer to the Federal Register, Volume 44, No. 190, September 28, 1979, pp. 55812-55815, for more detailed guidelines.

USASDC-37
10/30/96

Figure 8.2 Sample Grand Jury Subpoena (cont.)

COMPLIANCE WITH GRAND JURY SUBPOENA .

Grand Jury Subpoena Ref. No. 00-139-

    Re:

    This subpoena may be complied with my mailing the requested documents
to:

                  UNITED STATES ATTORNEY'S OFFICE
                  880 FRONT STREET, ROOM 6293
                  SAN DIEGO, CA 92101-8893
                  ATTENTION:

NOTE:　 Please return a copy of the subpoena with the records.

Figure 8.2 Sample Grand Jury Subpoena (cont.)

Another way to collect evidence is to take it out of the trash of the suspect. When a person places their trash on the sidewalk or in the alleyway, off their curtilage, for the trash collectors they are considered to have abandoned their right to that trash. The trash can be a treasure trove of information. You can find copies of bank statements, credit card receipts, notes, phone numbers, mail, packaging material used in criminal activity, correspondence and many other valuable information. Be prepared to get dirty and take some disposable gloves.

TYPES OF DOCUMENTARY EVIDENCE

Hotel Records

Hotel records can give you credit card information, telephone calls made, and membership numbers to hotel clubs (e.g. Hilton Honors) that will lead to more information. Hotel records can provide proof of where a person was on certain dates and times. Sometimes you will get the identity of the person or persons staying with your suspect, and other reservations made at the same time linking your suspect to other individuals. The hotel may record license plates of vehicles being used by their guest.

Airline tickets

Airline tickets will provide you proof of where the suspect was and when, credit card numbers for additional leads, what travel agency your suspect uses, if any, other persons traveling with your suspect and airline clubs membership numbers for additional trips. You want to note if the ticket was round trip or one way. In some drug cases the suspect travels on one-way tickets and return by vehicle with the drugs or money.

Credit Card Receipts

Credit card receipts will provide you an account number to subpoena the records. Those records will provide you with all the purchases that person has made with the credit cards. In financial cases the receipts will help as proof of tax evasion using the expenditure method. Don't forget to get the credit application when you subpoena information. That may give you employment history, friend names, and the name of relatives, social security number and a copy of his credit history giving all his other credit cards, sources of income and possibly property owned. The application may also give you the name of the spouse or better yet an ex-spouse. Ex-spouses may be willing to provide all sorts of good information and they are motivated by a get even attitude.

Corporate Records

Corporate records will list the officers of the corporation, the address of the corporation, minutes of corporate meetings, and other information about the organization and its business. Some of these records are sent to the Secretary of State for the state in which the corporation is registered.

Records keep by the corporation can provide you with financial information, bank records, list of employees including their personnel records, list of clients, and a list of their suppliers.

Phone Bills

Phone bills will help show who had control and use over the location of the phone, who was paying for the phone bill, what numbers were being called on the phone, and what other service that person had in the past. Again don't forget to subpoena a copy of the application for the phone service with the same information that you got on the credit card application.

Bank Records

Bank records are going to require a grand jury subpoena. The United States Attorney pays for the cost for the copying of those records. You can obtain copies of statements, checks, deposit slips, deposited checks, loan applications, request for opening the account, all credit information, all wire transfers and any safe deposit boxes. Depending on the case and what you need, the bank will first provide copies of the statements and you can choose what records you need. If the suspect has his paycheck deposited every week, it may not be necessary to get copies of every check and if needed you can get copies from the employer.

Photographs

Photographs can be used to connected people together like co-conspirators and at certain important times and places. Some of the cameras put the date and time on the photos, other times the processing date is imprinted on the back of the photo establishing a date for which the photo had to have been taken before. There has been more than one case where a defendant just had to take photos of himself standing on top of the drugs before they were hidden in his vehicle or of them loading the drugs in his vehicle. For child pornography cases the photos are very important. Frequently they take photos in their own house with the minors.

Video

For the same reasons as listed above you need to look at the videos. The videos offer an additional benefit of having voice for potentially more powerful evidence.

Computers

Today everyone has a computer. They use it to communicate with friends and associates, do their banking and pay their bills, to research on the Internet, to purchase goods and services, to process their own photographs. All of these offer the opportunity to find evidence. They also use computers to commit crimes, make false identification, and counterfeit certificates. There are a number of electronic storage devices that connect to the computer that may contain evidence, CDs, DVDs, floppy disks, Personal Digital Assistants (PDA) and other removable storage media. Computer forensics is a recent and evolving science.

For law enforcement purposes, only a certified computer forensic expert should be used to search computers. Specialized and ongoing training is required to develop the necessary skills to properly handle and analyze digital evidence. The evidence must be preserved in certain ways to be entered into court to survive defense challenges. Digital evidence is volatile and can easily be destroyed or corrupted by improper handling. The simple process of turning on a computer that utilizes the Microsoft Windows 98 operating system causes access to more than 200 files and permanently modifies or updates 18 files.

The investigator will be asked to provide the computer forensic agent with certain information to help with the examination. They will be asked for biographical information on the suspect to help in breaking any passwords used. They will be asked for key words or phrases for the type of investigation they are working to help the computer forensic agents find the files needed by using a data string search, an automated process where by data is scanned for occurrences of specified data strings.

When seizing computers there must be a basis for seizing each particular item. If you are searching for information, it may be senseless to seize hardware that cannot store information. However, many hardware devices have information that can be retrieved. Generally monitors, keyboards, and printer do not permanently store data, but some devices are used to send data to, and receive data from the computer. A trained computer forensic agent can retrieve data or other evidence from laser printers, hard disk print buffers, print spooler devices, ribbon printers, monitors, keyboards, hard cards, scanners and fax machines.

Electronic bulletin board systems (BBS) are another problem for law enforcement. A bulletin board system is a computer dedicated, in whole or in part, to serving as an electronic meeting place. A BBS computer system may contain information, programs, and e-mail, and is set up so that users can dial the bulletin board system, read and leave messages for other users, and download and up load software programs for common use. Some BBSs also have gateways, which allow users to connect, to other bulletin boards or networks. A BBS can have multiple telephone lines for many users at a time or a single line for first-come service. BBSs can have several levels of access called sub-boards or conferences. A user may store documents, data, programs, messages, and even photographs in the different levels of the BBS. A bulletin board system may be located anywhere telephone lines go. Therefore, if a suspect may have stored important information on a BBS, a pen register may be needed to reveal the location of these stored files.

A determination will have to be made to seize the computers and take them to the forensic lab for examination or do an on site digital image of the computers. In either case the computer forensic agents will make a duplicate digital evidence of the original devices. The duplicate digital evidence contains a bit stream image of the original evidence. In some circumstances, the duplicate digital evidence is considered to be the "best evidence" for court purposes.

Figure 8.3 U.S. Department of Justice Press Release

For Immediate Release August 4, 2004

Department of Justice Central District of California
United States Attorney Debra W. Yang Thom, Thom Mrozek, Public Affairs Officer (213) 894-6XXX

Six Internet Fraudsters Indicted In International Conspiracy To Steal More Than $10 Million From World's Largest Technology Distributor

LOS ANGELES - A federal grand jury this morning indicted a Romanian computer hacker and five Americans on charges that they conspired to steal more than $10 million in computer equipment from Ingram Micro in Santa Ana, California, the largest technology distributor in the world.

The indictment alleges that Ctalin Mateias hacked into Ingram Micro's online ordering system and placed fraudulent orders for computers and computer equipment. He directed that the equipment be sent to dozens of addresses scattered throughout the United States as part of an Internet fraud ring.

The 14-count indictment charges:

Mateias, 24, of Bucharest, Romania, who used the online nickname "Dr. Mengele";

Olufemi Tinubu, 21, of Atlanta;

Tarion Finley, 20, also of Atlanta;

Valeriu Crisovan, 27, of Hallandale, Florida;

Jeremy Long, 28, of Richmond, Virginia; and

Warren Bailey, 21, of Anchorage, Alaska.

The five defendants in the United States will be ordered to appear in United States District Court in Los Angeles for arraignment later this month. The Justice Department is working closely with Romanian authorities to ensure that Mateias is brought to justice, whether in Romania or the United States.

According to the indictment, Mateias began hacking into Ingram Micro's online ordering system in 1999. Using information obtained from his illegal hacking activity, Mateias bypassed Ingram's online security safeguards, posed as legitimate customers and ordered computer equipment to be sent to Romania. When Ingram Micro blocked all shipments to the Eastern European country in early 1999, Mateias recruited Tinubu, Crisovan, Long and Bailey from Internet chat rooms to provide him with United States addresses to use as "mail drops" for the fraudulently ordered equipment. Crisovan,

Figure 8.3 U.S. Department of Justice Press Release (cont.)

Tinubu, Finley and Long, in turn, recruited others, including high school students, to provide additional addresses and to accept the stolen merchandise. The defendants in the United States would either sell the equipment or send the proceeds to Mateias, or they would repackage the equipment and send it to Romania.

Mateias and his co-conspirators allegedly fraudulently ordered more than $10 million in computer equipment from Ingram Micro. However, Ingram Micro was successful in intercepting nearly half the orders before the items were shipped.

All six defendants are charged with conspiring to commit mail fraud by causing Ingram Micro to ship computer equipment based on the false pretenses that the equipment was ordered by legitimate customers. In addition to the conspiracy count, Mateias is charged with 13 mail fraud counts; Tinubu and Finley are charged with three mail fraud counts; Crisovan is charged with six mail fraud counts; and Long is charged with four mail fraud counts for shipments.

An indictment contains allegations that a defendant has committed a crime. Every defendant is presumed innocent until and unless proven guilty beyond a reasonable doubt.

If convicted of all counts, Mateias faces a maximum statutory sentence of 90 years in federal prison; Tinubu faces a maximum statutory sentence of 35 years; Finley faces a maximum statutory sentence of 35 years; Crisovan faces a maximum statutory sentence of 35 years; Long faces a maximum statutory sentence of 25 years; and Bailey faces a maximum statutory sentence of five years.

This international investigation was handled by the Cyber Crimes Squad in the Los Angeles Field Office of the Federal Bureau of Investigation, which received substantial assistance from the Romanian National Police and the FBI Legal Attaché Office in Bucharest. Additionally, the FBI Field Offices in Atlanta; Richmond, Virginia; Miami; Chicago; Albuquerque, New Mexico; El Paso, Texas; Newark, New Jersey; Norfolk, Virginia; Omaha, Nebraska; San Francisco; Seattle; Tampa, Florida; Albany, New York; and San Diego assisted in the investigation.

In a separate case, the United States Attorney's Office for the Western District of Pennsylvania today announced the unsealing of an 11-count indictment charging Mateias in another scheme involving shipments of fraudulently ordered merchandise that was sent to co-conspirators in Pennsylvania, Georgia and Louisiana.

PHYSICAL EVIDENCE

Physical evidence found at a crime scene or seized can be connected to people. Many criminal cases are made using circumstantial evidence. There may not be any witnesses to the crime, so in order to prove that the crime was committed by a certain individual, the investigator must piece together evidence that leads the jury to the conclusion that beyond a reasonable doubt that individual committed the crime. This may be done with fingerprints or DNA. Many murders are convicted when blood is found on their clothes, or vehicles or possessions and they are unable to explain how the blood of the victim ended up on them or their possessions.

DNA

DNA is Deoxyribonucleic acid. DNA is analyzed in body fluids, stains, and other biological tissues recovered from evidence. The results of DNA analysis of questioned biological samples are compared with the results of DNA analysis of known samples. This analysis can associate victim(s) and/or suspect(s) with each other or with a crime scene.

There are two sources of DNA used in forensic analyses. Nuclear DNA (nDNA) is typically analyzed in evidence containing blood, semen, saliva, body tissues, and hairs that have tissue at their root ends. Mitochondrial DNA (mtDNA) is typically analyzed in evidence containing naturally shed hairs, hair fragments, bones, and teeth.

If DNA evidence is not properly documented, collected, packaged, and preserved, it will not meet the legal and scientific requirements for admissibility in a court of law. If DNA is not properly collected, biological activity can be lost. If it is not properly packaged, contamination can occur. If it is not properly preserved, decomposition and deterioration can occur.

Figure 8.4 Los Angeles CA Police Department Press Release

LOS ANGELES POLICE DEPARTMENT PRESS RELEASE
Monday, July 26, 2004

"13 Year Old Homicide and Sexual Assault Case Solved through DNA"

What: News Conference

WHEN: Monday, July 26, 2004, 2:00 p.m.

WHERE: Los Angeles Police Department Headquarters, In front of Parker Center, 150 North Los Angeles, 90012

Los Angeles: On April 12, 1991, Ms. Soo Hoo Quon, 93 years of age, was found murdered in her residence located in the 2400 block of North Eastern Avenue. Ms. Quon was attacked by an intruder in her senior citizen assisted-living residence and sexually assaulted before being murdered.

At the time the case was assigned to Hollenbeck Area Detectives. All available leads were followed but the case remained unsolved.

In July 2003, Detectives Cliff Shepard and Jose Ramirez, Robbery Homicide Division, Cold Case Homicide Unit, had the evidence from the crime scene processed for DNA. Scientific Investigation Division found DNA evidence and forwarded it to the California Department of Justice Laboratory.

On July 20, 2004, Cold Case Homicide Detectives were notified that a DNA match was made from the crime scene evidence to a registered sex offender who was in the California's Combined DNA Index System (CODIS) database. Detectives determined the suspect, Albert Rodriguez Salinas, 42 years of age was on parole and living in the Los Angeles area.

On July 22, 2004, Cold Case Homicide Detectives took Salinas into custody with the assistance of State Parole.

This news release was prepared by Los Angeles Police Department's Media Relations Section, at 213-485-3XXX.

COMBINED DNA INDEX SYSTEM (CODIS)

The Combined DNA Index System (CODIS) program provides software and support services to enable state and local laboratories to establish databases of convicted offenders, unsolved crime scenes, and missing persons. CODIS allows these forensic laboratories to exchange and compare DNA profiles electronically, thereby linking serial violent crimes, especially sexual assaults, to each other, and to identify suspects by matching DNA from crime scenes to convicted offenders.

CODIS has recorded more than 500 matches linking serial violent crimes to each other or identifying suspects by matching crime scene evidence to known convicted offenders. These matches have aided more than 1,000 violent crime investigations.

This indexing system is installed in 104 laboratories in 43 states and the District of Columbia. All 50 states have enacted DNA database laws requiring the collection of a DNA sample from specified categories of convicted offenders. More than 500 federal, state, and local DNA analysts have received CODIS training, and the FBI Laboratory has provided CODIS software and training to criminal justice agencies in other countries. Examiners conducting DNA analyses can exchange and compare their samples electronically using CODIS.

More than $16 million in grant funding transferred to the Bureau of Justice Assistance has been awarded to the states to establish, develop, and upgrade computerized identification systems compatible with CODIS, the FBI's National Crime Information Center, and automated fingerprint systems compatible with the FBI's Integrated Automated Fingerprint Identification System.

CODIS Case Highlights

Using CODIS, the Illinois State Police Laboratory linked a 1999 solved sexual assault case to three other sexual assaults in which the suspect was previously unknown. The 1999 case involved a sexual assault on two female college students who were unable to identify the offender. Police, however, were able to develop a suspect from witnesses' descriptions and circumstantial evidence. CODIS matched this suspect's DNA profile to three other cases that occurred in 1994 and 1995.

A DNA profile developed by the Virginia Division of Forensic Science in Richmond resulted in the resolution of an unknown subject rape case. In March 1997, a man raped and sodomized a woman after breaking into her home. The police had no suspects in the case but were able to retrieve biological evidence from the crime scene. This evidence was sent to the Richmond laboratory, where a DNA profile was developed and searched in CODIS. In March 1999, CODIS linked the crime to a profile in Virginia's Offender Index. At the time of the identification, the offender was serving time in a New York prison for robbery, with a prior conviction in Virginia for grand larceny.

NATIONAL DNA INDEX SYSTEM (NDIS)

The FBI Laboratory began operation of the National DNA Index System (NDIS) on October 13, 1998. NDIS is the final level of CODIS and supports the sharing of DNA profiles from convicted offenders and crime scene evidence submitted by state and local forensic laboratories across the United States. All 50 states have laws authorizing the establishment of state DNA databases and the collection of DNA samples from convicted offenders. Twenty four states and the FBI Laboratory participate in NDIS, and the FBI Laboratory has added approximately 600 DNA profiles in NDIS.

Through use of NDIS, the FBI Laboratory linked six sexual assault cases that occurred in Washington, DC, to three sexual assault cases under investigation by the Jacksonville, Florida, Sheriff's Office. Without this link to the Florida cases, it is likely that these sexual assaults would have remained unsolved.

INTEGRATED AUTOMATED FINGERPRINT IDENTIFICATION SYSTEM (IAFIS)

In March 1997, the FBI Laboratory began using the FBI Criminal Justice Information Services Division's Integrated Automated Fingerprint Identification System (IAFIS) at a limited level of capability. On July 28, 1999, this system became fully operational, providing the capability to search latent fingerprints against the largest criminal fingerprint repository in the world, which contains more than 35 million individuals' known fingerprints.

Using the full capability of IAFIS, FBI examiners made 92 latent print identifications in two months. This is the same number of IAFIS assisted latent print identifications made during the previous 26 months.

IAFIS allows examiners to compare latent print evidence to a repository of known prints

All of these identifications were made without benefit of a named suspect and helped solve a variety of crimes, including homicides, rape, bombing matters, organized crime, extortion, drug crimes, and financial institution fraud.

LATENT PRINTS

The laboratory is the best place to develop latent prints; however, it is sometimes necessary to develop latent prints at the crime scene. Caution should be taken to prevent destroying latent prints. Photographs of latent prints are taken before any processing and each step in the processing sequence before moving to the next process. When processing latent prints the technicians apply black, gray or white powder to the surface with a long hair brush. The color of the powder should contrast with the color of the surface. They then use a short hair brush to remove the excess powder. Once the print is developed, they use transparent tape or black and white rubber lifts to lift latent prints. When transparent tape is used, it is placed on a card of a contrasting color of the powder.

The investigator provides the lab with fingerprints for anyone who might have touched evidence at the crime scene who is not a suspect, and these are called elimination prints. They also provide the prints they have of any suspects or the identity of any suspects for which they do not have prints.

Fingerprint evidence is very strong proof in proving a connection to evidence or a crime scene to link co-conspirators.

INK

Examining inked writing in conjunction with other techniques, such as handwriting analysis, watermark identification, can provide details regarding document preparation. The composition of writing inks varies with the type of writing instrument (e.g. ballpoint pen, fountain pen, porous-tip pen) and the date of the ink manufacture. In general, inks are composed of dyes in solvents and other materials that impart selected characteristics. Ink analysis is usually limited to comparisons of the organic dye components. When ink formulations are the same, it is not possible to determine whether the ink originated from the same source to the exclusion of others. Examinations cannot determine how long ink has been on a document.

ADHESIVES, CAULKS, AND SEALANTS

Adhesives, caulks, and sealants can be compared by color and composition with known sources. The source and manufacturer of adhesives, caulks, and sealants cannot be determined by compositional analysis.

TAPE

Tape composition, construction, and color can be compared with known sources. Comparisons can be made with the torn end of tape and a suspect roll of tape.

TOOLMARK

Tools can bear unique microscopic characteristics due to manufacturing processes and use. These characteristics can be transferred to surfaces that contacted the tools. Evidence toolmarks can be compared to recovered tools. In the absence of a questioned tool, toolmark examinations can determine the type of tool(s) that produced the toolmark and whether the toolmark is of value for comparison. The same is true for lock and key examinations.

TOXICOLOGY

Toxicology examinations can disclose the presence of drugs and poisons in biological specimens and food products. The examinations can determine the circumstances surrounding drug or poison related homicides, suicides, and accidents. Because of the large number of potentially toxic substances, it may be necessary to screen for classes of poisons.

FIREARMS

Firearm examinations can determine the general condition of a firearm and whether the firearm is mechanically functional or in a condition that could contribute to an unintentional discharge. Trigger-pull examinations can determine the amount of pressure necessary to release the hammer or firing pin of a firearm. Examinations can determine whether a firearm was altered to fire in the full-automatic mode. Obliterated and/or altered firearm serial numbers can sometimes be restored. Firearms can be test-fired to obtain known specimens for comparison to evidence ammunition components such as bullets, cartridge cases, and shot shell casings.

Fired bullets can be examined to determine the general rifling characteristics such as caliber and physical features of the rifling impressions and the manufacturers of the bullets. The microscopic characteristics on evidence bullets can be compared to test-fired bullets from a suspect firearm to determine whether the evidence bullet was fired from that firearm.

Cartridge cases or shot shell casings examinations can determine the caliber or gauge, the manufacturer, and whether there are marks of value for comparison. The images of questioned cartridge cases and shot shell casings can be scanned into the National Integrated Ballistics Information Network to compare with evidence from other shooting incidents. The microscopic characteristics of evidence cartridge cases and shot shell casings can be examined to determine whether they were fired from a specific firearm.

TRACE EVIDENCE

Trace Evidence can be identified and compared for specific types of trace materials that could be transferred during the commission of a violent crime. These trace materials include human hairs, animal hairs, textile fibers and fabric, ropes, feathers, and wood. The physical contact between a suspect and a victim can result in the transfer of trace materials such as hairs and fibers. The identification and comparison of these materials can often link a suspect to a crime scene or to physical contact with another individual. Torn pieces of fabric can be positively associated to a damaged garment, and broken pieces of wood can be positively fit together.

Hairs

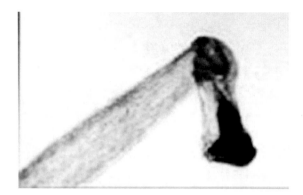

Hair examinations can determine whether hairs are animal or human race, body area, method of removal, damage, and alteration (e.g. bleaching or dyeing) can be determined from human hair analysis. Examinations can associate a hair to a person on the basis of microscopic characteristics in the hair, but cannot provide absolute personal identification. The animal species and family can be determined from hair analysis. The hairs can also be submitted for examination for mitochondrial DNA analysis.

Fibers

Fiber examinations can identify the type of fiber such as animal (wool), vegetable (cotton), mineral (glass), and synthetic (manufactured). Questioned fibers can be compared to fibers from victim(s) and suspect(s) clothing, carpeting, and other textiles. A questioned piece of fabric can be physically matched to known fabric. Fabric composition, construction, and color can be compared, and impressions on fabric and from fabric can be examined. Clothing manufacturers(information can be determined by label searches.

Ropes and Cords

A piece of rope or cord can be compared with a questioned rope or cord. The composition, construction, color and diameter can be determined. If a tracer is present, the manufacturer can be determined.

Figure 8.5 Major Cases By The FBI Laboratory

The services of the FBI Laboratory have proven to be crucial to law enforcement agencies. Throughout 1999, the FBI Laboratory provided forensic analysis, technical expertise, tactical communications, and operational support for investigative and intelligence activities as well as effective communications and surveillance capabilities to support essential FBI national and international responsibilities. In addition, trained and equipped laboratory and field evidence response, crisis response, hazardous materials, communications, and bomb technician personnel were deployed to remote locations throughout the United States and around the world in response to emerging crisis situations.

Kosovo War Crimes

The International Criminal Tribunal for the Former Yugoslavia (ICTY) requested FBI forensic assistance in direct support of the six count international indictment of Yugoslavian President Slobodan Milosevic and four Serbian leaders. Director Louis J. Freeh approved the deployment of a 65-person FBI forensic team to Kosovo, a small province between Macedonia and the Adriatic Sea. The mission of this team of expert investigators and forensic specialists was to document and photograph crime scenes; locate, collect, and preserve evidence at the massacre sites; and perform forensic examinations of the deceased victims to determine identity, sex, approximate age, and cause of death.

Kosovo Recovery Efforts

News accounts and preoperational briefings provided advance warning of the horrors committed by Serbian nationals. However, nothing prepared investigators and examiners for the devastation

Figure 8.5 Major Cases By The FBI Laboratory (cont.)

present at what Director Freeh called "the largest crime scene in history."

The FBI forensic team processed seven sites in Gjakove, Kosovo, and two sites in the town of Peje from June 20, 1999 through July 3, 1999. The majority of these sites were burned houses in which Serbian forces had allegedly murdered more than 75 individuals. The FBI forensic team recovered seven bodies, the remains of numerous others, jacketed rifle bullets, cartridge cases, hand grenade fragments, and evidence for positive presumptive blood test. Field autopsies conducted on the seven bodies determined the cause of death to be multiple gunshots to the head for all seven victims.

A second forensic team was deployed in response to a United Nations request for the provision of continued crime scene assistance to the ICTY. This team processed 21 crime scene sites from August 28, 1999 through September 8, 1999. The majority of these multiple gravesites were located near the town of Glogavac in the Vrbovac Valley, an area approximately 15 km by 6 km in size. Serbian forces allegedly occupied the main road surrounding this area and began an offensive during March and April of 1999, during which Albanian villagers hiding in the woods were captured, tortured, and killed. Local villagers under the cover of darkness buried those killed in remote graves. More than 250 Albanians are estimated to have been killed in the Vrbovac area.

The FBI forensic team exhumed the bodies of 124 victims from 15 sites and processed six "killing" areas. Field autopsies determined the cause of death to be multiple gunshots for the majority of the victims, although some, including a four-year-old girl, died from bluntforce trauma. Victims ranged from a two-year-old boy to a 94-year-old female.

Figure 8.5 Major Cases By The FBI Laboratory (cont.)

For more information about the FBI Laboratory's role in the Kosovo investigation, see the Kosovo section of the FBI Web site.

Egypt Air Flight 990

Essential forensic and operational support was provided by the FBI Laboratory in the recovery efforts of Egypt Air Flight 990, which crashed off the Massachusetts coast on October 31, 1999. Onsite support was provided by examiners from the DNA, Chemistry, Explosives, and Latent Print Units of the Laboratory and by Special Agents, Evidence Response Team members, and electronics technicians, who assisted in the collection and separation of human remains, personal effects, and aircraft parts. Evidence Response Teams from Boston, Little Rock, New York, and Newark responded to the initial crash investigation and additional teams from Buffalo, Cincinnati, and Baltimore provided assistance with the salvage operation at sea.

Columbine High School Shootings

The FBI Laboratory's Investigative and Prosecutive Graphic Unit served as the lead for the collection and documentation of the crime scene survey data during the Columbine High School shooting investigation, which followed the April 20, 1999 incident in Littleton, Colorado. This Unit, in combination with the Laboratory's Structural Design Unit, created scaled crime scene reconstructions of each segment of the incident.

Columbine High School, Littleton, Colorado

These reconstructions depicted the locations of victims, evidence, and explosive devices; diagramed bullet trajectories; and exhibited the movement of specific individuals as well as the sequence of events that took place.

The Laboratory's Forensic Audio, Video and Image Analysis Unit duplicated, enhanced, and conducted imaging work on a series of tapes of the cafeteria area at Columbine, and the Computer Analysis and Response Team analyzed and restored data to assist in the investigation. Additional crime scene processing support was provided by the Denver Evidence Response Team.

Figure 8.5 Major Cases By The FBI Laboratory (cont.)

Hacker Ring Pleads Guilty

As the daily frequency of communication through computer networks increases, criminal use of computer technology is becoming common. Evidence of this prevalence of computers as tools in crime is apparent in the case of the Phonemasters, an international ring of hackers who were able to gain access to major telephone networks, portions of the national power grid, air traffic control systems, and numerous databases. This hacker ring provided calling card numbers, credit reports, criminal records, and other data to individuals in Canada, the United States, Switzerland, and Italy who willing to pay for the information. The investigation of this case required the capture of Phonemasters' data communications under a Title III order and was successfully accomplished by collecting and analyzing the analog modem signals from the target phone lines. Phonemasters suspects Calvin Cantrell and Cory Lindsay were convicted in September 1999, for theft and possession of unauthorized access devices and unauthorized access to a federal interest computer. Cantrell was sentenced to two years in prison while Lindsay received a sentence of 41 months.

To support future cases of this nature, the FBI Laboratory is working to develop network intercept techniques and to produce software tools that view and analyze captured data. The intercept of data communications is becoming more common, and some of the

---

SUMMARY

It is not what you know that counts; it is what you can prove. Evidence is what is used to prove your case in court. The evidence must be legally obtained to use in court, at least as it relates to the defendant. If the evidence was obtained by violating the rights of a non-defendant, the defendant would not have standing to object.

DISCUSSION QUESTIONS

1. What evidence would you likely get with the different investigative techniques from Chapter 7?
2. How would trace evidence help prove a conspiracy case?
3. With permission, do a trash run from a couple of neighbors and determine what information you found and what you know about their lifestyle.

ADDITIONAL READINGS

Trace Evidence - The Hunt for an Elusive Serial Killer, Bruce Henderson, Hardcover, A Lisa Drew Book, 1998

Elements of Iinvestigations, Paul B. Weston and Charles A. Lushbaugh, Hardcover, Prentice Hall, 2003

Fingerprints - The Origins of Crime Detection and the Murder Case That Launched Forensic Science, Colin Beavan, Hardcover, Hyperion, 2001

BIBLIOGRAPHY

FBI Handbook of Forensic Services, 2003

United States Customs Service, Law Course for Customs Officers

Chapter 9

Ethics

CHAPTER OVERVIEW

In this chapter you will look at how ethics affects both your personal and professional life. You will see the how ethics in your personal and professional life are interrelated. You will examine some every day personal and professional ethical dilemmas and see how your decisions not only affect you, but your family, friends and co-workers. You will learn why poor ethical decisions can end your career and ruin your personal life.

CHAPTER OBJECTIVES

1. Understand the meaning of ethics.
2. Learn some tools to help you make the correct ethical decisions in your personal and professional life.
3. Learn the general police ethics.
4. Understand ethics from the prospective of an investigator.
5. Understand ethics for managers.

ETHICS

Ethics is doing the right things when no one is looking. Law enforcement officers have a unique position of public trust. For that reason, they cannot separate their personal life from their professional life. They cannot make poor ethical decisions in their personal life and still be trusted to do the right thing on the job. And while it may seem unfair, there are times when a law enforcement officer can do something perfectly legal and ethical on or off the job and still be perceived as unethical. Perception is fact, therefore, even if it right it is wrong. Most agencies have a table of offenses for unethical behavior that includes punishing officers for deeds that are perceived unethical.

Here is an actual example of how perception can make a perfectly innocent act appear to be unethical. It happened at a small port of entry on the U.S./Mexican border. At the primary inspection booth a male pulled his vehicle up to the booth for inspection. The male and the inspector were seen engaging in conversation. The male handed the inspector some money and very shortly there after proceeded into the U.S. without further inspection. The act was seen by fellow inspectors and others waiting in line to be inspected. The act was reported to the Office of Internal Affairs as a potential corrupt inspector.

An investigation determined that the male in the vehicle was the brother-in-law of the inspector. The brother-in-law owed the inspector twenty dollars from a family function. The money that was handed to the inspector was just paying back the brother-in-law's share for the money the inspector had spent on a family picnic. There was nothing illegal or unethical about paying a fair share of a family picnic. However, the perception by the inspector's co-workers and other individuals waiting to enter the United States was that the inspector received money for allowing the vehicle and its occupant to enter the United States without being properly inspected.

How could the inspector have handled this situation? He could have told his brother-in-law to wait until they saw each other when he was not on duty. The inspector needed to be aware of how his actions, that were perfectly legal and ethical, might be perceived by others. While the co-workers could have been informed of why the inspector received the money, what about the individuals waiting in line? They would never know the truth about what they saw. Their perception of that inspector and possibly the agency he worked for may have been changed forever.

Unethical behavior by law enforcement officers makes big headlines in the news. Think about the Rodney King beating by police officers in Los Angeles. The image of the Los Angeles Police Department has changed forever. The perception by the public of an entire police department was changed by the actions of only a few. Furthermore, the financial lost to the City of Los Angeles for the civil suit was substantial.

PERSONAL ETHICAL DILEMMAS

The following two examples are for class discussions.

Ethical Dilemma Number 1

A family consisting of a father, mother and two children are going to Disneyland for the day. The entrance fee is $40 for adults and children 13 and older, and $20 for children less than 13. The two children are ages 11 and 14. As the family approaches the booth to purchase tickets the father tells the 14-year-old child to tell them he is 12 years old if he is asked.

- Is this ethical?
- Whom does it really hurt, after all Disney is a large profitable company so $20 is nothing to them?
- What message does this give the children about cheating?

Ethical Dilemma Number 2

You are at the grocery store paying for a quart of milk costing $2. You give the clerk a $10 bill and she gives you back change for a $20.

- Do you tell her you gave her a $10 bill not a $20? Store policy is that the shortage will come not out of the clerk's paycheck?
- If you knew that shortage of money would come out of the clerk's pocket would it change your answer?

No one is saying that by telling your child to lie about their age or by keeping $10 extra from the change you life will be ruined forever, but these can be building blocks for more devastating decisions later. If it is $50 instead of $10 does that make a difference? What about a store owner who gives a police officer an extra special discount to watch out for his store? What about looking the other way when a small store owner is also a small time bookie? As you accept small unethical behavior as acceptable, you become sensitized to it and your level of acceptance can creep up until you find yourself in trouble. Where that line is drawn is a personal decision that only you can make.

WARNING SIGNS

A number of people have reported that when they come across an ethical dilemma their minds immediately start to beginning thinking of justifications for their action in case they got caught or they start justifying to themselves reasons why their actions are acceptable. If this happens to you, you must train yourself to recognize this as something you probably do not want to do. An example that comes up often is the misuse of a government vehicle that can only be used for work. An employee wants to make a detour on the way home to pick up something he needs. He does not want to go home to pick up his privately owned vehicle and back track to the store. His mind immediately starts to calculate what reason he would give for being in that part of town if he were in an accident.

If you find yourself justifying your actions, stop and think it through. As you will see later in this chapter, the consequences of your actions can change your life. If he is in an accident he will have to come clean or file a false report, and if he gets caught filing a false report that can be the end of his career.

CAREER ETHICS

Ethics in the work place starts at the top. If the workforce perceives that the senior management is not ethical and does not care about ethical behavior from their employees there is no incentive for employees to act ethically. However, if the senior management is perceived to be ethical and embraces it by promoting employees who do good work and are ethical then the culture of the organization will encourage ethical behavior as the norm. Ethics must be taught from the very beginning of an employee's entrance on the job and continue throughout their career with in-service training. Training is not enough; everyone on the job must practice ethics. When employees act in unethical ways on the job, they must be punished in a fair and equitable manner.

In the federal court system, defense attorneys routinely ask for a "Giglio" request on all government employees who provided a sworn statement in the case (e.g. affidavit for search warrant), or will be testifying as a witness for the government. The purpose of a "Giglio" request(is to uncover misconduct that reflects upon the truthfulness or possible bias of an employee, including a finding of lack of candor during an administrative inquiry. It covers past or pending criminal charges brought against the employee and credible allegation of misconduct that reflects upon the truthfulness or possible bias of the employee that is the subject of a pending investigation. If any "Giglio" information exists, it must be turned over to the Office of the United States Attorney. They will review the information. If the Office of the United States Attorney determines the information must be revealed, two things can happen, first they may decide that the information will not hurt the credibility of the witness. In those cases the information will be presented to the judge who will determine if it can be entered into evidence by the defense during the trial to impeach the witness. If this happens, the assistant United States attorney will likely bring out the information during the direct testimony of the witness in an attempt to take the issue away from the defense. It then becomes a factor for the jury to decide the credibility of the witness. The second thing that can happen is that the Office of the United States Attorney will decide not to prosecute the case or any other case where that witness is the only person who can testify about key elements of the crime. If that happens, it is mostly like that the employee will be removed from their job and placed in a job where they do not have to testify or totally removed from the agency. Now you can see one way how unethical behavior can end your career.

GENERAL POLICE ETHICS

Public service is a public trust, requiring employees to place loyalty to the Constitution, the laws, and ethical principles above private gain. It is the right of every citizen to have complete confidence in the integrity of the government.

Figure 9.1 The International Association of Chiefs of Police (IACP) Law Enforcement Code of Ethics

As a law enforcement officer, my fundamental duty is to serve the community; to safeguard lives and property; to protect the innocent against deception, the weak against oppression or intimidation and the peaceful against violence or disorder; and to respect the constitutional rights of all to liberty, equality and justice.

I will keep my private life unsullied as an example to all and will behave in a manner that does not bring discredit to me or to my agency. I will maintain courageous calm in the face of danger, scorn or ridicule; develop self-restraint; and be constantly mindful of the welfare of others. Honest in thought and deed both in my personal and official life, I will be exemplary in obeying the law and the regulations of my department. Whatever I see or hear of a confidential nature or that is confided to me in my official capacity will be kept ever secret unless revelation is necessary in the performance of my duty.

I will never act officiously or permit personal feelings, prejudices, political beliefs, aspirations, animosities or friendships to influence my decisions. With no compromise for crime and with relentless prosecution of criminals, I will enforce the law courteously and appropriately without fear or favor, malice or ill will, never employing unnecessary force or violence and never accepting gratuities.

I recognize the badge of my office as a symbol of public faith, and I accept it as a public trust to be held so long as I am true to the ethics of police service. I will never engage in acts of corruption or bribery, nor will I condone such acts by other police officers. I will cooperate with all legally authorized agencies and their representatives in the pursuit of justice.

I know that I alone am responsible for my own standard of professional performance and will take every reasonable opportunity to enhance and improve my level of knowledge and competence.

I will constantly strive to achieve these objectives and ideals, dedicating myself before God to my chosen profession... law enforcement.

From late 1995 until 1997, the IACP established an Ad Hoc Committee on Police Image and Ethics. The committee conducted the most extensive ethics training survey ever conducted by law enforcement. As a result of that survey and the information gathered by the committee, the report stated that, "Ethics is our greatest training and leadership need today and into the next century." The report points out that unethical behavior subjects the agencies to civil litigation and that defending against such allegations drains the organization financially and has a long-term reputation effect sometimes stigmatizing the agency forever.

As you read the entire report below, pay attention to how the leaders of our police departments feel about the importance of ethics. Pay attention to the cost of unethical behavior in terms of dollars, lost careers, lost families and lost lives. According to the report, "Each year, considerably more officers commit suicide than are murdered. Many times, these suicides are a result of officers' failure to deal with unethical acts in which they were personally or summarily involved."

Figure 9.2 Ethics Training in Law Enforcement

Ethics Training Subcommittee of the IACP Ad Hoc Committee on Police Image and Ethics

Established in late 1995 by then-President David Walchak, continued through 1997 under President Darrell Sanders and working under the guidance of Fourth Vice President Chief Bill Berger, IACP's Ad Hoc Committee on Police Image and Ethics has generated a tremendous amount of positive interest in and anticipation of the final report. Based on two years of research and numerous meetings among co-chairs Berger, Neal Trautman and Michael Cosgrove, who oversaw the efforts of the 60+ members of the committee, the following is a final compilation of the committee report to IACP members, along with a list of the ad hoc recommendations and a detailed analysis of the first-ever IACP ethics survey.

Our Greatest Need

Ethics is our greatest training and leadership need today and into the next century. In addition to the fact that most departments do not conduct ethics training, nothing is more devastating to individual departments and our entire profession than uncovered scandals or discovered acts of officer misconduct and unethical behavior. The effects of unethical acts and behavior take many forms.

One of the more detrimental consequences of unethical behavior is the subjecting of an agency to civil litigation. Litigation now comes in many forms: excessive use of force, racial discrimination, sexual discrimination, age discrimination, religious discrimination and sexual harassment suits. Violations of civil rights under Titles 18 and 42 are becoming too commonplace. Defending against such

Figure 9.2 Ethics Training in Law Enforcement (cont.)

allegations both drains an organization financially and has a long-term reputation effect in many cases, stigmatizing the agency forever.

These forms of civil litigation are more than tempting to the media; they are irresistible. The negative publicity generated is devastating, regardless of the type of employer. A single incident of unethical behavior can take you from one of the most-admired agencies to one of the least-respected, literally overnight.

Another reason is the personal consequences individual supervisors suffer. Simply being in the "chain of command" when substantial misconduct is discovered can literally destroy a career. When a scandal hits, heads will roll. Many supervisors lose their jobs or are demoted. Others are more fortunate by retaining their jobs, but may never be promoted again. Many of the violations that resulted in disciplinary actions or terminations were due to supervisory omissions or failure to take appropriate actions when dealing with acts of unethical conduct.

Professional destruction through termination does not end with these leaders. Finding one's name or picture on television or the focus of a newspaper story about corruption is an overwhelming public humiliation for any officer and his family; even if later exonerated, he can never recover. The stigma of association resulting from an allegation of unethical behavior lasts forever, even into one's personal life.

For officers who lose their jobs, the future is bleak, to say the least. Many times, unemployment compensation is not offered for such situations. Few employers would want to hire someone fired for being unethical. Without an income, domestic problems arise, often leading to divorce or separation and complicating an already strained and stressful situation.

Each year, considerably more officers commit suicide than are murdered. Many times, these suicides are a result of officers' failure to deal with unethical acts in which they were personally or summarily involved. Thus, by preventing unethical acts, you will be literally saving the lives of fellow officers.

The Ethics Training Survey

If we in law enforcement do not know what our problems are, how do we know how to properly address these issues? Based on our committee's recommendation, the solution is to create and conduct a needs assessment.

Figure 9.2 Ethics Training in Law Enforcement (cont.)

During the spring of 1997, the most extensive ethics training survey ever conducted by law enforcement was undertaken. Over 4,500 surveys were sent out to members of IACP; 20 percent (or 900 completed surveys) were returned. Though on the surface this percentage may seem low, private-sector marketers will tell you that anything over 10 percent is considered extraordinary. The large response was collected, and the interpretation of the results analyzed. This has produced solid recommendations for change in how we as a profession must address ethics today and in the future.

The survey research instrument utilized both qualitative and quantitative methodologies. It was believed that by using the two distinct research designs, the special demands of this specific project could be strengthened.

The survey was constructed using both fixed-answer questions and statements and/or open-ended questions. Consideration was given to formulating questions or statements that measured specified variables in an articulate and meaningful way. The initial contents of the survey design comprised a large number of questions and statements related to ethics in law enforcement. The survey was ultimately refined to contain questions or statements that were judged most relevant to the subject matter. The intention was to enhance the integrity and effectiveness of the survey by securing the comments of specific external evaluators regarding both the quality and substance of the items contained in the survey.

Reading the complete survey questions from each section will provide an intelligible understanding of the data provided in the report. This report incorporates one primary statistical factor: a mean. A brief description of the methodology follows: The mean is the sum of a set of mathematical values divided by the number of values for that series of data. The intention was to focus on the manner in which responses to the various questions were distributed and how they might inform members of IACP.

Synopsis of Findings on Questions 1 – 69

Questions 1-69 were check-off questions addressing a wide range of ethical topics. An overwhelming number of agencies (80.3 percent) reported that they commit resources to train instructors offering ethics courses; and over 60 percent (62.4 percent) reported that they also provide their ethics trainers additional training in adult learning theory. The major approaches these agencies employed in teaching ethics were reported as lecture (78 percent), readings and

Figure 9.2 Ethics Training in Law Enforcement (cont.)

discussion (67.3 percent), videotapes (53 percent) and video scenarios (49 percent).

Other methods, such as role play (26 percent), computers and games (about 7 percent) were used much less often. Sixty-three percent of the responding departments said that they employed a "standardized lesson plan" for ethics instruction, which means that over a third of the agencies did not equip ethics instructors with planned teaching materials.

The survey results regarding Field Training Officers (FTOs) ethics instruction were not as overwhelming as the reported statistics for instructors in general. Sixty-three percent received some formal training, while only 52 percent indicated they were trained in adult learning theories of education. Quite unexpectedly, only about a third (34.4 percent) of the agencies said they had an ethics category for the evaluation reports filled out by FTOs on their trainees. In other words, ethics-related categories were not included among those used to assess recruits' qualifications and skills in about two-thirds of the agencies surveyed.

When asked about ethics curriculum topics such as decision-making skills, values, code of ethics, officer safety, etc., a significant majority (generally 75 to 90 percent) of the departments reported that these topics were provided in their courses for recruits, in-service and management personnel. One exception to this general observation was in the area of "management responsibility"; only two-thirds (65.9 percent) of the agencies included this ethics topic for their managers. In other curriculum categories, there was very little difference in programs offered for recruits, in-service and management personnel.

One point that was clearly revealed in the survey was that a vast majority (83.3 percent) of the departments were engaged in some form of ethics training for newly sworn officers. Over 505 of the respondents saw this training as fulfilling a "high" need among officers, supervisory personnel and command-level staff. These item responses clearly suggested that there were important concerns about ethics training, and that an emphasis on ethics should be a top priority for all levels of the organization. To address this need, 72 percent of the agencies said that they provide some ethics-related training beyond the basic academy experience.

Questions about how much time was devoted to ethics training provided for some interesting findings. A majority of the respondents (70.5 percent) said that they provided four classroom hours or less of

Figure 9.2 Ethics Training in Law Enforcement (cont.)

programming. Only 16.8 percent of the respondents mentioned an eight-hour day of training reserved for ethics. For supervisors, 65.1 percent of the departments said they received some kind of ethics training, but again it was generally offered for four hours or less. Interestingly, although most saw a high need for ethics training, the amount of time earmarked for this activity was far less than what might be expected.

In resource commitment for ethics training, 56.9 percent of the agencies said that they sought external assistance in developing their ethics programs. Only about a third (30.4 percent), however, invested in formal training in teaching ethics for their FTOs, while almost two-thirds (63.5 percent) provided ethics training for narcotic and undercover officers. Whether this percentage for drug enforcement activities should be higher or not is difficult to decide. Perhaps it does reflect a concern about the ethical temptations inherent in that kind of work, and represents an effort by at least some agencies to aid in preventing more serious difficulties.

Other findings came from the items asking departments whether or not they addressed ethical issues in specific areas, such as gratuities (81 percent said "yes"), conflicts of interest (76 percent), abuse of force (90 percent), abuse of authority (78.9 percent), corruption (68.6 percent), discretion and the public trust (78.2 percent), cultural diversity (82.4 percent), off-duty ethics (70.9 percent), personal values (61.4 percent) and management of ethics (64.9 percent). What was interesting was the hourly breakdown regarding these issue areas. More time was spent discussing issues related to the use of force and cultural diversity than the other areas. This emphasis probably reflects major concerns in most agencies over the past several years, in which the issues of racial discrimination and use-of-force incidents were highly publicized, not to mention highly expensive concerns related to defending against civil litigation.

One major finding was that the amount of time devoted to ethics training did not appear to be consistent with how important the needs were, based on the responses. There seems to be a recognized demand for expanded training hours, more quality training resources and greater involvement with ethics training at all levels of the organization, but the number of hours remains rather insignificant in terms of this recognized demand. It is possible that the gap revealed in this survey between "high need" and training hours devoted to ethics actually reflects changes that are occurring, and there is simply a resource lag while the gap closes. Whether this is the case, only time

Figure 9.2 Ethics Training in Law Enforcement (cont.)

will tell. Generally speaking, these survey results support the general conclusion that ethics training is considered important by law enforcement agencies, and they are continuing to commit training resources, seeking outside assistance and generally providing some ethical training to recruits as well as in-service and management personnel.

Synopsis of Findings on Questions 69-73

Questions 69-73 consisted of open-ended, narrative and short-answer questions.

Overall, some of the answers were very thoughtful; some respondents provided typewritten pages with attached value statements clearly demonstrating that there was some time, effort and interest in the subject matter.

Other answers were so brief that the answers are subject to varying interpretations and are of little or no value. Some answers contained one or two words, and sometimes the answers were very cynical, such as, "A tiger can't change his stripes." Some answers were not responsive to the questions, and it is believed that these respondents did not understand how serious the ethical issues confronting law enforcement officers are. One respondent provided no answers to these questions.

Responses to the survey research instrument and in particular to the open-ended questions varied considerably, and by agency, with some responding to all of the questions and others to none. A breakdown follows:

Overall Survey # sent 4,784 # returned 874 % total 18% Open-ended Questions Full response 52% Partial response 28% No response 18%

While the total percentage returned was within acceptable limits, it was somewhat low and, by extension, a disappointment. Moreover, the overall findings should be a relatively accurate reflection of the concerns of most agencies regarding ethics training. Furthermore, the responses to the open-ended questions revealed a paradox between a "clearly perceived need for ethics training" and a lack of "demonstrated concern in the responses."

Question #69: What do you see as the more pressing ethical issues in law enforcement today?

The findings for this question are as follows, and reflect the perceptions of a very significant number of respondents.

Figure 9.2 Ethics Training in Law Enforcement (cont.)

- Cultural diversity/racism/sexism
- Corruption/gratuities
- Public trust
- Morals/personal values of officers/lack of values in new officers
- Honesty
- Abuse of force/abuse of authority
- Decision-making
- Code of silence
- Off-duty issues/behavior
- Poor work ethic of new recruits
- Lack of a sense of responsibility
- Lack of role models
- Issues considered critical:
- Honesty in official reports
- Police unions supporting unethical officers
- Fabricating evidence/honesty in official reports and embellishing testimony
- Temptation to embellish testimony or belief that the truth needs help
- Proliferation of drugs with money available to corrupt the police
- Lowered standards
- Professionalism
- Respect
- Loyalty
- Media

The above offer a substantial reflection of the concerns noted in the surveys. In part, these are evidence of previous "case study" analysis, but they bring a greater level of reliability to the findings. Moreover, the responses reveal some interesting common themes. Those who responded mentioned the importance of a set of agreed-upon foundations for behavior and the need for involvement of supervisors and managers. Further, many of the respondents spoke of the importance of role modeling in an agency and emphasis on the consequences of behavior.

Figure 9.2 Ethics Training in Law Enforcement (cont.)

Question #70: If you could design an ethics training program, which topics would you include?

This question was, to some extent, a reflection of responses posited in question #69. However, there were many occasions where there was substantial divergence. That is, problems as perceived in question #69 did not agree with the responses in question #70. This, perhaps, suggests that there is some level of disarray in terms of what the "critical issues are" and "what should be taught."

Question #71: Please provide us with any "working definitions of ethics" your organization uses.

In this particular case, most of those responding provided members of the committee with various codes of conduct and ethical behavior (e.g., department mission/ vision statements, IACP code of ethics, other specific codes), while only a handful provided any "working definition." To the extent that this occurred, it could suggest that the notion of what ethical behavior is should be more precisely defined as time progresses. In essence, this would provide some common ground from which to determine how to address issues related to ethical behavior.

Question #72: What do you consider to be the most important (or essential) elements or components of ethics training, and why?

One of the indicators that was focused on most frequently was the provision of a definition of ethics. Thus, further support was gained for question #71 (provision of a working definition of ethics).

Question #73: Further comments/suggestions/remarks.

This question was provided as a way in which to provide an opportunity for additional information. Very few agency representatives utilized this chance.

Summary/Conclusions

The overall perceptions of the members of the committee regarding the answers to these five questions was one of some level of disappointment and concern. Nevertheless, committee members do believe that a sufficient number of respondents answered the questions dealing with pressing ethical issues in law enforcement to provide some food for thought and critical insights. While it is impossible to scientifically categorize the poor responses to these questions, an educated guess is that the respondents would generally agree that the following represent the most serious ethical issues that confront law enforcement today.

Figure 9.2　Ethics Training in Law Enforcement (cont.)

Ad Hoc Committee Recommendations

If the effort to weave ethics training deeply into the fabric of police agencies is to succeed, it must be undertaken with a clear understanding of the very nature of the law enforcement profession. Police officers take risks and suffer inconveniences to protect the lives and secure the safety of fellow citizens, and they endure such risks and tolerate such inconveniences on behalf of strangers. Consequently, police work is one of the more noble and selfless occupations in society. Making a difference in the quality of life is an opportunity that policing provides, and few other professions can offer.

Therefore, police leadership must meet the highest ethical standards in order to keep the public's trust. As role models for officers as well as the community, police chiefs have an obligation to act in ways that avoid even the appearance of impropriety. In other words, integrity in word and deed, consistent with democratic principles, is one of the better ways to ensure that our organizations can live up to the noble promise of democratic public service.

Recommendation I: Increase visibility of ethics through the adoption of and support for a "Law Enforcement Oath of Honor."

As the effort to incorporate ethics training fully within law enforcement community begins, it will be important to heighten the visibility and awareness of ethics across the profession. A public affirmation to adhering to the current code of ethics and the adoption of an Oath of Honor will have to be undertaken, along with role modeling and mentoring, which are very powerful vehicles for changing behavior. To be successful at enhancing integrity within an organization, leaders must ensure that ethical mentoring and role modeling are consistent, frequent and visible. Therefore, the committee wholeheartedly supported the creation of a symbolic reverberance and public affirmation to attest a commitment to ethical conduct. After numerous drafts and conferences, the following Law Enforcement Oath of Honor was recommended as the IACP symbolic statement of commitment to ethical behavior:

On my honor, I will never betray my badge, my integrity, my character, or the public trust. I will always have the courage to hold myself and others accountable for our actions. I will always uphold the constitution and community I serve.

Before any officer takes the Law Enforcement Oath of Honor, it is important that he understands what it means. An oath is a solemn pledge someone makes when he sincerely intends to do what he says.

Figure 9.2 Ethics Training in Law Enforcement (cont.)

Honor means that one's word is given as a guarantee.

Betray is defined as breaking faith with the public trust.

Badge is the symbol of your office.

Integrity is being the same person in both private and public life.

Character means the qualities that distinguish an individual.

Public trust is a charge of duty imposed in faith toward those you serve.

Courage is having the strength to withstand unethical pressure, fear or danger.

Accountability means that you are answerable and responsible to your oath of office.

Community is the jurisdiction and citizens served.

The Oath of Honor's brevity allows it to be constantly referred to and reinforced during conversations with FTOs and line supervisors. In addition, administrators while communicating with others can also refer it to; placed on the back of all academy students' name cards, ensuring that they are looking at it all day; strategically and visibly placed in all police academies and law enforcement agencies; signed by each academy student, framed and hung on the wall; given at all official police ceremonies and gatherings; printed on labels that are placed on equipment; and used as a backdrop in citizens' meetings and news media events.

In conclusion, it is strongly recommended that the IACP adopt the Law Enforcement Oath of Honor and support a nationwide Oath of Honor sign-up campaign. Having officers take an oath will reconfirm the significance of integrity within the agency and help bring the entire profession together to show that the vast majority of law enforcement officers not only are good, decent individuals, but also will step forward to stop unethical acts by any members of our profession.

Recommendation II: Provide job-specific training on ethics.

While the approach to ethics training within a given agency should be viewed as universal in nature, it will be critically important to ensure that specific groups within a department have access to training tailored to their specific needs. Overall training content will be addressed in this section, but specific groups may include:

Recruits: Officers new to the profession must discuss the rules and regulations of an agency, while coming to understand the power

Figure 9.2 Ethics Training in Law Enforcement (cont.)

of the police culture. Recruits should be armed with decision-making tools so they are prepared to make intelligent/ethical choices.

Field training officers: FTOs are the most important link in developing a strong ethical foundation and culture within a police organization. FTOs must be schooled in the adult learning process so they are equipped to assist their trainees in learning to behave ethically. FTOs must understand the critical position they fill. It is not uncommon that an ethical situation will surface within the first 60 minutes spent with a new officer. The best illustration of this is exposing the new trainee to a half-price or free meal dilemma. More than any level within a police organization, the very finest, most ethical employees must be recruited and retained as FTOs. FTOs should become a gateway to first-line supervision within an agency.

In-service police officers: Tenured officers must be equipped with the tools necessary to identify and analyze ethical dilemmas, and thereafter must possess the ability to make appropriate ethical choices.

Supervisory personnel: Supervisors and first-line managers within a police department must understand their role in the development and maintenance of a healthy ethical climate in an agency. Supervisors can no longer absolve themselves of responsibility for misbehavior or personnel under their command. The prevailing attitude of being a popular supervisor rather than being an ethical supervisor must be reversed. This level of the organization, more than any other, must be constantly inundated with ethical situational training and scrutinized for indications of unethical behavior or dilemmas. The consensus of all members of the ad hoc committee identified this level of the police organization as essential in setting the ethical culture in the police profession.

Executive personnel: Command-level executives must take the lead in setting an ethical standard for the agency. Development of value statements and a readiness to "walk the line" (serve as a role model) must be critical benchmarks.

Civilian personnel: Often overlooked, civilians must understand the vital role they fulfill in the development of a fully ethical agency. Contract issues, records and financial matters are but a few of the areas open to discussion and examination.

Specialized unit categories: While much ethics training could be described as "one size fits all," certain specialized groups within an agency have very particular needs. Among those groups are

Figure 9.2 Ethics Training in Law Enforcement (cont.)

undercover drug personnel, detectives, traffic units, evidence collection teams, DARE officers, property custodians and SWAT officers.

Training focus: It is critically important, from an integrity and ethics perspective, that we not just "talk the talk" but also "walk the walk." Training bridges the gap between written integrity and ethics guidance and direction in the form of policy and procedure (talk the talk) to behavior change in the performance of duties and responsibilities (walk the walk) in police agencies.

Training will ensure that police personnel will know what to do, given integrity and ethical applications.

Supervision ensures that the policy and procedure and training curriculum are implemented at the operational level. Accountability systems ensure that all components of the integrity and ethics system are working, to include policy and procedure, training and supervision. Training becomes a critical and integral part of this process.

It is our recommendation that integrity and ethics training occur during police recruit training and throughout an individual's police career. Integrity and ethics training should be both general and agency specific in nature. General training would include generic applications that are applicable to all agency personnel. Agency-specific training would include examples of integrity and ethics violations and issues that have occurred in the past within the agency and how agency personnel should have responded to those situations.

Reasoning for recommendation: As with other training topics, ethics training is most effective when it is focused upon the specific needs of those being trained. The development and use of customized ethics training tools, techniques, processes and programs should provide personnel with more skills, knowledge and abilities for preventing unethical acts.

Recommendation III: Enhance training curriculum content.

As training programs are created and put into place within agencies, several important points should be carefully considered for inclusion:

Decision-making models: Officers should walk out of a training program with a set of tools readily available for use in analyzing ethical dilemmas and choosing among available options. Simply talking about ethics in a class is inadequate; an effective program will

Figure 9.2 Ethics Training in Law Enforcement (cont.)

provide usable tools available for immediate use outside the classroom. Discussion of specific values or moral anchors: As the tools described above are put to use, officers should be able to look toward a universally agreed-upon set of values to determine whether specific behavior is defensible and appropriate.

Examinations of ethical thinking outside the law enforcement arena: In the interest of learning from the mistakes of other groups, regular reading and discussion of a variety of classic cases in ethical thinking should be considered. Roll call, in-service training, and staff and line meetings should be the stage for discussion of ethical situations, with an emphasis on "why" and "how," followed by discussions of how it was resolved and what would be the most appropriate way if time were not a factor to resolve the situation. Feedback, feedback, feedback, combined with development of ethical solutions, must be continually emphasized.

Recommendation IV: Develop the appropriate training style.

Any attempt to incorporate training within the law enforcement community must be carried out within the framework of an "adult learning environment." Too often in the past, ethics training programs have consisted of little more than a lecture or sermon presented in a threatening and offensive tone. In such cases, it is little wonder that officers walk out of the classroom feeling they have, for all intents and purposes, wasted their time. The conscious decision should be made to treat police personnel attending ethics programs as adults, and to utilize the tenets of the adult learning process.

Reasoning for recommendation: The training of police personnel is most effective when the instructors concerned create a training style and environment that lends itself to the learning of adults. In particular, employees must fully appreciate how they will benefit from ethics training.

Recommendation V: Constantly reinforce ethics.

Police administrators must acknowledge that the development of a lasting and fully entrenched sense of positive ethical behavior within an agency will be arrived at only through continuing discussion of these issues. Ethics must be viewed as more than just a "Band-Aid" to be utilized after a scandal has arisen. Instead, personnel at all levels (and at all career stages) must have the opportunity to be reminded of these issues, and to have their decision-making skills refreshed and reinforced as discussed in examples given above.

Figure 9.2 Ethics Training in Law Enforcement (cont.)

Reasoning for recommendation: The ultimate solution for officer misconduct is for ethics and integrity to become ingrained throughout every aspect of an organization. Constant reinforcement, whether through training or leading by example, is a necessary element of organizational integrity.

Recommendation VI: Insist on strong recruit ethics training.

Executive summary: It is the recommendation of the ad hoc IACP Police Image and Ethics Training Committee that academies emphasize two major areas concerning ethics: ethical dilemma simulation training, and ethical perspectives on each training topic presented.

Specific recommendations:

- Incorporate an ethical perspective to all topics covered in the police academy curriculum.

- Have the academy director, when addressing the new recruit class for the first time, emphasize ethics and integrity, and stress that these two concepts are the highest priorities of the academy.

- Have every instructor in each training topic area address the ethical perspectives of each specific topic, and require them to substantiate such perspectives in lesson plan construction.

- Prominently display motivational posters or other similar types of signs within police facilities. Such signs might include the Value Statement, Oath of Honor, Code of Ethics, short articles of an ethical nature and reports of positive ethical behavior by members of the local agency or other departments.

- Distribute wallet cards with the Oath of Honor or key information on ethical decision-making models for ready reference.

- Print an honor code, Oath of Honor or ethics statement on desk nametags so officers can be constantly reminded of the issues they represent.

- Present a formalized four- to eight-hour interactive ethics training presentation. Primary focus should be on dealing with current, real-life ethical dilemmas.

- Create ethical decision-making "tests" to be given periodically to recruits and in-service trainees.

Figure 9.2 Ethics Training in Law Enforcement (cont.)

- Require recruits to read a current book that discusses ethics and promotes integrity. The book should then become the basis for class discussion and written examination.

- Facilitate lecture and emotional role-play scenario training that teaches officers the need for intervention, as well as how to professionally intervene when another officer appears about to commit an unethical act.

Reasoning for recommendation: Ethics instruction has not been a high priority within basic police academies. As such, academies sometimes conveyed the message that ethics was not a critical issue. Every instructor should address the ethical perspectives of each training topic and use the most effective tools and techniques available.

Recommendation VII: Focus on FTO ethics.

Executive summary: As mentioned previously, FTO programs must immediately become a major focus of law enforcement's efforts to prevent officer misconduct. FTOs should conduct ethics training in two major ways: through ethical dilemma simulation training focusing on previously documented unethical cases involving new recruits, and by including ethical situational training components on the Training Checklist.

Specific Recommendations:

- Make the integrity and positive mental outlook of potential FTOs a high priority in their selection.

- Ensure that FTOs thoroughly understand that they create the "organizational culture" of the patrol division, accept the responsibility, and have received FTO training that addresses this fact.

- Enlist administrators' deep support for the FTO program.

- Ensure that administrators follow the document-supported recommendation for termination of a recruit by FTOs, unless not doing so is truly justified.

- Have FTOs address each academy class to explain the upcoming FTO process.

- Add "Integrity/Ethics" to the trainee daily observation/evaluation report.

- Ensure that background investigator(s) have FTO experience.

Figure 9.2 Ethics Training in Law Enforcement (cont.)

- View members of the FTO program as part of the hiring process.
- Officially place "Integrity/Ethics" on the FTO training topic checklist.
- Confirm that each new officer has identified whom he talks to about any ethical dilemma, as a means of support.
- Provide lecture and emotional role-play scenario training that teaches officers the need for and how to intervene when another officer appears to commit an unethical act.
- Train FTOs in how to use audio and/ or video ethics simulation training for new officers.

Reasoning for recommendation: FTOs have a substantial impact upon the prevention or creation of unethical acts by patrol officers. Historically, law enforcement has not recognized this fact. The result was that ethics was seldom a training topic within FTO programs. In addition, the fact that the beliefs and attitudes of FTOs are usually replicated by recruits was not considered.

Recommendation VIII: Provide continual in-service training.

Executive summary: Ethics must immediately become a major focus of law enforcement's in-service training efforts. Departments should conduct internal ethics training in two fundamental ways: provide mandatory annual ethical dilemma simulation training, and require that instructors of each training topic address the ethical perspective of the topic they are presenting.

Specific recommendations:

- Ensure that every instructor of each in-service class addresses the ethical perspective of what he is training.
- Use internal e-mail, newsletters or other correspondence to disseminate words, quotes or verbiage dealing with ethics.
- Develop lectures and emotional role-play scenario training that teaches officers the need for and how to intervene when another officer appears about to commit an unethical act.
- Reasoning for recommendation: Ethics training must become a component of all internal instruction. Taking advantage of current ethics training techniques and tools can assist and enhance in-service ethics training. The neglect of in-service ethics training has frequently been present when employee misconduct occurred.

Comments

> ### Figure 9.2 Ethics Training in Law Enforcement (cont.)
>
> In order to have a viable and effective integrity and ethics impact within a police organization, it is critical that an integrity and ethics emphasis be infused into an agency's policy and procedure, training, supervision and accountability systems. This integrity and ethics infusion should have generic and specific applications. It should be generic in that certain integrity and ethics principles are applicable to all personnel in every assignment and at every level within the agency. It should be specific in that there are unique integrity and ethics applications to each assignment and position in a police agency.

Ethics For The Investigator

An investigator must be fair and impartial. How many times have you heard on the news in major cases accusations from attorneys and suspects that the investigators were bias against the suspects and failed to look at other suspects who may have committed the crime? The burden then shifts to the investigators to show that they followed all the leads. For the investigator the only thing that matters is the truth, no matter where it leads. But the investigator has the burden of getting to the truth by following the law and acting in an ethical manner. Their failure to follow the rules can lead to the dismissal of the case, a failure of the system to get justice for the victim, and a negative effect on the reputation of their agency.

The investigator must deal with the evidence and witnesses in an ethical manner. As discussed in the prior chapter, the defense will have access to the investigator(s notes, reports, witnesses'(statements, and other evidence. The defense will be looking for mistakes, intentional and unintentional by the investigator. Mistakes are made and can be explained or responsibility for those mistakes can be accepted. Covering up or lying about those mistakes can jeopardize the case and ruin a reputation. Changing or coloring a witness(testimony is unacceptable behavior, if not criminal. No case is so important as to jeopardize a career.

Below is a sample of a department(s ethical code of conduct. This particular one belongs to the United States Treasury Department and is dated October 15, 2000.

Figure 9.3 OFFICE OF THE TREASURY INSPECTOR GENERAL FOR TAX ADMINISTRATION, DATE: 04/01/2004

(700)-30 <u>Ethics</u>

This section contains general instruction and guidance for Treasury Inspector General for Tax Administration (TIGTA) personnel regarding the Standards of Ethical Conduct for Employees of the Executive Branch. The instruction and guidance do not serve as substitutes for the Standards of Ethical Conduct for Employees of the Executive Branch. If you have any questions or concerns, please consult with the Deputy Ethics Officer. It is the usual practice of the Deputy Ethics Officer to issue an ethics opinion, in writing, addressing any issues raised.

<u>Note</u>: This section does not address the additional ethical rules that may govern the different professions of TIGTA employees, e.g., attorneys, auditors.

30.1 <u>History and Background.</u>

In 1978, Congress enacted The Ethics in Government Act of 1978 (the Act), 5 U.S.C. app. 4 (1996). Section 401(a) of the Act established the Office of Government Ethics (OGE) as a separate agency in the executive branch. In addition, OGE received the authority to provide overall direction of executive branch policies to prevent conflict of interests on the part of officers and employees of any executive agency.

In 1989 and 1990, President George Bush signed two Executive Orders detailing The Standards of Ethical Conduct for Employees of the Executive Branch (the Principles). The Principles establish fair and exacting standards of ethical conduct and ensure that every citizen can have complete confidence in the integrity of the Federal Government. Exec. Order No. 12674, 54 Fed. Reg. 15159 (1989), *modified,* Exec. Order No. 12731, 55 Fed. Reg. 42547 (1990). The Executive Orders also authorized each agency to supplement any regulations issued by OGE with regulations of special applicability. The Department of the Treasury has issued supplemental regulations for its employees, which can be found at 5 C.F.R. pt. 3101 (2000). The Executive Orders also granted OGE the authority to promulgate, in consultation with the Attorney General and the Office of Personnel Management, "regulations that establish a single, comprehensive, and clear set of executive-branch standards of conduct that shall be objective, reasonable and enforceable." In addition, OGE was granted the authority to promulgate regulations interpreting the provisions of the post-employment statute (18 U.S.C. § 207); the general conflict-of-interest statute (18 U.S.C. § 208); and the statute prohibiting supplementation of salaries (18 U.S.C. § 209). OGE was tasked to promulgate regulations establishing a system of confidential financial disclosure pursuant to the Ethics in Government Act of 1978.

Pursuant to its authority, OGE has also enacted the following ethics regulations: Executive Branch Financial Disclosures, Qualified Trusts, and Certificates of Divestiture, 5 C.F.R. pt. 2634 (2000); The Standards of Ethical Conduct of Executive Branch Employees (the Standards), 5 C.F.R. pt. 2635 (2000); Limitations on Outside Employment and Prohibition of Honoraria, Confidential Reporting of Payments to Charities in Lieu of Honoraria, 5 C.F.R. pt. 2636 (2000); Regulations Concerning Post Employment Conflict of Interest, 5 C.F.R. pt. 2637 (2000); Interpretation, Exemptions and Waiver Guidance Concerning 18 U.S.C. § 208 (Acts Affecting a Personal Financial Interest), 5 C.F.R. pt. 2640 (2000); Post Employment Conflict of Interest Restrictions, 5 C.F.R. pt. 2641 (2000).

The Chief Counsel is the Deputy Ethics Officer for TIGTA.

30.2 TIGTA's Ethics Program

30.2.1 General Rule: TIGTA must have an ethics training program educating employees on ethics laws and rules and notifying them where to go for ethics advice. The training program must include, at a minimum, an initial agency ethics orientation for all employees and annual ethics training for covered employees. 5 C.F.R. § 2638.701.

30.2.2 Ethics Orientation: As part of its orientation program, TIGTA's Office of Management Services provides each new TIGTA employee with copies of the Standards of Ethical Conduct for Employees of the Executive Branch and Treasury's supplemental standards to keep or review, as well as the names, titles, office addresses and telephone numbers of TIGTA's ethics officer and other agency officials available to advise the employee on ethics issues. New TIGTA employees are entitled to a total of one hour of official duty time to review the standards and/or attend ethics training. The employee's manager will advise the employee of when this time will be granted.

30.2.3 <u>Annual Ethics Training For Public Filers:</u>

- Each calendar year, agencies must provide one hour of in-person ethics training to employees who are required by 5 C.F.R. § 2634 to file public financial disclosure reports.

- This training should include reviewing a combination of the Principles; the Standards; agency supplemental standards; federal conflict of interest statutes; and the names, titles, and office addresses and telephone numbers of the designated agency ethics official and other agency ethics officials available to advise the employee on ethics issues.

30.2.4 <u>Annual ethics training for other employees</u>: Each calendar year, agencies must train the following employees:

- Employees appointed by the President;

- Employees of the Executive Office of the President;

- Employees defined as confidential filers in 5 C.F.R. § 2634.904;

- Employees designated by their agency under 5 C.F.R. § 2634.601(b) to file confidential financial disclosure reports;

- Contracting officers; and,

- Other employees designated by the head of the agency or his or her designee based on their official duties.

30.3 <u>Outside Employment Activities.</u>

Pursuant to the Standards of Ethical Conduct for Executive Branch Employees, 5 C.F.R. §§ 2635.801-809, an employee may not engage in outside employment or activity that conflicts with the official duties of his or her position. An activity conflicts with official duties if: a) it is prohibited by statute or regulation; or b) the activity would require the employee to be disqualified from matters so central to the performance of the employee's official duties as to materially impair the ability to carry out those duties. An employee who wishes to engage in outside activities must comply with all relevant provisions of 5 C.F.R. §§ 2635.801-809 (Subpart H – Outside Activities). These provisions apply to uncompensated as well as to compensated outside activities. In addition, employees must endeavor to avoid action creating an appearance of violating any of the ethical standards in this part and the prohibition against use of official position for an employee's private gain or for the private gain of any person with whom he/she has employment or business relations or is otherwise affiliated in a non-governmental capacity.

The Supplemental Standards of Ethical Conduct for Employees of the Department of the Treasury require prior written approval for all Treasury employees before engaging in any outside employment or business activity. 5 C.F.R. § 3101.104(a). Approval shall be granted only upon a determination that the employment or activity is not expected to involve conduct prohibited by statute, section 2635 or any other provision. 5 C.F.R. § 3101.104(b).

Pursuant to the authority set forth in 5 C.F.R. § 3101.104(b), TIGTA has determined the following types of activities do not require written approval:

A. Membership and volunteer services (including holding of office) in civic, scout, religious, educational, fraternal, social community, veterans, and charitable organizations, including corporations, where such office or services do not entail the management of a business-type activity such as the direct operation of a commercial-type clubhouse;

B. Membership and services (including holding of office) in Federal employee organizations, credit unions, and Federal employee unions, as otherwise permitted by law;

C. Uncompensated services as a notary public;

D. A sale to co-workers, friends, relatives, and neighbors not involving a sale to, and solicitation of, the general public, provided that such sale does not constitute a business activity and is not solicited or transacted during duty hours or in space occupied by TIGTA offices, and is otherwise permitted by law;

E. Rental of personally-owned real or personal property, provided that the employee is not engaged in a commercial business venture; and

F. Minor services and odd jobs for friends, relatives or neighbors.

The determination as to whether one of the above-listed exemptions applies is fact specific, and employees may not engage in activities otherwise prohibited. Depending upon the circumstances, similar facts may produce a different result. Therefore, an employee who has a question regarding whether an outside employment or business activity requires prior written approval should consult with TIGTA Counsel through that employee's supervisor.

Figure 9.3 OFFICE OF THE TREASURY INSPECTOR GENERAL FOR TAX ADMINISTRATION, DATE: 04/01/2004 (cont.)

TIGTA functions may require its employees to adhere to additional procedures. Each TIGTA employee is responsible for becoming familiar with and following any specific   function requirements. A TIGTA employee currently engaged in or wishing to start outside employment in an activity not exempted above must submit a Form 7995, Outside Employment or Business Activity Request, through his or her manager to the Chief Counsel for approval. The employee's manager is to indicate approval or disapproval of the request before forwarding it to the Chief Counsel's Office. The Chief Counsel will review each request, seeking additional information from the employee, through the manager, as needed. Employees must ensure that any outside employment request on file reflects current outside employment and that no outside employment is changed or begun without prior approval. Employees must renew requests for outside employment annually, on a calendar year basis. The Office of Chief Counsel will maintain on file all outside employment requests and will return a copy of the approved or disapproved request through the manager to the employee.

30.4 Financial Disclosures, Qualified Trusts, and Certificates of Divestiture.

30.4.1 Rule for Public Filers. Public filers (Inspector General and TIGTA Senior Executive Service (SES)) who perform the duties of the position or office for a period in excess of sixty (60) days, must file a public financial disclosure report, Standard Form 278, Executive Branch Public Financial Disclosure Report, disclosing their financial interests as well as the interests of their spouses and minor children, on or before May 15 of the succeeding year. 5 C.F.R. pt 2634.

30.4.2 General Rule for Confidential Filers. Confidential filers who perform the duties of the position for a period in excess of sixty (60) days during the twelve-month period ending September 30, including more than sixty (60) days in an acting capacity, must file a confidential report, OGE Form 450, Confidential Financial Disclosure Report, on or before October 31 immediately following that period. The information contained in a completed OGE Form 450 generally tracks the approach of the public disclosure system with some differences. TIGTA makes the determination as to which employees must file confidential reports based on the following criteria: GS-15 employees, COTRs, auditors involved in contract reviews, employees who process procurements, and employees involved in reviewing or making recommendations on procurements.

30.4.3 <u>**Filing of Report.**</u> TIGTA's Deputy Ethics Officer or his or her delegate will review each financial disclosure report to determine that:

- Each required item is completed; and,

- No interest or position disclosed on the form violates or appears to violate applicable statutory provisions or regulations.

After completing its internal review, TIGTA will transmit copies of public financial disclosure reports to the Director of OGE.

30.4.4 <u>**Access to Public Reports.**</u> TIGTA shall, within thirty (30) days after any public report is received by the agency, permit inspection of the report by, or furnish a copy of the report to, any person who makes a written application as provided by agency procedure. The report shall be made available for a period of six (6) years. After the six-year period, the report shall be destroyed unless needed in an ongoing investigation.

An application to obtain a public report must be made to TIGTA's Deputy Ethics Officer and include the following:

- The requesting person's name, occupation, and address;

- The name and address of any other person or organization on whose behalf the inspection or copy is requested; and,

- That the requesting person is aware of the prohibitions on obtaining or using the report for any unlawful purpose; for any commercial purpose, other than by news and communications media for dissemination to the general public; for determining or establishing the credit rating of any individual; or for use, directly or indirectly, in the solicitation of money for any political, charitable, or other purpose.

30.5 <u>Post Government Employment.</u>

30.5.1 The following statutes and regulations govern post government employment for Executive Branch Employees:

- Restrictions on former officers, employees, and elected officials of the executive and legislative branches, 18 U.S.C. § 207 (1999);

- Penalties and Injunctions, 18 U.S.C. § 216 (1999);

> ## Figure 9.3 OFFICE OF THE TREASURY INSPECTOR GENERAL FOR TAX ADMINISTRATION, DATE: 04/01/2004 (cont.)
>
> - Office of Government Ethics, regulations concerning post employment conflict of interest, 5 C.F.R. pt. 2637 (1997);
>
> - Office of Government Ethics, Post-Employment conflict of interest restrictions 5 C.F.R. pt. 2641 (1998); and,
>
> - Office of the Secretary of the Treasury, administrative enforcement of post-employment conflict of interest, 31 C.F.R. § 15.737-7 (1999).
>
> **30.5.2 Ethical Restrictions.** Certain applicable statutes and regulations bar certain acts by former TIGTA employees which may reasonably give the appearance of making unfair use of prior Government employment and affiliations. Requests for guidance in determining whether post Government employment is authorized in a certain situation should be made to the Chief Counsel, as TIGTA's Deputy Ethics Officer. The Office of Chief Counsel will respond with written guidance.
>
> - Restrictions on any former Government employee's acting as representative as to a particular matter in which the employee personally and substantially participated, 18 U.S.C. § 207(a) (1999) and 5 C.F.R. § 2637.201 (1997).
>
> - Two-year restriction on any former Government employee's acting as representative as to a particular matter for which the employee had official responsibility, 18 U.S.C. § 207(b)(i) (1999) and 5 C.F.R. § 2637.202 (1997).
>
> - Two-year restriction on a former senior employee's assisting in representing as to a matter in which the employee participated personally and substantially, 18 U.S.C. § 207(b)(ii) (1999) and 5 C.F.R. § 2637.203 (1997).
>
> - One-year restriction on a former senior employee's transactions with former agency on a particular matter, regardless of prior involvement, 18 U.S.C. § 207(c) (1999) and 5 C.F.R. § 2637.204 (1997).
>
> ## 30.6 Gifts
>
> The following statutes and regulations govern the acceptance of gifts for Executive Branch Employees:
>
> - The Emoluments Clause, U. S. CONST., art. I, § 9, cl. 2;
>
> - Foreign Gifts and Decorations Act of 1966, as amended, 5 U.S.C. § 7342 (20030);

> ## Figure 9.3 OFFICE OF THE TREASURY INSPECTOR GENERAL FOR TAX ADMINISTRATION, DATE: 04/01/2004 (cont.)
>
> - Standards of Ethical Conduct for Executive Branch Employees, 5 C.F.R. pt. 2635 (2002);
>
> - Utilization, Donation and Disposal of Foreign Gifts and Decoration, 41 C.F.R. pt. 102-42 (2003);
>
> - Department of the Treasury Employee Rules of Conduct, 31 C.F.R. § 0.203 (2003);
>
> - General Services Administration, Office of Government Wide Policy, 65 Fed. Reg. 45539 (2000);
>
> - General Services Administration, Office of Government Wide Policy, 64 Fed. Reg. 13700-01 (1999); and,
>
> - Treasury Directive 61-04, Foreign Gifts and Decorations.
>
> ### 30.6.1 <u>Gifts From Outside Sources.</u>
>
> 30.6.1.1 Generally, an Executive Branch Employee is prohibited from soliciting or accepting any gift from a prohibited source or given because of the employee's official position, unless the item is excluded from the definition of a gift or falls within one of the exceptions set forth in this subpart. Prohibited source means any person who is either seeking official action by the employee's agency; does business or seeks to do business with the employee's agency; conducts activities regulated by the employee's agency; has interests that may be substantially affected by performance or nonperformance of the employee's official duties; or is an organization a majority of whose members have been previously described.
>
> In addition, an employee shall not
>
> - Accept a gift in return for being influenced in the performance of an official act;
>
> - Solicit or coerce the offering of a gift;
>
> - Accept gifts from the same or different sources on a basis so frequent that a reasonable person would be led to believe the employee is using his public office for private gain;
>
> - Accept a gift in violation of any statute. Relevant statutes applicable to all employees include: 18 U.S.C. § 201(b), which prohibits a public official from seeking, accepting, or agreeing to receive or accept anything of value in return for being influenced in the performance of an official act or for being induced to take or omit to take any action in violation of his official duty; 18 U.S.C. § 209, which prohibits an

Figure 9.3 OFFICE OF THE TREASURY INSPECTOR GENERAL FOR TAX ADMINISTRATION, DATE: 04/01/2004 (cont.)

employee, other than a special Government employee, from receiving any salary or any contribution to or supplementation of salary from any source other than the United States as compensation for services as a Government employee; or

- *Accept vendor promotional training contrary to applicable regulations, policies or guidance relating to the procurement of supplies and services for the Government, except pursuant to 5 C.F.R. § 2635.204(l).

30.6.1.3 Exceptions

- Gifts of $20.00 or less. Except for cash or investment interests, such as stock, bonds, or certificates of deposit, an employee may accept unsolicited gifts having an aggregate market value of $20.00 or less per occasion, provided that the aggregate market value of individual gifts received from any one person under this exception shall not exceed $50.00 in a calendar year;

- Gifts based on a personal relationship. An employee may accept a gift given under circumstances which make it clear that the gift is motivated by a family relationship or personal friendship rather than the position of the employee;

- Discounts and similar benefits;

- Awards and honorary degrees. An employee may accept gifts, other than cash or an investment interest, with an aggregate market value of $200.00 or less, if such gifts are a bona fide award or incident to a bona fide award that is given for meritorious public service or achievement by a person who does not have interests that may be substantially affected by the performance or nonperformance of the employee's official duties or by an association or other organization the majority of whose members do not have such interests;

- Gifts based on outside business or employment relationships.

Figure 9.3 OFFICE OF THE TREASURY INSPECTOR GENERAL FOR TAX ADMINISTRATION, DATE: 04/01/2004 (cont.)

- An employee may accept meals, lodgings, transportation and other benefits either resulting from the business or employment activities of an employee's spouse when it is clear that such benefits have not been offered or enhanced because of the employee's official position; resulting from his outside business or employment activities when it is clear that such benefits have not been offered or enhanced because of his official status; or customarily provided by a prospective employer in connection with bona fide employment discussions;

- Gifts in connection with political activities permitted by the Hatch Act Reform Amendments;

- Widely attended gatherings and other events. A gathering is widely attended if it is expected that a large number of persons will attend and that persons with a diversity of views or interests will be present. When an employee is assigned to participate as a speaker or panel participant or otherwise to present information on behalf of the agency at a conference or other event, his or her acceptance of an offer of free attendance at the event on the day of the presentation is permissible when provided by the sponsor of the event. When there has been a determination that an employee's attendance is in the interest of the agency because it will further agency programs and operations, the employee may accept an unsolicited gift of free attendance at all or appropriate parts of a widely attended gathering of mutual interest to a number of parties from the sponsor of the event or, if more than 100 persons are expected to attend the event and the gift of free attendance has a market value of $250.00 or less, from a person other than the sponsor of the event. Payment may be accepted from non-Federal sources for travel, subsistence, and related expenses with respect to attendance of the employee; an employee facing such an offer should consult with Management Services regarding the procedures for acceptance (e.g., whether payment must be made directly to TIGTA). Additional guidance is available at the Office of Government Ethic's website. In addition, TIGTA Counsel is available to offer assistance if needed;

Figure 9.3 OFFICE OF THE TREASURY INSPECTOR GENERAL FOR TAX ADMINISTRATION, DATE: 04/01/2004 (cont.)

- Social invitations from persons other than prohibited sources. An employee may accept food, refreshments and entertainment, not including travel or lodgings, at a social event attended by several persons where: a) the invitation is from a person who is not a prohibited source; and b) no fee is charged to any person in attendance;

- Meals, refreshments and entertainment in foreign areas, if certain conditions are met;

- Gifts authorized by supplemental agency regulation; and,

- Gifts accepted under specific statutory authority. For example, the Foreign Gifts and Decorations Act of 1966, authorizes a federal employee to accept from an agent or representative of a foreign government a gift of minimal value tendered as a souvenir or mark of courtesy. Foreign Gifts and Decorations Act of 1966, 5 U.S.C. § 7342(c)(1) (A) (2003).

30.6.2 Gifts Between Employees.

30.6.2.1 An Executive Branch Employee is prohibited from giving, donating to, or soliciting contributions for, a gift to an official superior and from accepting a gift from an employee receiving less pay than himself/herself, unless the item is excluded from the definition of a gift or falls within one of the exceptions set forth in this subpart.

Gifts to superiors. Except as provided in this subpart, an employee may not

- Directly or indirectly, give a gift to or make a donation toward a gift for an official superior; or

- Solicit a contribution from another employee for a gift to either his own or the other employee's official superior.

30.6.2.3 Gifts from employees receiving less pay. Except as provided in this subpart, an employee may not, directly or indirectly, accept a gift from an employee receiving less pay unless the two employees are not in a subordinate-official superior relationship; and there is a personal relationship between the two employees that would justify the gift.

30.6.2.4 Limitation on use of exceptions. Notwithstanding any exception provided in this subpart, an official superior shall not coerce the offering of a gift from a subordinate.

Figure 9.3 OFFICE OF THE TREASURY INSPECTOR GENERAL FOR TAX ADMINISTRATION, DATE: 04/01/2004 (cont.)

30.6.2.5 Exceptions

On an occasional basis, including any occasion on which gifts are traditionally given or exchanged, the following may be given to an official superior or accepted from a subordinate or other employee receiving less pay:

- Items, other than cash, with an aggregate market value of $10 or less per occasion;

- Items such as food and refreshments to be shared in the office among several employees;

- Personal hospitality provided at a residence, which is of a type and value customarily provided by the employee to personal friends;

- Items given in connection with the receipt of personal hospitality if of a type and value customarily given on such occasions; and,

- Leave transferred under subpart I of part 630 of this title to an employee who is not an immediate supervisor, unless obtained in violation of Sec. 630.912 of this title.

Special, infrequent occasions. A gift appropriate to the occasion may be given to an official superior or accepted from a subordinate or other employee receiving less pay:

- In recognition of infrequently occurring occasions of personal significance such as marriage, illness, or the birth or adoption of a child; or

- Upon occasions that terminate a subordinate-official superior relationship, such as retirement, resignation, or transfer.

Voluntary contributions. An employee may solicit voluntary contributions of nominal amounts from fellow employees for an appropriate gift to an official superior and an employee may make a voluntary contribution of a nominal amount to an appropriate gift to an official superior:

- On a special, infrequent occasion as previously described;

- On an occasional basis, for items such as food and refreshments to be shared in the office among several employees

An employee also may accept as gifts such items as food and refreshments to be shared in the office among several employees.

> **Figure 9.3 OFFICE OF THE TREASURY INSPECTOR GENERAL FOR TAX ADMINISTRATION, DATE: 04/01/2004 (cont.)**
>
> **30.6.3 <u>Proper Disposition of Prohibited Gifts.</u>** An employee who has received a gift that cannot be accepted shall:
>
> - Return any tangible item to the donor or pay the donor its market value;
>
> - When it is not practical to return a tangible item because it is perishable, the item may, at the discretion of the employee's supervisor or an agency ethics official, be given to appropriate charity, shared within recipient's office, or destroyed;
>
> - For any entertainment, favor, service, benefit or other intangible, reimburse the donor the market value; or
>
> - Dispose of gifts from foreign governments or international organizations in accordance with 41 C.F.R. § 101-25.103.
>
> An employee who, on his own initiative, promptly complies with the above mentioned requirements of this section will not be deemed to have improperly accepted an unsolicited gift. An employee who consults with TIGTA's ethics official to determine whether acceptance of an unsolicited gift is proper and who, upon the advice of the ethics official, returns the gift or otherwise disposes of the gift in accordance with the ethical requirements, will be considered to have complied with the ethical requirements on his or her own initiative.

Ethics For The Manager

As a manager, you are responsible for modeling ethical behavior and providing advice and guidance to employees regarding ethics. This is to ensure compliance with the regulations of your agency.

A first line supervisor in a typical investigative agency will have a number of investigators and at least one administrative person under his command. The manager must be the person to lead the ethical behavior through example.

The manager should look for signs of abuse that can lead to unethical behavior. Some of these signs are indicators of alcohol or drugs abuse, martial problems, and financial problems. These signs can include living above their means, poor attendance, and a reduction in the quality of their work product. As a manager, you should become involved when an employee's problem becomes severe enough to affect his/her work performance and/or conduct. You can play a critical role in early detection of developing problems by observing and documenting deficient performance and unacceptable conduct and referring the employee to the Employee Assistance Program when you recognize a pattern of deterioration.

INTEGRITY AND OBJECTIVITY

As a law enforcement officer you can not allow your prejudices, emotions or surmises to effect your judgment or your work without losing your integrity; your code of honor. You must remain objective in the way you deal with suspects, witnesses, and evidence. You will come in contact with individuals with different believes, and cultures. You will need to have the patience to listen to them and keep an open mind and try to understand their point of view. How you act will have will have an effect on how you, your agency and may be your country is perceived by these individuals and those influenced by what those individuals tell them.

Typical Ethical And Integrity Issues

To assist their employees, the United States Customs Services published a pamphlet entitled Plain Talk About Conduct and Ethics, that provided an overview of the most common conduct and ethical issues their employees faced. They felt that knowing what the standards are and abiding by them can prevent problems before they occur. Some of the topics covered that are applicable to most law enforcement positions are listed below.

- Off-duty conduct
- A full day(s work for a full day(s pay
- Regular and punctual attendance
- Prohibition against discrimination
- Basic courtesy
- Truthful Statements
- Protection of official information
- Taking care of government money and property
- Firearms
- Misuse of vehicles
- Misuse of badges, credentials, and identification
- Use of illegal drugs

- Reporting arrests and formal charges (of employee)
- Reporting violations of laws and employee misconduct
- Reporting attempted bribes
- Associating with criminals
- Accepting gifts
- Conflicting financial interests
- Borrowing or lending money among employees
- Impartiality in performing official duties
- Conflict of interest - family members
- Outside activities
- Misuse of Position
- Public disclosure and use of nonpublic information

Below you will read the Complaint for violation of 18 U.S.C., Section 1030, computer related fraud in the case of the United States of America vs. Beverly Jean Jordan. Beverly was a special agent with the United States Customs Service. I knew Beverly from attending advance training with her on several occasions and we worked together for a short while in San Diego. She was well thought of in the office and considered a good person. The point is that if a person like Beverly can get caught up in a situation that ended her career and gave her a criminal history, it can happen to anyone. Beverly is one of the last persons who I would of thought of who would have betrayed their public trust.

Beverly was single and became involved with an unethical defense attorney who used her to his benefit. In paragraph 32 of the complaint, it talks about an ex-internal affairs agent giving her advice on not disclosing official information to aid an outsider, that ex-internal affairs agent was me.

Figure 9.4 Criminal Complaint

ORIGINAL

FILED

JUN – 3 1997

CLERK, U.S. DISTRICT COURT
SOUTHERN DISTRICT OF CALIFORNIA
BY: _____ DEPUTY

UNITED STATES DISTRICT COURT
SOUTHERN DISTRICT OF CALIFORNIA

'97 MG 1360

UNITED STATES OF AMERICA)

VS.   )   Magistrate's Case No.

Beverly Jean JORDAN   )   COMPLAINT FOR VIOLATION OF
)   18 U.S.C. && 1030 –
)   Computer Related Fraud
)

The undersigned complainant being duly sworn states:

COUNT ONE

That on or about August 6, 1996 through approximately March 13, 1997, within the Southern District of California, defendant Beverly Jean JORDAN did knowingly and intentionally utilize the TECS Computer, and databases accessible through TECS, to commit unauthorized computer queries in violation of Title 18, United States Code, Section 1030.

And the complainant states that this complaint is based on the attached Statement of Facts incorporated herein by reference.

_____
Lorraine Concha
Special Agent – U.S. Customs Service

Sworn to before me and subscribed in my presence, June 3, 1997.

_____
United States Magistrate Judge

Figure 9.4 Criminal Complaint (cont.)

STATEMENT OF FACTS

1.   According to Customs Service personnel files, Beverly
Jordan is currently employed as a Special Agent with the Customs
Service, Office of Investigation, in San Diego, California. Jordan has
been employed in this capacity since August 12, 1990 and is assigned to
the Fraud Group, which is physically located in the Customs Service's
Otay Mesa Commercial Facility, 9777 Via de la Amistad, Suite 203, San
Diego, California.

2.   I conducted a TECS User Profile computer query for
Beverly Jordan, which indicated that she completed and passed the TECS
Security Procedures Course and Certification Test on June 17, 1996 and
completed and passed the NCIC Policies and Procedures Course and
Certification Test on January 3, 1996. According to a review of the
TECS system sign-on screen and Customs Service personnel files, TECS
number 403920331 is Beverly Jordan's social security number and user
identification number (hereinafter, "Jordan's TECS number").

3.   On January 6, 1997, San Diego Police Department detective
Cindi L. Stetson contacted me regarding a case in which a Customs
Service employee, later identified as Beverly Jordan, was allegedly
involved. I subsequently spoke to Detective Stetson and reviewed
surveillance reports from the San Diego Police Department.

4.   According to Detective Stetson, on December 19, 1996, she
directed a confidential source (hereinafter, "CS-1") to meet Attorney
Nicholas Cimmarrusti at his law office. For purposes of recording all
conversations during this meeting, CS-1 was equipped with a nagra
recording device. I have reviewed the tape recording that resulted

1

Figure 9.4 Criminal Complaint (cont.)

1   therefrom.   The tape reveals that during this meeting, Nicholas

2   Cimmarrusti requested two pounds of methamphetamine from CS-1 and took

3   possession of eight rings, which CS-1 claims were stolen by Terry

4   (Terrance) Murray. According to State of California, San Diego Superior

5   Court records (case number P8028901), Terry Murray is a client of

6   Nicholas Cimmarrusti. Nicholas Cimmarrusti informed CS-1 that he would

7   keep the rings and have them appraised.

8   5.   During this meeting of December 19, 1996, between CS-1

9   and Nicholas Cimmarrusti, Detective Stetson observed a black female,

10   later identified as Beverly Jordan, arrive outside the office in her

11   assigned Customs Service vehicle (a gold-colored Cutlass Cierra, bearing

12   California license plate number 3JOP762), and walk into the 301 West A

13   Street address.   Having listened to the recording of the meeting, I

14   heard Beverly Jordan's voice evaluating the rings in an attempt to

15   determine their value.

16   6.   I have conducted a TECS history query for the name of

17   Nicholas Cimmarrusti, which revealed that the name was queried by

18   Jordan's TECS number on February 12, 1997. The name "N Cimmarrusti" was

19   also queried by Jordan's TECS number on that date.   In addition,

20   Cimmarrusti's law office address was also queried on that date.   The

21   aforementioned TECS history query also demonstrated that the name of

22   Nicholas Cimmarrusti was queried by user identification number 561733028

23   on December 4, 1996. According to a review of the TECS system sign-on

24   screen, and Customs Service personnel files, TECS number 561733028 is

25   Jeanette Martin's social security number and user identification number

26   (hereinafter, "Martin's TECS number").   Jeanette Martin is the

27

28   2

Figure 9.4 Criminal Complaint (cont.)

1   Investigative Aide to the Fraud Group to which Beverly Jordan is

2   currently assigned.

3   7.   State of California Department of Motor Vehicles

4   (hereinafter, "DMV") records indicate that Nicholas Cimmarrusti is the

5   registered owner of a 1967 Alfa Romeo, bearing California license plates

6   1FYN394. I conducted a TECS history query, which revealed that this

7   vehicle plate was queried by Martin's TECS number on September 19, 1996.

8   8.   Based upon my training and experience, a review of

9   documents and other relevant information I believe to be reliable, and

10   discussions with other federal agents, I believe that Beverly Jordan

11   either conducted TECS queries herself utilizing Martin's TECS number or

12   requested that Martin conduct TECS queries on her (Jordan's) behalf.

13   9.   Further TECS research has revealed that the

14   aforementioned license plate (1FYN394) was also queried by Jordan's TECS

15   number on August 6, 1996. On August 12, 1996, telephone number 619-231-

16   1181 was queried by Jordan's TECS number. I have reviewed subscriber

17   information from the Pacific Bell Telephone Company indicating that

18   Nicholas Cimmarrusti's law office telephone number is listed as 619-239-

19   1181.

20   10. DMV records indicate that Pietro Cimmarrusti, residing at

21   6042 Tamilynn Drive, San Diego, California, is the registered owner of

22   a 1987 Alfa Romeo, bearing California license plates 1RWW222. This

23   vehicle plate was queried by Jordan's TECS number on November 12, 1996.

24   11. Further TECS research has revealed that the name of

25   Nicholas Cimmarrusti was queried by Jordan's TECS number for Warrants

26   and Restraining Orders on January 2, 1997.

27

28   3

Figure 9.4 Criminal Complaint (cont.)

1   12. Further TECS research reveals that just prior to the

2 aforementioned TECS query of license plate 1FYN394, Vehicle

3 Identification Number (VIN) 4EMEL2E21SN147408 was queried on September

4 19, 1996, by Martin's TECS number. According to DMV records, this VIN

5 number belongs to a 1995 Harley Davidson motorcycle currently registered

6 to Cimmarrusti's client, Terry Murray. I have also discovered that this

7 same VIN number was queried on October 31, 1996, by Jordan's TECS

8 number.

9   13. Further TECS research has revealed that the names of

10 Nicole Bradley and Nicole Rene were each queried by Jordan's TECS number

11 at least once on November 13, 1996; at least four times on November 15,

12 1996; and at least once on March 13, 1997. According to DMV records,

13 Nicole Bradley changed her name to Nicole Rene when she renewed her

14 driver's license on February 27, 1997, and listed the name of Nicole

15 Michelle Bradley as her "other name."

16   14. According to State of California, San Diego Superior

17 Court records (People v. Nicole Michelle Bradley, case number P8550301),

18 Nicole Bradley is a client of Nicholas Cimmarrusti, who on October 23,

19 1996 was arrested for violation of State of California Health & Safety

20 Code Section 11360(a) - Transportation of Marijuana, and Section 11359 -

21 Possession of Marijuana. According to Deputy District Attorney (DDA)

22 Richard Clabby, on April 9, 1997, Nicole Bradley pled guilty to all

23 charges and is scheduled to be sentenced on May 20, 1997.

24   15. I have learned from DDA Clabby that on April 7, 1997, the

25 Nicole Bradley criminal case was set to begin trial at San Diego County

26 Superior Courtroom Number 31. Nicholas Cimmarrusti was retained as

27 defense counsel, and DDA Clabby was the assigned prosecutor. I have

28   4

Figure 9.4 Criminal Complaint (cont.)

1 further learned from DDA Clabby that the Bradley trial had previously

2 been set to begin on Friday, March 14, 1997, but Cimmarrusti requested

3 a continuance, allegedly due to illness.

4   16. I have listened to a tape recorded answering machine

5 message for March 12, 1997, at approximately 10.19 p.m., left by Beverly

6 Jordan for her Group Supervisor, David McClintock, stating she (Beverly

7 Jordan) had cut the business trip short, due to "personal business."

8 Beverly Jordan requests, via the telephone message, that she be placed

9 on Annual Leave for Thursday and Friday, March 13, 14, 1997,

10 respectively.

11   17. I have spoken with Beverly Jordan's supervisor, Dave

12 McClintock, who informed me that Beverly Jordan was scheduled to be in

13 the Washington D.C. area from March 2, 1997 through Friday, March 14,

14 1997. On March 12, 1997, at approximately 6:40 p.m., Customs Service,

15 Office of Internal Affairs Special Agent David Hughes saw Beverly Jordan

16 talking to the female driver of a Lexus with California license plates

17 3CLB099. According to DMV records, license plate 3CLB099 is registered

18 to Nicole M. Bradley, at 2232 River Run Drive, #208, San Diego,

19 California.

20   18. Based upon my training and experience, a review of

21 documents and other relevant information I believe to be reliable, and

22 discussions with other federal agents, I believe that Beverly Jordan

23 conducted TECS queries and curtailed her business trip in order to

24 return to the San Diego area and assist Nicholas Cimmarrusti in the

25 preparation of the Bradley case, originally scheduled for trial on March

26 14, 1997. Further TECS research has revealed that on March 13, 1997,

27 the name of Everton McKnight was queried by Jordan's TECS number.

28   5

Figure 9.4 Criminal Complaint (cont.)

19. I have learned from DDA Clabby that on April 7, 1997, just before arguments on a defense motion were to be heard by presiding Judge Joan Weber, DDA Clabby was handed two sheets of paper by defense attorney Cimmarrusti. One sheet represented a defense "List of Witnesses," while the other set forth a list of defense "Exhibits" Cimmarrusti anticipated using during the Bradley criminal trial set to commence that day. Listed as item number one on the defense "Exhibits" list was a "Photograph of Everton McKnight."

20. I have learned from a search of the San Diego County Superior Court civil case index that on October 26, 1995, civil case number 693900, under the case name of <u>Cimmarrusti, Nicholas v. Baldassini-Jordan Studios</u> (Jordan, Eric) was filed. This civil complaint was filed by Nicholas Cimmarrusti (Plaintiff/Petitioner) against Eric Jordan (Defendant/Respondent). Further review of the file by your affiant revealed the case concerned a dispute over a $26,000 bank draft, which Nicholas Cimmarrusti "entrusted" to Eric Baldassini-Jordan. This case was dismissed July 22, 1996.

21. DMV records indicate that California driver's license number A4746843 is currently assigned to Eric Baldassini-Jordan.

22. Further TECS research has revealed that the name of Eric Jordan was queried by Jordan's TECS number at least eight times on August 6, 1996; at least once on August 12, 1996; at least once on August 13, 1996; at least once on September 24, 1996; at least three times on October 28, 1996; at least three times on November 27, 1996; at least once on November 30, 1996; at least four times on December 4, 1996; at least once on December 30, 1996; at least once on January 27, 1997; and at least once on February 11, 1997.

6

Figure 9.4 Criminal Complaint (cont.)

23. I have further discovered that in Beverly Jordan's research of Eric Baldassini-Jordan, the names of Alison Gabriel, Olivier Bernard, and Olivier Watrelot were encountered (as a result of her queries), and, in turn, queried by Jordan's TECS number. On August 6, 1996, the name of Alison Gabriel surfaced in a query of address 2881 Beldon Drive, Los Angeles, California. This is the address listed on a vehicle registered to Eric B. Jordan, which Jordan discovered via DMV database, which was in turn accessed via TECS. Jordan's TECS number then queried the 2881 Beldon Drive, Los Angeles, CA address via the Criss-Cross real estate database. Jordan received the name of Alison Gabriel as the owner of the residence.

24. On December 4, 1996, California Driver's License A6008805 was queried by Jordan's TECS number, which license, according to DMV records, is assigned to Olivier Bernard. San Diego Sheriff's Department records indicate an incident in which Bernard, Olivier was listed as a victim, in January of 1995. In those records, Olivier Bernard listed his employer as The Sound Company, located at 767 Center Drive, San Marcos, California. I have reviewed a "Proof of Service" declaration in the civil case of <u>Cimmarrusti, Nicholas v. Baldassini-Jordan Studios</u> (Jordan, Eric), in which four attempts to serve Eric Jordan with a summons/complaint were made at The Sound Company 's San Marcos address.

25. On December 4, 1996, the name of Olivier Watrelot was queried by Jordan's TECS number. DMV records indicate that Olivier Watrelot's California driver's license lists under "other address," 2152 Ramona Lane, Vista, California. The address of 2152 Ramona Lane, Vista, California is listed by Eric Baldassini-Jordan as his residence on his California driver's license.

7

Figure 9.4 Criminal Complaint (cont.)

1   26.   Further research has revealed that the following queries

2   were conducted by Jordan's TECS number:

3   Barnett, Steve, DOB: 01-23-51 (February 14, 1997);

4   Breipohl, Joel Robert, DOB: 06-08-61 (September 24, 1996);

5   Cacioppo, Alfonso (December 4, 1996);

6   Commereau, Patricia (December 4, 1996);

7   Hill, Felicia (March 25, 1997);

8   Holden, Raymond, DOB: 08-21-35 (January 24, 1997);

9   Kelly, Matt, DOB: 05-20-66 (aka: Kelly, Kerry Matthew; Kelly

10   Matthew) (September 24, 1996 and October 11, 1996);

11   Lanz, Marvel Elaine, DOB: 06-12-39 (October 5, 1996);

12   Morgan, David, DOB: 11-07-71 (August 1, 1996);

13   Ritelli, Adrio Fabio, DOB: 09-23-66 (September 24, 1996);

14   Szabo, Brent Kelly, DOB: 05-15-69 (October 23, 1996);

15   Rothman, Michael (December 18, 1996);

16   Vehicle License Number 1LSA624 - 1984 Alfa Romeo; R/O: Kelly,

17   Matthew Wade, 8125 El Paseo Grande, La Jolla, CA (July 29,

18   1996);

19   Vehicle License Number 2CXR692 - 1972 Ferrari; R/O:

20   Cohanarieh, Farzaneh, 10750 Lindbrook Dr., Los Angeles, CA

21   (February 11, 1997);

22   Vehicle License Number 3RQE050 - 1977 Porsche; R/O: Morgan,

23   David Wayne, DOB: 11-07-71, 2889 Poplar Meadow Lane, Jamul,

24   CA (August 1, 1996); and

25   Vehicle License Number HCSTORE - 1989 Porsche; R/O: Rothman,

26   Michael U., 1809 Hidden Oaks, El Cajon, CA (December 18,

27   1996).

28   8

Figure 9.4 Criminal Complaint (cont.)

1   27. I have conducted TECS queries of the names "N.

2 Cimmarrusti" and "Nicholas Cimmarrusti," which revealed that no agent in

3 the Customs Service, Office of Investigation, including Beverly Jordan,

4 has an on-going investigation involving Nicholas Cimmarrusti.

5   28. I have also conducted TECS queries of California license

6 plate 1FYN394, VIN 4EMEL2E21SN147408, and the name of Terrance/Terry

7 Murray, which queries revealed that no agent in the Customs Service,

8 Office of Investigations, including Beverly Jordan, has an on-going

9 investigative case involving the aforementioned license plate, VIN

10 number, or the name of Terrance/Terry Murray.

11   29. I have further conducted TECS queries of the name Nicole

12 Bradley, Nicole Rene, Rene Bradley, and Everton McKnight, which revealed

13 that no agent in the Customs Service, Office of Investigations,

14 including Beverly Jordan, has an on-going investigative case involving

15 any of the aforementioned individuals.

16   30. I have also conducted TECS queries of the name Eric

17 Jordan, Eric Baldassini, and Eric Baldassini-Jordan, which revealed that

18 no agent in the Customs Service, Office of Investigations, including

19 Beverly Jordan, has an on-going investigation case involving Eric

20 Jordan, Eric Baldassini, Eric Baldassini-Jordan.

21   31. In addition, I have conducted TECS queries of the names

22 and license numbers listed in paragraph 26 above, which revealed that no

23 agent in the Customs Service, Office of Investigations, including

24 Beverly Jordan, has an on-going investigative case involving any of the

25 aforementioned individuals or license numbers. Moreover, on May 7,

26 1997, I spoke to Supervisor McClintock, who reviewed the above-listed

27 individuals and vehicle license plates to determine if he recognized

28   9

Figure 9.4 Criminal Complaint (cont.)

1 them as part of any case that Beverly Jordan or any of his group agents

2 were investigating. Group Supervisor McClintock told your affiant that

3 he did not recognize any of the individuals or vehicle license plates.

4   32. According to Supervisor McClintock, on Monday, March 31,

5 1997, while he was having lunch with Beverly Jordan and two other fraud

6 group agents, the subject of TECS information disclosure was raised by

7 one of the other agents who had served in the Office of Internal Affairs

8 (hereinafter, "OIA"). Supervisor McClintock stated that, following

9 Jordan's question regarding possible conflict of interest between a

10 spouse employed in the Importation business and a Customs Inspector

11 working at the Commercial Facility, OIA's ability to conduct research

12 and playbacks of TECS users activities on TECS was also discussed as

13 casual lunch conversation. According to Supervisor McClintock, it was

14 at this time that the ex-Internal Affairs agent mentioned that the

15 employee could encounter trouble if he disclosed TECS information to aid

16 the spouse, which assistance could be traced back through TECS

17 playbacks.

18   33. Based upon my training and experience, a review of

19 documents and other relevant information I believe to be reliable, and

20 discussions with other federal agents, I believe that Beverly Jordan has

21 conducted TECS queries and provided Nicholas Cimmarrusti confidential,

22 computer-database-generated information to assist Cimmarrusti in the

23 preparation of his criminal and civil cases.

24   34. Based upon my experience and training, I know that the

25 TECS system contains a number of separate databases, each of which

26 contains specific types of information about individuals, such as the

27 California Law Enforcement Telecommunications System (CLETS). By

28   10

Figure 9.4 Criminal Complaint (cont.)

1　accessing CLETS, a user can obtain several categories of records: 1) DMV

2　records, including driver's license information, information on license

3　plates, and vehicle identification numbers, 2) the personal history of

4　an individual, including the date of birth and address of a said

5　individual, and 3) the individual's criminal history information.

6　　　　35. Based upon my experience and training, I also know that

7　through the TECS system, an authorized user can access the National

8　Crime Information Center System (NCIC), which is maintained by the

9　Federal Bureau of Investigations. By accessing the NCIC system, a user

10　can obtain information and records regarding the arrest and conviction

11　of an individual.

12　　　　36. Based upon my experience and training, I further know

13　that through the TECS system, an authorized user can access the National

14　Law Enforcement Telecommunications System (NLETS). By accessing the

15　NLETS system, a user can obtain information and records through from the

16　DMV and criminal history information from any state in the United

17　States.

18　　　　37. A TECS system user is capable of printing out the results

19　of their queries that constitute government records. According to the

20　Privacy Act of 1974, law enforcement employees are prohibited from

21　accessing and obtaining confidential information and records from the

22　aforementioned systems unless required for official law enforcement

23　purposes.

24　　　　38. Based on all of the above, my experience and training,

25　discussions with other federal agents, and all the above facts and

26　circumstances, it is my belief that the aforementioned TECS system

27　queries performed by Beverly Jordan were not authorized queries to TECS

28　　　　　　　　　　　　　　　　11

Figure 9.4 Criminal Complaint (cont.)

1 or the various databases accessed through TECS but for her own gain or

2 the personal gain of Nicholas Cimmarrusti.

3   39. Based on all of the above, my experience and training,

4 discussions with other federal agents, and all the above facts and

5 circumstances, I submit that there is probable cause to believe that

6 there have occurred, and are now occurring, violations of federal law by

7 Beverly Jordan, as specified herein.

8

9

10 _____
    Lorraine Concha
    Special Agent - U.S. Customs Service

11

12 SWORN AND SUBSCRIBED TO before me this ___3ᵈ___ day of June, 1997.

13 1.

14 _____
    UNITED STATES MAGISTRATE JUDGE

15

16

17

18

19

20

21

22

23

24

25

26

27

28

12

Figure 9.5 Sample Record of Proceedings and Judgement

UNITED STATES DISTRICT COURT
SOUTHERN DISTRICT OF CALIFORNIA
RECORD OF PROCEEDINGS AND JUDGMENT

FILED
00 FEB 23 AM 10: 17

CLERK. U.S. DISTRICT COURT
SOUTHERN DISTRICT OF CALIFORNIA

UNITED STATES OF AMERICA,

vs.

BEVERLY JEAN JORDAN

CASE NO. 97CR2164-
SUPERSEDING
INFORMATION FILED: June 22, 1999

Tape No: JFS00-1:1000-3640

VIOLATION: CT 1 and 2: 18 USC 1905 Disclosure of Confidential Information Generall;
(misd)

PROCEEDINGS: DATE: 2/22/00

___X___ Defendant informed of charges, right to trial and right to counsel.
___X___ Attorney: EUGENE IREDALE, RETAINED
___X___ Filed "Consent to be Tried by U.S. Magistrate Judge".

PLEA: ___X___ Guilty on Count 1,2.

JUDGMENT AND COMMITMENT

___X___ Defendant adjudged guilty on count 1,2. UNDERLYING INDICTMENT DISMISSED.
___X___ Penalty Assessment of $50.00. ___Remitted   ___X___Forthwith
___X___ Fine of $ _NONE_   ___Waived ___Forthwith ___Within_____
_____ Restitution of $_____ ___Forthwith ___Within_____

___X___ SUPERVISED Probation for a period of _TWO (2) YEARS_ on condition:
_X_ she obey all laws Federal, State and Municipal;
_X_ she comply with all lawful rules and regulations of the Probation Department;
_X_ she not possess any narcotic drug or controlled substance without a lawful
    medical prescription;
_X_ she not possess any firearm or other dangerous weapon;
_X_ she complete 200 hours of community service, at the rate of 100 hours each year of
    supervised probation, in a program approved by the probation officer;
_X_ she report all vehicles owned or operated, or in which she has an interest, to the
    probation officer;
_X_ she submit to one drug test within 15 days of being released on probation and two
    random drug tests during the probation period, if funds are available;
    _X_ This final condition is hereby ordered waived.

    IT IS ORDERED that the Clerk deliver a certified copy of this judgment and
commitment to the United States Marshal or other qualified officer and that the copy
serve as the commitment of the defendant.

I have executed within PROBATION
Judgement and Commitment on 2/28/00
        James M. Sullivan
        United States Marshal

By: _____
    USMS Criminal Section

JAMES F. STIVEN
United States

ENTERED ON

47cr2164

SUMMARY

Law enforcement officers have a position of public trust that requires them to be ethical in their public and private life. Being ethical is doing the right thing when no one is looking. Many careers have been ruined by unethical behavior like the Beverly Jordan case.

DISCUSSION QUESTIONS

1. If a criminal is a threat to society without question and you, as a law enforcement officer, obtained the key evidence by illegal means and only you know that, is it ok to lie about how you obtained that evidence for the good of the community?
2. Is taking office supplies home for personal use ok?
3. If a business offers free food to police officers as a citizen how do you feel about that? How do you feel about the police officers? How does the business owner feel about it?

ADDITIONAL READINGS

Elements of Investigation, Paul B. Weston and Charles A. Lushbaugh, Hardcover, Prentice Hall, 2003

Lines of Defense - Police Ideology and the Constitution, *Chuck Klein, paperback, Institute of Police Technology, 1999*

BIBLIOGRAPHY

United States Treasury Department, Directive 700-30 dated October 15, 2000

International Association of Chiefs of Police, Law Enforcement Code of Ethics

International Association of Chiefs of Police, Report on Ethics Training in Law Enforcement

United States Customs Service, Plain Talk About Conduct and Ethics

Chapter 10

Case Preparation For Trial

CHAPTER OVERVIEW

Preparation is the key to a successful prosecution. In this chapter you will learn when to start preparing for trial, witness demeanor and image including appearance, voice and manner of speaking, what happens during direct examination, what happens in the cross examination and the duties of the case agent.

CHAPTER OBJECTIVES

1. Know when to start preparing for trial.
2. Know the duties for the case agent.
3. Learn how to testify on direct and during cross-examination.
4. Know the proper appearance for court.
5. Know how to speak in a courtroom.

INTRODUCTION

The job of the investigator is to investigate the crime, find those responsible for committing the crime and to provide the prosecutor with the evidence needed to obtain a conviction. This means that the investigator must obtain the evidence in a legal manner so that it can be used in court. The investigator must conduct the investigation in an ethical manner. The investigator must find the truth.

WHEN TO START PREPARATION FOR TRIAL

Preparation for trial begins the first day of your investigation. Everything you do from the first day on will be subject to scrutiny by the defense attorney and the courts. As you get close to the actual trial there will be a number of things you will do to assist the prosecutor. However if mistakes are made during the investigation they could be fatal to the case and it may never get to trial. An example would be a fabricated statement in an affidavit for a search warrant where evidence crucial to prove the case is seized.

Preparations Needed As The Trial Date Gets Near

As the trial date nears, the case agent has a number of responsibilities. The investigator should verify the location of all of the witnesses that may be required to testify. Depending on the length of time between the conclusion of the investigative stage of the case and the trial stage, some witness may have retired, moved or died. You do not want to wait for the last minute before trial to find out you cannot find a key witness. Hopefully, during your investigation you will have asked them to stay in touch with you if they change jobs or move. You may need to check the criminal history of the key non-law enforcement witnesses for credibility issues.

The investigator should go to the evidence vault and make sure that the evidence is still there. This includes checking the chain of evidence to be sure the chain has not been broken. If there is a problem with the chain of evidence, the investigator should prepare a memorandum to explain the problem. If the chain has been broken and the evidence has been subject to a scientific test, it may need to be retested.

The investigator should review the case folder. He needs to be sure any lab reports are in the folder with the results. He may wish to check with the lab to see if any new test have been developed that should be preformed prior to trial.

Trial

When the trial begins, the case agent will set at the table with the prosecutor. Together they will work as a team for a successful prosecution. It is the responsibility of the case agent to be sure that the evidence is brought to trial each day. It is also the case agent's responsibility to be sure the evidence is secured the entire time and the chain of evidence is not broken.

Normally, the case agent will keep track of exhibits and evidence as they are entered for trial. This is a two-step process. First, the evidence is introduced. Having a witness testify about the evidence does this and how it was acquired. The defense can object to the evidence. After this is done, the court accepts the evidence. The case agents must keep track of when the evidence is introduced and accepted.

The case agent is responsible for being sure that the witnesses are at the courthouse and available to testify when needed. This can mean arranging for transportation for those witnesses who cannot get to court on their own.

The case agent knows the entire case, so he is responsible for listening carefully to the testimony of all the witnesses. He should let the prosecutor know if he misses any important points during direct examination. The case agent should also listen carefully to the defense witnesses and advise the prosecutor of any issues that may need to be brought out on cross examination.

If this is your first trial, it is a good idea to sit in on a trial. You will become more comfortable with the courtroom and the procedures. You will get use to how the judge controls the courtroom.

Trials are fun and exciting, but the hours are long. The days begin early getting what is needed for court and meeting with the prosecutor. At the conclusion of court for the day, it is back to the prosecutor's office to get ready for the next day.

Witnesses

As a witness in a trial it is perfectly natural to be nervous. You do want to become as comfortable as possible so you do not appear overly nervous so that the jury might perceive your nervousness as untrustworthiness. There are steps you can take to help you prepare for your testimony. You must review your notes, reports and memorandums. While you are allowed to refer to your notes, reports and memorandums while you are on the stand, you should be so familiar with the contents of your material that you rarely need to refer back to your materials. Constantly reading from notes, reports and memorandums tends to make the jury doubt the credibility of the information. Knowing your material will make you more comfortable and confident when you testify.

The prosecutor will help prepare you with one or more practice sessions. The prosecutor will ask questions to elicit the responses he needs to prove his case. He may also act as the defense attorney would on cross-examination in asking questions.

Appearance

Appearances count. You can best believe that the defendant that you arrested with the long unkempt hair, beard, and dirty clothes will show up in a suit and looking like a banker. You will be expected to make a professional impression. If you are a uniformed officer, you should show up in your uniform that is clean and pressed. Your shoes should be shined and with a fresh conservative hair cut. No flashy jewelry. While sitting at the prosecutor's table or on the witness stand you should maintain good posture with your leg crossed at the ankles and your hands folded on your lap. Beware of nervous mannerisms like rocking or tapping your foot.

Voice

You should speak clearly and in a tone loud enough to be heard by the jury. Listen to the question and then hesitate for a couple of seconds to allow your mind to work before you answer the question. This also gives the prosecutor time to object to the question before you answer it. When you answer the question, turn to the jury and speak. You do not want to appear to be argumentative or bias. You want to treat both the prosecutor and the defense attorney in the same courteous manner. You should refer to the prosecutor and defense attorney as sir or ma'am. Stay away from using slang or legal or law enforcement jargon.

Direct Examination

Direct examination is the questioning of a witness by the side that called that witness. The prosecutor will generally start off asking you your name, title, your job, and some background information like training and length of time of the job. Then the prosecutor will ask specific questions about the case. The questions will generally require a detailed response. They will be something like, "Tell the court what happened the night of December 5, 2003." The questions are not allowed to be leading questions like, "Isn't it true that ..." You should already know how much information the prosecutor wants you to give to questions. Be careful not to go off the point or with too much information that will confuse the jury.

Remember you must always tell the truth that is your duty. You should not slant your testimony. It is not your duty to convince the jury, only to answer the questions. If there is an objection, wait until the judge rules before answering the question. If the judge sustains the objection, you will not answer the question. If the judge overrules the objection, you will answer the question. Be certain of your facts, if needed, ask the judge for permission to refer to notes or reports.

Do not volunteer information. You are not to give hearsay or opinion testimony. Do not guess. If you don't understand a question, ask to have it explained. If you do not know the answer to the question, just say you don't know. If you are asked a question that demands exact knowledge like distance, only answer if you know or you can answer using "approximately."

Cross Examination

The job of the defense attorney is to make your testimony not credible or make the government's case unbelievable. The defense attorney has many tools to accomplish that task. Remember the defense attorney only has to convince one juror he has reasonable doubt. On cross-examination, the defense attorney may ask leading questions. Also remember that the defense attorney will have access to your notes, reports and memorandums prior to the trial. He will be looking for contradictory statements made during your direct testimony and your notes, reports and memorandums. Your notes, reports, and memorandums may also have weaknesses already in them that can be exploited by the defense. If you have done your trial preparations correctly, you will be ready for that. The defense attorney will attempt to rattle you in any way possible.

During cross-examination control your emotions. The defense attorney wants to get you angry or appear to be hostile and bias. Be sure you understand the question. If you don't understand the questions ask the defense attorney to explain it or rephrase the question. A common trick is to ask two questions at the same time. If that happens, ask the defense attorney which question he would like answered first, don't try to answer both at the same time.

Do not get into a verbal confrontation with the defense attorney or the judge. If you are asked a question and told to answer it "yes" or "no," but the question requires an explanation to be complete or accurate explain that the answer needs explanation. If the defense attorney does not allow you to answer the question accurately then ask the judge for permission to clarify your answer. Watch out for trick questions like, "Do you still beat your wife?" It assumes that you beat your wife. Another trick question is "Have you ever told a lie?" Of course you have told lies during your lifetime, but the correct answer should be, "Yes, but never under oath." Do not allow your answers to be interrupted by the defense attorney. When the defense attorney interrupts you answer, you should continue to answer the question, then ask the defense attorney to repeat the second question. The defense attorney may attempt to accelerate the pace of questioning to confuse you, but be sure you take your time and answer the questions. Also remember to hesitate a few seconds before you answer any question.

The defense attorney may ask you if you discussed the case with anyone prior to trial. The question suggests that it is improper to discuss the case prior to trial. That is not the case and of course you discussed the case with the prosecutor, other witnesses, and your supervisor.

Preparing For Cross Examination of the Defendant

The defendant is not required to take the witness stand. There are a number of reasons why he may not want to take the stand. There may be evidence against him that he cannot explain and his failure to be able to explain will not help his case with the jury. Another reason may be that the prosecutor may be allowed to bring in prior bad acts. Prior bad acts are convictions for crimes that are similar to the case being tried. If he was on trial for bank robbery using a handgun and a mask and he had a prior conviction using the same method, the judge may allow the prosecutor to use that prior bad act to impeach him. Now the jury will know that he is a convicted bank robber. Sometimes the prior bad acts are so prejudicial to the defendant the judge will not allow them to be entered into evidence.

The best time to prepare for the testimony of the defendant is at the time of his arrest. Get a statement and get his defense documented. If he has been arrested for smuggling narcotics, he may tell you that a friend asked him to drive the car back into the country for him. Get the name of the friend and the address. Ask him how long he was in Mexico and where he stayed. Get all the details, he will make mistakes. Prior to the trial, track down every detail of his story. If he takes the stand, the prosecutor will be able to break his story. If his story changes, he will be able to use the statements he gave you to impeach him.

If the suspect is not going to be arrested until his indictment, you can still find out his potential defense. You can do a non-custodial interview. If the suspect is not in custody he does not have to be advised of his rights under Miranda. For Miranda you need questioning and custody. You do want to be sure the suspect knows he is not under arrest and is free to leave. It is best to videotape the interview. The investigator can explain to the suspect pieces of evidence he has and ask the suspect to explain it. If he explains it, you are locking him in to a story. For example, you can show him documentary evidence of wrong doing by him.

Trial Exhibits

Most large prosecutors' offices have Litigation Support Units that prepare exhibits to be used in trials. They have special software and printers that make the exhibits. In order for an exhibit to be accepted by the courts, all the facts on the exhibit must have been introduced and accepted into evidence. Below is a chart used to compare the testimony of two witnesses in a case.

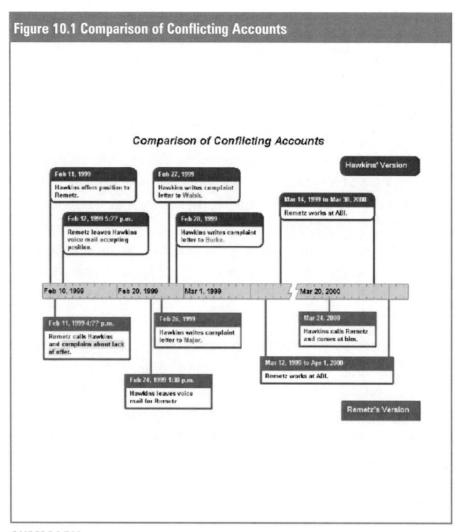

Figure 10.1 Comparison of Conflicting Accounts

SUMMARY

As a law enforcement officer, your job includes investigating the crime, obtaining evidence that proves who is legally responsible, present that case to a prosecuting attorney and help prepare the case for trial. Court preparation start the first day of your investigation, and everything you do is subject to scrutiny. How you conduct the investigation, how you obtained the evidence, and the chain of custody to keep the integrity of the evidence are examined by the defense.

DISCUSSION QUESTIONS

1. What steps can you take prepare for trial starting with day one of your investigation.

2. Is it better to keep your reports of investigation short and concise or more detailed.

3. Should an undercover agent who worked undercover with long hair and facial hair, cut his hair and be clean-shaven for court?

ADDITIONAL READINGS

Department of Justice, United States Attorney's Manual,
http://www.usdoj.gov/usao/eousa/foia_reading_room, Title, Section
9.18, Defenses

Department of Justice, United States Attorney's Manual,
http://www.usdoj.gov/usao/eousa/foia_reading_room, Title, Section
9.19, Documentary material held by third parties

BIBLIOGRAPHY

United States Customs Service, Law Course For Customs Officers